PERSPECTIVES ON WRITING
Series Editors, Susan H. McLeod and Rich Rice

PERSPECTIVES ON WRITING
Series Editor, Susan H. McLeod and Rich Rice

The Perspectives on Writing series addresses writing studies in a broad sense. Consistent with the wide ranging approaches characteristic of teaching and scholarship in writing across the curriculum, the series presents works that take divergent perspectives on working as a writer, teaching writing, administering writing programs, and studying writing in its various forms.

The WAC Clearinghouse and Parlor Press are collaborating so that these books will be widely available through free digital distribution and low-cost print editions. The publishers and the Series editor are teachers and researchers of writing, committed to the principle that knowledge should freely circulate. We see the opportunities that new technologies have for further democratizing knowledge. And we see that to share the power of writing is to share the means for all to articulate their needs, interest, and learning into the great experiment of literacy.

Recent Books in the Series

Asao B. Inoue, *Antiracist Writing Assessment Ecologies: An Approach to Teaching and Assessing Writing for a Socially Just Future* (2015)

Beth L. Hewett and Kevin Eric DePew (Eds) with Elif Guler and Robbin Zeff Warner (Assistant Eds), *Foundational Practices of Online Writing Instruction* (2015)

Christy I. Wenger, *Yoga Minds, Writing Bodies: Contemplative Writing Pedagogy* (2015)

Sarah Allen, *Beyond Argument: Essaying as a Practice of (Ex)Change* (2015)

Steven J. Corbett, *Beyond Dichotomy: Synergizing Writing Center and Classroom Pedagogies* (2015)

Tara Roeder and Roseanne Gatto (Eds.), *Critical Expressivism: Theory and Practice in the Composition Classroom* (2014)

Terry Myers Zawacki and Michelle Cox, *WAC and Second-Language Writers: Research Towards Linguistically and Culturally Inclusive Programs and Practices* (2014)

Charles Bazerman, *A Rhetoric of Literate Action: Literate Action Volume 1* (2013)

Charles Bazerman, *A Theory of Literate Action: Literate Action Volume 2* (2013)

Katherine V. Wills and Rich Rice (Eds.), *ePortfolio Performance Support Systems: Constructing, Presenting, and Assessing Portfolios* (2013)

Mike Duncan and Star Medzerian Vanguri (Eds.), *The Centrality of Style* (2013)

Chris Thaiss, Gerd Bräuer, Paula Carlino, Lisa Ganobcsik-Williams, and Aparna Sinha (Eds.), *Writing Programs Worldwide: Profiles of Academic Writing in Many Places* (2012)

WORKING WITH ACADEMIC LITERACIES: CASE STUDIES TOWARDS TRANSFORMATIVE PRACTICE

Edited by
Theresa Lillis, Kathy Harrington,
Mary R. Lea, and Sally Mitchell

The WAC Clearinghouse
wac.colostate.edu
Fort Collins, Colorado

Parlor Press
www.parlorpress.com
Anderson, South Carolina

The WAC Clearinghouse, Fort Collins, Colorado 80523-1052
Parlor Press, 3015 Brackenberry Drive, Anderson, South Carolina 29621

Printed in the United States of America

Library of Congress Cataloging-in-Publication Data

Names: Lillis, Theresa M., 1956-
Title: Working with academic literacies : case studies towards transformative practice / edited by Theresa Lillis, Kathy Harrington, Mary R. Lea, and Sally Mitchell.
Description: Anderson, South Carolina : Parlor Press ; Fort Collins, Colorado : WAC Clearinghouse, 2015. | Series: Perspectives on writing | Available in digital format for free download at http://wac.colostate.edu. | Includes bibliographical references and index.
Identifiers: LCCN 2015042472| ISBN 9781602357617 (pbk. : alk. paper) | ISBN 9781602357624 (hardcover : alk. paper)
Subjects: LCSH: English language--Rhetoric--Study and teaching. | Academic writing.
Classification: LCC PE1404 .W65 2015 | DDC 808/.04207--dc23
LC record available at http://lccn.loc.gov/2015042472

Copyeditor: Don Donahue
Designers: Tara Reeser and Mike Palmquist

Series Editors: Susan H. McLeod and Rich Rice

This book is printed on acid-free paper.

The WAC Clearinghouse supports teachers of writing across the disciplines. Hosted by Colorado State University, it brings together scholarly journals and book series as well as resources for teachers who use writing in their courses. This book is available in digital format for free download at http://wac.colostate.edu.

Parlor Press, LLC is an independent publisher of scholarly and trade titles in print and multimedia formats. This book is available in print and Adobe eBook formats from Parlor Press at http://www.parlorpress.com. For submission information or to find out about Parlor Press publications, write to Parlor Press, 3015 Brackenberry Drive, Anderson, South Carolina 29621, or email editor@parlorpress.com.

CONTENTS

Contents

WORKING WITH ACADEMIC LITERACIES: CASE STUDIES TOWARDS TRANSFORMATIVE PRACTICE

INTRODUCTION

Theresa Lillis, Kathy Harrington, Mary R. Lea and Sally Mitchell

WHY THIS BOOK?

The idea for this book arose from the many conversations over the years between researchers and practitioners about what it means to adopt, or perhaps more accurately as reflected in the title of this book to *work with* an "Academic Literacies" approach to writing, and more broadly language and literacy, in contemporary higher education. Whilst not necessarily distinct people or groups, a gap in understandings between researchers (those with a specific role in carrying out research about academic writing and reading) and practitioners (those with a specific role in working with students in their academic writing, such as teachers, curriculum designers, policy makers and academic administrators) often seems to be in evidence. The impetus to take forward a project that would bring together researchers, practitioners and researcher-practitioners to illustrate the specific ways in which they/we engage in and develop ideas from Academic Literacies came from the 2010 international *Writing Development in Higher Education* conference, London, following a plenary workshop on "Academic Literacies" by a group of researcher-practitioners, Sally Baker, Lynn Coleman, Theresa Lillis, Lucy Rai, and Jackie Tuck (http://www.writenow.ac.uk/news-events/wdhe-conference-2010). Three questions arising from this plenary were debated and are reflected in the framing and contributions of this book:

1. What does working with Academic Literacies mean "in practice"?
2. How can the transformative approach argued for in Academic Literacies' theorizing be instantiated in practice(s)?
3. In developing a transformative approach, how might work in Academic Literacies usefully draw on and engage with other approaches to writing?

Exactly how, when and in which specific contexts—geographical, institutional, disciplinary, stage of study—particular elements of Academic Literacies are valuable for developing a transformative approach to writing and reading in the academy were (and are) questions we all felt needed more consideration. This book is intended as a contribution to such a development, bringing together ideas, pedagogic case studies and critical commentaries from teacher-researchers working in a range of contexts, from undergraduate to postgraduate levels across a range of disciplines—including natural and social sciences—and a number of geopolitical regions—Australia, Brazil, Canada, Catalonia, Finland, France, Ireland, Portugal, South Africa, United Kingdom, United States. While some contributions are from within specific institutionally "writing designated" spaces (a well-known example being US Composition), many others engage with the question of writing from within disciplinary spaces. Contributions focus on issues such as: How to make language and writing visible in meaningful ways in disciplinary activity, including in areas as diverse as engineering, geography, nursing, natural sciences, graphic design, business studies and photojournalism? How can teachers across all disciplinary areas meaningfully engage with writing? How can and do writing/language specialists work collaboratively with disciplinary specialists? How can a wider range of semiotic resources including modes, media and genres fruitfully serve academic meaning and knowledge making? What kinds of writing-specific designated spaces do we need and how can these be facilitated, for example through postgraduate writing circles and one-to-one language/writing tutorials? How can theory and practice from Academic Literacies be used to open up debate about writing and language at institutional and policy levels?

WHAT IS ACADEMIC LITERACIES?

What is the "Academic Literacies" that contributors are seeking to *work with* in this collection? While acknowledging that the phrase is used in a number of ways (see Theresa Lillis & Mary Scott, 2007), here we briefly set out the particular tradition we are referring to and engaging with.

"Academic Literacies" is a critical approach to the researching and teaching of writing and literacy and to the role and potential of these activities for individual meaning making and academic knowledge construction in higher education. In broad terms, "Academic Literacies" draws attention to the importance, for research and pedagogy, of adopting socially situated accounts of writing and text production. It also draws attention to the ways in which power and identity (at the levels of student, teacher, institution, discipline) are inscribed in literacy practices, and the need to explore the possibilities for adopting transformative approaches to academic writing, which includes working to extend the range of semiotic resources—linguistic, rhetorical, technological—that are legitimized in the academy of the twenty-first century. Key areas of research have included: the nature of academic writing from the perspective of student-writers; the impact of power relations on student writing; the contested nature of academic writing conventions; the centrality of identity and identification in academic writing; academic writing as ideologically inscribed knowledge construction (for overviews see Theresa Lillis & Mary Scott, 2007; David Russell et al., 2009; Jackie Tuck, 2012a; Joan Turner, 2011). More recent work has continued with a focus on student writing but also extended into areas such as the everyday writing of academics (Mary Lea

& Barry Stierer, 2009), disciplinary teachers' perspectives on their engagement with students' writing (Tuck, 2012b), academic writing for publication (Theresa Lillis & Mary Jane Curry, 2010) and digitally mediated literacy practices inside and outside the academy (Lynn Coleman, 2012; Mary Lea & Sylvia Jones, 2011; Robin Goodfellow & Mary Lea, 2013). The approach has a particularly vigorous research base in the United Kingdom and South Africa (see for example, Awena Carter et al. (Eds.), 2009; Roz Ivanič, 1998; Cecilia Jacobs, 2010; Carys Jones et al., 1999; Mary Lea, 2005; Mary Lea & Barry Stierer (Eds.), 2000; Mary Lea & Brian Street, 1998; Theresa Lillis, 1997, 2001, 2003; Lillis & Scott (Eds.), 2007; Lucia Thesen & Linda Cooper, 2013; Lucia Thesen & Ermien van Pletzen, 2006) and has strong connections/resonances with critical arguments found in a number of pedagogical and theoretical traditions across a range of national contexts, for example, critical EAP (Sarah Benesch, 2001; Nigel Harwood & Gregory Hadley, 2004), "basic writing" (e.g., Bruce Horner & Min-Zhan Lu, 1999), *didactique* or *littéracies universitaires* (Isabelle Delcambre & Christiane Donahue, 2011), writing across the curriculum and writing in the disciplines, WAC and WiD (e.g., Charles Bazerman et al., 2005; Donna LeCourt, 1996; David Russell, 2001) and multilingual academic writing (e.g., Suresh Canagarajah, 2002). (See Reflections 1, 3, 4, 6 this volume).

There are strong points of convergence in the ways in which researchers and teachers define or co-opt the notion "Academic Literacies" in their/our research and practice, as well as considerable points of debate and areas in need of development. A core point of convergence (and indeed the imperative driving much research and pedagogy) is a deep and consistent concern with the limitations of much official discourse on language and literacy in a rapidly changing higher education world. This includes the prevailing deficit approach to language, literacy, and indeed students, whereby the emphasis tends overwhelmingly to be on what student writers *don't* or *can't do* in academic writing rather than on what they can (or would like to), and where—even whilst discourses of diversity and internationalization populate university mission statements globally—"variety" of linguistic, semiotic and rhetorical student repertoires tends to be viewed as "a problem rather than resource" (Brian Street, 1999, p. 198). A core area of debate is how best to draw and act on Academic Literacies' critiques of contemporary approaches to language and literacy, in particular, how to design policy, curriculum, assessment and pedagogy which engage with a commitment to "transformation"—rather than solely induction or reproduction—and indeed, to examining what we understand by "transformation" in contemporary higher education. The goal of this book is to focus explicitly on how practitioner-researchers (mainly teachers) are grappling to theorize and develop "transformation" in their/our practice, within the constraints and demands of specific disciplines and institutions within a range of higher education systems globally, each of which have their specific social and geopolitical histories.

WHERE DOES "ACADEMIC LITERACIES" COME FROM?

The use of the phrase "Academic Literacies" to signal a critical and social practice perspective on writing and reading in the academy seems to have been forged out of conversations taking place at different times and in different places by people with similar concerns. From the late 1980s onwards, the term was regularly used, for example, at monthly Academic Literacies sessions at the Institute of Education, London, chaired by Mary Scott—and the related extensive international mail and discussion list—and in ongoing discussions by scholars in South Africa, such as Lucia Thesen and Cecilia Jacobs. The principles underpinning what would come to be labelled as "Academic Literacies" were also evident in some innovative language pedagogy and policy work without the use of this label: for example, in a UK polytechnic in 1989, which subsequently became a "new" university,[1] the Language Policy, written by Phyllis Creme, was designed to both recognize and value diversity and the language practices that students brought with them to the university (see Phyllis Creme & MaryLea, 1999). More widely at the time, the response of many of the new universities to both their students and their attempts to compete with other high status institutions was to develop targeted study skills provision. This frequently included "fixing" student writers with generic approaches, focused on surface features of form, grammar, punctuation, spelling etc.—what Lea and Street in their 1998 paper termed the "study skills" model. However, many practitioners working directly with student writers were increasingly finding these approaches unsatisfactory when faced with actual students completing real assignments.

In the context of policies of access and widening participation in higher education, "Academic Literacies" came to be used to challenge the strongly deficit orientation towards the writing (and reading) of students, in particular of students who were the first generation in their families and communities to go into higher education and to signal the need for a more questioning and critical stance towards what students were doing and meaning in their academic writing. Available linguistic, theoretical and pedagogic frames just did not seem to articulate or help account for the experiences and practices of the student-writers. Lillis, for example, was struck that student-writers often did not use discourses that their academic teachers were expecting, not because they didn't know these, but because they were not what they wanted to use, to mean, *to be* (Lillis, 2001). Key writers offering ways of articulating such phenomena were Norman Fairclough (1992) and other critical discourse analysts (Romy Clark & Roz Ivanič, 1991). In particular, Roz Ivanič used critical discourse analysis (CDA) to explore students' practices and texts, foregrounding the question of identity (1998). Teacher-researchers in the United Kingdom and in other parts of the world grappled with finding a frame that would enable them to explore issues that were often treated as background or secondary—where the job of the teaching discipline-based academic writing, if visible at all, was often construed as teaching conventions (as if these were uncontested) that students must adopt (rather than critically engage with).

Of course the work that is central to articulating an "Academic Literacies" orientation—and widely cited across this book—is the 1998 paper by Lea and Street. In this paper they outlined three ways or "models" to articulate different approaches to student writing in the academy which they described in terms of "skills," "socialization," and "academic literacies." Whereas "study skills" was primarily concerned with mastery of the surface features of texts, "academic socialization" pointed to the acculturation of students into the discourses and genres of particular disciplines as an essential prerequisite for becoming a successful writer. Lea and Street saw "academic literacies" as subsuming many of the features of the other two, illustrating that the three models were not mutually exclusive. Nevertheless, they claimed that the academic literacies model was best able to take account of the nature of student writing in relation to institutional practices, power relations and identities, therefore offering a lens on meaning making that the other two models failed to provide.

An important point to signal about this 1998 article was that Lea and Street were adamant that it should speak to both practitioners and researchers—of writing, language and literacy—and chose their target journal carefully. However, getting the article published was not without its challenges. They had to persuade the editor and reviewers that their approach "counted" as research in higher education and that the literacies as social practice frame was legitimate in a context dominated by psychological models of student learning. Its theorized and practitioner-focused orientation is still at the heart of the field that we call Academic Literacies although individual researchers and practitioners occupy different institutional positions and orientations. Some are centrally concerned with finding ways of providing immediate support to students, often in demanding institutional settings against a backdrop of institutional accountability; others are endeavouring to engage critically and make visible issues of power and control over knowledge and meaning making; and many are seeking to do both, as evidenced in the contributions to this volume.

So what was it that the framing and the phrasing "academic literacies"—that was definitely in the air but was honed in Lea and Street's 1998 paper—seemed to be offering? It provided a name for a whole cluster of research and pedagogic interests and concerns that many were grappling to articulate and it anchored concerns around academic writing to a larger scholarly project relating to literacy more generally (New Literacy Studies, e.g., David Barton & Mary Hamilton, 1998; David Barton & Uta Papen, 2010; James Gee, 2007; Mary Hamilton, 2001; Mastin Prinsloo & Mignonne Breier, 1996). Furthermore, the ethnographic impulse in New Literacy Studies in particular—paying particular attention to emic perspectives—connected strongly with progressive voices in adult education and access movements and thus captured the intellectual imagination of many educators and language/writing researchers both in the UK and other national contexts. Thus whilst the phrase 'academic literacy' and even the plural form were in use in some contexts,[2] the publication of the work by Lea and Street fulfilled three important scholarly functions in configuring the field:

1. It helped generate an intellectual space for the many scholars who were dissatisfied with dominant pedagogical and institutional approaches to student writing.

2. By indexing "New Literacy Studies" and Street's robust critique of "autonomous" approaches to literacy, it opened up routes of intellectual inquiry that differed from the strongly "textualist" (Bruce Horner, 1999) and normative approaches available with which many scholars were also dissatisfied (across a number of traditions, such as English for Academic Purposes and Systemic Functional Linguistics).

3. It helped create a theoretically and empirically robust position from which to challenge the prevailing ideology of deficit which centered on what students could *not* do (rather than what they could) and also shifted attention towards disciplinary and institutional practices.[3]

WHAT DOES "TRANSFORMATION" MEAN IN ACADEMIC LITERACIES?

At the heart of an Academic Literacies approach is a concern with "transformation" and the "transformative." But what does this mean? How is "transformation" to be understood, and what does it look like when using an Academic Literacies lens to investigate and design writing practices in the academy? In this section, the book's editors each offer a perspective on these questions—but without a desire to close them down. We recognize that individual practitioner-researchers will define and work with the notion of transformation somewhat differently depending on their/our particular institutional and/or disciplinary positions and the specific questions they/we ask. An examination and elucidation of this contextual diversity is, indeed, one of the main aims of this volume.

THERESA LILLIS: TOWARDS TRANSFORMATIVE DESIGN

As a teacher, researcher and participant in contemporary academia I am involved in both working with(in) and against powerful conventions for meaning making and knowledge construction. I am committed to exploring what it is that prevailing academic conventions for meaning making have to offer—and to whom—and what it is they constrain or restrict. My concern (based on many years of teaching and researching) is that we—as teachers, researchers, writers, policy makers—may often adopt prevailing conventions, including those surrounding which specific semiotic practices are valued, simply because they have become routinised rather than because they offer meaningful, valid and creative resources for knowledge production, evaluation and participation in the contemporary world. The challenge, I think we all face, is to become aware of the vast array of semiotic resources potentially available to us and others (however we construe "us" and "others"—and in positions of both producers and receivers/evaluators) and to explore how these can be harnessed for meaning and knowledge making.

As part of this broader concern with conventions, why is *transformation* an important notion to discuss? In an opening paper of a Special Issue on Academic Literacies in the *Journal of Applied Linguistics* Mary Scott and I set out what we saw as a map of the field of "Academic Literacies" in its current state as well as offering a position statement on what the field could be, some ten years after Lea and Street's influential 1998 paper. In addition to pointing to the key epistemological framing of "Ac Lits"—notably a social practice approach to language and literacy with a particular emphasis on ethnography as a research methodology—we also pointed to the ideological orientation of Ac Lits as being one of transformation. In broad terms, we made a contrast between two common stances (in research and pedagogy): those which could be characterized as "normative" and those that could be characterized as "transformative". Normative stances and approaches to writing and literacy tend to work within a framework which raises questions about writing and literacy in the following terms: What is the nature of the writing and literacy required—at the level of genre, grammar, style, rhetoric? How can these most usefully be researched (made visible) and taught? A normative stance is often considered essential when seeking to induct people into the literacy practices that have become legitimized in academia to the extent that in order for people to participate in existing academic practices, these practices have to be taught and literally "practised". However, we argued that Ac Lits has also encouraged a transformative stance towards writing and literacy which foregrounds additional questions such as: how have particular conventions become legitimized—and what might alternatives be? To what extent do they serve knowledge making—and are other ways of making knowledge, and other kinds of knowledge/knowing possible? Whose epistemological and ideological interests and desires do these reflect and enable—and whose interests and desires may be being excluded?

As transformation/transformative is a key theme in this book, I'd like to quote what Mary Scott and I wrote here:

> The ideological stance toward the object of study in what we are calling "academic literacies" research can be described as explicitly transformative rather than normative. A normative approach evident for example in much EAP work can be summarized as resting on the educational myths that Kress (2007)

describes: the homogeneity of the student population, the
stability of disciplines, and the unidirectionality of the teacher-student relation. Consonant with these myths is an interest
to "identify and induct": the emphasis is on identifying academic conventions—at one or more levels of grammar, discourse
or rhetorical structure or genre—and on (or with a view to)
exploring how students might be taught to become proficient or
"expert" and developing materials on that basis (for examples,
see Flowerdew, 2000; Swales & Feak, 2004). A transformative
approach in contrast **involves an interest in such questions
but in addition is concerned with**: a) locating such conventions in relation to specific and contested traditions of knowledge making; b) eliciting the perspectives of writers (whether
students or professionals) on the ways in which such conventions impinge on their meaning making; c) exploring alternative
ways of meaning making in academia, not least by considering
the resources that (student) writers bring to the academy as
legitimate tools for meaning making. (Lillis & Scott 2007, p.
12-13, emphasis added)

A key point we were seeking to make was that the normative stance is the default position in much practice in academia (pedagogy and policy) and a necessary
stance in order to participate (and enable participation) successfully in academic
institutions as currently configured. However we also argued that there was a considerable amount of additional work to be done—thinking, research, engagement
and reflection on practice—in order to harness the full range of semiotic practices
to intellectual labour.

One conceptual way forward is to acknowledge the importance of critique which
is strong in Academic Literacies research (for example the critique of the dominant deficit discourse on writing, the critique of an autonomous approach—Street
(1984)—to language and literacy, the concern with issues of power and identity in
academic writing) but at the same time to work with the notion of *design*. Gunther Kress usefully offers "design" as an epistemological and ideological move which
builds on critique but moves beyond it:

Design rests on a chain of processes of which critique is one: it
can, however, no longer be the focal one, or be the major goal
of textual practices. Critique leaves the initial definition of the
domain of analysis to the past, to past production. (Kress, 2000,
p. 160)

The question of design—or what I am referring to as "transformative design" in order to signal the critical basis for Kress's notion—has been explored by colleagues and myself, Lillis (2003, 2006) and Lea (2004) in specific relation to the relevance and use of Academic Literacies to practice in higher education but we have both pointed to the need for considerably more work to be done. For this book, the four editors came together to begin to engage in this *design work*, each of us committed to the importance of interrogating possibilities for transformation and interested in exploring the potential of "Ac Lits" in designing pedagogy and policy and all aware that working towards transformative design in higher education is a large and challenging project, possible only through extensive collaboration. We see this collection as reflecting examples of transformative design and as therefore a part of this larger collaborative project.

KATHY HARRINGTON: BORDER CROSSING

My interest in transformation, how I think about and understand what this might mean in the context of Academic Literacies, stems from the position I occupy as a relative newcomer to the field, coming in from the outside and bringing with me questions and perspectives from other domains of knowledge, experience and work. In her book on encounters between science and other disciplinary fields in nineteenth century Britain, Gillian Beer (1996) suggests that "ideas cannot survive long lodged within a single domain. They need the traffic of the apparently inappropriate audience as well as the tight group of co-workers if they are to thrive and generate further thinking" (p. 1). I have been intrigued and stimulated by Beer's ideas since coming across her work while writing my PhD in Victorian Studies in the late 1990s. What happens, I have been wondering more recently, when ideas harvested in other domains are trafficked into the field of Academic Literacies? What transformation might become possible in my own thinking and practice, particularly in my role as a teacher on academic and professional development programmes for other teachers in the academy?

I am interested in boundaries, how and why edges lie where they do, how we demarcate and decide what's inside and what's outside, and the transformative, or restrictive, possibilities this field mapping allows. I am interested in the potential for transformation as located within self-understandings, in the perceptions we have of ourselves as students and as teachers, and in the fluidity of the relationship between these identities. I am interested in the connection between transformation and being able to take the risk of not knowing whether the destination will be better than what has been left behind. None of these questions is specifically about, or originates from my engagement with, writing practices in the academy. They come from outside, from my personal history and experiences of border crossings, and from other fields—from perspectives gleaned from psychoanalysis and group analysis, group relations and open systems theory.

So, what does this mean in practice? What "further thinking" do these perspectives and questions generate in the context of Academic Literacies? In her application of open systems theory to the study of organizations, Vega Zagier Roberts notes that "a living organism can survive only by exchanging materials with its environment, that is, by being an *open system*" (1994, p. 28). In keeping something alive, boundaries are important. They can provide a helpful frame and hold a space within which something can live and flourish, such as a research or teaching community, ideas and people. But if drawn too tightly, boundaries can isolate and close down dialogue and growth. Boundary setting happens both from within and outside a field, and there are gains to be had by questioning which interests are being served by these processes. Where are the lines around Academic Literacies being drawn, by whom, and why? The rich and various contributions in this volume attest, I think, to the inspiring fecundity of thought and practice that comes of questioning and constantly re-thinking where the edges of the field might lie, and how permeable, and to which outside influences, they might most vitally remain open.

There is another sense in which working with a notion of boundaries informs my sense of the transformative potential of Academic Literacies. Boundaries can delineate an intellectual and professional field, but also an internal space, where *one's own norms and assumptions*—about the nature of writing and learning, about oneself as a teacher/authority and about the other/student—and one's own experiences of difference, inequality and power situated in specific contexts and relationships, can be brought to the surface and worked with. In my understanding, this questioning, self-reflective attitude and challenging work of seeing and confronting one's own assumptions is integral to the practice of teaching as informed by an Academic Literacies approach—and it is itself transformative, and empowering, for both teachers and students.

Transformation as I see it, and as distinguished from induction or reproduction, is essentially about this increased level of awareness. Whether the focus of a particular piece of work is on students, teachers, resources, institutional culture, or classroom practices, what is transformed through a "transformative approach" is fundamentally a way of seeing and being—and in particular, seeing and being with respect to *one's own* contribution to variously perpetuating, subverting and re-writing exclusionary narratives of power and identity inscribed in the practices and discourses of "academic writing". This is about daring to be curious, to ask difficult questions and to be honest about the answers. For example, it might be interesting to ask how requiring the "submission" of written work—and how one's own attitudes to the authority and power of the teacher in this relationship—influences the nature of the knowledge it is possible to create within formal writing and assessment processes. From a place of self-awareness, it becomes possible to step back, imagine and actually begin to do things differently—more creatively, more thoughtfully, and more radically. Rather than set the 'transformative' against the "normative, " as has sometimes been implied, it is through this critical process of nurturing transformation in self-understandings, uncertainties and identifications as teachers in higher education that I believe *the normative has the potential to enable the transformative.*

Returning to the notion of an *open system*, my sense of the transformative potential of Academic Literacies lies in being able to delineate living, creative yet protected spaces—within the curriculum and in institutional structures, in the interactions and relationships between and among students and teachers, in academic professional development programmes where discussions about assessment and literacy inevitably bring deficit and autonomous models of student writing to the surface, and, perhaps most importantly, in ourselves—where diverse and often conflicting beliefs, values and knowledges about writing in the academy can be made available for further thinking and ongoing transformation.

MARY R. LEA: HEURISTIC THINKING, INSTITUTIONS AND TRANSFORMATIONAL POSSIBILITIES

My interest has always been around the contested nature of textual practice. The ethnographic perspective—which permeates our Introduction and many contributions in this book—has been crucial here. It has helped me to develop my earlier work, which was concerned with making visible the detail of encounters between students and teachers around meaning making, towards the consideration of broader institutional perspectives.

So what do I mean by transformation when I am thinking institutionally? As I argued in Lea (2004), I believe that we need to attend to the workings of academic literacy practices, more widely, rather than focus our attention solely on students who may appear marginalized from the dominant practices and cultures of the academy. I think there is a danger that if we concentrate our attention on the latter it can mask the implications of academic literacies research and practice for laying bare the ways in which textual practices become instantiated through institutional processes and procedures. In fact, many of the chapters in this volume attest to how broader institutional practices are implicated in many day-to-day encounters around writing, assessment and feedback between students and their teachers. Deficit views of student writing still hold significant sway in higher education despite the extensive body of work in both academic literacies and other traditions of writing research which offers evidence to the contrary. My belief is that, in order to counter these deficit stances, we need to be interrogating practice at both an institutional and sectoral level, since the complexity and diversity of textual practices are evident across the institution and not merely in the practices of writing students. This might help us also to deal with the ongoing tension that is evident between conceptualizing "academic literacies as a heuristic" and more normative approaches associated with "teaching academic literacies". As a heuristic—one that is in progress as illustrated in this book—Academic Literacies has illuminated and helped me to understand more about the contested space of knowledge making and to build on this in practical ways in a range of practice settings in higher education. In contrast, I see the normative approach as more orientated towards inducting students into academic and disciplinary writing conventions, what Brian Street and I have referred to as "academic socialization". Although in some ways these may appear to be rather crude distinctions, I have found them invaluable when it comes to examining institutional practice within the changing landscape of higher education. Indeed, they emerged for us from our own research.

The development of academic literacies as a field of study in the early 1990s reflected a very different landscape from that which is in evidence today. The last decade has seen a combination of both structural and technological change, reflected in emergent textual practices around teaching and learning. Potentially these signal a breaking down of old boundaries and opening up of new spaces for meaning making in higher education. In this regard, my own curiosity about writing and academic professional practice (Lea, 2012; Lea & Stierer, 2009) was sparked by my teaching role in academic and professional development with Open University teachers. This signaled to me how different experiences of writing, values about writing in relation to academic identity and the models of writing associated with specific professional fields all suggest a contested space for teachers' own writing and their students' writing (see Lea, 2012; Tuck, 2013).

When Brian and I undertook the research for our 1998 paper, the use of digital technologies was still in its infancy. As these have gained centre stage, practitioners and researchers—including myself—committed to an academic literacies orientation in their work have begun to explore the relationship between literacies and technologies (Robin Goodfellow & Lea, 2007; Bronwyn Williams 2009; Goodfellow & Lea, 2013; Lea & Jones, 2011; Colleen McKenna, 2012; Bronwyn Williams, 2009). Williams (2013) discusses how certain virtual learning environments reinforce conservative views of knowledge-making practices, for example where the software and design of the online teaching environment privileges print and makes it difficult for students to engage in multi-modal text making. Colleen McKenna and Jane Hughes (2013) take a literacies lens to explore what technologies do to writing practices, in particular the ubiquitous, institutional use of plagiarism detection software and how this is reframing the concept of plagiarism for students and their teachers, taking them away from useful discussions, in disciplinary learning contexts, around attribution and knowledge-making practices. Research I carried out with Sylvia Jones offered an alternative to the representation of students as "digital natives" (Marc Prensky, 2001), purportedly comfortable online but unable to engage in more conventional study practices, such as academic reading and writing. Our project explored this issue through a literacies lens, illustrating the complex interrelationship between literacies and technologies with the potential to disrupt traditional academic literacy practices. We argued that in order to understand the changes that are taking place for learners in today's higher education more attention needs to be paid to textual practice around learning and less upon the technologies themselves and their applications. While on the one hand students accessed online resources and engaged in a wide range of digital and print-based textual practices, on the other we found that assignment rubrics did not generally reflect or engage with the rhetorical complexity of these practices. This meant that the opportunity for teachers to work explicitly with the processes of meaning making with their students was being missed. These examples signal to me the intransigent dominance of normative perspectives towards learning and literacies in a changing landscape and, therefore, the pressing need to think about transformation institutionally if we are going to work across the myriad nature of textual practices emerging in today's higher education.

SALLY MITCHELL: OPEN-ENDED TRANSFORMATION: ETHNOGRAPHIC LENS AND A SUSPICIOUS TENDENCY

In my experience transformation is not to be understood as a finished state, something that is fully achieved, rather it is an inclination towards envisaging alternative understandings of, and actions within any particular context. In this sense transformation is set against the normative and the status quo. And there are many things within educational settings which can become the object of transformative thinking. Clifford Geertz lists some of them when he calls for an "ethnography of thought, " a consideration of thought's "muscular matters":

> … translation, how meaning gets moved, or does not, reasonably intact from one sort of discourse to the next; about intersubjectivity, how separate individuals come to conceive, or do not, reasonably similar things; about how thought frames change (revolutions and all that), how thought provinces are demarcated ("today we have naming of fields"), how thought norms are maintained, thought models acquired, thought labor divided. (p. 154)

If an ethnography is a description and an interrogation of "what is" in a particular setting, to this I would add a suspicious orientation towards findings, and, after that, a tendency to pose the next question—the transformative question—"what if"?

Suspicion is a term I borrow from Paul Ricoeur who in *Freud and Philosophy* (1970) talks about the "hermeneutics of suspicion" as compared to the "hermeneutics of obedience". A suspicious tendency is a willingness to question how things—especially dominant things—are as they are, and *why*, and to seek for alternatives.

For me similar powerful ideas are the notion of taking a "paradigmatic" approach to "knowledge" (Aram Eisenschitz, 2000), and of acknowledging the crucial role of "warrants" and "backing' (Stephen Toulmin, 1958) in establishing, and hence critiquing, any position (Sally Mitchell & Mike Riddle, 2000). These ways of unpacking knowledge claims help to make sense both of what I observe in practice and of how I might want to respond.

Looking at a fraction of data from my study of "argument" in educational settings in the 1990s (Mitchell, 1994; Richard Andrews, 1995) may help to anchor what I mean. Picture an upper secondary school sociology class where students are gathered in small groups around tables to discuss Ivan Illich's (1976/1990) theory of "Iatrogenesis. " In one group, two students dominate: Andrew—questioning the value of hospital treatment and pointing out that treatment ultimately doesn't stop people from dying and is also costly; Susan—strongly resisting this view.

> Susan: Rubbish. No sorry Andrew, I don't agree.
>
> Andrew: Why?
>
> Susan: Because I wouldn't want to die and I don't think you
> would and if it comes to the choice where you'd got a chance of
> living, you would have it. You would have it!

In this scene "argument"—the object of my study—emerges as a conflict between what Susan knows and feels to be the case in her everyday experience and Andrew's espousal of the new, counter-commonsensical idea. She's annoyed, it seems, by his detaching *himself* (what *he* would do if he were ill and needed treatment) from the discussion. And indeed Andrew is getting more abstract in his thinking, becoming more "sociological. " Towards the end of the discussion he seems to grasp—to arrive at for himself—the "bigger picture" argument being put forward by Illich. Referring to the Health Service, he says:

> Andrew: So it's an excuse for, like, the government not interven-
> ing in causes of ill health, isn't it?

Andrew's aha! moment isn't the end of the story however: I observed how much of the argument that had emerged collaboratively and antagonistically through the peer to peer discussion dropped out of the writing the students subsequently did (see Mitchell, 1995). What accounted for this disappearance? Was it control over the medium, the medium itself, the fact that the writing would be read and assessed by the teacher as part of working towards a public exam, a resultant reluctance to take risks?

These kinds of question about "translation, how meaning gets moved, or does not …", about "intersubjectivity, how separate individuals come to conceive, or do not, reasonably similar things …" make clear that it was not possible thinking about what I observed, to conceive of "argument" simply as a text or simply as talk. It was also absolutely necessary to think about beliefs, identities, permissions, what was tacit or silenced as well as what was shared—by whom and for what purposes.

Then comes the shift to new kinds of question. What other kinds of transformation besides those achieved through the class dialogue, would Andrew and Susan have had to make to express their insights powerfully in their written texts— and to have them recognized against official assessment criteria? What might have been done differently and by whom? What might make a difference? To what and to whom? What *kind of a difference*? And why? Seeking to address these questions suggests that there would be no such thing as straightforwardly "better argument." This is absolutely not to say that change shouldn't be tried—and my study gave rise to numerous suggestions, including ways of bridging the gaps between generative and formal writing, meta-discussion of what counts as knowledge and so on.

To return to where I started, however. The combination of an ethnographic lens with a suspicious tendency, means that any transformative goal is never finalized; being socially, politically, ideologically constructed, what counts as "good" or "better" is always rightly the object of further scrutiny. Many of the contributions to this book suggest a willingness to engage in such scrutiny.

THE CONTENTS OF THE BOOK

The goal of this book is to offer examples from a range of institutional contexts of the ways in which teacher-researchers are working with Academic Literacies, engaging directly with the three questions set out in the first section of this Introduction. The contributions are 31 "case studies," a term we use here to refer to the detailed discussion and/or illustration of specific instances of "transformative design" which are often also anchored to specific theoretical concerns. Contributors have worked hard to offer concise snapshots of their practice and key challenges in order to:

- illustrate how they have sought to "work with" Academic Literacies
- offer their perspectives on what constitutes transformative design in current practice
- provide resources for teacher-researchers working in a range of contexts which are practical in nature whilst being theoretically robust.

We have also included six contributions that we have called *Reflections*. These are comments and dialogue from scholars from different traditions and geolocations and reflect some of the "troublesome" areas we are all seeking to grapple with, both theoretically and practically. These are interspersed across the book.

We have organized the contributions into four main sections, the sections determined by the key focus of each contribution: Section 1—Transforming pedagogies of academic writing and reading: Section 2—Transforming the work of teaching: Section 3—Transforming resources, genres and semiotic practices: Section 4—Transforming institutional framings of academic writing. Whilst we provide an introduction at the beginning of each section, we do of course recognize that there is considerable overlap in themes, questions and issues across the contributions and we strongly encourage readers to move back and forth across the book to follow threads of particular interest.

NOTES

1. "New" universities were created in 1992 in the United Kingdom, with the abolition of the binary divide between polytechnics and universities. Initially, they took students from the local community and had close links with colleges providing "Access to Higher Education" courses. Many of their students were the first in their family to attend university.

2. Tracking the use of terms is not straightforward. This is discussed in Lillis and Scott 2007.

3. These three points are discussed in more detail in Lillis 2013.

REFERENCES

Andrews, R. (1995). *Teaching and learning argument*. London: Cassell.

Barton, D., & Hamilton, M. (1998). *Local literacies: Reading and writing in one community*. London: Routledge.

Barton, D., & Papen, U. (Eds.). (2010). *The anthropology of writing. Understanding textually-mediated worlds*. London: Continuum International Publishing Group.

Bazerman, C., Joseph, L., Bethel, L., Chavkin, T., Fouquette, D., & Garufis, J. (2005). *Reference guide to writing across the curriculum*. West Lafayette, IN: Parlor Press/The WAC Clearinghouse. Retrieved from http://wac.colostate.edu/books/bazerman_wac/

Beer, G. (1996). *Open fields: Science in cultural encounter*. Oxford, UK: Oxford University Press.

Benesch, S. (2001). *Critical English for academic purposes*. Mahwah, NJ: Erlbaum.

Brew, A. (2006). *Research and teaching: Beyond the divide*. Basingstoke, UK: Palgrave Macmillan Publishing.

Canagarajah, A. S. (2002). *Critical academic writing and multilingual students*. Ann Arbor, MI: University of Michigan Press.

Carter, A., Lillis T., & Parkin, S. (Eds.). (2009). *Why writing matters: Issues of access identity and pedagogy*. Amsterdam: John Benjamins Publishing Company.

Chang, H. (2005). Turning an undergraduate class into a professional research community. *Teaching in Higher Education, 10*(3), 387-394.

Clark, R., & Ivanic, R. (1991). Consciousness-raising about the writing process. In C. James & P. Garrett (Eds.), *Language awareness in the classroom* (pp. 168-185). London: Longman.

Coleman, L. (2012). Incorporating the notion of recontextualisation in academic literacies research: The case of a South African vocational web design and development course. *Higher Education Research and Development, 31*(3), 325-338.

Creme, P., & Lea, M. R. (1999). Student writing: Challenging the myths. In P. Thompson (Ed.), *Academic writing development in higher education: Perspectives, explorations and approaches* (pp. 1-13). Reading, Berkshire: Centre for Applied Language Studies, University of Reading.

Delcambre, I., & Donahue, C. (2011). University literacies: French students at a disciplinary "threshold"? *Journal of Academic Writing, 1*(1), 13-28. Retrieved from http://e-learning.coventry.ac.uk/ojs/index.php/joaw/article/view/6/47

Eisenschitz, A. (2000). Innocent concepts? A paradigmatic approach to argument. In S. Mitchell & R. Andrews (Eds.), *Learning to argue in Higher Education* (pp. 15-25). Portsmouth, NH: Boynton/Cook.

Fairclough, N. (1992). *Discourse and social change.* Cambridge, UK: Polity Press.

Flowerdew, J. (2000). Discourse community, legitimate peripheral participation, and the nonnative-English-speaking scholar. *TESOL Quarterly, 34*(1), 127-150.

Gee, J. (2007). *Sociolinguistics and literacies* (3rd ed.). London: Taylor & Francis.

Geertz, C. (1993). *Local knowledge.* London: Fontana Press.

Goodfellow, R., & Lea, M. R. (2007). *Challenging e-learning in the university: A literacies perspective.* Maidenhead, Berkshire, UK: Society for Research into Higher Education/Open UniversityPress/McGraw Hill.

Goodfellow, R., & Lea, M. R. (Eds.). (2013). *Literacy in the digital university: Critical perspectives on learning, scholarship and technology.* London/ New York: Routledge.

Hamilton, M. (2000). Expanding the new literacy studies: Using photographs to explore literacy as social practice. In D. Barton, M. Hamilton, & R. Ivanič (Eds.), *Situated literacies* (pp. 16-34). London: Routledge.

Harwood, N., & Hadley, G. (2004). Demystifying institutional practices: Critical pragmatism and the teaching of academic writing. *English for Specific Purposes, 23*, 355-377.

Horner, B. (1999). The birth of basic writing. In B. Horner & M.-Z. Lu (Eds.), *Representing the other: Basic writers and the teaching of basic writing* (pp. 3-29). Urbana, IL: NCTE.

Horner, B., & Lu, M. (Eds.). (1999). *Representing the "other" basic writers and the teaching of basic writing.* Urbana, IL: NCTE.

Illich, I. (1976/1990). *Limits to medicine, medical nemesis: The expropriation of health.* London: Penguin.

Ivanič, R. (1998). *Writing and identity: The discoursal construction of identity in academic writing.* Amsterdam: John Benjamins Publishing Company.

Jacobs, C. (2010). Collaboration as pedagogy: Consequences and implications for partnerships between communication and disciplinary specialists. *Southern African Linguistics and Applied Language Studies, 28*(3), 227-237.

Jones, C., Turner, J., & Street, B. (Eds.). (1999). *Students writing in the university: Cultural and epistemological issues*. Amsterdam: John Benjamins Publishing Company.

Kress, G. (2000). *Multimodality*. In B. Cope & M. Kalantzis (Eds.), *Multiliteracies: Literacy, learning and the design of social futures*. London: Routledge.

Kress, G. (2007). Thinking about meaning and learning in a world of instability and multiplicity. *Pedagogies. An International Journal, 1*, 19-34.

Lea, M. R. (2004). Academic literacies: A pedagogy for course design. *Studies in Higher Education, 29*(6), 739-756.

Lea, M. R. (2012). New genres in the academy: Issues of practice, meaning making and identity. In M. Castelló & C. Donahue (Eds.), *University Writing; Selves and texts in academic societies studies in writing* (pp. 93-109). Bingley, UK: Emerald Group Publishing.

Lea, M. R., & Jones, S. (2011). Digital literacies in higher education: Exploring textual and technological practice. *Studies in Higher Education, 36*(4), 377-395.

Lea, M. R., & Stierer, B. (Eds.). (2000). *Student writing in higher education: New contexts*. Buckingham, UK: Society for Research into Higher Education/Open University Press.

Lea, M., & Stierer, B. (2009). Lecturers' everyday writing as professional practice in the university as workplace: New insights into academic literacies. *Studies in Higher Education, 34*(4), 417-428.

Lea, M. R., & Street, B. (1998). Student writing In higher education: An academic literacies approach. *Studies in Higher Education, 23*, 157-172.

LeCourt, D. (1996). WAC as critical pedagogy: The third stage? *JAC: A Journal of Advanced Composition Theory, 16*(3), 389-405.

Lillis, T. (1997). New voices in academia? The regulative nature of academic writing conventions. *Language and Education, 11*(3), 182-199.

Lillis, T. (2001). *Student writing: access, regulation, desire*. London: Routledge.

Lillis, T. (2003). An 'academic literacies' approach to student writing in higher education: Drawing on Bakhtin to move from critique to design. *Language and Education, 17*(3), 192-207.

Lillis, T. (2006). Moving towards an academic literacies pedagogy: Dialogues of participation. In L. Ganobscik-Williams (Ed.), *Academic writing in Britain: Theories and practices of an emerging field*. Basingstoke, UK: Palgrave Macmillan Publishing.

Lillis, T., & Curry, M. J. (2010). *Academic writing in a global context*. London: Routledge.

Lillis, T., & Scott, M. (2007). Defining academic literacies research: Issues of epistemology, ideology and strategy. *Journal of Applied Linguistics, 4*(1), 5-32.

Lillis, T., & Scott, M. (Eds.). (2007). Special issue—New directions in academic literacies. *Journal of Applied Linguistics*, *4*(1).

McKenna, C. (2012). Digital texts and the construction of writerly spaces: Academic writing in hypertext. *Pratiques: Littéracies Universitaires: Novelle Perspectives*, *153-154*, 211-229.

McKenna C., & Hughes, J. (2013). Values, digital texts, and open practices—a changing scholarly landscape in higher education. In R. Goodfellow & M. R. Lea (Eds.), *Literacy in the digital university: Critical perspectives on learning, scholarship and technology* (pp. 15-26). London/New York: Routledge.

Mitchell, S. (1994). *The teaching and learning of argument in sixth forms and higher education: Leverhulme final report.* Kingston upon Hull, UK: Centre for Studies in Rhetoric, Hull University.

Mitchell, S. (1995).Conflict and conformity: The place of argument in learning a discourse. In P. Costello & S. Mitchell (Eds.), *Competing and consensual voices: The theory and practice of argument* (pp. 131-146). Clevedon, UK: Multilingual Matters.

Mitchell, S. (2000). Putting argument into the mainstream. In S. Mitchell & R. Andrews (Eds.), *Learning to argue in higher education*. Portsmouth NH: Boynton/Cook.

Mitchell, S., & Riddle, M (2000*). Improving the quality of argument in higher education: Leverhulme final report.* London: School of Lifelong Learning & Education, Middlesex University.

Prensky, M. (2001). Digital natives, digital immigrants. *On the Horizon, 9*, 5. Retrieved from http://www.nnstoy.org/download/technology/Digital%20Natives%20-%20Digital%20Immigrants.pdf

Prinsloo, M., & Breier, M. (Eds.). (1996). *The social uses of literacy: Theory and practice in contemporary South Africa*. Amsterdam: JohnBenjamins Publishing Company.

Ricoeur, P. (1970). *Freud and philosophy*. New Haven, CT: Yale University Press.

Roberts, V. Z. (1994). The organization of work: Contributions from open systems theory. In A. Obholzer & V. Z. Roberts (Eds.), *The unconscious at work: individual and organizational stress in the human services*. London: Routledge.

Russell, D. R. (2001). Where do the naturalistic studies of WAC/WID point? A research review. In S. McLeod, E. Miraglia, M. Soven, & C. Thaiss (Eds.), *WAC for the new millennium: Strategies for continuing writing-across-the-curriculum programs* (pp. 259-298). Urbana, IL: National Council of Teachers of English.

Russell, D. R., Lea, M., Parker, J., Street, B., & Donahue, T. (2009). Exploring notions of genre in "academic literacies" and "writing across the curriculum": Approaches across countries and contexts. In C. Bazerman, A. Bonini, & D. Figueiredo (Eds.), *Genre in a changing world* (pp. 395-423). Fort Collins, CO: The WAC Clearinghouse/Parlor Press. Retrieved from http://wac.colostate.edu/books/genre/

Street, B., & Street, B. V. (1984). *Literacy in theory and practice*. New York: Cambridge University Press.

Street, B. (1996). Academic literacies. In J. Baker, C. Clay, & C. Fox (Eds.), *Challenging ways of knowing in English, Mathematics and Science*. London: Falmer Press.

Street, B. (1999). Academic literacies. In C. Jones, J. Turner, & B. Street (Eds.), *Students writing in the university: Cultural and epistemological issues*. Amsterdam: John Benjamins Publishing Company.

Swales, J. M., & Feak, C. B. (2004). *Academic writing for graduate students*. Ann Arbor, MI: University of Michigan Press.

Thesen, L. (2001). Modes, literacies and power: A university case study. *Language and Education, 15*, 132-145.

Thesen, L., & van Pletzen, E. (2006). *Academic literacy and the languages of change*. London/New York: Continuum.

Thesen, L., & Cooper (2013). *Risk in Academic writing: Postgraduate students, their teachers and the making of knowledge*. Bristol, UK: Multilingual Matters.

Toulmin, S. (1958.). *The uses of argument*. Cambridge, UK: Cambridge University Press.

Tuck J. (2012a). "Academic Literacies": Débats et Développements Actuels. *Recherches En Didactiques. Les Cahiers Theodile, 14*, 159-173

Tuck, J. (2012b). Feedback-giving as social practice: Teachers' perspectives on feedback as institutional requirement, work and dialogue. *Teaching in Higher Education, 17*(2), 209-221.

Tuck, J. (2013). *An exploration of practice surrounding student writing in the disciplines in UK Higher Education from the perspectives of academic teachers* (Unpublished doctoral thesis). The Open University, UK.

Turner, J. (2011). *Language in the academy: Cultural reflexivity and intercultural dynamics*, Bristol, UK: Multilingual Matters.

Williams, B. T. (2009). *Shimmering literacies: Popular culture and reading and writing online*. New York: Peter Lang Publishing Group.

Williams, B. (2013). Control and the classroom in the digital university: The effects of course management systems on pedagogy. In R. Goodfellow & M. Lea (Eds.), *Literacy in the digital university: Critical perspectives on learning, scholarship and technology*. London: Routledge/Taylor & Francis.

SECTION 1
TRANSFORMING PEDAGOGIES
OF ACADEMIC WRITING AND READING

INTRODUCTION TO SECTION 1

Section 1 focuses on the ways in which teachers are seeking to transform pedagogies around academic writing and reading and re-negotiate opportunities for teaching and learning. A key theme running across the chapters is a commitment to making visible the dominant conventions governing academic writing so as to facilitate access to such conventions, whilst at the same time creating opportunities for student choice and active control over the conventions they use in their writing. At the heart of this section is a concern with the pedagogic relationship and the ways in which teachers seek to transform this relationship in order to enhance students' academic writing, reading, meaning making and knowledge making practices. Transformation is explored along a number of dimensions drawing on a range of theoretical traditions and using a range of data, including teacher-researcher reflections, extracts from students' writing, drawings and sketches, students' talk about their writing and examples of curriculum design and materials. The section opens with a paper by Julio Gimenez and Peter Thomas who offer a framework for what they call a "usable pedagogy" or *praxis*. In offering this framework the authors are tackling head on the question of the *usability* of theory and principles developed in academic literacies work (and indeed theory more generally). Their framework for praxis includes three key goals: to facilitate accessibility, to develop criticality, to increase visibility. Transformation in their work draws on traditions of "transformative learning" foregrounding the importance of making students "visible participants of academic practices." They illustrate the use of their framework with undergraduate students in Art and Design and Nursing. The following chapter by Lisa Clughen and Matt Connell also centres on the transformation of the pedagogic relationship by explicitly connecting issues of concern in academic literacies work with the psychotherapeutic approach of Ronald David Laing (1965, 1967). They explore in particular two key challenges: how tutors can validate students' struggles around writing and reading without trapping them into feelings of stupidity, passivity or self-condemnation; and how tutors can share their power with students. Their dialogue is an instantiation of the collaborative relationship between "academic literacy" facilitator and discipline specialist—a relationship that is also explored in many chapters in the book—as well as an illustration of an alternative model of writing that can be used in knowledge making and a theme that is focused on in detail in Section 3.

Transformative pedagogy in the following two chapters seeks to tackle old or familiar problems with new approaches. Jennifer Good tackles what she describes as "theory resistance" by undergraduate photojournalism students through the active encouragement to use a semiotic resource they are more at ease with—visual metaphor. She describes how she encouraged students to visually represent their feelings around attempting to engage with difficult texts and argues that an academic literacies model "provides a framework for acknowledging the pressure faced by students as they negotiate unfamiliar literacy practices."

Joelle Adams likewise foregrounds the academic learning potential in the pedagogic use of visual rather than verbal (only) resources. Adams returns to a question that is nested in all contributions—how is "academic literacies" understood and taken up by practitioners?—focusing in particular on students taking on a tutoring role as part of an elective module in a Creative Writing course. Adams provides details of the kind of writing tutoring that student-tutors engage in, including designing subject specific writing workshops, but her main aim is to consider the ways in which student-tutors engage with academic literacy theory. Using sketches made by student-tutors as well as written extracts from their journals, she illustrates the ways in which student-tutors grapple with and take meaning from a key text in Academic Literacies (Lea & Street, 1998) and apply it to both their teaching and understandings about their own writing.

A theme prominent in Academic Literacies research and running across all contributions in Section 1 is the implicit nature of many conventions in which students are expected to engage and the challenges teachers face in working at making such conventions visible. The paper by Adriana Fischer, focusing on an undergraduate engineering course in Portugal, seeks to explore the extent and ways in which the implicit or "hidden features" (Brian Street, 2009) of academic literacy practices can be made visible to both students and tutors. Fischer outlines a specific programme of interventions involving an academic literacy facilitator working with discipline specialists and highlights both the possibilities and limits to practices involving 'overt instruction' (Bill Cope & Mary Kalantzis, 2000). Transformation in Fischer's work centres on combining attention to overt instruction, alongside the creation of spaces for ongoing dialogue between subject specialists, academic literacy facilitators and students. She argues that overt instruction is important but that given the ideological nature of academic literacy practices, many specific understandings about these practices will inevitably remain implicit, an argument also made by Lawrence Cleary and Íde O'Sullivan in Section 4.

The final three contributions in this section focus on transforming pedagogic orientations towards language and literacy at graduate level. The paper by Kathrin Kaufhold explores specific instances of thesis writing by a sociology student, Vera, foregrounding the uncertainties the writer experiences and the choices she makes, particularly in relation to her decision to include both what she saw as "more traditional" sociological writing and her more alternative "auto-ethnographic" writing. A key emphasis in this paper is the relationship between supervisor and student-writer, which Kaufhold characterizes as dialogic, evidence of which she carefully traces in the text. The paper by Cecile Badenhorst, Cecilia Moloney,

Jennifer Dyer, Janna Rosales and Morgan Murray also focuses on graduate writing, outlining a programme of workshops in a Canadian university aimed at supporting graduate students' explicit knowledge of academic and research discourses, whilst encouraging their creative engagement with these. At the centre of this paper is a focus on "play," with the authors arguing that play is an important way to encourage "participants to move out of their usual ways of writing and thinking." The paper draws on comments by workshop participants to illustrate the value of the approach adopted and to explore the extent and ways in which such involvement can be considered transformative. The question as to what counts as transformative in graduate writing is also addressed in the final paper in this section by Kate Chanock, Sylvia Whitmore and Makiko Nishitani. Co-authored by a writing circle facilitator with a background in Applied Linguistics and two writing circle participants in an Australian context, the paper focuses on the question of "voice" and the relationship between writer voice, disciplinary field and the specific object being investigated. Using extracts from writers' texts and their concerns about these texts, the authors discuss how the writing circle provided a space for the consideration of how "academic socialization had shaped their writing" and opened up opportunities for taking greater discursive control. The authors argue for the value of "informed" choice around acts of writing.

This section of the book closes with reflections by Sally Mitchell on a conversation with Mary Scott, one of the key researcher-teacher participants in the development of Academic Literacies as a field. The question in the title, "How can the text be everything?"signals a key position in Academic Literacies which is that in order to understand what writing is and does we need to carefully explore written texts but not limit our gaze to texts alone. *Reflections 1* foregrounds the importance of personal trajectories and biography in the development of individual understandings how these are powerfully bound up with the ways in which areas of knowledge grow and develop.

CHAPTER 1

A FRAMEWORK FOR USABLE PEDAGOGY: CASE STUDIES TOWARDS ACCESSIBILITY, CRITICALITY AND VISIBILITY

Julio Gimenez and Peter Thomas

This chapter presents case studies of pedagogical applications of an academic literacies approach to the development of academic reading and writing. They were designed for degree programmes at a London university within the context of UK policies of widening participation.[1] In most widening participation contexts the student profile is varied in terms of, inter alia, relationship with English,[2] previous educational experiences, and length of time away from formal education. These elements of the student profile have a direct bearing on academic achievement, so we argue that academic literacies practices in contexts like that described in this chapter must take account of this variety and provide students with a balance between language learning, language development and literacy enhancement.

The two case studies here represent attempts to develop what we call a "usable pedagogy" informed by, and complementing, theoretical considerations of academic literacy (e.g., David Barton, Mary Hamilton, & Roz Ivanič, 2000; Mary Lea, 2004; Mary Lea & Brian Street, 1998; Theresa Lillis, 2001, 2003; Joan Turner, 2012). This interrelation of theory and practice draws on Paulo Freire's (1996) conceptualization of *praxis*, or research-informed action through which a balance between theory and practice is achieved. This balance, we believe, is important for widening participation contexts.

Our approach to academic literacies as praxis is based on three core principles which aim to offer students opportunities for: 1) gaining access to and mobilizing the linguistic and analytical tools needed for active participation in their academic and professional communities; 2) developing a critical approach to not only academic discourses but also the broader contexts where these discourses are produced and consumed (e.g., their disciplines and institutions); and 3) increasing their visibility as active participants in the processes of knowledge telling, transformation and creation through dialogue and authorial presence. These three principles form the basis of our framework for usable pedagogy which will be discussed in the next section.

The framework has been developed with the purpose of providing students with opportunities for transformative practices through which they can gain control over their own personal and educational experiences. Alongside most of the literature on transformative learning (e.g., Jack Mezirow, 2000; Edmund O'Sullivan, 2003), we would argue that transformative practices involve shifts in a number of human spheres: thinking, feelings and actions. These shifts require changes in how we have learned to think of, feel about and act upon the world around us, including ourselves, the relations of power underlying institutional structures, opportunities for access to knowledge and resources, as well as opportunities for success. Transformative practices thus aim to help learners to develop a deep understanding of themselves as main agents in processes such as knowledge creation and discourse construction and co-construction, their own location and positioning, their relationship with other learners and their teachers, and their feelings about themselves. Like constructivist approaches to education (e.g., Lev Vygotsky, 1978), transformative practices recognize that knowledge in all its forms—technical, practical, propositional and procedural—is central to transformation and that learners can become more visible participants of academic practices through inquiry, critical thinking, and dialoguing with peers and lecturers.

Our approach is not a rejection of text-based approaches to academic writing instruction, often known as "English language support"[3] (e.g., EAP), in favor of an academic literacies approach which emphasizes "social practices". We contend that an either-or view is problematic in the context of universities committed to widening participation. Instead, we support Turner's call for a balance or synergy, "whereby a focus on social practice feeds back into an awareness of textual practice" (Joan Turner, 2012, p. 19) (see also Turner Chapter 28 this volume; for relationship between Ac Lits and EAP, see Theresa Lillis and Jackie Tuck 2015).

Despite having developed in "quite different socio-political contexts" (Ken Hyland & Liz Hamp-Lyons, 2002, p. 4), EAP and academic literacies approaches both aspire to provide students with a more successful educational experience. Our approach couples text-centred pedagogy, which highlights how particular textual and genre-related features are used in specific disciplinary contexts, with the socio-political dimension emphasized by academic literacies. The former allows us to raise novice "home" and "international"[4] student writers' awareness of the rules that govern disciplinary academic discourses.[5] The latter provides opportunities for students to become more aware of, and more confident in, their roles and positioning within their educational contexts.

In the next section we discuss the framework for usable academic literacy pedagogy that we have designed, then illustrate how the framework was implemented in two degree programme subject areas: Art and Design and Nursing. The final section concludes the chapter with a brief evaluation of the three underlying principles that make up the framework and the way in which they materialise social inclusion in higher education.

A FRAMEWORK FOR USABLE ACADEMIC LITERACY PEDAGOGY

Paying attention to context, in particular the contextualization of pedagogical practices, is central to our understanding of academic literacies. Contextualization in our work includes a macro level of theorizing (the student's individual and social realities before their institutional experiences, their individual and social identities, their new institutional realities, and the identity of their institution and disciplines) and a micro level of praxis, involving the modules and the lecturers for whom the students are writing. Our aim is that these levels of theory and practice should enable students to empower themselves in their reading and writing, as will be illustrated in the case studies.

Thus our framework aims to—

Facilitate accessibility by:

- Challenging the "institutional practice of mystery" (Lillis, 2001; Turner, 2011) and, by means of analytical tools, helping students to gain access to the often tacit disciplinary expectations (Julio Gimenez, 2012);
- Helping students to develop effective means of expression through raising their awareness of the constitutive nature of language (Turner, 2011) in their construction and representations of knowledge.[6] One common route to this is the identification of key textual and discursive features in their disciplines (by using linguistic tools), the consideration of alternatives and their impact, and the development of informed student use of such features.

Develop criticality by:

- Helping students to understand the role they play in the academic world that surrounds them. It is only through this understanding that students will be able to fully comprehend "the way they exist in the world *with which* and *in which* they find themselves" and most importantly to "come to see the world not as a static reality, but as a reality in process, in transformation" (Freire, 1996, p. 64, emphasis in the original);
- Helping students to critically analyze the multiplicity of factors intervening in the processes of producing and consuming texts to avoid collapsing them into monolithic entities (e.g., good and bad writing) (Freire &

Donald Macedo, 2002).

Increase visibility by:

- Encouraging visibility and writer's voice development through a process we refer to as "dialogics," that is, by establishing co-operation and dialogue between all the people involved in academic literacy practices. This idea resonates with Bakhtin's views of dialogue as an aspiration to struggle for, "a range of possible truths and interpretations" (Lillis, 2003, p. 198);
- Empowering students to find ways of becoming more visible (to themselves, their lecturers and institutions) and thus less peripheral to the processes of knowledge telling, transformation and creation, getting their voices as writers heard, and their writer authority respected.

Figure 1.1 illustrates how the elements in the framework are interrelated: visibility depends to a certain extent on criticality and both on accessibility. The diagram also aims to show the proportional relationship between the elements: the more visible the students become as participants of knowledge-making processes, the wider the range of resources, linguistic and otherwise, they can access and control. However, the relationship between the elements is fluid; their sequence is not

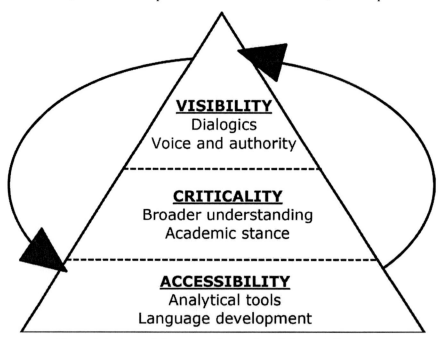

Figure 1.1: Accessibility, criticality and visibility—A framework for usable academic literacies pedagogy.

fixed as will be demonstrated in the case studies.

PUTTING THE FRAMEWORK TO WORK: CASE STUDIES IN ART AND DESIGN AND NURSING

This section examines how the framework was applied in the context of three core modules; "Introduction to History of Art, Architecture and Design," a first year BA module for a number of programmes in Art and Design; and "Foundations for Nursing Practice" (first year) and "Nursing the Patient with long-term Conditions" (second year), two BSc Adult Nursing modules. The students in these two subject areas differed in terms of their ages (most Art and Design students were in their early twenties whereas most Nursing students were in their early or mid-thirties) and in terms of their relationship with the English language (for most of the nursing students, English was their second or additional language but the majority of the art and design students used English as their first—or only—language). However, almost all students on both programmes can be classified as "non-traditional students," that is, they are from social groups which have historically been largely absent from higher education: students from working class backgrounds, older than 18 when starting university, some with learning difficulties, and as a group representing a variety of cultural and linguistic backgrounds. Against this context, pedagogical interventions representing the framework discussed here were designed and planned by two academic literacy lecturers, the authors of the chapter, in collaboration with the content lecturers in charge of the modules and in discussion with the vice-chancellor of the university. Interventions were delivered as small seminars, which meant they were repeated a number of times. They were scheduled within the degree timetable and most of them were co-taught with the content lecturers.

The following sections of the chapter present two case studies which illustrate how we implemented the framework in the context of the two degree subject areas: Art and Design and Nursing.

A USABLE PEDAGOGY FOR ART AND DESIGN

This case study illustrates an approach to reading *required texts,* which was used in interventions designed for a first year History of Art, Architecture and Design module that runs alongside studio modules. The texts on the module are often part or all of seminal texts (e.g., Benjamin's *The Work of Art in the Age of Mechanical Reproduction*) and as such are not introductory. Students can find these texts off-putting because the language is not moderated to suit the non-expert reader, and conceptually the texts can be complicated. The *authoritative* discourse (Bakhtin, in Erik Borg, 2004, p. 195) of texts like these can be perceived to leave little room for the student-reader, and the text-based practices of contextual studies/ history of art, can be seen as restrictive by studio-based art and design students. In contrast, the more *internally persuasive* discourse (ibid.) of object-based practices of the studio tends to be seen as comparatively liberating, because it encourages forms of self-discovery that these texts seem to deny. Reading these texts brings to the fore an epistemological tension between the *distinct worlds* (Michael Biggs & Daniela Büchler, 2012, p. 231) of text- and object-based research practices.

The students on the module share the broadly mixed profile of the university, but many of them also have dyslexia or another SpLD (Special Learning Difficulties).[7] Biggs (2007, p. 99) identifies that dyslexics seem to favor, "forms of thinking that aid creative work in the arts," or cognitive activity characterized as a preference for holistic, visual and spatial thinking, rather than sequential and auditory (word-based) thinking.[8]

DEVELOPING CRITICALITY

An important feature of the session is that it draws on studio-related practices, to encourage students to make use of the kind of criticality that they exercise in the studio, with which they often feel more competent. The sessions begin with an image that is relevant to the studio area (e.g., Figure 1.2 for Photography students),

Figure 1.2: Dorothea Lang, Migrant Mother, 1936
[permission under Creative Commons].

and we consider questions like: *How do we look at an image? What do our eyes settle on? Is there a prescribed order of looking and what to look at?*

Students tend to suggest that they start to look at what they *want* to start with, and work on from there, selecting their own route-of-looking through the image. In the case of "Migrant Mother," some of the students have mentioned looking first at her eyes, others start with the backs of the heads of her children, one student mentioned being drawn to the edges of the image, which provide evidence that it has not been cropped, but is a print of the full, original negative.

The session continues with another image of the floor plan of an exhibition, and more questions, this time related to how we encounter an exhibition, like *Do we follow a prescribed order?* Students tend to suggest that to an extent, they do because of curatorial decisions. However, they also speak of following an alternate order, their own, particularly if the exhibition is busy or they have specific interests. Some speak of working backwards, which means encountering the work in counter-cu-ratorial order. We consider whose order is correct, whether meaning remains the same, and whether this matters (see also Good, Chapter 3 and Adams Chapter 4 this volume).

Facilitating Accessibility

Next we address the *required text*. The sessions propose an interpretation of *interactive* reading (David Eskey, 1986, p. 11) that draws on different approaches to reading as necessary. We *objectify the text*, which includes breaking it up (literally, removing the staples and laying it out on the floor, if the text is short enough, see Figure 1.3.). This allows students to see the whole text at once, to examine it as a visual object and look for areas, or *centres*, of interest to them.

They are encouraged to *walk around* the text, literally and figuratively, to consider it from different angles, and to see component parts in a different order, as they might elements in an exhibition. These *centres of interest* are not necessarily at the beginning of the text; the students skim it, as they might a magazine, to find their own starting points. They are encouraged to notice clues (visual elements, repetition of words, etc.) that indicate topics. Having identified centres of interest, students investigate around them, forwards, backwards or sideways, to establish where they seem to start and end.

We address meaning making with initial discussions about the discourse of the text, its genre and purpose, framing linguistic features as language choices that the author has made. The students generally characterize the language as "compli-cated," so we look at simplifying strategies like removing modifying language (see simplification of a passage on early cinema in Figure 1.4). The students do this type of activity in small groups on their individual centres of interest, generating interpretations of them.

Discussion and dialogue are important elements of the sessions, which are often co-taught by a content lecturer and an academic literacy lecturer. We encourage dialogue between all those present in the session, which generates a process of collective meaning making, drawing on Freire's (1996, p. 56) idea of humanistic education. For the last part of the sessions, students are asked to explain one of their centres of interest in the text, and to relate it to their studio practice.

Access here is gained to potentially off-putting texts, and to the process of dialogue towards meaning. We challenge the misconception that less confident student-readers can have, that reading means word-for-word decoding of a hidden message, which reinforces their sense of *incapacity* (Pierre Bourdieu & Jean-Claude Passeron, 1990, p. 111.)

Increasing Visibility

The *visibility* of the studio in the session is an important feature. In drawing on epistemologies of the studio in this non-studio setting, we acknowledge the central role it plays for the student. This responds to the gap/tension between studio/object and text-based practices through emphasising a synergy between art/design and language (Joan Turner & Darryl Hocking, 2004).

The visibility of student decisions or agency is also key. The act of selecting their own centres of interest encourages them to question their role in the reading-writing process. It draws their attention to the possibility that they are reader-creators, generating new knowledge from texts, rather than merely reader-conductors. Also, making choice visible at the level of language accentuates a sense of possibility and

Figure 1.3: Text objectified.

relevance which, for these students, is present in the studio but is often lacking in writing-related activities.

Our approach encourages student-readers to exercise criticality in accessing texts on their own terms. In challenging textual norms they alter the power-relationship between the author and the reader, and *loosen the sway of the author* (Roland Barthes, 1977, p. 143). This does not mean that the author's authority is denied, but as the students navigate the text and map it for their own purposes, it becomes a usable resource for them, rather than an inaccessible holder of secret meaning.

A USABLE PEDAGOGY FOR NURSING

Most nursing students in this and similar institutions are faced with two significant challenges when writing academically: returning to education after some

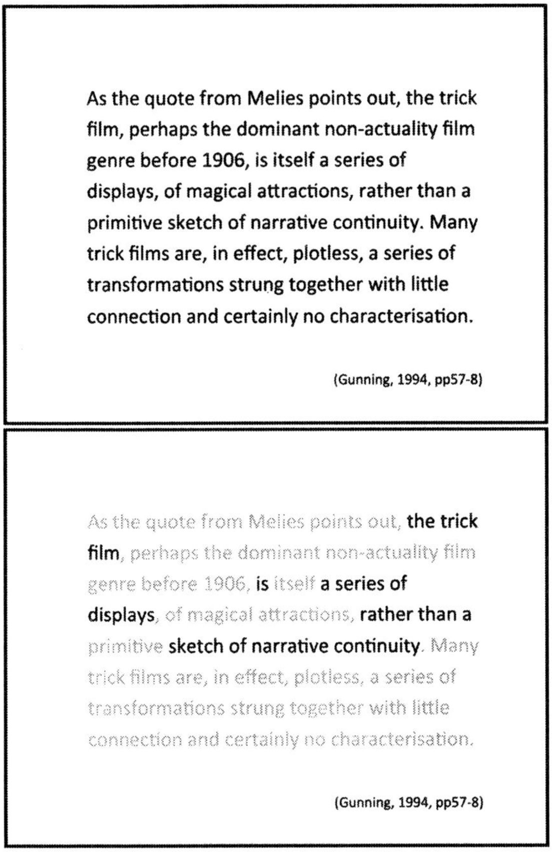

As the quote from Melies points out, the trick film, perhaps the dominant non-actuality film genre before 1906, is itself a series of displays, of magical attractions, rather than a primitive sketch of narrative continuity. Many trick films are, in effect, plotless, a series of transformations strung together with little connection and certainly no characterisation.

(Gunning, 1994, pp57-8)

As the quote from Melies points out, **the trick film,** perhaps the dominant non-actuality film genre before 1906, **is** itself **a series of displays,** of magical attractions, **rather than a** primitive **sketch of narrative continuity.** Many trick films are, in effect, plotless, a series of transformations strung together with little connection and certainly no characterisation.

(Gunning, 1994, pp57-8)

Figure 1.4: Text simplified: A slide used in an intervention with communication arts students (excerpt from Gunning, 1994, pp57-58).

considerable time away and writing in their second or additional language. The case study presented here discusses how the framework was implemented within two nursing modules.

Facilitating Accessibility

One of the first pieces of writing that nursing students are asked to produce is a reflective account. Reflective writing is in itself a rather complicated process that requires a set of distinctive analytical and linguistic skills. Research on reflective writing has shown that writers need to distance themselves from the situation reflected upon in order to analyze it critically and suggest a course of action to improve it (Gimenez, 2010; Beverly Taylor, 2000). It also depends on a fluent command of language so as to present a coherent sequencing of events supported by the correct use of tenses to make complete sense (Kate Williams, Mary Woolliams, & Jane Spiro, 2012). All this poses a real challenge to most of the students on the nursing programme described here.

A number of language development tasks were designed to help students write their first reflective account for the module. In these tasks, the academic literacy and content lecturers start by asking students on the "Foundations for Nursing Practice" module to discuss their previous experiences in writing reflectively, how successful these experiences were, and the challenges they faced. Next, led by the content lecturer, students examine the general role of reflective writing in nursing before they set out to analyze the discourse of reflection. For the discoursal analysis, we focus on an "incident in practice" account a student from another cohort has written (see activities in Figure 1.5). We examine questions such as *Who wrote it?*, *For whom?*, *For what purposes?*, and *How has the writer positioned him/her self?* Then, a textual analysis of the account provides insights into its generic structure, organizational patterns, sequential arrangement, and textual patterning. Linguistically, students de-construct the account to examine its language and register. This linguistic exercise is followed by transformation activities that require students to manipulate the discoursal, generic and linguistic elements in the account so that it can be located in a different context: a different writer-reader relationship, a different situation, a different outcome. This aims to help students realize the effects of their linguistic choices and the relationship between language and discourse (see also English chapter 17). An example of the texts and activities for this type of intervention is shown in Figure 1.5.

Developing Criticality

In our framework, developing criticality means providing students with opportunities to evaluate the context where they are operating as students and as future professionals, assess their roles and actions, and establish a reflective link between the present (as student writers) and their future (as professional nurses).

To help students to develop their criticality, a number of activities were designed around a care plan for the "Nursing the Patient with long-term Conditions" module. The first activity requires students to write a care plan by filling in a template typically used in hospitals for these purposes. Following this, a number of activities provide opportunities for critical evaluation. Students critically examine the care provided by a female nurse to an Asian man with a type 2 diabetes condition, taking into account contextual elements (who the patient is, the relationship with his GP, his nurse and the hospital consultant, and his culture and beliefs), their roles as student writers (writing for knowledge telling and knowledge transforming), their role as future nurses (the care provided and how it could be improved), and in what ways writing this text can help them as future nurses

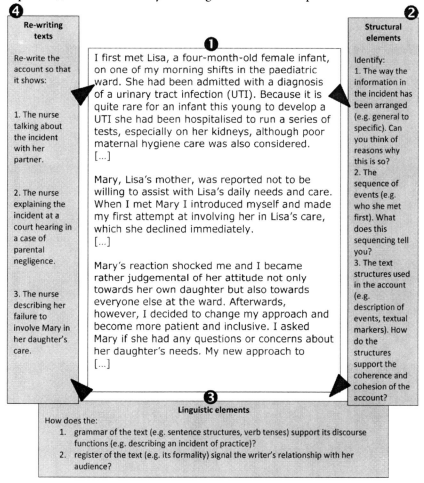

❹ Re-writing texts

Re-write the account so that it shows:

1. The nurse talking about the incident with her partner.

2. The nurse explaining the incident at a court hearing in a case of parental negligence.

3. The nurse describing her failure to involve Mary in her daughter's care.

❶

I first met Lisa, a four-month-old female infant, on one of my morning shifts in the paediatric ward. She had been admitted with a diagnosis of a urinary tract infection (UTI). Because it is quite rare for an infant this young to develop a UTI she had been hospitalised to run a series of tests, especially on her kidneys, although poor maternal hygiene care was also considered. [...]

Mary, Lisa's mother, was reported not to be willing to assist with Lisa's daily needs and care. When I met Mary I introduced myself and made my first attempt at involving her in Lisa's care, which she declined immediately. [...]

Mary's reaction shocked me and I became rather judgemental of her attitude not only towards her own daughter but also towards everyone else at the ward. Afterwards, however, I decided to change my approach and become more patient and inclusive. I asked Mary if she had any questions or concerns about her daughter's needs. My new approach to [...]

❷ Structural elements

Identify:
1. The way the information in the incident has been arranged (e.g. general to specific). Can you think of reasons why this is so?
2. The sequence of events (e.g. who she met first). What does this sequencing tell you?
3. The text structures used in the account (e.g. description of events, textual markers). How do the structures support the coherence and cohesion of the account?

❸ Linguistic elements

How does the:
1. grammar of the text (e.g. sentence structures, verb tenses) support its discourse functions (e.g. describing an incident of practice)?
2. register of the text (e.g. its formality) signal the writer's relationship with her audience?

Figure 1.5: Analyzing, deconstructing and transforming text.

(initiating dialogue with their lecturers, markers and also future patients with similar conditions). In this way, criticality becomes both a "textual" activity and an attitude towards self and others.

Increasing Visibility

One way of achieving greater visibility is by students initiating dialogue and co-operation (dialogics) between themselves and key participants in academic literacy practices: other students, lecturers, and markers. In the example about reflective writing provided above, nursing students in their role of academic writers are encouraged to use their outlines and first drafts to continue the dialogue with their lecturers and other students initiated with the analysis of reflective texts and the co-operation in co-constructing the meaning of their own texts. Through this process of dialogics, students are able to discuss how the drafts they have produced represent a range of possible interpretations of the task set by their lecturer and of the disciplinary discourses the assignment is supposed to encapsulate.

By speaking about their texts from their authorial stance, students make it clearer for themselves and others how they are involved in processes of knowledge telling, transformation and creation. Dialogic encounters also offer the students the opportunity to situate their writing within the context of their professional communities, their discipline, and their institutions.

DISCUSSION AND CONCLUSION

One central aspect of our development of a praxis of academic literacies, shown in the case studies here, is the need to provide opportunities for students to access and mobilize a variety of linguistic resources. Thus language development is at the heart of the *accessibility* component of our framework. Key sociolinguistic studies (e.g., Jan Blommaert, 2005; James Gee, 1999; Dell Hymes, 1996) demonstrate that success in education, and society as a whole, is largely determined by the linguistic resources individuals have access to and are thus familiar with.[9] Social systems, of which education is just one, are characterized by structural inequalities including differential access to and distribution of these resources (Blommaert, 2005). By offering opportunities for student writers to engage in analytical tasks, which required not only deconstructing different genres but also transforming them by mobilising a variety of linguistic resources, a process akin to what English calls "regenring" (2011; see also English chapter 17 this volume), our framework afforded students the opportunity to gain a better understanding of the role and impact of language choices in performing specific academic actions.

By the same token, the activities in our framework aim to demystify a number of academic practices in the context of the degree programmes and, in particular, the modules for which students were writing. Thus the students are not only able to explore formal aspects of the texts they are writing but also examine the value of those texts within their disciplines and modules, as well as their own expectations as writers and those of their lecturers.

The framework also provides opportunities for the students to critically evaluate their academic and professional contexts to comprehend their present and future roles and actions, and to consider how the reality they are part of is not static but open to negotiation and change. This, we argue, is mainly achieved through dialogue. The students gain a better understanding of their positions as writers of academic texts, and as future professionals, by dialoguing about the processes involved in discipline-specific knowledge creation and transformation; a process of finding their own voice through speaking about their interpretations of the contexts in which they operate.

NOTES

1. Widening participation, according to the Higher Education Funding Council for England (HEFCE), "addresses the large discrepancies in the take-up of higher education opportunities between different social groups. Under-representation is closely connected with broader issues of equity and social inclusion, so we are concerned with ensuring equality of opportunity for disabled students, mature students, women and men, and all ethnic groups" (HEFCE, 2011).

2. For some students English is their mother tongue, for others their second, third, or additional language.

3. A discussion of approaches to teaching and learning academic writing is beyond the remit of this chapter. Readers are referred to Turner (2011, 2012) and Wingate (2012).

4. Like most other categories used to describe groups of people and their behaviour, these categories are also problematic and far from being straightforward but they present a more "realistic" alternative to the "native" and "non-native" labels usually used in these contexts.

5. These rules are familiar to expert writers but are usually left unexplained to students (Turner, 2011).

6. As opposed to the view that language is merely referential (Filmer, et al., 1998, in Turner, 2011, p. 41).

7. Art and design programmes attract some of the largest numbers of students with a Specific Learning Difficulty (SpLD), like dyslexia, at the university. More than 15% of recent applicants for art and design courses identified themselves as dyslexic. The proportion of dyslexics tends to increase as the year progresses because many students are not assessed for dyslexia until they enter HE.

8. Generalized correlations like this should be treated with caution because dyslexia is a highly debated phenomenon, for which a universally accepted definition is elusive (Reid, 2009, p. 2).

9. These resources are theorized variously as a linguistic code (Bernstein, 1971) and a form of social capital (Bourdieu, 1986).

REFERENCES

Barthes, R. (1977). Death of the author. In R. Barthes, *Image, music, text* (pp. 142-148). London: Fontana Press.

Barton, D., Hamilton, M., & Ivanič, R. (Eds.). (2000). *Situated literacies: Reading and writing in context*. London/New York: Routledge.

Berstein, B. (1971). *Class, codes and control: Theoretical studies towards a sociology of language*. New York: Routledge/Kegan Paul.

Biggs, I. (2007) Art, dyslexia and creativity. In M. Kiziewicz & I. Biggs (Eds.), *Cascade—creativity across science, art, dyslexia, education*. Conference Proceedings, Cascade—creativity across science, art, dyslexia, education, Bath University. Retrieved from http://www.bath.ac.uk/cascade/pdf/cascadefullbook.pdf

Biggs, M., & Büchler, D. (2012). Text-led and object-led research paradigms: Doing without words. In G. Lees-Maffei (Ed.), *Writing design: Words and objects* (pp. 231-241). London: Berg.

Blommaert, J. (2005). *Discourse: a critical introduction*. Cambridge, UK: Cambridge University Press.

Borg, E. (2004). Internally persuasive writing in fine arts practice. *Art, Design & Communication in Higher Education, 3*(3), 193-210.

Bourdieu, P. (1986). The forms of capital. In J. Richardson (Ed.), *Handbook of theory and research for the sociology of education* (pp. 241-258). New York: Greenwood Publishing Group.

Bourdieu, P., & Passeron, J. C. (1994). Introduction: Language and relationship to language in the teaching situation. In P. Bourdieu, J-C. Passeron, & M. de Saint Martin (Eds.), *Academic discourse: Linguistic misunderstanding and professorial power* (pp. 1-34). Cambridge, UK: Polity Press.

English, F. (2011). *Student writing and genre: Reconfiguring academic knowledge*. London: Continuum International Publishing Group.

Eskey, D. E. (1986). Theoretical Foundations. In F. Dubin, D. E. Eskey, & W. Grabe (Eds.), *Teaching second language reading for academic purposes* (pp. 3-23). Reading, MA: Addison-Wesley.

Freire, P. (1996). *Pedagogy of the oppressed*. Harmondsworth, UK: Penguin Books.

Freire, P., & Macedo, C. (2002). *Ideology matters*. Lanham, MD: Rowman & Littlefield

Gee, J. D. (1999). *An introduction to discourse analysis: Theory and method*. New York: Routledge.

Gimenez, J. (2012). Disciplinary epistemologies, generic attributes and undergraduate academic writing in nursing and midwifery. *Higher Education, 63*(4), 401-419.

Gimenez, J. (2010). Academic writing in the disciplines: Practices in nursing, midwifery and social work. In M. F. Ruiz-Garrido, J. C. Palmer-Silveira, & I. Fortanet-Gomez. (Eds.), *English for professional and academic purposes* (pp. 197-211). Amsterdam: Rodopi.

Gunning, T. (1994). The cinema of attractions: Early film, its spectator and the avant-garde. In T. Elsaesser (Ed.), *Early cinema: Space frame narrative* (pp. 56-62). London: British Film Institute.

Higher Education Funding Council for England (HEFCE). (2011). *Widening participation*. Retrieved from http://www.hefce.ac.uk/widen

Hyland, K., & Hamp-Lyons, L. (2002). EAP: Issues and Directions. *Journal of English for Academic Purposes, 1*(1), 1-12.

Hymes, D. H. (1996). Two types of linguistic relativity. In W. Bright (Ed.), *Sociolinguistics* (pp. 114-158). The Hague: Mouton.

Lea, M. (2004). Academic literacies: A Pedagogy for course design. *Studies in Higher Education, 29*(6), 739-756.

Lea, M., & Street, B. V. (1998). Student writing in higher education: An academic literacies approach. *Studies in Higher Education, 23*(2), 157-172.

Lillis, T. (2003). Student writing as "academic literacies": Drawing on Bakhtin to move from critique to design. *Language and Education, 17*(3), 192-207.

Lillis, T. (2001). *Student writing. Access, regulation, desire*. London: Routledge.

Lillis, T. and Tuck, J. (2015) Academic Literacies: a critical lens on writing and reading in the academy. In K. Hyland & P. Shaw (Eds.) *The Routledge handbook of English for academic purposes*. London: Routledge.

Mezirow, J. (2000). *Learning as transformation: Critical perspectives on a theory in progress*. San Francisco: Jossey Bass.

O'Sullivan, E. (2003). Bringing a perspective of transformative learning to globalized consumption. *International Journal of Consumer Studies, 27*(4), 326-330.

Reid, G. (2009). *Dyslexia: A practitioner's handbook*. Chichester, UK: John Wiley & Sons.

Taylor, B. J. (2000). *Reflective practice: A guide for nurses and midwives*. Buckingham, UK: Open University Press.

Turner, J. (2012). Academic literacies: Providing a space for the socio-political dynamics of EAP. *Journal of English for Academic Purposes, 11*(1), 17-25.

Turner, J. (2011). *Language in the academy. Cultural reflexivity and intercultural dynamics*. Bristol, UK: Multilingual Matters.

Turner, J., & Hocking, D. (2004). Synergy in art and Language: Positioning the language specialist in contemporary fine art study. *Art, Design and Communication in Higher Education, 3*(3), 149-162.

Vygotsky, L. S. (1978). *Mind in society: The development of higher psychological processes.* Cambridge, MA: Harvard University Press.

Williams, K., Woolliams, M., & Spiro, J. (2012). *Reflective writing.* Basingstoke, UK: Palgrave Macmillan Publishing.

Wingate, U. (2012). Using academic literacies and genre-based models for academic writing instruction: A "literacy" journey. *Journal of English for Academic Purposes, 11*(1), 26-37.

CHAPTER 2

WORKING WITH POWER: A DIALOGUE ABOUT WRITING SUPPORT USING INSIGHTS FROM PSYCHOTHERAPY

Lisa Clughen and Matt Connell

Harnessing the potential of writing for self-transformation through exchanges with students can be a struggle indeed. Students, it often seems, wish to hand control over their writing to their tutor,[1] who struggles to resist this. Academic literacies perspectives can help elucidate some of the reasons for such tussles, inviting us to consider "hidden" aspects of writing (Brian Street, 2009), such as relationships between writing, subjectivity and power (Romy Clark & Roz Ivanic, 1997), and asking how such relationships may enable or disable the transformative potentialities of writing. Moreover, academic literacies researchers argue, it is through open dialogue that students and tutors may engage with these complex facets of writing (Theresa Lillis, 2006). However, as Lillis suggests, the nature of dialogue itself needs examination if it is to become genuinely transformative, and spaces for writing generated where the 'creative,' rather than the 'compliant' life might thrive (Sarah Mann, 2001, pp. 9-13).

In this chapter, we construct a dialogue between its co-authors[2] which examines struggles in writing support encounters from a psychological perspective, arguing that transformative exchanges over writing are quasi-therapeutic. Framing writing support as a negotiation of struggles with power and subjectivity, we offer tutors a way of thinking about relationships with students and their writing. We have chosen this dialogic form because it reflects the way our position on these topics has developed through conversation and co-writing, and also resonates with the conversational medium of academic supervision itself. We also think that this form can work as an example of alternative modalities of academic writing that can retain the author's voice, something students often find difficult.

Our dialogue follows psychotherapists who have argued for the application of certain insights from psychotherapy to pedagogy (Carl Rogers, 1993), and writing tutors who already use psychotherapy to inform their practice (Amanda Baker, 2006;

Phyllis Creme & Celia Hunt, 2002). However, we would avoid conflating the separate spheres of writing support and psychotherapy, simply noting that writing support encounters may take on the flavour of counselling, with issues of self-esteem, rejection and alienation being their everyday stuff (Helen Bowstead, 2009; Lisa Clughen & Matt Connell, 2012; Tamsin Haggis, 2006; Mann, 2001; Barbara Read, Louise Archer & Carol Leathwood, 2003). We aim not to pathologize students but to recognize that difficulties with writing are "normal," that struggles within writing tutorials are to be expected, and that psychotherapeutic discourse can offer strategies to negotiate them. Attitudes and methods that seek to recognize and redistribute power, such as a realness in the tutor-student exchange, a focus on non-directive modes of language and a reframing of powerlessness through normalizing strategies and non-judgment have as much of a place in writing support as they do in the therapy session. These are just some of the themes we touch on in our dialogue.

> Lisa: My writing support sometimes veers toward counselling, especially if students position themselves as stupid or as lacking in what it takes to succeed. I try to bolster their confidence to help them to help themselves, but it's a struggle to enter into the open, transformative exchange Carl Rogers talks about (1993). Often they just want me to tell them what to do and, understandably, ask me to judge their work, as if I am the final arbiter of truth: "Is that ok?" "Is that better?" They may refuse to own their power, seek to give it to me, and then resist my attempts to give it back to them!

> Matt: That sounds like a psychotherapeutic client saying "Doctor, I'm sick; cure me." The therapist has to carefully avoid reinforcing their passivity and self-pathologization. Have you got an example from your sessions?

> Lisa: Well, the opening of sessions often sets the scene for this— a student showed me her writing today and said: "I really need you to fix it for me." And read this email from a very self-aware student: "I hate to admit this—and I'm embarrassed that I have to admit it—but I think I need to be spoon-fed."

> Matt: "Spoon-fed" is an interesting choice of language psychoanalytically speaking, since it has infantile connotations. Writing tutorials can certainly seem like power struggles over dependency and independence. How do you avoid positioning the tutor as the dispenser of authoritative knowledge and the student as its recipient?

Lisa: Well, passivity is often a response to being rendered passive by, for example, alienating language and the pressure to succeed—so I try to resist becoming another alienating force. I take seriously the language I use so that it does not represent me as author of their text. I aim to foreground the student-writer as governor of their writing and to downplay my own authority: "what would you like to discuss today?" "I can only comment as a reader, you don't have to accept my points." "Am I right in thinking that …?" I sometimes talk about questions I ask myself when writing "that you may or may not find helpful" such as: "Is this really what I'm trying to say here?" "Does that language really get over my meaning?" This positions them as in being control, emphasising that only they can know what they want to say.

Matt: I'm afraid I find it very hard to resist students' desire to give away their agency by positioning me as their editor, and too easily get sucked into giving them what they often want—an editorial critique that can "fix" a specific piece of work.

Lisa: But if you do that, or only that, you run the risk of affirming their self-critical tendencies, feeding feelings of powerlessness and dependency. Subsequently, they may feel they can't do it without you.

Matt: Yes. Negative feelings and self-critique crop up a lot when students are struggling with writing—that's another reason for the parallels with therapy.

Lisa: What Rogers (1993) says about learning is definitely what I experience in my writing support—students bring the whole self to the exchange about writing, not just a simple request to go over, for example, sentence construction. Have a look at these statements from recent writing support sessions:

> I feel too stupid to be here. It's not a nice feeling at all.

> I deleted my work in anger, so I couldn't send it to you. You get a bit frustrated don't you, because you feel a bit thick.

> I … got myself in a right mess. I lost the ability to write so cried for a while.

Matt: You can really feel the pain in these cries for help. I'm sure you need a box of hankies in your office, just like a counsellor! Humanistic psychotherapy tries to avoid reinforcing the client's self-pathologizing tendencies, refusing the power of clinical classification and labelling (Thomas Szasz, 1974). In our context the question is: how can we avoid making the student who says they are stupid feel it even more? I wonder if the cognitive mode of academic teaching often side-lines such feelings, exacerbating students' self-condemnation for getting emotional?

Lisa: Oh yes, approaches to writing that are purely rational (for example, conceiving academic support as "skills teaching") often ignore the relationship between writing and emotion. But emotions affect both sides of the support encounter. Being "real" in the exchange by, for example, owning one's feelings about it could mean that while students might complain of their frustrations if the tutor will not edit their work for them, tutors might have to admit to their own feelings of irritation if students believe they are, or should be, telling them what to write, rather than engaging in an open exchange about both of their responses to the student's text (Rogers, 1993).

Matt: And to other people's texts and discourses? I'm interested in the way in which language use can sustain or disturb power in the writing exchange—those impediments to writing caused by engagements with alienating academic language. Tutors don't even have to assume the mantle of this intimidating linguistic power, it unconsciously colonizes the space between teachers and learners, being always already part of the cultural imaginary around education.

Lisa: One student told me that her strategy for coping with her tutor was to use dictionary.com afterwards because she "didn't have a clue what she was trying to say to me." She didn't feel able to ask at the time, due to the fear of looking stupid. Here's another student emailing me their experience of reading: "I've read all these theory books and they sound posh and are just too hard to understand. If I don't pick at each sentence, I won't have a clue what they are on about."

Matt: Here, students are imagining that it's different for us, whereas in reality, everyone struggles at one level or another with "theory books." I have to pick at each sentence too, and I find that if I explain this to students, it can help to transform their self-perceptions, mitigating their fantasies about our power. Radical psychotherapy can work like this too—one of the insights of "co-counselling" was that empathy can be generated more easily when professional hierarchies are eroded rather than reinforced (Mann, 2001).

Lisa: I sometimes explicitly give up my power by mentioning my own struggles with writing and what I do to cope with them, then ask students if they can suggest anything to help me.

Matt: Even Freud, a bad offender when it comes to jargon and power-bound interaction, knew that the struggles of the so-called "mentally ill" are only exaggerated versions of the every-day struggles that dog us all. If we can normalize what students are feeling, that helps them enter the community of scholars as potential equals, not competing supplicants.

Lisa: Yes. Normalizing both feelings and the typical gamut of unproductive writing behaviors can be a potentially powerful strategy. A PhD student who said she wanted me to tell her "how to write efficiently and effectively" told me that she was panick-ing that she was not a good writer as some days she could write a thousand words and other days none at all. It was as if she was looking for a magic formula for writing, something outside of herself (Bowstead, 2009). Instead, I drew on ideas about mind-fulness and encouraged her gently to see this just as a part of her own writing process (and said it was mine too, in fact)—it was neither good nor bad, but just the way it was at that moment. My hope was that her self-diagnosis ("bad writer") and the panic that ensued from it might be assuaged by establishing a climate of non-judgment. You've mentioned R. D. Laing when we've talked about this before, haven't you?

Matt: Yes—he's the big figure when it comes to avoiding the pathologizing gaze, normalizing distress and trying to avoid the pitfall of therapy becoming a lesson in power-bound conformity to an existing social order (Laing, 1967).

Lisa: But Matt, these students DO have to conform in order to succeed, they aren't living in a cultural free-for-all. The university and their employers determine which language games win and which lose.

Matt: Yes, but if they can become conscious of this on their own terms with their integrity intact, rather than feeling "retarded" because it doesn't come automatically, as one student shockingly described it, then that's a big thing. This may mean they need to find the sense hidden in what they are trying, but failing, to articulate in their writing, and to present it a different way. Laing provided a lot of analysis of distorted communications—especially a peculiar type of jumbled psychotic discourse colloquially known as "schizophrenese" or "word-salad" (Laing, 1965). Traditional psychiatry is uninterested in this discourse, seeing it simply as a symptom of a diseased brain. Following Freud's (1991) notion that all symptoms had a sense, Laing instead tried to tease out what meanings underpinned the confusing speech (Laing, 1965).

Lisa: Aren't you coming close to pathologizing students here? We don't want to suggest they are psychotic!

Matt: Of course not! Firstly, I mean this as an analogy, as a metaphor. But secondly, Laing was, precisely, trying to avoid the pathologizing of psychosis itself—where some would dismiss it as nonsense, he reframed it as a "normal" expression of the human head and heart, and as a communication strategy that made sense to the person deploying it.

Lisa: So, applied here, can we say that there must always be a logic behind even the most confused writing, the kind of text that tutors may highlight with a big question mark, if only we could find out what that logic is?

Matt: Right! In Laing's case studies the jumbled discourse is indicative of repressed and conflicted personality fragments. In a much less extreme way, jumbled writing may be indicative of conflicts in students' understanding and expressions. The further twist is that Laing suggests the "word-salad" may operate as a defensive measure when the sufferer feels pressurized or misunderstood by those exerting power over them (Laing, 1965). I think sometimes there's a parallel here with student writing—students may be trying to mimic a scholarly register as a defensive reaction to criticism, but trying to sound clever to avoid seeming stupid usually only makes it worse.

Lisa: So, the task is to somehow negotiate the power while knowing that the required language game cannot be completely avoided—just as those experiencing psychosis in the end have to find ways to talk using the rules of conventional discourse.

Empathy is the key to this—Rogers' (1989, pp. 225-226) "unconditional positive regard," where we refrain from judging the student no matter what they say, is central, but it's a struggle to maintain it: when confronted with very frustrating writing, or confused students asking me to sort it out for them, value judgments—and even anger—can be hard to avoid. I have to be constantly mindful of the suffering individual and strive to remain compassionate.

Matt: It's interesting that you say "negotiate" rather than "remove" the power. With that distinction, I think you are opening up a critique of the sort of theory which frames power simply as something to be escaped.

Lisa: Do you mean the Nietzschean criticism deployed by Foucault (1988), which he aims at Freudo-Marxists and existentialists like Laing?

Matt: Yes, bang on—for Foucault, there's a naiveté to theories which claim power is a purely negative thing, operating via constraint. For the theorists he criticizes, power always stops things happening, it limits freedom, and they want us to strive to remove it so that freedom can blossom free of its baleful effect.

Lisa: Whereas in his Nietzschean model, power is constitutive, it creates things …

Matt: … and, moreover, it simply cannot be "removed": it can only be re-deployed, swapped for another form of power or channelled in another way. We could say it has to be owned, consciously exploited and used, rather than refused. The refusal to own power may simply be a sort of passive-aggressive strategy—in fact, a disavowed form of power. Maybe we have to help students work with power because, as you said, we simply can't remove power when it comes to academic writing. We might harbour a hope that students' personal growth can be central to the university experience, à la Rogers, or that we can help them shrug off the shackles of conformity and develop their true self, à la Laing—but if we overdo it, we may be giving them rope to hang themselves with. If we removed academic structure and expected "freedom" to emerge, it would just be a mess!

Lisa: Yes. On the one hand, it is certainly important to critique the dominating force of didactic academic socialization, which can deny students the right to their own voice. For that, the strategies of humanistic psychotherapy for opening up dialogue and empowering students through an understanding of the complex role of emotion and self-identity are really useful. But on the other hand, we can't simply throw the baby out with the bathwater, and can accept that scholarly frameworks and writing conventions can be an enabling force too, a form of power that can be appropriated and used. For example, writing conventions are not just a straight-jacket, they're a means of achieving clarity: if you can learn them, you can communicate more powerfully.

Matt: So, what we need is for writing support to function as a sort of "critical socialization" that helps to foster the students' nascent membership of the academic community. We can help students to find the parts of academic culture where they feel at home, and to resist those parts of the culture that alienate them.

Lisa: And the task of academic literacies work is to do this concretely, not only at the level of theory. So, for example, other ways of writing academically might be offered that would allow for a freer engagement with academic ideas. Perhaps what we are doing here is one model for this: writing an academic analysis as a conversation can allow for a discussion that is research-informed, critical, and also more immediately inclusive of the writer's own voice, as it allows for a language that is closer to this voice. This isn't necessarily the case with the formal language required by the academic essay.

NOTES

1. By "tutor" we mean anyone in HE, whether they work as a subject lecturer or within a writing development service, who discusses students' writing with them.

2. Lisa is a Spanish subject lecturer and also leads a School/Faculty-level academic support service, and thus has a specialist writing development role. Matt is a lecturer in the Social Theory subject area.

REFERENCES

Baker, A. (2006). What else do students need? A psychodynamic reflection on students' need for support from staff at university. *Active Learning in Higher Education*, 7(2), 171-183.

Bowstead, H. (2009). Teaching English as a foreign language—a personal exploration of language, alienation and academic literacy. *UK Journal of Learning Development in Higher Education, 1.* 1-10.

Clark, R., & Ivanič, R. (1997). *The politics of writing.* London: Routledge.

Clughen, L., & Connell, M. (2012). Using dialogic lecture analysis to clarify disciplinary requirements for writing. In L. Clughen & C. Hardy (Eds.), *Writing in the disciplines* (pp. 123-141). Bingley, UK: Emerald Group Publishing.

Creme, P., & Hunt, C. (2002). Creative participation in the essay writing process. *Arts and Humanities in Higher Education,* 1(2), 145-166.

Foucault, M. (1988). Power and sex. In L. D. Kritzman (Ed.), *Politics, philosophy, culture: Interviews and other writings of Michel Foucault, 1977-1984* (pp. 110-124). New York/ London: Routledge.

Freud, S. (1991). The sense of symptoms. In J. Strachey (Trans.), *Introductory lectures on psychoanalysis* (pp. 296-312). Harmondsworth, UK: Penguin Books.

Haggis, T. (2006). Pedagogies for diversity: Retaining critical challenge amidst fears of "dumbing down." *Studies in Higher Education,* 31(5), 521-535.

Laing, R. D. (1965). *The divided self.* Harmondsworth, UK: Penguin Books.

Laing, R. D. (1967). *The politics of experience and the bird of paradise.* Harmondsworth, UK: Penguin Books.

Lillis, T. (2003). Student writing as "academic literacies": Drawing on Bakhtin to move from critique to design. *Language and Education,* 17(3), 192-207.

Lillis, T. (2006). Moving towards an academic literacies pedagogy: Dialogues of participation. In L. Ganobcsik-Williams (Ed.), *Teaching academic writing in UK higher education: Theories, practices and models* (pp. 30-45). Basingstoke, UK: Palgrave Macmillan Publishing.

Mann, S. (2001). Alternative perspectives on the student experience: Alienation and engagement. *Studies in Higher Education,* 26(1), 7-19.

Read, B., Archer, L., & Leathwood, C. (2003). Challenging cultures? Student conceptions of "belonging" and "isolation" at a post-1992 university. *Studies in Higher Education,* 28(3), 261-277.

Rogers, C. (1989). The necessary and sufficient conditions of therapeutic personality change. In H. Kirschenbaum and V. Land Henderson (Eds.), *The Carl Rogers Reader* (pp. 219-235). London: Constable.

Rogers, C. (1993). The interpersonal relationship in the facilitation of learning. In M. Thorpe, R. Edwards, & A. Hanson (Eds.), *Culture and processes of adult learning* (pp. 228-242). London/ New York: Open University.

Street, B. (2009). 'Hidden' features of academic writing. *Working Papers in Educational Linguistics,* 1(24), 1-17. Retrieved from http://www.gse.upenn.edu/sites/gse.upenn.edu.wpel/files/archives/v24/Street.pdf

Szasz, T. S. (1974). *The myth of mental illness.* New York: Harper and Row.

CHAPTER 3

AN ACTION RESEARCH INTERVENTION TOWARDS OVER-COMING "THEORY RESISTANCE" IN PHOTOJOURNALISM STUDENTS

Jennifer Good

"THEORY RESISTANCE"

What follows is an account of a small-scale action research intervention designed to tackle a problem I have called "theory resistance," among undergraduate photojournalism students. By this I mean the resistance often expressed by these students to theoretical reading and writing, encountered in the required "Contextual Studies" unit of their course (also called the "History and Theory" unit). This is often related to a perceived or artificial polarization of "theory" and "practice." In this context, "practice" denotes the act of taking photographs, as opposed to the critical reading and writing that supplements and underpins this activity. Many students express a belief that this reading and writing is at best alienating and difficult, and at worst, a waste of time or a distraction from the "real work" of photography (see also Gimenez and Thomas Chapter 1, Adams Chapter 4 this volume).

Action research is a process in which a specific problem is identified and an experimental "intervention" designed and tested with a view to gaining insight into the problem and ultimately solving it (John Elliott, 2001; David Kember, 2000). This particular intervention, undertaken at a large Arts and Design university in the United Kingdom, explored the experiences of students in reading weekly set critical texts for this unit in their second year. It is based on the pedagogic principle that effective engagement with such texts is crucial in students' development as photojournalists, and that "theory resistance" is detrimental to their engagement with higher education as a whole, as well as to this photographic practice.

Because I have found that using metaphors is often helpful in explaining the value of critical texts, as well as how to tackle the reading involved—imagery such as sieves, onions, chopsticks and maps, for example, can help illustrate selective or step-by-step approaches to reading—I designed an intervention based on visualization, in which students could collaboratively create visual models or metaphors by making simple drawings, and then discuss the implications of their drawings (Sarah Pink, 2006; Gillian Rose, 2007). Arlene Archer (2006) argues that rather than being tied solely to verbal representation, academic literacies can and should account for other modalities, notably the visual. Visualizing ideas through drawing might be understood both as a *way of communicating*, inasmuch as visual literacy is an academic literacy, and as a *practice* that might usefully "cut through" the power relations around difficult language, inasmuch as it transcends verbal language. This validation of a visual or pictorial approach is particularly useful among photojournalism students, who are often more comfortable communicating through (and about) images than words (see also Coleman Chapter 18, Stevens Chapter 19 this volume).

The intervention was based upon the following hypotheses: 1) students would find drawing helpful in articulating their feelings about reading; 2) they would benefit from recognizing that they were not alone in their concerns; 3) they would be able to create models for more effective reading; and 4) I would learn from seeing how the students represented their struggles, enabling me to design better teaching and learning activities. Of these hypotheses, the first, second and fourth were proved correct, while the third did not turn out as expected. Transformation for the teacher is a key part of the findings of my action research. More important than this however is the movement for students from "resistance" to acceptance of the contribution that reading theoretical texts can make to their practice as photographers, and also from a place of intimidation and shame in the face of difficult theoretical language to empowerment and (following bell hooks, 1994) freedom. In this process, the atmosphere within the teaching space is completely transformed, as trust is built between teacher and students through making explicit the tacit "oppression" of language.

DRAWING ON/AS AN ACADEMIC LITERACIES APPROACH

Students embark on the BA (Hons) Photojournalism course with a view to becoming photographers: from the beginning of the course they are practitioners of photography first and foremost, rather than writers or theorists. My approach in teaching theory must be sensitive to this. I aim to encourage students to take what they "need" from texts—to gain the confidence to be selective in what they read based on their own interests and practice, without being dismissive of the rest. There are a number of hurdles involved in this. My view is that while it tends to manifest itself as a dismissal of the value of theory, "theory resistance" is most often rooted in a lack of confidence; a belief that critical texts are too difficult, provoking a defensive and/or fearful reaction. The academic literacies model provides a framework for acknowledging the pressure faced by students as they negotiate unfamiliar literacy practices (Mary Lea & Brian Street, 1998). These are understood as social practices that often "maintain relationships of power and authority" (ibid., p. 168). A key element distinguishing the academic literacies model as the basis for this intervention is its attention to the problem of tacit-ness or implicitness, which is rooted in power relations: the student experience of having to adapt to "academic" language is often stressful, and as Lea and Street (1998, p. 2006) argue, teachers often fail explicitly to acknowledge this, instead maintaining a tacit expectation that students must either navigate these differences independently or fail to progress. Students thus either occupy a privileged position "inside," with access to academic discourse, or are excluded and disempowered, particularly in relation to the teacher. Theory resistance is an understandable response to this situation, in which, according to the academic literacies model, there is a clear need to make tacit assumptions about academic language more explicit, and to find ways of empowering students in relation to language. Tamsin Haggis suggests that "collective inquiry"—open dialogue or negotiation between students and teachers—is one important way of working at this empowerment (2006, p. 8).

Feeling that a text is too hard is one issue. Another, which I encounter frequently among students, is that it is irrelevant. Writing in the context of feminism, bell hooks spells out the urgent political stakes implicit in this assumption, explaining how language can widen the perceived theory/practice gap in dangerous ways:

> many women have responded to hegemonic feminist theory that does not speak clearly to us by trashing theory, and, as a consequence, further promoting the false dichotomy between theory and practice …. By internalizing the false assumption that theory is not a social practice, they promote … a potentially oppressive hierarchy where all concrete action is viewed as more important than any theory written or spoken. (hooks, 1994, pp. 66-67)

The complexity of theoretical language is often seen by photojournalism students as a sign that it is not useful; that it is firmly divided from practice or "concrete action." hooks presents this in hierarchical terms that arguably contrasts with what Lea and Street say about power relationships, highlighting a tricky double standard: students recognize that some types of language are of a higher, more exclusive order than others. They often conclude, however, *as a direct consequence of this,* that academic language is not valuable. Rather than aspiring to be part of the conversation, they reject it in principle because of its very exclusivity; objecting to an "oppression" which in part they themselves are implicated in constructing. hooks' work signals a valuable link that needs to be made between academic literacies work which centers primarily on language and literacy with other fields in which there is an essential relationship between political activism and theory, such as feminism, and, indeed, photojournalism.

THE ACTION RESEARCH INTERVENTION

The action research intervention involved gathering data over the course of one ten-week term. In keeping with an action research approach, this data took a number of forms. It included drawings, questionnaires and detailed notes made in the course of a number of sessions in which I recorded what students said.

In week one of the autumn term, I asked the students to read a fairly complex chapter from Roland Barthes's (1977) book, *Image Music Text*. The following week I conducted two identical hour-long sessions with the two halves of the student cohort. Each began with an informal discussion about the experience of reading the text, during which I noted particularly how it had made the students *feel*. I then introduced the concept of academic literacies, firstly by explaining that in academic reading and writing, *power relations* are in play because of the power that language has to both include and exclude; and secondly that an important step in addressing this power imbalance is to have an explicit, clear and inclusive discussion about such issues rather than leaving them unspoken. I explained my belief that creating visual models of what difficult academic reading "looks like" might be helpful, and that it was important that we do this collaboratively, to explode the myth that, "I'm the only one who doesn't get it."

I asked the students, in collaborative groups of four or five, first to draw their negative experiences of reading the Barthes text, visualizing what it was like. I then asked them to imagine and draw a more positive reading experience. Overall, twenty-four drawings were made in the course of the two sessions, using colored marker pens on A2-sized paper. In some cases the collaboration involved one student doing the drawing based on suggestions and directions by others; in other cases several students worked on different parts of the drawing at once, or added elements one after another as ideas developed. We then discussed the drawings, and in the weeks that followed I asked the students questions about how this exercise had affected their experience of reading, recording their answers in my notes. Most importantly:

- How did they approach/tackle the text(s)?
- How did it feel?

In the final week students filled in an anonymous questionnaire about the term's reading experiences overall.

INITIAL FINDINGS: DRAWING READING

When reflecting on the initial experience of reading a difficult text, students' comments, which I noted during our group discussion, ranged from the very emotional—"I felt stupid", "it made me angry"—to critical judgments about the text itself—"I felt it was badly written", "there was too much assumed prior knowledge of words and concepts"—and accounts of strategies that they used to try to tackle the text. These included reading particular paragraphs "again and again," constantly having to refer to a dictionary, "or I wouldn't have got through it," and beginning by reading in close detail but eventually giving this up and just skim reading because, "I felt fed up." The fact that much of the language used was so emotive confirms hooks's assertion that students can perceive theory as "oppressive" in a very real way and consequently feel compelled to "trash" it (1994, pp. 66-67).

Illustrations 1 through 7 in Figure 3.1 are scans made from a selection of the students' original drawings, and highlight some overarching metaphorical themes. Firstly, the linear journey, race, climb or obstacle course (illustrations 1, 2 and 3 in Figure 3.1)—these implying an assumption that reading is necessarily a rigidly linear process of "getting from A to B". Secondly, the appearance of incomprehensible symbols and codes (illustration 4) brings to mind Lea and Street's point that students must adapt to, organize and interpret entirely "new ways of knowing" within the university (1998, p. 157). Most significant, though, was the number of symbols pertaining to access or barriers, as evidenced in all of the drawings illustrated here, but particularly in illustrations 5, 6 and 7 in Figure 3.1. I noted a comment from one student who had drawn circles representing inclusion and exclusion, that, "the circle has to let us in. It has to be accessible." From an academic literacies perspective in which the negotiation of access is an important concept, this was revealing—particularly the implication that access is controlled by the text (or the author of the text), which may or may not "let us in," rather than the power of access lying with the reader.

Having been asked to make "negative" drawings and then "positive" ones, the students seemed to find the former much easier than the latter, indicating that (imagined) success was harder to visualise than (experienced) failure. It is perhaps unsurprising, then, that the "positive" drawings illustrate feelings and states of being (illustration 6) rather than models or strategies for action. As the development of strategies was one of the goals of the project, this was rather disappointing. However in light of some of the other findings, it began to seem less relevant.

When we discussed the drawings together, I noted two key conclusions that were reached by the students. The first was that adopting a non-linear approach to a text—for example skim reading it and then going back to the most relevant sections—might be "okay." This illustrates that while strategies for action were not necessarily represented in the drawings themselves, discussion *of* the drawings pointed towards them. Interestingly, the second conclusion was that there might be other things to gain from a text than comprehension, such as an appreciation of language, or even relishing the challenge of reading. While the first conclusion was related to action, the second was more about attitude. Overall, the exercise confirmed that effective reading practices cannot be taught or "delivered" as such. As Haggis has argued, they can only be "described, discussed, compared, modelled

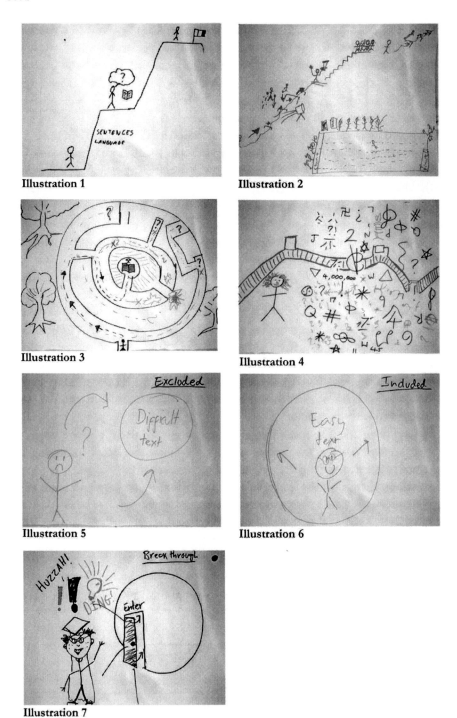

Illustration 1

Illustration 2

Illustration 3

Illustration 4

Illustration 5

Illustration 6

Illustration 7

Figure 3.1: Drawing "theory resistance."

and practiced" (2006, p.10). This exercise involved the first four of these. The fifth would come later as the term progressed.

ONGOING FINDINGS: PRACTISING READING

As I continued to ask students about their perceptions of reading in subsequent weeks, I tried different methods of structuring our seminars in response to what they said, looking for the best ways to facilitate discussion about the weekly set texts. Many continued to express frustration, and while the number of students actually doing the reading increased, some were still reluctant to engage. When asked if the earlier drawing exercise had impacted how they approached texts, most said no, but as we talked further, it became apparent that some were beginning to approach reading in a more flexible, non-linear way, as we had discussed, and were finding this helpful. In week five, sensing that many in the group still felt disempowered, I set up a small group activity which involved them in looking through that session's set text in small groups for any "nuggets" that particularly related to the theme of the seminar. This worked well for the following reasons:

- It was achievable even for students who hadn't done the reading in advance.
- It encouraged independent exploration of the text according to their own initiative and/or interests rather than the teacher's agenda.
- It explicitly demonstrated and validated a selective approach to reading according to specific goals and lessened the pressure to "take in" and comprehend the whole of the text. Some students wanted to engage at a deeper or more thorough level, but for others who felt excluded, this was a valuable first step.

Through this exercise, most students were able to identify something, however small or basic, and thus "access" a text that had previously seemed to exclude them. I encouraged them to adopt a similar approach when they read the following week's text, so that each person could come to the seminar prepared to offer an observation. The following week's discussion flowed more easily and there seemed to be less frustration. Subsequently I developed the above small-group exercise by asking students to look at the text together, identifying one point they agreed with and one they disagreed with. This had the same benefits as above, with the added benefit of encouraging critical thinking (David Saltmarsh & Sue Saltmarsh, 2008), giving students permission to agree or disagree with the author in their own terms, and providing an accessible framework in which, at the very least, every student could feel empowered to have something to say.

At the end of the term, students were asked to complete an anonymous questionnaire about their experiences. The sample was small (twelve out of twenty-eight students responded), but the results were striking, and can be summed up as follows:

- The majority (7/12) seemed to see (or remember) the drawing exercise as being primarily about *feeling and expressing* rather than learning, constructing or illustrating.
- A surprising number said that they found reading the weekly set texts both difficult *and* enjoyable/useful.
- Most (10/12) said that the drawing exercise caused them to think about/ approach/engage with the course readings in a different way.
- However, of those who said that the exercise had led to change, not many were able to describe this change in very specific detail.

It seems that the primary change experienced by these students was in attitude, feeling and perception about reading rather than a shift in comprehension or strategy. For example, two students wrote that they did not necessarily find the reading any easier as a result of the exercise, but that they did find it less intimidating.

CONCLUSIONS

Of my initial indicators of success, it is those relating to the atmosphere in the teaching space and levels of discussion and participation in which I have observed the most significant changes, and which represent the key outcomes of the project.

As I continued to work with this group of students throughout the following two terms, the atmosphere in our seminars was very different. Students seemed more open and relaxed, and perhaps the most obvious change was that they were much more willing to talk. Conversation about concepts and texts began to come more naturally. This, I think, was largely a result of what I learned and how I was able to use this knowledge to develop the structure of seminars in more effective ways. For example, for me it was hugely beneficial to literally see the problem of theoretical language as experienced by students. Seeing texts represented as marathons, black holes, tornadoes, and mazes helped me to identify with their difficulties in a very immediate way. As Lea and Street point out, difficulties in navigating different registers of academic practice are often attributable to the "contrasting expectations and interpretations of academic staff and students" (1998, p. 157). From my own perspective, this process helped to narrow this gap in expectations, and the change in atmosphere was largely due to an increased level of trust. The intervention in itself demonstrated that I am interested in the students' struggles, and that my goal in teaching theory is to contribute to their development as photographers—not just to foist my own (possibly irrelevant) interests on them. As noted in the questionnaire results, students seemed to relate to the drawing exercise more as a mode of expression than a strategy for constructing something for future "use." An important benefit of this was in confronting feelings of shame and isolation. Thus as well as building trust between myself and the students, the process of making struggles explicit increased trust between the students themselves, and perceived barriers to collaboration were broken down.

Overall, the transformations seen in the interpersonal dynamics within the classroom were as marked as changes in the students' individual reading practices. This was not what I had anticipated, but since the problem initially identified was "resistance," as opposed to lack of understanding, this can be seen as a successful outcome. I might conclude that my primary findings are emotional rather than intellectual, and, following bell hooks, account for students' holistic experience of learning as "the practice of freedom" (hooks, 1994, p. 4). More fundamentally, they should be understood in terms of the academic literacies view of literacies as social practices (Lea & Street, 1998, p. 158), in which power relations are played out and identities are forged. Some elements of the intervention might be usefully repeated with subsequent student groups, but most important for the future are the lessons learned about these social practices of literacy: listening to and negotiating with students, making tacit expectations explicit, acknowledging how serious the oppression of these expectations can be, and navigating them via a genuinely collaborative process.

REFERENCES

Archer, A. (2006). A multimodal approach to academic literacies: Problematizing the visual/verbal divide. *Language and Education, 20* (6), 449-462.

Barthes. R. (1977). *Image, music, text.* New York:Hill and Wang.

Elliott, J. (2001). *Action research for educational change.* Milton Keynes, UK: Open University Press.

Haggis, T. (2006). Pedagogies for diversity: Retaining critical challenge amidst fears of "dumbing down." *Studies in Higher Education, 31* (5), 521-535.

hooks, b. (1994). *Teaching to transgress: Education as the practice of freedom.* London: Routledge.

Kember, D. (2000). *Action learning and action research: Improving the quality of teaching and learning.* London: Kogan Page.

Lea, M. R., & Street, B. V. (1998). Student writing in higher education: An academic literacies approach. *Studies in Higher Education, 23* (2), 157-173.

Lea, M. R., & Street, B. V. (2006). The "academic literacies" model: Theory and applications. *Theory Into Practice, 45* (4), 368-377.

Pink, S. (2006). *Doing visual ethnography.* London: Sage Publications.

Rose, G. (2007). *Visual methodologies*. London, Sage Publications.

Saltmarsh, D., & Saltmarsh, S. (2008). Has anyone read the reading? Using assessment to promote academic literacies and learning cultures. *Teaching in Higher Education, 13*(6), 621-632.

CHAPTER 4

STUDENT-WRITING TUTORS: MAKING SENSE OF "ACADEMIC LITERACIES"

Joelle Adams

This chapter draws on a small-scale study of the student-tutor experience to illustrate how student-tutors make sense of the "academic literacies" framework, as set out by Mary Lea and Brian Street (1998). By "student-tutors" I am referring to students who engage in supporting other students' writing as part of their work on an accredited undergraduate module. The module is *Teaching Writing*, which offers third-year Creative Writing students an opportunity to develop their pedagogical knowledge and skills. Participants engage in a wide range of practices as student-tutors, including one-to-one peer tutoring in the university's Writing and Learning Center, designing and leading subject-specific academic writing and editing workshops within the university, and facilitating creative writing workshops in the community (see also Good Chapter 3, this volume).

In recognition of the challenges students often face in making sense of theory, I carried out a small scale intervention study which involved devising a series of activities to help student-tutors understand the key tenets of academic literacies theory and apply the principles in their tutoring practice. I asked students to create a diagram of based on Lea and Street's (1998) introductory article, to help them identify the key concepts, to apply the principles to practice through observation and in their own tutoring, and to record their reflections in their learning journals. These activities acknowledge the professional context of the module and some of the "signature pedagogies" (Lee Shulman, 2005) in education: that is, observation, application, and reflection.

Data extracts included in this chapter are drawn from diagrams and journal entries by student-tutors who studied the module in the academic years 2010/11 and 2011/12; permission has been given by student-tutors for their work to be used, but all names have been changed. In my attempt to make sense of their learning experience, I draw on Roz Ivanič's (1998) work to consider how "aspects of identity" and "possibilities for self-hood in the socio-cultural and institutional contexts" (Ivanič, 1998, p. 27) figure in the student-tutors' experiences.

STUDENTS' CONCEPTIONS AND OBSERVATIONS
OF ACADEMIC LITERACIES

Students read "Student Writing in Higher Education: an academic literacies approach" (Lea & Street, 1998) prior to one of the initial module workshops. In the session, students created diagrams to help them clarify the relationship between the three approaches to writing in higher education outlined by Lea and Street—study skills, academic socialization and academic literacies. Students then shared diagrams with the whole class and reflected on the exercise in their journals.

First, in Figure 4.1, Sally's representation clearly signals a hierarchical relationship between different elements. She positions being "academically literate" as being built on the foundation of study skills and academic socialization, but is informed by one's "previous experiences, etc." or what might be considered the "autobiographical self" aspect of identity (Ivanič, 1998, p. 24). These "previous experiences, etc." form the basis for students' academic experiences. The placement of the "really good graduate" at the pinnacle of the pyramid shows that Sally interprets the model as privileging being "academically literate" as part of achieving success; it would seem that Sally is interpreting Lea and Street's model referentially and normatively (as describing a particular level of literacy knowledge) and as applying to the whole student experience (and beyond).

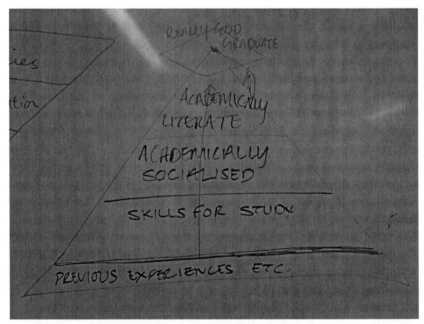

*Figure 4.1: Sally's conception of academic literacies
from reading Lea and Street (1998).*

In her journal, Alex uses a bull's-eye (see Figure 4.2) and, like Sally, a layered pyramid to demonstrate a sense of "construction"; however, Alex inverts the pyramid, with study skills at the narrow base and academic literacies situated at the wide top, demonstrating her conception of academic literacies as 'broader', all-encompassing approach, than the study skills or academic socialization approaches to teaching writing.

During the work around academic literacies on the module, students often claim that an academic literacies approach subsumes other approaches, an argument made by Lea and Street (1998); Alex's "bull's-eye" diagram is indicative of how students think of an academic literacies approach as encompassing both study skills and academic socialization. The idea that academic literacies subsumes other approaches is evident in the way both Sally and Alex place academic literacies theory at the "top" of pyramids; study skills and academic socialization are phases or goals one passes through on the way to the summit.

What is unclear is whether students like Sally and Alex see academic literacies as a theory—they seem to be using it as a description of a hierarchy of literacy expertise. Though the students are learning how to become writing teachers and tutors, their conceptions of the model seem to be understood through their experience as individual students and with concerns, as with Sally's note, about becoming a "really good graduate." The "student" part of their identity may be influencing their engagement with the academic literacies framework: they may not yet identify themselves as being in a position to step outside their current experience and concerns to

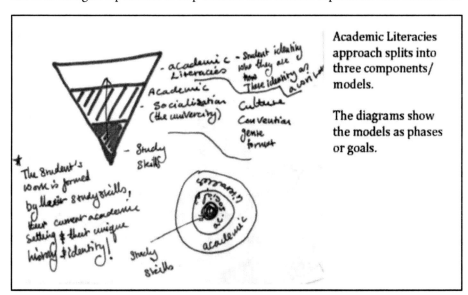

*Figure 4.2: Alex's conception of academic literacies
from reading Lea and Street (1998).*

work with theories of language and literacy in their own teaching practice.

WHAT WE SEE AND DO: HOW STUDENTS RELATE ACADEMIC LITERACIES PRINCIPLES TO PRACTICE

After the diagram activity, students commented in their learning journals: their comments illustrate the different ways in which they grappled with Lea and Street's framework and tried to connect it to their understanding of teaching and learning writing, as well as to their own experience and perspectives as writers. Extract 1 for example illustrates how Anne distinguishes between academic socialization and academic literacies:

EXTRACT 1: ANNE'S CONCEPTION OF ACADEMIC LITERACIES AFTER READING LEA AND STREET (1998)

> Academic socialization sees the tutor as a gateway between the student as a learner and the student as a professional. It address [sic] the way that students interact with their field and interpret tasks, but it fails to teach the students how write [sic] at an academic level. Academic literacies argue [sic] then that the problems with student writing lies [sic] in the level of knowledge and identity rather than skill or socialization. The student perceives academic literacies as the ability to write "in a certain way" for "for a certain audience."

Extract 1 illustrates Anne's attempt to understand the framework and a somewhat partial understanding. A key point she seems to be taking from the Lea and Street is a contrast between the theoretical position they advocate—a view of writing as to do with knowledge and identity—and the way in which students tend to view academic writing, that is as the ability to "write in a certain way for a certain audience." However, she then deconstructs her own experience of academic writing, as in Extract 2.

EXTRACT 2: ANNE'S APPLICATION OF ACADEMIC LITERACIES THEORY TO HER OWN EXPERIENCE

> This all rings true in my own experiences. When I write an essay I adopt a voice appropriate for a student audience at times and not a voice which comes from a place of knowledge, as an academic talking among other academics.

> Other times I stumble when I do have the right voice in my writing because I realize I don't KNOW very much about my subject. I don't know how to research, what to research or how to put all the facts together in a seamless piece of academic writing. It's forced, fractured. I believe that the more you know about the field the easier it is to write and present.

It's interesting to note that in the first extract Anne is attempting to express her learning/sense-making around academic literacies in a conventional impersonal academic style, whereas in Extract 2 she is expressing her sense-making as it relates to her *personally*, not only in the content, but in the language that she uses. Her anxiety about writing about the theoretical is perhaps signaled through the language errors at sentence level in Extract 1; in contrast, when she writes about the personal in Extract 2, Anne's writing contains fewer grammatical errors. Her "discoursal self" (Ivanič, 1998, p. 25) is less confident ("forced, fractured") when she struggles with the theoretical issues of academic literacies and more confident when she's writing about what she knows: her own experience.

In her attempts to make sense of academic literacies, in Extracts 3 and 4 Laura addresses the emancipatory possibilities of writing; Laura seems to see what Ivanič has called "possibilities for self-hood in socio-cultural and institutional contexts" (Ivanič, 1998, p. 27) in relationships between teachers and students engaged in creative writing and the wider contexts of "political and social power."

EXTRACT 3: LAURA'S UNDERSTANDING OF THE EMANCIPATORY POWER OF AN ACADEMIC LITERACIES APPROACH TO TEACHING WRITING

> [academic literacies theory] treats literacy as political and social power, acknowledging the variety of communicative practices whilst also taking into account the identity of the learner and institution.

Laura's reflection on the effect of applying academic literacies principles, in Extract 4, shows great emotion; her use of italics and punctuation, such as the exclamation mark, highlights the importance of this insight to her. What Ivanič refers to as her "discoursal self" is excited by the "possibilities for self-hood" in her disciplinary context.

EXTRACT 4: LAURA'S REFLECTION ON THE EMANCIPATORY POWER OF THE ACADEMIC LITERACIES APPROACH

> This is incredibly important to creative writing! I see teaching

creative writing as teaching a social and political form of power, as well as a subject in which identity is fundamentally important.

Laura's analysis of the relationship of academic literacies theory indicates that she understands core principles of the framework, including its focus on power and identity, and that she sees possibilities for application. In Extract 5, Laura reflects on how the diagram activity affected her understanding of academic literacies and begins to consider how she will apply this knowledge.

EXTRACT 5: LAURA'S REFLECTION ON THE DIAGRAM EXERCISE

I found [the diagram exercise] to be an extremely clever method for clarifying the teaching in our minds, discussing it with our peers and contextualizing it. I found it incredibly useful because it made me simplify the teaching for myself.

Students on the module find the reading troublesome at first because they often have not read much critical or scholarly writing to this point in their degree programme; making meaning from the text in groups encourages them to share and debate their understanding, while the diagram encourages simplification of complex ideas. The following examples show the range of conceptions students have of academic literacies principles, and highlight some similarities in how they privilege the approach above other ways of teaching writing.

In Extract 6, Christine reflects on her observation of tutorials in the Writing and Learning Centre, a service providing academic writing advice to students on any course at the university.

EXTRACT 6: CHRISTINE'S OBSERVATIONS OF TUTORING PRACTICE

The writing tutors didn't simply tell the students what was right and wrong with their work, instead they asked many questions and got the student thinking and analyzing their own work in order to understand for themselves how they could improve their work. This demonstrates the academic literacies theory because the student is made to develop their own knowledge and understanding and to adapt these within each subject that they study.

Christine sees academic literacies principles in practice when students are encouraged to take responsibility for their own learning. Similarly, Edie tries to explicitly use an academic literacies approach to structuring her peer-led session on professional copy-editing; Edie has chosen to run a workshop on editing because it closely aligns to the course outcomes. She analyzes her tutoring approaches in Extract 7.

EXTRACT 7: EDIE'S ANALYSIS OF HER OWN TEACHING

- A study skills approach: practical assessment of students' editorial skills;
- an academic socialization approach: open discussion within the class about why editing is important; and
- an academic literacies approach: checking to see that students have improved understanding of the importance of editing and what is required of them.

For Edie, an academic literacies approach means engaging students at a meta-cognitive level. Edie does not simply wish to teach editing skills; she also hopes to clarify the rationale for learning how to edit and empower students to meet expectations.

In her tutoring practice, Laura explores the issue of identity, making a connection between academic literacies and creative writing. The following extract demonstrates her explicit exploration of identity for students on a Creative Writing course, where creative outputs constitute the "academic" assessed work (as opposed to traditional critical essays, for example). Laura seems to be making connections between what Ivanič (1998) refers to as "autobiographical identity" ("we tend to write what we know") and "possibilities for self-hood" in the relationship between student and teacher.

EXTRACT 8: LAURA'S CONSIDERATION OF IDENTITY WHEN TEACHING WRITING

> In an unusual way I [as a student-tutor] will have an insight into the student's identity from looking at their writing; we tend to write what we know, in fact this is encouraged in creative writing, so it will be possible to gain an understanding of my student's psychology more so than in other subjects.

DISCUSSION AND CONCLUSION: MAKING SENSE OF ACADEMIC LITERACIES AND ISSUES OF IDENTITY IN LEARNING

The design of the learning activities on the *Teaching Writing* module encourages students to define the key concepts of academic literacies theory (including the concepts' relationship to one another), apply the theory, and then reflect on the experiences to deepen their knowledge. I ask students to keep a reflective journal precisely because of the connection between writing and meaning-making; this low-stakes and relatively informal writing provides an opportunity for students to develop their understanding of theories introduced on the module before they attempt to critically discuss them in a traditional essay. Anne's discomfort around finding a voice when writing about areas she feels she has little knowledge highlights the need to allow students a safe environment in which they can practice articulating their thoughts (without being formally assessed). The learning activities on the module are designed to move away from a "study skills" approach to teaching students how to write, teach writing, and write about teaching and not only socialize them into the academic conventions, but provide a platform for considering how their own identities and contexts might influence their own writing, learning, and teaching practices.

The issue of identity also influences the ways students on the *Teaching Writing* module experience learning, teaching, and assessment. The *Teaching Writing* students often have not written (what they consider) "academic" pieces of work before: their previous output is mainly creative or reflective texts rather than critical, academic essays. Again, Anne's uneasiness with writing about theory demonstrates how little these third-year students may have been required to engage with scholarly literature before taking this module, which raises questions about how the "signature pedagogies" of Creative Writing develop students' critical thinking and rhetorical communication skills.

The diagrams show how students define academic literacies, while the journal extracts demonstrate how students reflect on their experience of applying the theory. There is some evidence that students accept the benefits of using an academic literacies approach over a "study skills" or "academic socialization" approach, particularly when they begin applying the principles to their peer-tutoring practices. Laura sees a connection between concepts of identity and her practice as a creative writing student and teacher, Christine sees deeper learning fostered through students' self-assessment of their own writing, and Edie's application of the academic literacies theory leads her to design teaching activities that focus on students' understanding, rather than simple skills.

Laura considers how issues of identity might affect teacher/student relationships in Creative Writing and makes a connection between academic literacies and creative writing. Her reflections raise interesting questions about how we might view other forms of writing through an academic literacies lens. For Creative Writing students, creative output *is* "academic writing" because it is how they are assessed. The issues of privileged ways of writing, power, epistemology and identity raised by Lea and Street (1998) may influence debates about the craft and teaching of "creative" writing as much as they do the conversations about "academic" writing. The work the students do to critically analyze and apply principles of the academic literacies framework challenges aspects of their identity, but also opens up, as for Laura and Edie, possibilities for self-hood in their identity as teachers when they focus on the empowerment of others.

Analysis of the extracts above is only a small beginning towards exploring how student-tutors can use principles of academic literacies theory in relation to their pedagogic practice and their own writing (both academic and creative).

REFERENCES

Ivanič, R. (1998). *Writing and identity: The discoursal construction of identity in academic writing.* Amsterdam: John Benjamins Publishing Company.

Lea, M. R., & Street, B. (1998). Student writing in higher education: An academic literacies approach. *Studies in Higher Education, 23*(2), 157-172.

Shulman, L. (2005). Signature pedagogies in the professions. *Daedalus, 4*(3), 52-59.

CHAPTER 5

"HIDDEN FEATURES" AND "OVERT INSTRUCTION" IN ACADEMIC LITERACY PRACTICES: A CASE STUDY IN ENGINEERING

Adriana Fischer

Project-based report writing is currently a regular academic literacy practice in Portuguese medium Engineering Programmes at the University of Minho (UM), Portugal. Such work aims to position students as professional engineers building scientific and professional knowledge. However, one recurring problem in the writing of the project based reports is the gap in understandings and expectations between students and teachers about the forms and norms governing the reports. This gap in understanding has been highlighted in "academic literacies" work more generally (Mary Lea, 2004; Mary Lea & Brian Street, 1998; Theresa Lillis, 2006) and the question of how we might address this gap is the focus of this contribution. Specifically, my aim is to explore the extent to which "overt instruction" (The New London Group, 2000) on report writing as a genre can resolve the gap in understanding and whether features considered to be often "hidden" in pedagogy (Brian Street, 2009) can be addressed through overt instruction (see Street, Lea and Lillis Reflections 5 this volume).

Two main questions motivated my pedagogic research and analysis:

1. Are "hidden features" inevitably constitutive of academic literacy practices?
2. Can overt instruction disclose the features hidden in academic literacy practices?

THE PEDAGOGIC CONTEXT AND THE INTERVENTIONIST ROLE OF THE "LANGUAGE EDUCATOR"

Between 2010 and 2011 I worked on an Industrial Engineering and Management (henceforth IEM) Integrated Master's Degree Programme at the University of

Minho, Portugal. I was invited by the teachers to work as an Assistant Researcher at IEM between September 2010 and January 2011 in order to support the students and the teaching staff in producing and disseminating the outcomes of project reports. In total 12 teachers (subject specialists), four educational researchers working alongside the teachers and six student groups with seven students in each were involved. I was one of the "educational researchers" and the only person specifically focusing on language and literacy: the teachers explicitly sought my cooperation— as a "language educator." Considerable effort overall was put into supporting the programme and the students' activities.

Students in their first semester of the academic year regularly work with a Project-Based Learning (PBL) methodology to develop technical competencies associated with four particular courses. A Project Based Learning (PBL) methodology typically involves students working on a group project drawing on a number of disciplinary fields (Sandra Fernandes, Anabela Flores, & Rui Lima 2012: Natascha van Hattum-Janssen, Adriana Fischer, & Francisco Moreira, 2011). In this course, the PBL involved four key disciplinary/ knowledge areas: industrial engineering, calculus C, computer programming, and general chemistry.

The project in this instance was entitled Air_2Water and the task was to design a portable device capable of producing drinking water from air humidity. The final report writing that students needed to produce had a word length of 60 pages, including three main sections—Introduction, Development and Final Remarks. Students were provided with a "Guide" and a list of assessment criteria which included the following: clearly stated objectives, a clear structure, evidence of sound

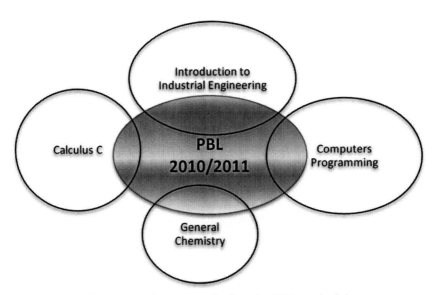

Figure 5.1: Courses involved in the PBL methodology.

reasoning and conceptual rigor, evidence of the capacity to reflect and engage in critical analysis with group members, appropriate use of formatting and layout, and appropriate referencing. Overt instruction with regard to academic literacy on the part of the teachers included the formulation and sharing of these explicit assessment criteria and giving oral feedback on reports at different stages of drafting. However, it was considered that additional overt instruction in academic literacy was needed in order to narrow the gap in understandings between students and teachers which led me to develop, with another educational researcher, three key "interventions" to take place at three key points in the 19 week course (see Figure 5.2 for schedule). The first involved a workshop focusing on the groups' spoken presentation of the project, the second a workshop focusing on the writing of the project report, and the third a series of sessions with each group where I fed in comments and concerns by teachers and listened to students' perspectives on their writing. The goal of these interventions which took the form of workshops involving students and teachers (see for example, Figure 5.3) was to provide additional overt instruction in language, discourse and writing conventions that seemed to remain hidden despite explicit guidelines and teachers' oral feedback throughout the programme of work around the project.

As I discuss below, the interventions constituted an additional form of overt instruction. However, it's important to note that they also made visible specific features of this particular literacy practice that had remained more deeply hidden, often to both teachers and students. Drawing on academic literacies ethnographic

Course Schedule	Course Tasks and Workshop Interventions
Week 2	(1) Pilot Project presentation
Week 5	*Intervention 1: speaking in public*
Week 5	(2) Project Progress presentation
Week 7	*Intervention 2: the written report*
Week 8	(3) Intermediate Report (max. 20 pages)
Week 9	(4) Extended Tutorial
Week 12	*Intervention 3: individual sessions with each group— talk around written report*
Week 13	(5) Preliminary draft of the final report (max. 30 pages)
Week 18	(6) Final Report (max. 60 pages) (7) Delivery of Prototype (Portable Device)
Week 19	(8) Final Exam (9) Final Presentation and discussion (10) Poster Session

Figure 5.2: Course tasks and workshop interventions.

approaches (see for example Lea & Street, 1998; Lillis, 2001, 2008) I sought to tease out these more hidden features using the following tools: observation of academic literacy practices within course based instruction, analysis of preliminary and final drafts of project reports, and reflections (mine and teachers') on the intervention workshops. In the rest of this paper I outline the programme of work, the specific workshop interventions I designed and facilitated and discuss brief data extracts drawn from one of the six groups of students at IEM, working together to produce a project report.

PROJECT REPORT AT IEM:
OVERT INSTRUCTION AND HIDDEN FEATURES

The project was developed over 19 weeks; it had ten key pedagogic tasks—designed by the subject specialists—and three workshop "interventions" (see Figure 5.2).

The first draft of the project report was handed in by the students in week 8. Until that moment, overt instruction had been given in different ways: the students had received assessment criteria and oral feedback (based on the assessment criteria) from the teachers on student presentations. Giving oral (rather than written) feedback on this programme is in line with feedback practices in higher education more generally in Portugal. The teachers' oral feedback comments on presentations had involved several recurring criticisms. These included: 1) lack of justification for the choices and decisions that were made; 2) lack of explanation about what was innovative; and 3) lack of critical reflection. What's important to note here is that the teachers were both critical of the students for not fulfilling these expectations and therefore meeting the assessment criteria, but also concerned about how to provide adequate support to enable students to meet such criteria. In a fundamental sense, the specific nature (conceptual and discoursal) of these three elements that teachers were critical of were hidden in some ways to teachers as well as to students. In a meeting (week 5), one of them stated how difficult it was to "manage feedback," and it was agreed that "giving students written feedback" might be helpful.

Given the concerns that the oral feedback were proving insufficient to support the students in developing the three elements mentioned above in their reports, I designed a workshop where I aimed to explicitly raise and address teachers' concerns (see Figure 5.3).

After the workshop, Group 2—the group I am focusing on in this paper—made efforts towards responding to the concerns raised. For example, in their draft report they explicitly signaled the innovative nature of their project:

> Because this project is complex and innovative, it needs good

management and staff organization. (Intermediate Report[1]);

and they wrote that their goal was:

> ... to lead a creative and dynamic project that can make a differ-
> ence in the market ... to contribute to finding a solution in a
> responsible and realistic fashion. (Intermediate Report)

The explicit mention of creativity and dynamism—and the contribution that the project seeks to make—indicated that the group understood to some extent the teachers' expectations about explicitly marking innovation. The group also provided some justification for their choices and decisions pointing to the need for "good management and group organization."

They also made efforts towards signalling group processes and collective group decision making, an element that is mentioned in the assessment criteria and one that teachers were looking for:

> A proposal was made to create a company .... At first, Angola
> and Sudan were defined as target markets ... it was concluded
> that there was no average relative humidity in that country,
> hence this option was discarded. (Intermediate Report)

Reference to the group processes that were involved are signaled in phrases such as:

Areas of Focus	Questions/Activities
Report Planning	Target audience? Project objectives? Group objectives? Requirements for project design? Assessment criteria? How to make explicit group decisions about the structure of the project?
Making sense of teachers' comments (from Week 5)	Need to clarify: steps of the project; justifications for decisions; explanation of innovative nature of the project: organise the sequencing and cohesion of paragraphs and sections; aligning of objectives with the overall report and the introduction with the conclusion. Analysis of excerpts of a successful report (2009/2010)
Argument and Discourse Features	Academic language; types of arguments; discourse modalisation.
Report Introduction	Contextualisation? Objectives? Introduction and overview of sections?
Report Conclusions	What is innovative about the project? How is knowledge from the four areas integrated? Benefits of the type of teaching/learning to the group? How is the critical positioning of the group signalled linguistically?

Figure 5.3: Intervention workshop, week 7.

"were defined … as target markets," "it was concluded," and "hence."

ONGOING TEACHER CONCERNS AND TEASING OUT HIDDEN FEATURES

While all the groups' reports indicated evidence of progress towards responding to teachers' comments, by week 9, teachers still had major concerns about the project report writing. In an extended tutorial (week 8) these concerns surfaced when each group presented their written report—accompanied by an oral summary—to seven teachers of the programme. In this tutorial the seven tutors who had by this stage read the "intermediate" draft of the project report discussed their concerns with the group members. I observed all tutorials and recorded the feedback from the teachers to students. Based on a transcription of their feedback, key ongoing areas of concern were as follows:

- Lack of focus and coherence across sections of the report
- Lack of sufficient integration of course content from the four subject areas (see Figure 5.1)
- Insufficient discussion of the proposed device
- Need for greater clarification about the innovative nature of the project
- Need for clearer justification for the different decisions made

Because these comments by teachers were recurrent and the students were not succeeding in responding in ways expected while writing the intermediate report, I consider it useful to describe them as "hidden features" in this particular pedagogic context; as already stated these features were hidden from both the teachers/tutors and the students. The teachers did not explicitly articulate what they meant, e.g.,

	Talk Around the Intermediate Report
	(1) Integration of course content areas. How is this evident in the Table of Contents and in the report sections?
	(2) Textual coherence. What is the "common thread" of the report?
	(3) Where and how is innovation signalled? What are the arguments or the justifications associated with the portable device and the objectives of the project?
	(4) Critical view of the work and the results. Where is it signalled?
	(5) Introduction. How is the theme contextualised? Are the objectives of the group and the project presented? Is the structure of the sections appropriate?
	(6) Conclusions. What can be highlighted as innovative in the study? Was the group able to integrate the content areas? How? Are there any limitations to the study? What are the benefits to the group of this type of teaching/learning? What are the benefits of PBL from a technical-scientific point of view?

Figure 5.4: Intervention workshop 3: Talk around the intermediate report.

how innovation could be shown and evidenced in the project report and the students could not grasp what the teachers felt they were intimating. Rather, teachers made evaluative comments about what was not being achieved, leaving students guessing at what teachers seemed to actually require.

Based on the comments in the extended tutorial with teachers, I designed a third intervention workshop (week 12): this involved talk with students around the Intermediate Report. I designed the workshop discussion with students around the

Table of contents week 8 (group 2)	Table of contents week 18 (group 2)	Additions made
Introduction. Project Management. Phases of Project Management. Project Specification. Project Planning. Leading Techniques and take meetings more informal. (see sections 1, 2—week 18)	1—Introduction, 1.1) Project Framework; 2—Project Methodology and Management and Team Management; 2.1) Project Management; 2.2) Team Management;	Industrial engineering
	3—Potable Water treatment method; 3.1) Thematic Framework;	*Critical dimension*
WE—Water Everywhere. Methods of Production. Objects of production. Tools. Transportation Methods. Production management. Optimization of production. Labor Service. Area, volume and length. (see sections 6, 7 , 8, 9—week 18)	4—Understanding the Process of Obtaining Water from Air humidity; 4.1) Introduction, 4.2) Advantages and disadvantages; 5—The Water; 5.1) Molecule of water; 5.2) Molecular Structure of Water and its physical properties; 5.3) Chemical equilibrium and condensation; 5.4) Salt concentration in water;	Chemistry *Critical dimension*
Theoretical Framework. (see sections 4, 5—week 18)	6—WE-Water Everywhere; 6.1) A We, the Logo and Slogan; 6.2) Target Market and Relative Humidity; 6.2) Plant location; 6.3) Product: AirDrop; 6.4) Plant Departments; 7—Production System; 7.1) Production factors;	
Target market and Relative Humidity. (see sections 6, 7 ,8, 9—week 18)	7.2) WE´s Productive System; 7.3) Enterprise Deployment Overview; 8—WE´ Process manufacturing and Dynamics of Production; 8.1) Manufacturing Cycle Analysis and Rate and Production; 8.2) Time Crossing; 8.3)	Integration of 4 subject areas (Industrial engineering, Chemistry, Calculus and Computer Programming) in outline of production of innovative project.
Enterprise Management Softwares. (see section 12—week 18)	Productivity; 8.4) Labor service Rate occupancy; 9—Health and Safety; 9.1) Factors affecting health and safety; 9.2) Number of extinguishers and evacuation routes;	*Critical dimension*
Conclusion.		
Bibliography	10—Cost Analysis; 11—WE´s Energy Resources Optimization; 12—Prototype LEGO's Mindstorms; 13—WEP—Water Everywhere Program; 14—Conclusion; 15—Bibliography.	Calculus *Critical dimension* Computers *Critical dimension*
(Intermediate Report, Contents, week 8)	(Final Report, Contents, week 18)	

Figure 5.5: Changes in report focus as evident in table of contents.

key concerns expressed by teachers (see Figure 5.4).

In the Intervention Workshop 3, where students and I talked through key points derived from teachers' comments and concerns, students were able to recognize some of the concerns of teachers that I presented to them. For example, following discussion of the teacher comments in relation to their specific report, one student reflected on the changes they had made while also mentioning the difficulties they continued to face:

> We have added sections—in the Contents and in the Report—that
> were missing. The relationship between some aspects—"the com-
> mon thread of the Report" was not noticeable .... Related to the
> area of Introducing Industrial Engineering we wrote about project
> management, we wrote all the techniques. But, in addition, we have
> to apply the concept of chemical equilibrium, for example, our
> equations, our experiments, our device. I think it's quite difficult. I
> feel that in PBL—we need more help. (Student 1).

Indications that the workshop intervention helped students produce a report more aligned with the assessment criteria and teacher expectations can be illustrated by comparing a table of contents at week 13 with one at week 18 (see Figure 5.5). Some of the key changes are listed in Figure 5.5.

However even at this stage students said that they struggled to make sense of the comment for the need for "clarification about the innovative nature of the project".

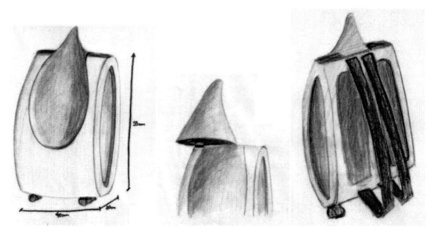

Strengths: easy to construct and to carry with backstraps, facilitates easy access to any situation and space
Weaknesses: if the material used to construct the device is heavy and/or if too much water is in the portable device, it may damage people's backs

Figure 5.6: Strengths and limitations of the device.

They felt that innovation—the way that they proved that the device was really portable—was already clearly stated in their report:

> We were **the only group to explain certain aspects**. In one of the oral presentations, we mentioned that we believe our device is different from those of all other groups. We were **the only group that effectively worked with the portable device** .... This was **our understanding of innovation ...** (Student 3: emphasis added)

The group had also presented images of the device (named "AirDrop") as well as showing weakness and strengths (see Figure 5.6).

Following both overt instruction from subject specialists and three intervention workshops, students were both making progress towards understanding expectations as evidenced both in their report drafting and talk around their writing, but students were also still confused about why and how they were failing to meet teacher expectations.

DRAWING CONCLUSIONS FROM THE PROJECT

I opened this paper with two questions:

1. Are "hidden features" inevitably constitutive of academic literacy practices?
2. Can overt instruction disclose the features hidden in academic literacy practices?

With regard to the first question, on the basis of the programme and the considerable intervention discussed here, I would argue that hidden features are inevitably constitutive of academic literacy practices. Subject specialist and teachers often "know" what they are expecting students to produce but: a) they are not used to articulating such discursive knowledge; b) it may be that it is far from clear what the nature of the knowledge expected is—this may be particularly the case when the knowledge to be produced cuts across disciplinary and theoretical/applied frames of reference, as in project based learning; and c) the ideological nature of literacy practices—that is, the doing of any literacy practice inevitably involves fundamental issues of epistemology (what counts as knowledge here now) and power (who can claim what counts as knowledge) even though this ideological nature of literacy is not acknowledged. Furthermore, the dominant autonomous model of literacy (Street, 1984) encourages a transparency approach to language and a transmission understanding of language pedagogy (Lillis, 2006) whereby both teachers and students assume that taking control over language and knowledge making is (or should be) a relatively straightforward issue. But as this pedagogic research study indicates, this is far from being the case. Teachers in this project were aware that they were not articulating what was required and unsure of how to do so. They were also frustrated at the students' incapacity to act on explanations. At the same time, students were convinced that they had produced what was required but their voices were not listened to in some key moments of the process. Students also recognized some of the difficulties they faced without necessarily having the resources to resolve them.

With regard to the second question, I collaborated with the PBL teachers and designed specific interventions aimed at making visible the academic literacy practices required in this specific context. These were partly successful, as evidenced by the changes students made to reports, the decision by teachers to use additional forms of feedback in future programmes (to include written as well as spoken feedback) and a general awareness raising of the many aspects of producing a report that are not easily or quickly communicated. The interventions also signaled the limitations in overt instruction: after a range of interventions involving overt instruction, at the end of the programme students still did not understand why their reports failed to do what was required and important gaps between students and teachers perspectives—for example whether "innovation" had been explicitly signaled—remained. Producing knowledge from across a number of disciplinary boundaries is a complex task: ongoing dialogue between teachers and language educators and students, facilitated by ongoing research into perspectives and understandings, as was begun to be carried out in this project, would seem to be the most promising way forwards.

NOTE

1. All data extracts and extracts from course materials have been translated from Portuguese into English.

REFERENCES

Fernandes, S., Flores, A., Lima, R. M. (2012). A aprendizagem baseada em projetos interdisciplinares no Ensino Superior: Implicações ao nivel do trabalho docente. *Proceedings of the International Symposium on Approaches in Engineering* Education (PAEE). São Paulo, Brazil.

Lea, M. R. (2004). Academic literacies: A pedagogy for course design. *Studies in Higher Education, 29*(6), 739-754.

Lea, M. R., & Street, B. V. (1998). Student writing in higher education: An academic literacies approach. *Studies in Higher Education, 23*(2), 157-172.

Lillis, T. (2001). *Student writing: Access, regulation, desire.* London: Routledge.

Lillis, T. (2006). Moving towards an academic literacies pedagogy: Dialogues of participation. In L. Ganobscik-Williams (Ed.), *Academic writing in Britain: The-*

ories and practices of an emerging field. (pp. 30-45). Basingstoke, UK: Palgrave Macmillan Publishing.

Lillis, T. (2008). Ethnography as method, methodology, and "deep theorizing": Closing the gap between text and context in academic writing research. *Written Communication, 25*(3), 353-388.

The New London Group. (2000). A pedagogy of multiliteracies. Design of social futures. In Cope, B., & M. Kalantzis (Eds.), *Multiliteracies: Literacy learning and design of social futures* (pp. 9-37). London/New York: Routledge.

Street, B. (1984). *Literacy in theory and practice.* Cambridge, UK: Cambridge University Press.

Street, B. (2009). "Hidden" features of academic paper writing. *Working Papers in Educational Linguistics, 24*, 1. Retrieved from http://www.gse.upenn.edu/sites/gse.upenn.edu.wpel/files/archives/v24/Street.pdf

Van Hattum-Janssen, N., Fischer, A., Moreira, F. (2011). Presentation skills for engineers: Systematic intervations in a project-based learning course. *Proceedings of the 1st World Engineering Education Flash Week, Lisbon.*

CHAPTER 6

MAKING SENSE OF MY THESIS: MASTER'S LEVEL THESIS WRITING AS CONSTELLATION OF JOINT ACTIVITIES

Kathrin Kaufhold

I would like to thank Sue Smith,* for her patience, and seemingly never ending questioning to make me decide what really interests me.

Sue Smith is a pseudonym for the supervisor

The above quote is an acknowledgement preceding a master's thesis. The author, Vera, was a sociology master's student when I met and interviewed her about her thesis. This acknowledgement underlines Vera's perception of her supervisor as playing a key role in the evolution and success of her thesis. What is remarkable about this case is how Vera was encouraged to draw on her creative writing experience which she gained through her leisure time activities in the past. Vera incorporated aspects of this experience when writing her thesis largely as an autoethnographic account. Moreover, her supervisor not only expressed her excitement about the project but also engaged with Vera's topical interests. In the following, I will introduce Vera and aspects of her thesis development. The focus will be on the interaction with her supervisor and their negotiation of standards for thesis writing within the institution and the sub-discipline they were working in. I will demonstrate how, unaware of the existence of an academic literacies perspective, Vera and her supervisor exemplified certain key aspects of the transformative approach that academic literacies aims to encourage. These were the exploration of different ways of knowledge making, the role of creative approaches to language use and the negotiation of accepted institutional norms. In broad terms, "transformation" here pertains to opening up textual forms that are understood to be standards of thesis writing, both by the institution of higher education and the writer.

The discussion is based on a notion of "doing a thesis" as a constellation of activities that are carried out jointly by the student and other co-participants, and as influenced by students' past experiences and future-oriented goals. My aim is to show how master's theses viewed as a constellation of joint activities (Theodore Schatzki, 1996) potentially provide a space for a dialogic pedagogy and, in this process, contribute to ever evolving understandings of what it is to do a thesis.[1]

VERA AND HER THESIS

I met Vera on a postgraduate module on research methods and asked her later if she wanted to participate in my study on academic writing of master's theses. In our three subsequent interviews we talked about her thesis development based on samples of her academic writing. We drew links to past writing as part of her literacy history (David Barton & Mary Hamilton, 1998) and imagined futures (David Barton, Roz Ivanič, Yvon Appleby, Rachel Hodge, & Karin Tusting, 2007). Vera researched a particular British seaside resort as place of liminality and carnival. Her thesis commenced by describing the status and historical reception of the place. The main part focused on an analysis of her personal experience of the resort. Vera explained her methodology in a separate chapter where she linked it to feminist autobiographical approaches. Her autoethnographic section was written in a style that oscillates between literary fiction and sociological theory complete with flashbacks to childhood episodes. Writing her thesis made her reflect not only on her experience of the place but also on how to use language in order to convey this as experiential narrative yet with academic rigor. Vera's work on her thesis thus highlighted issues at the heart of an academic literacies approach, such as reflecting on and exploring alternative ways of meaning making (Theresa Lillis & Mary Scott, 2007). To gain a fuller understanding of Vera's work within the sociology department, I observed departmental thesis workshops, researched literature foregrounded in our conversations, and interviewed Vera's supervisor and other students.

Education was very important to Vera. She had attended a grammar school, then started an undergraduate degree in psychology and theology, changed university and completed a degree in sociology. As her secondary and undergraduate education was influenced by having to deal with illness, she described starting the sociology master's at her new university to be a great achievement. What struck me most about her story was her wealth of experience in creative writing. In our first interview, she told me how, as a teenager, she wrote poems, songs, an autobiography and, together with a friend, material around a sci-fi TV series. She finished off this list proudly announcing that she submitted a piece of fan fiction for her GCSE[2] in creative writing and received a very good mark. With this mark, her leisure time writing had been validated by a formal education institution and it seemed important for her to add this point. Being complimented for her writing style was a recurring topic in our conversations. She mentioned how she had regularly been chosen as scribe for group work assignments in her undergraduate studies and how her supervisor expressed enjoyment in reading Vera's work. From the start, Vera insisted that in both her writing for leisure and for formal education she was creative in the sense of "putting something into the world". In our third meeting, she explicitly returned to this link and mused on how writing the autoethnographic part of her thesis reminded her of her past autobiographical writing. Nevertheless, her references to her undergraduate writing activities also underline her practical knowledge and experience in academic writing.

At the same time, Vera was uncertain about her thesis. As suggested in her acknowledgement (at the beginning of this chapter), finding a suitable topic was complicated and lengthy. She felt that Sue accompanied her in this process with "patience". She had indicated a topic area in her proposal that was to be handed in before May, the start of the dissertation period that lasted till the first week of September. Yet it took her until June before she felt able to outline her topic. This insecurity became most visible in a work-in-progress meeting at the end of June. Here students presented their topics to-date to each other. When it was Vera's turn, she appeared rather nervous. Bent over her paper, she read out her presentation quickly while showing some photos from the research site projected to the whiteboard. My field notes of the day describe my impression of her presentation:

> Vera was very uncertain about it all, started reading a print out very quickly, her supervisor said 'slow down' and then it got better. This idea apparently just came a week before or so. Vera later said that it felt like the creative writing piece for English lit.
>
> Seems to be at the periphery in the academic culture although she used complex expressions and lots of theory stuff that made it hard to follow at the start. (Extract from field notes, 23 June 2010).

This impression of insecurity was supported by Sue's comment in our interview in which she characterised Vera as "a bit shy".

Yet, Vera had not chosen a safe and traditional topic but worked, encouraged by her supervisor, at the periphery of what was possible under the wider umbrella of sociology and within the specific subfields and neighbouring areas represented in the department. She perceived it as connected to a more literary, impressionistic approach which was familiar to her from her creative writing. At the same time, her text was dense with abstract, sociological concepts. The interweaving of a more literary style and more mainstream academic elements are particularly evident in the following excerpt from her thesis. The passage is part of her introduction to a section on the meaning of the beach as a constitutive element of seaside resorts:

> There is a kite hovering skilfully in the sky, young children pad-
> dling in the pools that have settled full of seawater near the steps,
> a few people have dared to venture into the sea, but not as many
> as are in the pools. Some of the children, and the adults, are
> building sandcastles. In the paper "Building Castles in the
> Sand …", Obrador-Pons wants to create a "livelier account of
> the beach that incorporates a sense of the ludic and the perfor-
> mative" (Obrador-Pons, 2009, p. 197). He argues that descrip-
> tions of the beach are focused on the visual; and that they are
> unable to fully explain the meaning of the beach. (Extract from
> Vera' thesis, p. 30)

In the initial description of this extract Vera evokes the dynamicity of the scene. People are involved in numerous activities. They paddle, venture and build. There is a change in pace from the peaceful "hovering" and "paddling" to the dramatic "venture." Starting with the wider scene, she zooms in on the focus of this section. With this scene-setting based on her experience, Vera leads into a discussion of an extended meaning of sandcastles orientated on academic literature. She uses a direct quote and a paraphrase, standard conventions of academic writing, to indicate different ways of theorizing the beach. This was not just a story. Vera provided a theoretical discussion. As suggested by my observations above, Vera was clearly negotiating the boundaries between her experience and expectations of what sociological work entailed and new possibilities that had opened up for her gradually. Specifically during her master's course, she encountered and deepened her understanding of new research approaches through participation in course modules, literature, conversations and guidance from her supervisor.

In our third meeting Vera spoke more confidently about her choices. When I mentioned this to her, her mixed feelings towards her approach became apparent:

> V: It's probably because I've actually written the autoethnograph-
> ic—started the autoethnographic. Because that was the bit I was
> scared about.
>
> K: The stepping into the unknown.
>
> V: Yea. Yea. It was like, ok, let's take a great big jump into some-
> thing crazy. (Extract from interview 3).

Vera acknowledges her initial insecurity. She talks about it in the past tense indirectly acknowledging the change. She characterizes her work not just as something different and new, as I suggested, but also as "something crazy". Vera enjoyed her fieldwork and her writing building on her creative work but she was also aware that she was following a more risky route as she had not worked in this way before academically and she did not consider her approach as mainstream.

VERA'S THESIS AS SPACE FOR DIALOGUE AND NEGOTIATION OF STANDARDS

As indicated in the acknowledgement, this "jump" was supported by her supervisor, Sue. Vera appreciated that she had been asked many questions to clarify her own interests. This seems to point to an open dialogue between supervisor and student, a genuine engagement with the interests of the author (Theresa Lillis, 2003). I did not have the opportunity to observe a supervision session as Sue felt it would not be a good idea with Vera being shy. Nevertheless, the interviews with Vera and Sue provide a number of insights into the nature of the dialogue that characterized their relationship in supervision.

A concrete example of how Vera felt supported by her supervisor, besides discussing literature and data was given in our second meeting. At that point, Vera had written a draft of her first chapter and started to write about her methodology. She had discussed her draft with Sue the day before. When we talked about the way she wanted to approach the autoethnographic part, Vera commented on the previous supervision:

> I said to [Sue] yesterday, I should have done a creative writing degree because she um she started reading it and she goes, oh, don't you write nicely. And I said, people have said that before. I should have done creative writing not, um, not sociology. And she said, well, in a way, sociology is creative writing and this is definitely creative writing. Because if I hadn't got some sort of— if I hadn't got an ability to write then I wouldn't be able to do an autoethnography at all. (Extract from interview 2)

In this "small story" (Michael Bamberg & Alexandra Georgakopoulou, 2008; James Simpson, 2011), Vera recounts a conversation about her writing on a meta-level in which Sue complimented her style. For Vera this fitted with previous comments on her writing and the pride she expressed in listing her past leisure time writing in the previous interview. Moreover, she repeatedly characterized her academic writing as less mainstream and underlined her enjoyment in playing with words. Vera had encountered feminist approaches before. And she had read critiques and challenges of autoethnographic approaches. Thus, she was aware that more than her experience in creative writing was required for her project. Sue did not only encourage Vera in rejecting Vera's sense of insecurity but also linked creative writing explicitly to sociology, specifically the methodological approach of feminist-inspired autoethnography. With the above story, Vera demonstrated how her desire to be creative in her writing matched the value system of the sub-discipline in which she and her supervisor worked. In reporting her supervisor's speech, she constructed an authoritative legitimation.

On the other hand, it's clear that Vera also acted on her idea about existing conventions that would still apply for her thesis. This aspect can be illustrated poignantly in an instance from our conversation about her draft in the second interview. Looking at her draft, Vera quoted some language related feedback from Sue:

> V: "Don't use the word don't" and "paraphrase some quotes."
> Because it makes it sound better if I use "do not" or "'cannot.'"
>
> K: Ok.
>
> V: Which is a fair enough comment, really.
>
> K: Yea. Which is interesting though. Because it—it puts it back to kind of standard.
>
> V: Yea, well, that is the standard section, though. (Extract from interview 2)

Here Vera immediately evaluates Sue's feedback by providing reason and agreeing. Although Sue's comments first of all refer to the surface structure of the text, they reveal that in all its freedom there are still certain expectations that are shared or easily accepted by Vera. When I voice my surprise about this convention, Vera opens up a distinction between her initial two sections, which she identified as "standard," and her autoethnography.

Both Vera and Sue were aware of tensions between the possibilities afforded by the approach and those afforded by the thesis as assignment format. They did not discuss these differences explicitly—contrary to pedagogic initiatives based on an academic literacies approach (see Mary Lea & Brian Street, 2006). Instead, Vera had realized this because of the different purposes of sections in her thesis:

> I wanted that more traditional sociological bit so that it had still got, you know, some of the features of a real [thesis]. Because it needed the history in it and I don't think I could have done that autoethnographically and I don't think I could have done the research method bit autoethnographically. It had to be different. I just don't think it would have worked. (Extract from interview 3)

Vera had a notion of a generic "traditional sociological" thesis formed through a mixture of her undergraduate experience, her expectations, and the initial thesis workshop in which general advice was given and sample theses discussed. Again, she positioned her thesis as different, yet felt she needed to fulfil some requirements. She could not imagine introducing the background and the methods section in an alternative way. Moreover, she could not imagine writing a thesis without such elements. In her and Sue's understanding of the thesis, these were necessary.

The idea of unconstrained creative writing was challenged even within her autoethnographic section. Vera listed in her thesis some features she found in the literature to be included in an autoethnography such as reflexivity, others' voices and theoretical analysis. These guidelines provided some orientation for her as a novice in the field as well as a quotable legitimation for her approach: "It's cause I do want it to be academically acceptable and I don't want them to turn round and go, it's not." In this quote she also positions herself as less powerful than the faceless "them," an institutional body who decides about academic acceptability. She felt compelled to play to their rules but within the logic of her alternative approach. Sue facilitated this experiment through encouragement and providing space for an open dialogue. Vera's case demonstrates a two-way interaction between working with more diverse approaches that become established at the periphery of mainstream academia (Mary Hamilton & Kathy Pitt, 2009) as well as "accommodating to institutional norms" (Mary Scott & Joan Turner, 2004, p. 146), more specifically, marking regimes and conventional expectations.

TRANSFORMATION IN THE LIGHT OF HISTORY, FUTURE AND NORMATIVE STRUCTURES

Vera's thesis was influenced by a plethora of factors some of which have been discussed in this chapter. She expressed this point when looking back at her work: "Well, I think I wouldn't have done it had I not been at [xx university]. I'd never have done that," that is, she would never have considered drawing so extensively on her experience and love for using language more playfully. She felt that possibilities of knowledge making were opened up to her at this particular university in which she completed her master's studies through the combination of people and theoretical perspectives she encountered here. Her ability to use these possibilities for her own purposes also depended on her interests as well as the practical experience and knowledge she had acquired while participating in various writing-related activities within and outside formal education. Building on these repertoires (Jan Blommaert & Ad Backus, 2011) to the extent she did entailed reflections on the way she was using language. Our interviews certainly contributed to this too.

The format of one-to-one supervision sessions together with Sue's approach provided space for Vera's specific interests and perspectives. Within the assessment format of a thesis, Vera was able to make choices about her topic, her methodological approach and her language. The specific way she chose to structure her autoethnography, rejecting other possibilities, was intricately connected to who she wanted to be in her work. After talking about the relations of her thesis to creative writing, she half-jokingly explained how she wanted to write her autoethnography: "I have got this like imaginary thing like vision in my head of me just some sort of bohemian in a café on the seafront with my laptop". With the word "bohemian" she signaled an imagined self as artist, underlining her affinity to creative work. She could now see how to use this side of her as a resource for her academic work to an extent she could never do before. Her approach, which emphasized a narrative style, could incorporate this image.

As there were possibilities, there were also constraints. Norms emerged in the interplay of the requirement for the thesis to be assessed, Sue's notions of surface features of academic texts, the values of the sub-discipline indexed in the guidelines for autoethnographic research, and Vera's expectations of what a "real thesis" entails (see also Badenhorst et al. Chapter 7 this volume). While each thesis is unique in its specific constellation of activities influenced by a variety of historically situated factors, these norms allow us to make sense of a piece of writing and to recognise a "thesis" (Anis Bawarshi & Mary Jo Reiff, 2010). For instance, Vera started her autoethnographic section with a description of pondering questions that came to her mind at her arrival at the seaside place. I immediately interpreted them as research questions which she confirmed. While Vera's instantiation of a master's thesis contributed to the constant evolution of understandings of what it is to do a thesis, these changes are constrained through normative structures that govern what can be imagined as a thesis. These norms derive from historically situated shared understandings of thesis practices, that is, activities, ways of writing and feelings that can be accepted as belonging to what it is to do a thesis. These understandings also include practical knowledge of how to do something and are connected to a range of goals and desires the order of which can shift from situation to situation (Schatzki, 1996). Explicit guidelines can therefore only be orientations and never capture every possibility. Vera's choices and interpretations of advice made sense to her and Sue as part of the thesis research and writing. Thus, Vera's case demonstrates that master's theses can provide a space for negotiating alternative ways of knowledge making within a complex web of activities, experiences, expectations and purposes as well as notions of norms in academic writing.

ACKNOWLEDGEMENT

This work was supported by the Economic and Social Research Council [grant number ES/H012974/1].

CHAPTER 7

THINKING CREATIVELY ABOUT RESEARCH WRITING

Cecile Badenhorst, Cecilia Moloney, Jennifer Dyer, Janna Rosales and Morgan Murray

Writing is an essential requirement of any graduate student's programme. Over the course of their graduate career a student will write hundreds of pages, much of it for assessment purposes, and will be expected to do so in complex ways. Yet, in spite of the centrality of writing to their academic success, formal instruction is often uncommon. At many universities in Canada, in many cases, the only explicit writing instruction graduate students will have received by the time they complete their programme is a requisite undergraduate English Literature course, possibly an English Second Language class for international students, and perhaps a visit with a peer-tutor at an overworked writing centre. For the most part, learning to write academically takes place, or is expected to take place, implicitly. However, in a context where language, genre, and stylistic conventions are governed by disciplinary norms that are constituted by competing and conflicting discourses, implicit learning becomes problematic. What counts as evidence, for example, will be different in philosophy and anthropology. Many of the conventions and norms of academic writing are subtle even for experienced writers, yet students are expected to learn and practice them without explicit instruction (Sharon Parry, 1998). From an academic literacies approach, we argue that academic writing is a social practice constituted by prevailing ideologies (Theresa Lillis & Mary Scott, 2007), rather than a transparent generic skill.

The purpose of this pedagogic intervention was to offer an intensive co-curricular, multi-day (7) workshop to graduate students on "thinking creatively about research." The workshop was developed from an academic literacies perspective and had a central focus of explicit pedagogy. Memorial University is the only university in Newfoundland and Labrador, Canada and has some 17,000 students enrolled annually. The university is situated in St John's on the remote island of Newfoundland. There are few opportunities for graduate academic development and our team proposed "thinking creatively about research" to introduce a more collegial and interactive approach to research writing than was currently being experienced. We conceptualized "creatively" as different, new, and innovative.

We applied for and received funding to pilot the workshop in two faculties. We then invited a volunteer cohort of students from Memorial University's Graduate Program in Humanities and the Faculty of Arts in Fall 2011 (nine participants) and a second offering occurred in Winter 2012 with graduate students from the Faculty of Engineering and Applied Science (13 participants). In this chapter, we focus on the Arts cohort. The majority of those who attended were international students from Eastern Europe, China and South America, others were from mainland Canada and only a few were local. All the students attended the workshop voluntarily in addition to their regular coursework and teaching duties. Students in the Arts cohort came from Philosophy, Anthropology, Music, and the inter-disciplinary graduate programme. The evaluation of the intervention was framed by one overarching question: Did students find the pedagogy to be transformative and empowering in their approach to research writing? (For overview of workshop schedule, see Table 7.1.)

TRANSFORMATIVE PEDAGOGIES

Antonio Gramsci (1971), Michel Foucault (1995) and Paulo Freire (1986) have all argued that certain ways of thinking and doing become dominant over time, and begin to appear as natural parts of our taken-for-granted world. Transformative education, which challenges the normalizing forces inherent in most education, has two complementary components. First, it allows the individual to learn new ways of "seeing" the world, and to act upon that. Second, it makes visible the tension created between living within the system but thinking outside it; from contending with issues on a daily basis while, at the same time, moving incrementally towards something new (Peter Mayo, 1999).

Like other practices in academic environments, writing is shaped by accepted "norms" of particular disciplinary discourses. There are rules that govern how to cite, what to cite, what questions to ask, and what constitutes an acceptable answer (Robin Lakoff, 1990). Lakoff (1990) further argues that academic language is oblique and implicitly understood practices maintain the exclusivity and authority of the discourse, distinguishing those who understand discourse conventions from "others" who do not. Writing assessment practices that require students to reproduce the "voice" of the discourse in their writing often "militate against creativity and individuality" (Liz Cain & Ian Pople, 2011, p. 49). Rather than exploring innovation in their research and writing, students find themselves trying to act as ventriloquists for their disciplines (Amanda Fulford, 2009).

Dealing with this problem from an academic literacies perspective, this project uses a pedagogy of explicit instruction, and non-traditional approaches to research writing in an attempt to open students' eyes to their positions and roles within their respective disciplinary discourses, and provide them with a range of techniques and perspectives to allow them to engage the tension of living inside the system but thinking outside it.

THE WORKSHOPS

The 7-morning workshop was based on a curriculum developed at a South African university in a context of transformation and change in higher education. The curriculum was encapsulated in a book (Cecile Badenhorst, 2007); the workshops for the Faculty of Arts cohort were adapted from this source. The workshop takes a participant—who has already started their graduate research and has collected data or achieved some results from this research—through the process of research writing from conceptualization to final draft. There are two parts to the workshop to simulate two stages in the writing process: *composition* (Part 1: four consecutive mornings) and *revision* (Part 2: three consecutive mornings) with homework assigned after each morning's workshop. Between the two parts, participants had a month to write the first draft of their chosen research project. While we emphasized the iterative and recursive nature of writing, we found the two part structure useful for focusing on specific issues. Three key questions informed the design of the pedagogy and shaped the activities and materials:

1. What does the writer need to know about academic and research discourses?
2. What does the writer need to know about writing and creativity?
3. What does the writer need to understand about him/herself as an academic researcher/writer?

These questions guided the content, materials and activities. The pedagogy was experiential (David Kolb, 1984). Participants were given *information* often in the form of examples, research articles, and theories to deconstruct; they then had to *apply* what they had learned; they *reflected* individually and in groups; then they extracted key learning points and *reapplied* this in new learning situations. The curriculum was continuously spiralling and hermeneutical. For example, an issue such as "extracting a focus from the complexity of their research topics" was introduced in the morning, participants would complete an activity on it in class, they would read their activity to the group and the group would give feedback. The students then applied that activity to their research in the homework activities. That homework was debriefed in groups the following morning and learning was mediated again by the facilitator after the group work. The following day's activities built on the previous day's ones. All activities contained scaffolding—mini-activities that built on one another—to cultivate participant confidence: developing a safe environment was an important element, as were group work and dialogue.

Each workshop morning was divided into three sections (see Table 7.1). In Part 1, through dialogue, activities, and handouts (research articles, samples of research writing) participants each day discussed issues such as academic discourses (e.g., what counts as evidence in different disciplines, how arguments work, research writing genres and so on) and they were taken through theories on writing (e.g., writing as a process, what goes into writing, why writing is so difficult, how self-criticism can paralyze a writer, how academic writing is situated in a discourse of criticism and what constitutes a writing identity). Although we provided information on current research in this area, for example, work on disciplinarity by Ken Hyland (2008), our purpose was not to present "best practices" or solutions but rather to allow participants to develop an understanding of the epistemological nature of academic writing and to allow them to decide how they would write from the range of choices we presented. The final part of the day was devoted to "play." Play was important to the pedagogy because it encouraged participants to move out of their usual ways of writing and thinking. The play activities used concept mapping, free-writing and sketching to revise sections or thinking in their drafts and involved activities to do with developing authority in writing, seeing research from

Table 7.1: Thinking creatively about research—workshop structure

Part 1:	Day One	Day Two	Day Three	Day Four
Half hour	Introduction	Group work	Group work	Group work
One hour	Issues in research writing	Issues in research writing	Issues in research writing	Issues in research writing
Half hour	Theories of writing and creativity	Theories of writing and creativity	Theories of writing and creativity	Pushing the boundaries with language, words and writing
One hour	Pushing the boundaries with language, words and writing	Pushing the boundaries with language, words and writing	Pushing the boundaries with language, words and writing	Concluding activities

There was a break between Part 1 and 2 of approximately a month. Participants were expected to write a draft of their chosen research project during this time.

Part 2:	Day Five	Day Six	Day Seven
Half hour	Introduction	Group work	Group work
One hour	Creative Revision 1	Creative Revision 2	Creative Revision 3
Half hour	Feedback	Dealing with criticism	Writing strategies
One hour	Revision activities	Revision activities	Revision activities and conclusion

different points of view, trying out different voices, thinking about representation in the research (who we are representing, how and why). An example of "play" activity was to free-write about the research from the subject's point of view (e.g., the participant, the organization, the document) or to sketch a research project as if it were on a stage in a theatre

Part 2 followed the same pedagogy and emphasis on play. The focus in this section was on revision, structure and coherence, and the discourses around producing a finished product in a particular discipline. We also engaged with the emotional aspects of writing such as dealing with criticism, how to give and get feedback and what to do with feedback.

STUDENTS' EXPERIENCES

While there is much that can be said about these workshops, the participants and the pedagogy, we have chosen to focus on how explicit instruction and play lead to transformative learning since we feel these were catalyst elements.

EXPLICIT INSTRUCTION

Explicit instruction is most often used to make the invisibility of assessment more visible in education but as Sally Mitchell (2010) has argued the intentions of transparency are not always seen in the outcomes. Making assessment criteria clear can lead to a compliance attitude where the student focuses on the criteria and not on the learning task. This workshop was not assessed and we felt that explicit instruction—essentially a meta-instruction about activities—would promote dialogue and discussion. For example, when we proposed an activity, we asked students: Why have we included this activity? Why do we need to know this? We were explicit about the nature of academic discourses, about the pedagogy and about what we asked them to do. We provided no answers or solutions (since there are none) but allowed students to find their way through dialogue. For many students, their intuitive writing practices were at odds with the way they thought they ought to write as academics. The explicit instruction highlighted the epistemological nature of writing and how it is tied to particular perceptions of knowledge, some of which are privileged in university contexts. This allowed participants to see that there was no "wrong" way to write but rather there were choices about whether to conform, how much to conform or if to conform at all. Rather than "fixing" writing that was "weak" or "poor," we emphasized understanding their particular discourse/audience requirements and then making decisions based on their own epistemologies and power base. The following student comments, written during the workshop, illustrate a growing awareness of their own writing. These direct quotes from workshop participants are included with permission. All names have been changed:

> This class is interesting because it helps me to realize the way I write is not wrong. (Charlie, 5)

> I learned a fair deal about the writing process ... which was a pleasant surprise. (Ernest, 5)

We also emphasized that they could make choices about *what* they wrote about. This is where they could be innovative, creative and original. For many students, it was a relief to feel that there was a choice after years of being squeezed into a mould and not being allowed to do things differently:

> Yesterday's workshop was interesting to me because things started coming to me quicker than they usually do. At one point during our exercises I stopped thinking about what I was going to say about myself and my research and just wrote. I think I'm getting to a more honest place regarding where I'm at. (Veronica, 9)

We discussed the consequences of challenging disciplinary ways of writing, why one would want to do that and what the alternatives were. We related these discussions to their position in the discourse, and their roles in the university. We particularly focused on their identity as researchers and writers and how research writing was tied into developing an identity as a researcher/writer (Frances Kelly, Marcia Russell & Lee Wallace, 2011). We asked them to free-write about their identity, to sketch themselves in relation to their research and to constantly reflect on themselves, their research topic and their goals with this research project. The following comments indicate a re-connection with themselves as researchers:

> In my research and writing I have noticed that it is getting easier to focus on what I am looking for and what I want to say. I think I am going to start getting up early to do a little sketching in the morning so that I can give my mind a chance to warm up before I tackle things like Heidegger or Kant or God knows who else. (Veronica, 12)

> It's not that I discovered a magic formula to get rid of my academic obligations. But I realized I can commit to what I want to do, find my way and do it. I find that the ... discussions really help. (Jaromil, 11)

THE IMPORTANCE OF PLAY

Play was a central component of the pedagogy for two reasons. First, the element of play allowed participants to move out of their usual way of writing and thinking; and second, we wanted students to have "flow" experiences while writing. "Flow," argues psychologist Mihaly Csikszentmihalyi (1990), is an optimal experience that happens when people experience feelings of intense concentration and deep enjoyment. For the play activities we used metaphor, "illogical" questions about their research, concept mapping (Tony Buzan & Barry Buzan, 2006), free writing (Peter Elbow, 1973) and sketching (Yeoryia Manolopoulou, 2005). Participants enjoyed the coloured blank paper and coloured felt markers they were given to work with. We explained to participants that like the Billy Collins poem "Introduction to poetry" (Collins, 1996; also available at http://..loc.gov/poetry/180/001.html), we wanted them to drop a mouse in their research and see which way it ran, or to hold their research up to the light like a prism and watch the colors changing. We did not want them to tie their research in a chair and torture the truth out of it. Although sceptical and hesitant at first, students soon embraced "play" enthusiastically. They found that play allowed them to focus on ideas rather than rules and conventions. New and novel ways of looking at their research made them feel unique and showed them that they had something worthwhile to say, as these quotes illustrate:

> Some of the activities opened my eyes to the potential of creativity in [academic] writing that I had not thought possible. (Tip, 5)

> I thought about the problem [in] my problem statement, trying to pinpoint something out of several problems. We played with words and images, which was a fun way to deal with the task on hand. I don't know if these words and images are going to guide me toward clearer words or statements or even clearer ideas but they're there. (Sasha, 9)

TRANSFORMATIVE LEARNING

It is difficult to assess if an intervention results in transformation and we would not want to claim that a series of seven morning workshops over two months could generate such results. The process of transformative learning is often difficult to measure because it includes complex experiences that involve "cognitive questioning, invested deliberation, contradictions, new possibilities, risk-taking, and resolution" (Kathleen King, 2005, p. 92). It also includes developing confidence and self-efficacy in a particular domain. Our key evaluative tool was the students themselves and the writing they produced. We found that participants did leave the workshop with a new sense of themselves and their position within the system in which they worked. Our aim was not to change their epistemologies, but to open them to their own ontological and epistemological claims in their research and the epistemologies inherent in the writing tasks they were asked to do on a daily basis (Badenhorst, 2008). Participants discussed the myriad components of research such as conceptualizing research, designing a research project, developing a methodology, collecting data, analyzing data, synthesizing results and evaluating research contributions—not as generic concepts—rather as conceptions of what constitutes knowledge and what knowledge is valued. They recognized the tension of working inside the system while thinking outside it—but that the choice of action was their decision. The following quotes indicate this growing awareness:

> The workshop helped me to see where I stand in relation to my thesis. (Kei, 11)

> What surprised me the most about my writing during the break [the break between the two parts of the workshop] was how stable it felt. I wrote a little almost every day and it developed into something good and less stressful even though there were still some things I hadn't figured out. (Veronica, 37)

> What surprised me was that I actually understood what was going on, rather than writing in a lost way. (Farah, 38)

We discussed disciplinary norms regarding citations, evidence, authority and expectations regarding graduate writing. Towards the end of the workshop, this is what students articulated about the practical application of writing within a discipline:

> I was surprised at the very useful conceptual map (very colourful), which was the base of a successful and productive meeting with my supervisor. (Jaromil, 5)

> My supervisor has noted that I am beginning to write with more clarity or at least it is the best quality I have produced after two years. (Evals, 2)

> I realized my methodology, my area of inquiry [was] arts-based research. This has changed completely my understanding of what I would do if I continue [with] a PhD (Evals, 8)

CONCLUSION

Ultimately, our aim was to explore how the pedagogic intervention manifested in practical changes and to understand the choices participants made in relation to their disciplinary writing and perhaps even to see how this extended even further to other actors in the institution, such as research supervisors. To this end we are conducting in-depth interviews with students who participated in the workshops. This chapter's focus centred on the pedagogic intervention, particularly the elements of explicit instruction and play. The most interesting conclusion we drew from the intervention was the difficulty students faced when we could not provide them with a right or wrong answer to an activity. Used to being rule-bound, participants found themselves faced with unending possibilities. This same difficulty became their opening to innovation, enjoyment and insight. Rules were not abolished but revealed. The purpose of revealing the rules was not only to enable students to succeed but to allow them to make choices about how they wanted to succeed. The explicit instruction did not focus only on "best practice" or templates of conventions but on opening up critical dialogue and complex questioning about research and writing in disciplinary discourses. Through dialogue, intense writing and play, participants began to experience change in their approach to writing, the way they saw themselves as writers and their perceptions of writing research. While we cannot unreservedly label this "transformational," this research indicates that students did experience incremental movements towards something new. The following comment indicates the elusive nature of this change:

> I've barely had time to think over the past four days, and haven't really had time to do the [workshop] homework due to a lot of other obligations, yet when I finally got home from campus last night at 11p.m. and sat down to relax for a minute, I felt compelled to write, and not with any intent in mind or for any academic purpose and what came out was a kind of problem narrative of what I'm working on in a way I had never remotely conceived of before. (Neville, 11)

ACKNOWLEDGEMENTS

An Instructional Development Grant (2011-2012) from Memorial University of Newfoundland provided support for this research. Ethical approval was granted by the Interdisciplinary Committee on Ethics in Human Research at Memorial University.

REFERENCES

Badenhorst, C. M. (2007). *Research writing: Breaking the barriers*. Pretoria: Van Schaik.

Badenhorst, C. M. (2008). *Dissertation writing: A research journey*. Pretoria: Van Schaik.

Buzan, T., & Buzan, B. (2006). *The mind map book*. London: British Broadcasting

Corporation.

Cain, L., & Pople, I. (2011). The dialect of the tribe: Interviewing highly experienced writers to describe academic literacy practices in business studies. *Journal of Academic Writing, 1*(1), 46-53.

Collins, B. (1996). Introduction to poetry. *The apple that astonished Paris.* Fayetteville, AR: University of Arkansas Press. Retrieved from http://loc.gov/poetry/180/001.html

Csikszentmihalyi, M. (1990). *Flow: The psychology of optimal experience.* New York: Harper Collins.

Elbow, P. (1973). *Writing without teachers.* London: Oxford University Press.

Foucault, M. (1995). *Discipline and punish: The birth of the prison.* New York: Vintage Books.

Freire, P. (1970/1986). *Pedagogy of the oppressed* (M. B. Ramos, Trans.). New York: Continuum International Publishing Group.

Fulford, A. (2009). Ventriloquizing the voice: Writing in the university. *Journal of Philosophy of Education, 43* (2), 223-237.

Gramsci, A. (1971). *Selections from the prison notebook* (Q. Hoare, G. Nowell-Smith, Trans.). London: Lawrence & Wishart.

Hyland, K. (2008). Genre and academic writing in the disciplines. *Language Teaching, 41* (4), 543-562.

Kelly, F., Russell, M., & Wallace, L. (2012). Trouble in mind: Supporting the transition to graduate research in English. *Arts & Humanities in Higher Education, 11*(4), 1-16. doi:10.1177/1474022211416779.

King, K. (2005). *Bringing transformative learning to life.* Malabar, FL: Krieger Publishing.

Kolb, D. (1984). *Experiential learning: Experience as the source of learning and development.* Upper Saddle River, NJ: Prentice Hall.

Lakoff, R. T. (1990). *Talking power: The politics of language in our lives.* New York: Basic Books.

Lillis, T., & Scott, M. (2007). Defining academic literacies research: Issues of epistemology, ideology and strategy. *Journal of Applied Linguistics, 4*(1), 5-32.

Manolopoulou, Y. (2005). Unformed drawing: Notes, sketches, and diagrams. *The Journal of Architecture, 10*(5), 517-525.

Mayo, P. (1999) *Gramsci, Freire and adult education.* London: Zed Books.

Mitchell, S. (2010). Now you don't see it; Now you do: Writing made visible in the university. *Arts & Humanities in Higher Education, 9*(2), 133-148.

Parry, S. (1998). Disciplinary discourse in doctoral theses. *Higher Education, 36,* 273-299.

CHAPTER 8

DISCIPLINED VOICES, DISCIPLINED FEELINGS: EXPLORING CONSTRAINTS AND CHOICES IN A THESIS WRITING CIRCLE

Kate Chanock, Sylvia Whitmore and Makiko Nishitani

Each author has contributed to this account, but we do not attempt to speak with one voice, for we occupy different positions in the university and come from different perspectives, as will be seen. To avoid confusion, therefore, Kate has produced an "I" narrative in which Sylvia and Makiko speak within quotation marks. All of us have then considered and amended the resulting article before submitting it for publication.

When Mary Lea and Brian Street articulated the concept of Academic Literacies, it spoke to the concerns of many Australian teachers of what was then, and still is now, known generally as academic skills (a role with various labels, but most often "Learning Advisers"). Although we were employed to impart the habits, forms, and conventions of academic performance, we resisted the delineation of our role as "study skills" support. The "how-to" focus was neither pedagogically effective nor intellectually persuasive, and (led by Gordon Taylor et al., 1988) many of us were re-framing our teaching to start with the "why-to"—the purposes and values underlying the diverse forms, practices and language of academic work encountered in the disciplines. Such teaching can, however, remain "assimilationist," supporting students to produce writing that is "a demonstration of the acquisition of institutional, subject or disciplinary knowledge and insiderdom," without questioning the context within which this all takes place (David Russell, Mary Lea, Jan Parker, Brian Street, & Christiane Donahue, 2009, pp. 411-412). When Learning Advisers are asked to work with students to improve their "academic literacies," it is usually in conjunction with courses that discipline students and their writing in both senses of "discipline," that is, control and intellectual training (Russell et al., 2009, p. 413).

It is possible, however, in some classes that focus on writing in or across particular fields, to find ways to talk about what the conventions enable and what they constrain, and how much room there may be for "informed choice". It is this effort at opening up spaces in which we can encourage "informed choice" that we consider transformatory. This is an account of one such discussion, in the context of a Thesis Writing Circle for research students in the Faculty of Humanities and Social Sciences at an Australian university, to which the authors (the staff convenor, and two student members) belong—an example of an "alternative [space] for writing and meaning making in the academy" (Russell et al., 2009, p. 404, citing Theresa Lillis, 2006; for discussions of the purposes and benefits of writing circles, see Claire Aitchison & Alison Lee, 2006; Wendy Larcombe, Anthony McCosker, & Kieran O'Loughlin, 2007). For students engaged in the high-stakes enterprise of writing a thesis, where everything depends upon its acceptance by a few authorized and authorizing readers, the writing circle provides an alternative readership of people who are unconcerned with how the writing reflects on the writer (or the supervisor) in terms of mastery of content, theory or method, but who focus instead on how satisfying their texts can be for both writer and reader. This involves negotiating with each other on many levels simultaneously, about the grammar and punctuation, the sound and feel, the clarity and comprehensibility of their texts; and it suggests ways of negotiating further with supervisors about the possibilities that these discussions identify.

What I contribute, from a background in Applied Linguistics and long exposure to the faculty's disciplinary cultures and discourses, is what Sara Cotterall describes as "a guide who can help demystify the writing process and provide opportunities to discuss and experience different ways of writing" (2011, p. 415). Following my invitation on the faculty's postgraduate email list, interested students decided to meet fortnightly for an hour to share and respond to one another's writing. Our meetings follow participants' concerns, either flagged in the email accompanying their 1,000-word submissions, or arising in discussion at the meetings. These discussions exemplify the distinction Theresa Lillis has described between evaluative "feedback" focussing on "the student's written text as a product," and "talkback," which focuses on the "text in process," and recognizes "the partial nature of any text and hence the range of potential meanings, [in] an attempt to open up space where the student-writer can say what she likes and doesn't like about her writing" (2003, p. 204).

Our circle had been meeting only a few weeks, and several students had expressed an interest in knowing more about "voice," when Sylvia, whose turn it was to submit a piece for response, asked us to think about whether her writing was "pedestrian." This concern arose, she explains, because "I have always been extremely careful in my writing to ensure that I have not embellished or distorted archaeological evidence. Therefore (although perhaps not always consciously), I have generally avoided the use of the first person to prevent falling into the trap of becoming "too creative," particularly if the subject matter is not associated with direct personal experience." Sylvia's piece was, in fact, an exemplary piece of archaeological discussion, and it was probably fortunate that the second piece submitted that week, by Makiko, was very different, while also very appropriate for her discipline of anthropology. The texts suggested, and the discussion confirmed, that we were looking at "disciplined" voices, about which the writers had "disciplined" feelings. Their contrasts afforded a way of approaching Sylvia's question in terms of academic literacies, rather than in terms of a personal style derived simply from personality and constrained only by taste.

On receipt of both submissions I circulated an email ahead of that week's meeting, suggesting questions the members might like to bear in mind while reading them:

- Whose voices do we hear in each text?
- What is the relationship of the writer to the objects she's investigating?
- Is this different in different disciplines?
  In other words, how far is the writer's presence in, or absence from, the text a matter of personal choice and how far is it a convention of the discipline? Why do different disciplines have different conventions about this? (And do they change, and if so, why?)

I also attached a handout looking at voice as a constrained choice via a comparison of theses in different disciplines, and different sections within the same thesis, to facilitate consideration of how much choice a writer has (for full details of handout, see Chanock, 2007; for extracts see Figure 8.1). I included extracts from the writing of one writer who, while including a very unconventional, narrative and even lyrical "Prologue" in his front matter, had placed before it a highly conventional, analytical thesis "Summary" which would serve to reassure his examiners about his academic competence—absent from his published book (Christopher Houston, 2001) although the Prologue remains (a paragraph from each is shown in Figure 8.1).

Drawing on discussions of these examples and students' own writing, it was possible at the writing circle meeting to identify what it was about Sylvia's and Makiko's pieces that shaped the "voice" we heard as we read them. In Extracts 1 and 2, which are selected because each one explains a decision the researcher has made in relation to her analysis, I have indicated the features on which our discussion focussed, by putting grammatical subjects in bold and verbs in italics. I used the same "marking up" in copies I distributed to the writing circle members ahead of our discussion of these pieces.

In Sylvia's piece, which was an explication of the meaning of a particular month, the *wayeb'*, in the ancient Mayan calendar, the voice was formal, impersonal, and distant. This distance, from both her object of study and her readers, was created by particular language choices: a technical vocabulary, use of third person only, and

Summary

This thesis examines the Islamist political movement in Turkey, with special reference to its activities in Istanbul where I did my fieldwork from October 1994 to December 1996. The thesis identifies the particular characteristics of political Islam in the Turkish context. The movement's situating of itself in opposition to the enforced civilizing project of the Turkish Republic is argued to be the key to understanding its politics.

Prologue

Flags filing into Taksim Square. Flags teeming on the flagpoles outside the 5-star hotels. Flags draped over the balconies of offices, flags promenading down the boulevards. Shaking the hands of children sitting on fathers' shoulders, swishing over heads like snappy red butterflies. Abseiling down the face of the Ataturk Cultural Centre. Crawling out along the arm of the giant crane, swinging fearless as acrobats high over the unfinished hole of the Istanbul Metro. Flags pinning up the sky.

Figure 8.1: Extracts from writing circle handout.

a preference for passive verbs, with processes, practices, ideas, or texts more likely than people to be the grammatical subject of her clauses. Together, these choices created an objective stance congruent with the ethos of Sylvia's discipline, in which it is the object of study, not the researcher, that is the focus at all times. (Archaeology has developed, over the last hundred years, from an amateur pursuit to a science, and it seems possible that its avoidance of subjective language may reflect the desire to put its origins behind it.) In these extracts, ellipsis indicates minor factual details omitted in the interests of space.

EXTRACT 1: FROM SYLVIA'S WRITING

The most intriguing **month** in the Haab' calendar *is* the wayeb' …. The **wayeb'** *was perceived* by the Maya and the Mexicans **who** *had* a similar calendar, as an "unlucky and dangerous" period (Tozzer, 1941, p. 134; Boone, 2007, p. 17). This **reaction** *has been documented* by Landa and the other Spanish priests **who** *had* the opportunity to observe the behavior of the indigenous population after the Spanish conquest (Landa in Tozzer, 1941; Durán, 1971, p. 395, pp. 469-470). The **wayeb'** *represented* the transitional stage between the old year and the ensuing New Year. Hence, this short five day **month** also *had* cosmological associations for the Maya. The **intention** of this section *is* not to present an analysis of the entire New Year festival, but to focus on the transitional stage of the wayeb' because of the perceived negativity and danger associated with these five days. Wayeb' **events** relating to period endings, rituals, a death, an intriguing accession and a birth date, *have been detected* in the Maya inscriptions researched for this dissertation. Furthermore, **it** *is known* that the contemporary Kiché **Maya** still *regard* the five days of the wayeb' as ominous (Tedlock, 1992, p. 100). The **wayeb'** *has* an obvious literal meaning in relation to time. However, **it** *is* apparent that this short five day **month** *is* also *associated* with a profound metaphorical dimension connected with transition and change.

Makiko's piece for anthropology, in contrast to Sylvia's analytical treatment of her material, presented a narrative of Makiko's decision to use a particular term to describe the people she had chosen to study. The writing was relatively informal, personal, and engaging, an effect created, again, by particular language choices: largely everyday vocabulary, first person narration, and active verbs whose subjects were most often people (indeed, twelve of these are "I," the researcher herself). The most striking contrast with Sylvia's piece was that, in Makiko's, the subjectivity of the researcher was explicitly reflected upon, as an integral part of the object and process of study.

EXTRACT 2: FROM MAKIKO'S WRITING

Throughout my thesis, **I** *call* my main participants, women of Tongan descent in their twenties and early thirties, girls **which** *is* a native term in a sense that other **people** at Tongan churches or **people** in different age groups or men's groups *call* them girls …. The **reason** why **I** *employ* a non-cultural or non-ethnic term to refer to them *is derived* from my bitter experience when **I** *had* just *started* my fieldwork in the late 2006. **I** *attended* a Tongan church regularly to broaden my network among the congregation so that **I** *could ask* people to participate in my research. At that time, **I** *explained* to people that **I** *was studying* about Tongans in Australia. Then, a **girl** in her twenties *responded* by asking me, "Oh, so **you** *think* I'm Tongan?" **This** *was* one of my embarrassing moments because **I** *felt* like my naïve **stance** *had been revealed* even though **I** *had read* about how **identities** of children of migrants *were* diverse and often located in between where **they** *live* and Tonga. During my fieldwork, **I** actually *encountered* similar questions several times, especially when **I** *wanted* to talk to people **who** *distanced* themselves from Tongan gatherings. So what else *can* **I** *call* them?

The consensus of the writing circle was that Makiko's writing was livelier and more accessible than Sylvia's, but interestingly, members had different feelings about the language choices that made it so. Some admired the accessible first person narration of the writer's dilemma and its resolution; one member commented "from my film and media background," on the way in which "voice" in a piece of writing possibly creates pictures in reader's mind. "... I see [Makiko] talking directly to me (as TV presenters do) as well as see the moving images of her field work, her experiences and relations to research participants. I can imagine I walk behind her to the community." Others, however, were uncomfortable with the anecdotal and personal character of the writing, which they felt would undermine their authority and be unacceptable to readers.

In fact, neither of these students' discursive "voices" was unconstrained, despite the apparent freedom of Makiko's writing, for as Makiko confirmed in the discussion, it is part of the ethos of anthropology that the writer should reflect upon her own position in, and therefore influence on, the research she is reporting. Many scholars have remarked upon students' acquisition of a disciplined voice apparently by osmosis from the discussions they read and hear, a discourse that is "privileged, expected, cultivated, [and] conventionalized" (Patricia Duff, 2010, p. 175; see also Tony Becher & Ludwig Huber, 1990, p. 237; Sharon Parry, 1998). Both Sylvia and Makiko had evidently internalized a disciplined voice, which they experienced as more or less "transparent," to use David Russell's (2002) expression. Russell argues that because researchers' apprenticeship to the discourse of their discipline is gradual, their writing seems to them like "a transparent recording of speech or thought" rather than "a complex rhetorical activity, embedded in the differentiated practices of academic discourse communities" (Russell, 2002, p. 9).

The writing circle, however, created a space in which members could examine how their academic socialization had shaped their writing. It is this recognition of, and reflection upon, their own socialization as manifested in their writing that takes the discussion beyond that socialization and into the territory of Academic Literacies. It has been observed elsewhere that mixed disciplinary membership in writing groups proves very useful to participants because "it gives them other disciplinary examples against which they can position their experience of writing and allows them to make explicit issues and ideas that have been largely tacit" (Phyllis Creme & Colleen McKenna, 2010, p. 164; cf. Denise Cuthbert, Ceridwen Spark, & Eliza Burke, 2009; Ken Hyland, 2002, p. 393).

Makiko's reflections very much confirm this:

> Until I attended the writing circle, I had little idea about the
> diverse styles and voices among different disciplines. The mixed
> reaction toward my subjective writing in the circle surprised me
> because I had never thought that the way I wrote was difficult to

be accepted by people from different disciplines. Having majored only in anthropology since my undergraduate course, I think I naturally learned the appropriate styles without acknowledging that different disciplines have different styles. Of course, my thesis is not comprised of personal accounts: in some reflexive sections I use many subjective words, and in the other part which shows my research data, I write in rather impersonal ways. Since I had unconsciously written in different styles, the experience in the inter-disciplinary group led me discover the difference, and changed my perspective when I write. After the session, I became more conscious about my use of words, and started to think more about how potential readers would see the way I write.

In considering the pieces discussed in the meeting on which this chapter focusses, Sylvia and Makiko found that they appreciated the "fit" between their authorial voice and the ethos of their discipline. One minor aspect Sylvia decided to change was the repetition of "month" as the subject of so many of her clauses; but for the purpose of this passage justifying her choice of focus, she opted to preserve the authority that she felt derived from an objective voice (cf. Creme & McKenna, 2010, p. 162).

If exploring the constraints and choices involved in academic writing sometimes serves to make it more "internally persuasive" (Mikhail Bakhtin, 1981), as on this occasion, does this mean that the activity has failed to be transformative? I do not think so, for the discussion itself creates a space for thinking more deliberately about voice. In so doing, it enables the goals of "academic literacies": to make writing less "transparent" and to raise awareness of the multiple, yet constrained, possibilities for expression. Sylvia was satisfied that her "demonstration of ... insiderdom" was at the same time "a personal act of meaning making" (Russell et al., 2009, p. 413). However, in exploring alternatives, the group acquired the linguistic tools (such as the options of active or passive voice, concrete grammatical subjects or abstract nominalizations, first or third person, narrative or analysis, technical or lay vocabulary) to change their voice if any of them decide they want to—including Sylvia, who writes:

> Through the analysis and discussion of each other's work by the students in this multi-disciplined group, I have become more aware of the impact of one's writing style on the reader. It is apparent that the level of creative "control" in writing varies according to the discipline, with some subjects such as Media Studies enabling a greater level of freedom. Nevertheless, the feedback has helped me to improve the creativity in my writing

and not to be afraid of including my own "voice" where appropriate.

We see this, indeed, in a subsequent piece, where Sylvia takes first-person ownership of some reservations about her sources:

> I found it surprising that there is not a greater level of compatibility between Sahagún's auguries for the first days of the trecenas and those of the Telleriano-Remensis .... I consider there are some questionable aspects associated with the Telleriano-Remensis. For instance, in the section relating to the veintenas .... From my perspective, this indicates a surprising lack of understanding of this "unlucky" month and does call into question the reliability of some of the scribes and artists associated with this work.

Since the writing circle discussion on which this article focuses, our circle has talked about such strategies of negotiation as asking supervisors for their views on particular language choices; writing two versions for supervisors' consideration; voicing an oral presentation differently from a written chapter; or postponing experimentation in the belief that later, as "licensed" scholars, they will be able to take more risks. Research students are already well aware of their liminal status in the scholarly community, and the power relations surrounding their candidature; what the writing circle gives them is an awareness of the technology of expression, the interplay of discipline socialization and individual desires and aspirations, and the social nature of what can otherwise seem like individual concerns (see Kaufhold Chapter 8 this volume). What is transformative about the writing circle is not that it makes people write differently (although it may); but that instead of thinking of writers and writing as good or bad, they are thinking of both as situated. "Informed choice," in this context, is informed by a greater understanding of *how* they are situated by disciplinary voices (see also Horner and Lillis, Reflections 4 this volume).

REFERENCES

Aitchison, C., & Lee, A. (2006). Research writing: Problems and pedagogies. *Teaching in Higher Education, 11*(3), 265-278.

Bakhtin, M. (1981). Discourse in the novel. In M. Holquist (Ed.), *The dialogic imagination. Four essays by M. Bakhtin* (C. Emerson & M. Holquist, Trans.). Austin, TX. University of Texas Press.

Becher, T., & Huber, L. (1990). Editorial: Disciplinary cultures. *European Journal of Education, 25*(3), 235-240.

Chanock, K. (2007). Helping thesis writers to think about genre: What is prescribed, what may be possible. *The WAC Journal, 18*. Retrieved from http://wac.

colostate.edu/journal/vol18/index.cfm

Cotterall, S. (2011). Doctoral students' writing: Where's the pedagogy? *Teaching in Higher Education, 16* (4), 413-425.

Creme, P., & McKenna, C. (2010). Developing writer identity through a multidisciplinary programme. *Arts and Humanities in Higher Education, 9*(2), 149-167.

Cuthbert, D., Spark, C., & Burke, E. (2009). Disciplining writing: The case for multi-disciplinary writing groups to support writing for publication by higher degree by research candidates in the humanities, arts and social sciences. *Higher Education Research and Development, 28*(2), 137-149.

Duff, P. (2010). Language socialisation into academic discourse communities. *Annual Review of Applied Linguistics, 30*, 169-192.

Houston, C. (2001). *Islam, Kurds, and the Turkish nation-state.* Oxford, UK: Berg.

Hyland, K. (2002). Specificity revisited: How far should we go now? *English for Specific Purposes, 21*, 385-395.

Larcombe, W., McCosker, A., & O'Loughlin, K. (2007). Supporting education PhD and EdD students to become confident academic writers: An evaluation of thesis writers' circles. *Journal of University Teaching and Learning Practice,* (1), 54-63.

Lillis, T. (2003). Student writing as "academic literacies": Drawing on Bakhtin to move from critique to design. *Language and Education, 17*(3), 192-207.

Parry, S. (1998). Disciplinary discourse in doctoral theses. *Higher Education, 36*, 273-299.

Russell, D. (2002). *Writing in the academic disciplines: A curricular history* (2nd ed.). Carbondale, IL: University of Southern Illinois Press.

Russell, D., Lea, M., Parker, J., Street, B., & Donahue, T. (2009). Exploring notions of genre in "academic literacies" and "writing in the disciplines": Approaches across countries and contexts. In C. Bazerman, A. Bonini, & D. Figueiredo (Eds.), *Genre in a changing world. Perspectives on writing.* Fort Collins, CO: The WAC Clearinghouse/Parlor Press. Retrieved from http://wac.colostate.edu/books/genre

Taylor, G., Ballard, B., Beasley, V., Bock, H., Clanchy, J., & Nightingale, P. (1988). *Literacy by degrees.* Milton Keynes, UK: Society for Research into Higher Education & Open University Press.

HOW CAN THE TEXT BE EVERYTHING? REFLECTING ON ACADEMIC LIFE AND LITERACIES

Sally Mitchell talking with Mary Scott

One of the tenets of Academic Literacies research is recognition of the personal resources that an individual brings to any situation, practice, or text. In any inquiry the student writer is not bracketed off from the object that she or he produces. Students bring to their writing and study, experiences, values, attitudes, thoughts which are personal as well as "academic" or "disciplinary"—though they sometimes struggle to negotiate these, and can be constrained by the ways in which discourses silence as well as give voice to individual meaning-making. As for students, so, of course, for all of us …

In this piece Sally Mitchell reflects on a conversation with Mary Scott, one of the key participants in the development of Academic Literacies as a field, and explores what personal trajectories and biographical details can suggest about how a disciplinary (disciplined, theorized, academic) stance and ethos can develop.

Mary Scott (2013a) has recently written a personal, theorized account of her involvement, as a teacher and researcher, with the writing of university students. She frames this journey, which has taken place over a number of years, as "learning to read student writing differently". I was interested to talk to her about this, and how her biographies—personal, intellectual, professional and institutional—have shaped her thinking and work as someone who, if we think of Academic Literacies as a grouping of certain interrelated *people*, as much as interrelated *ideas*—is a key figure. The relationship between people and ideas—peopled ideas—seems significant, perhaps particularly when we are talking about a field which is also a profession and a practice. Certainly important texts in Academic Literacies explicitly use who the authors are, and where they have come from as part of what they have to say (I'm thinking of Roz Ivanič and Theresa Lillis both who drew on practice to begin theorizing).

When Mary opened our conversation by sharing what's new in the field—the idea of superdiversity—she talked about how the idea is being tested and contested by various *players*, differently located geographically and theoretically, politically and temperamentally. Her interest is in seeing new knowledge as *developing, multiply influenced and as voiced*, rather than as "presented," self-contained and abstract. This stance lies behind Mary's email list which distributes information to colleagues across the world about conferences, books and talks, as well as in the more grounded termly meetings she has hosted since the early/mid 1990s at the Institute of Education in London. Both are characterized more by their sense of plurality and capacity than by a particular framing. "I wanted [them] not to be doctrinaire," she says.

Mary studied for her first BA in English and Latin at Rhodes University, South Africa. This was followed by a postgraduate year for which she received a BA honours in English Literature. (The shifting meaning of university qualifications is a significant theme in the conversation). At Rhodes, she had an "inspirational" tutor, Guy Butler, who was also a poet. He wrote a poem called "Cape Coloured Batsman" when he was in the army in Italy, and was subsequently criticized for having neo-colonialist views: "It was the first time anybody had written a sympathetic poem about a colored man, but he wouldn't write it now." "Views," then, are not the sole property of individuals; they are caught up in time, part of social, political, historical moments and movements. So, for example, Butler set up a Study of English in Africa Centre, and it takes me a while to realize there might be any progressive significance to this; to me, it doesn't sound progressive at all—perhaps the opposite. But Butler was challenging the assumption that English meant *British English* taught in South Africa mainly by academics from Britain—a kind of colonialism within colonialism. Mary herself was entangled with this struggle over language and nation. She was "British by descent" and, at age 16, to fund her study she was given a grant by the "Sons of England Patriot and Benevolent Society" which committed her to teaching English in schools for three years. The Society was concerned at a shortage of good English teachers: "Afrikaans would take over, English would be excluded". The economic hand-up committed her to more than safeguarding English in schools however; it marked her positioning in English-Afrikaans politics. More or less the contract was: "Now if we give you this money ... you'll teach for three years—will you promise us you'll never vote for the Nationalist government?"

Having paid her dues teaching English (in fact it was largely Latin which the schools thought was more of a rarity), Mary took up an invitation from Guy Butler to return to Rhodes and teach—"poetry, drama, rather than the novel." Other pressures then saw her move to Cape Town; her father in particular was anxious that she should get a professional qualification and she enrolled to do a two year BEd with a teacher's certificate while teaching full-time in the Department of English at the University of Cape Town (UCT). It was a pre-requisite at the time that to do a BEd you should have another first degree in a subject discipline—not so today. Mary wrote her thesis on the teaching of Shakespeare in schools, though "schools" did not include black or coloured schools:

> I'm writing about South Africa, and education in South Afri-
> ca, with a thesis on the teaching of the Shakespeare play in the
> secondary school. And I'm looking at the kinds of theories that
> teachers were drawing on in what they were doing, and looking
> at some examples of students writing about Shakespeare. And it
> was all terribly much … something I think that would probably
> have been done in Britain. There was no local politics included
> in it. Well, why Shakespeare? It was taken for granted, you know,
> the classics, the canon, and Shakespeare at the top. … In all the
> education, there was an Anglocentric subtext all the time.

Experiences of this kind perhaps shaped in Mary a visceral mistrust of categories, an uneasy relationship with institutions and a scepticism about the orthodox-
ies of disciplinary meaning making. Another recollection from South Africa shows
the political subtext pushing into the foreground of her thinking:

> In the days when I did English Literature, there was an empha-
> sis on the close study of the text, even to a ridiculous extreme. I
> remember trotting out the received wisdom to a student at Cape
> Town University; he'd said something about the life history of
> some author. And I said, "Oh no, that's not relevant, you just look
> at the text." And he said, "Why is it not relevant?" And I went
> away and thought, "Gosh, I've been talking—you know—I'm just
> trotting out something without thought. Oh, he's got a point."

Mary's own scholarship still reflects the close attention/sensitivity to texts that
her literary training gave her, but recognizing the myopia of English's bracketing
of the text's producer perhaps prepared her to critique and challenge the bound-
aried-ness of disciplines and fields, domains, territories that she encountered, negotiated and was subject to. When finding less encouragement to pursue scholarship and teaching at UCT, than with Guy Butler at Rhodes, she along with other
contemporaries applied for grants to study overseas—and in the mid-1970s found
herself at the Institute of Education in London. She took the "Advanced Diploma
with special reference to the role of language in education" taught by Nancy Martin, Harold Rosen and Margaret Spencer, and she taught part time in secondary
and language schools while gradually taking on a fulltime academic post.

When Gunther Kress arrived at the Institute of Education in the early 1990s
he and Mary together set up the MA in the Learning and Teaching of English with
Literacy. Their collaborative work on this programme established a lasting respect
and interest in each others' work: there was perhaps a meeting of ex-colonial minds
(Gunther was born in Germany, brought up and educated in Australia) because

though their "official" disciplines were different—Literature, Linguistics—they shared insights into texts/language in and across contexts, how texts are received and how, and who produces them: a sensitivity to the importance not only of who you're writing *for (audience)* but of *who you are* writing:

> I think Gunther has always thought about the learner. And I
> liked that. And the writer in the text. So, he concentrates on
> texts but he doesn't leave out a view of the writer—it's a writer
> bringing certain resources and assumptions and expectations,
> and what those are.

Is she talking about "identity" here? Well no, for a South African, identity is a problematic term:

> It goes back to history again, personal history .... I think of it as
> Jan Blommaert's' "ascribed identity," and we had to carry identity
> cards in South Africa, and I had one saying I was white, and, you
> know, the Pass Laws and all that. That's what immediately comes
> into my mind—people putting others in brackets and racial
> categories ...

With Mary and with Gunther, recognition of the writer is never just a way of looking at texts, it's a way of interrogating where the power lies, what assumptions it rests on, how it maintains itself, how it subjects or subjugates those who come to it for a share. This is perhaps why Mary has preferred the notion of the "subject"— both agent and recipient of categories, discourses, agenda: "identity" for her doesn't admit of a two-way process (see discussions of Norman Fairclough and Gunther Kress in Mary Scott, 1999; see also Scott, 2013b).

During the 1970s and 1980s in the United Kingdom the increased recruitment of higher fee-paying international students led to a greater recognition at an institutional level of the utility of language teaching. Mary was conscious of the conflicting discourses here: literary texts/student texts, a discipline/training, home students/international students, literate/illiterate. In the implicit or explicit creation of binaries the "versus" often also brings about the creation of deficit. "What is being edited out in the terms we use?" she asked.

Some of the international students were sponsored by their governments and seeking qualifications of higher currency than those in their home country—higher currency, though not necessarily of higher intrinsic value (an echo of Mary's own experience of taking two degrees classed as bachelor's in South Africa, that elsewhere and in later years might be classed as bachelor followed by master's). At the same time, many practising UK teachers were taking their qualifications to degree level.

The Institute decided to offer a BEd for those teachers who had got certificates, from the days before there was a BEd, so a conversion BEd. They had Certificates of Education, they'd come from training colleges, and many of them were in very senior posts.

Mary offered a "morning programme" to the BEd students:

> So, what I tried to do then, with the morning programme, the students would meet on a Monday morning, and beforehand, they would have read some text relevant to the Tuesday evening lecture. And they'd be given a question to consider. Now, as time went on, they might have to read two texts, and the question would get more complicated. And then, on the Tuesday, a couple of them would present what they'd done and it would be discussed. So that when they went to the Tuesday … evening lectures, they'd have some background … it wasn't just English and language. And then we'd meet on a Thursday morning, where they could talk about any problems they'd had following the Tuesday lectures or any things that had come up that they hadn't thought of … it was very intensive.

Although this provision sounds like good teaching full stop, its existence also began in some way to create the role of "language and literacy service provider" in the institution. In 1994 it was given a more secure and prominent footing, when with the support of Gunther Kress, Mary got the backing of Senate to establish the Centre for Academic and Professional Literacy Studies (CAPLITS) with three important functions: teaching, research and consultancy.

In making this move Mary recognized that, despite her mistrust of prefixed distinctions or compartments, within institutions such compartments are often convenient. They attract resource and status and they allow innovation and perhaps resistance (agency), and even whilst they demonstrate compliance to, they are a symptom of an institutional framing. In this framing the institution is cast as providing the things people lack (its deficient recipients), and the ideology is one in which socialization is largely a one-way process towards the reproduction of institutional norms. This emphasis continues to pervade provision in the United Kingdom. Reflecting on a seminar being held later in the academic year to focus staff on the issue of assessment, Mary comments:

> From what I can understand, it's all about how to make the norms clearer, that sort of thing. No thought about the people who have been learning here, and how the institution needs to change.

Yet in a world of diversity which is increasingly becoming recognized as a world of superdiversity, the "meeting of norms seen in a very narrow way is not the solution".

While, like most institutions, the Institute does not easily cast a critical eye on its role in the education of students from across the globe, the process in the initial establishment of CAPLITS and in Mary's own thinking has been much more reflexive and developmental. As I've mentioned, Mary describes her progression as a researcher as "learning to see [students'] writing differently"; she refers elsewhere to seeing the student text as "a hypothesis" (Mary Scott & Nicholas Groom, 1999; see also Mary Scott & Joan Turner, 2009). But she is also aware of and acutely teased by the question of how research insights relate to, or translate into, practice:

> Alright, I can look at this text and see there are all these assumptions and things, but do I look at that simply in terms of how I must lead the student on—*the way they should be?*

Mary doesn't have any answers if answers were to be in a set of practices. And I'm not sure the tension she points to is a resolvable one, or a question that a teacher/researcher could be expected definitively to solve. Perhaps it is enough that the answer lies in the question; the act or acts of reflexive awareness. For me, I realize, this is what having an "Aclits" orientation means—not so much a pedagogy but a framing of pedagogy which keeps the questions open and keeps questioning, even itself. The question of what *moving the student on* might mean, or look like, without once again casting the student as deficient, could be said to be the key dilemma for the academic literacies practitioner/researcher, but the willingness to hold that question might also be thought of as their key *characteristic*. A kind of temperament. Reflecting on our conversation, this seems to hold true in Mary's case. She mistrusts the reductionism in simple or single explanations or models, resisting for example, the reading of "Study Skills, Socialisation, Academic Literacies" as distinguishable approaches ("are they models?"), and she is aware of complex framings that impinge on and shape the teacher—making her a pragmatist as well as an idealist.

REFERENCES

Scott, M. (1999). Agency and subjectivity in student writing. In C. Jones, J. Turner, & B. Street (Eds.), *Students writing in the university: Cultural and epistemological issues*. Amsterdam: John Benjamins Publishing Company.

Scott, M. (2013a). *A chronicle of learning: voicing the text* (Proefschrift). Tilburg, NL: University of Tilburg Press.

Scott, M. (2013b). From error to multimodal semiosis: Reading student writing differently. In M. Boeck & N. Pachler (Eds.), *Multimodality and social semiosis: Communication, meaning-making, and learning in the work of Gunther Kress* (pp. 195-203). New York: Routledge.

Scott, M., & Groom, N. (1999). Genre-based pedagogy: problems and pedagogy. In Thompson, P. (Ed.), *Issues in EAP writing research and instruction*. Reading, UK: Anthony Lowe Ltd.

Scott, M. & Turner, J. (2009). Reconceptualising student writing: From conformity to heteroglossic complexity. In A. Carter, T. Lillis, & S. Parkin (Eds.), *Why Writing Matters. Issues of access and identity in writing research and pedagogy* (pp. 151-161). Amsterdam/Philadelphia: John Benjamins Publishing Company.

SECTION 2
TRANSFORMING
THE WORK OF TEACHING

INTRODUCTION TO SECTION 2

This section continues a focus on pedagogy, but with the angle of investigation emphasising the teacher—identities, practices, normative assumptions and resources for change—as the site of transformation. The chapters cover such themes as the value of teachers learning from one another in collaborative partnerships, questioning and challenging their own assumptions and situating practice within disciplinary contexts of meaning-making.

Throughout, there is a focus on transformative pedagogical practice as intimately linked with transformations in teachers' own understandings of the possibilities for re-thinking prevailing norms and for generating new forms of meaning-making within the disciplinary and professional contexts in which they are working. Transformation is understood by the authors in this section as meaning more than simply "change," in that it incorporates a new degree of self-awareness and a greater ability to think about one's own beliefs and active role in the complex and difficult processes of engaging with a transformative stance in one's teaching practice. The chapters demonstrate the value for students' learning and sense of agency and potential for their own transformation that can be brought about through teachers negotiating with and allowing transformation in their own personal understandings and professional identities.

The section opens with Cecilia Jacobs's discussion of an institutional, cross-disciplinary initiative in South Africa that sought to challenge dominant framings of academic literacy, as taught in generic, skills-based courses, through the development of collaborative partnerships between Academic Literacies and disciplinary lecturers. These partnerships were shaped by a shift of focus away from students and deficit models of language proficiency to lecturers and their pedagogy, and the chapter shows how possibilities for more transformative understandings and pedagogical practices were enabled through the "doing" of teaching, including joint curriculum and assessment design and co-research. The author draws attention to the ways in which complementary outsider/insider positions can work to bring tacit disciplinary conventions into explicit awareness. The next chapter by Julian Ingle and Nadya Yakovchuk also considers the transformative potential of collaborative teaching and curriculum design, here in the context of sports and exercise medicine and the task of preparing BSc students to write a research project to publishable standard. The authors reflect on their experiences of developing a series of workshops that explicitly foregrounded questions of disciplinary knowledge construction, identity and power as a way of fostering greater insight and the ability to negotiate in a more conscious way some of the conventions and epistemological positionings found in medical research writing. Whilst acknowledging their experiences of limitations of an Academic Literacies approach, they suggest that becoming more aware of disciplinary meaning-making practices and one's emergent identity within this context is itself transformative, for teachers as well as students. Exploration of the transformative potential of collaboration, this time between disciplinary teachers and academic developers, continues in the paper by Moragh Paxton and Vera Frith, who consider the ethical imperative for, and challenges of, embracing a transformative pedagogy in the field of Biological, Earth and Environmental Sciences. Whilst the authors argue that in a South African context normative approaches are to an extent essential to bringing about greater equity amongst all students, they illustrate how working with teachers to help them recognize how actively working with students' prior knowledge and practices can be a resource for fostering change and empowering students to overcome barriers to learning.

The next two chapters look at the relationship between standard written (Anglo-American) English norms and the experiences of students who are using English as an additional language. Maria Leedham contributes to thinking about transformation by challenging a traditional framing of "non-native speaker writing" as deficient compared with that of the "native speaker" (taken as the norm)—an assumption found in many corpus linguistic studies. Instead, she brings a more nuanced perspective to bear and asks what we can learn from disciplinary lecturers about proficient student writing irrespective of the writer's first or second language. Through close textual analysis and interviews with lecturers, she shows that using visuals and lists (preferred by Chinese native speakers) is as acceptable as writing in extended prose (preferred by British-English native speakers) in the disciplines of Economics, Biology and Engineering. She argues that this disciplinary flexibility is often not acknowledged in approaches to writing tuition offered by EAP and academic writing teachers who are predominantly familiar with more essayist and discursive meaning-making conventions from their own, generally humanistic, backgrounds. She suggests that a willingness to question one's own normative views about writing is essential to a transformation of teaching practice towards recognizing the diversity, rather than the deficits, that writers bring with them to the academy.

The next chapter by Laura McCambridge focusses on the context of an international master's degree programme at a Finnish university, where English is used as the institutional *lingua-franca* and students come from widely diverse linguistic, cultural and academic backgrounds. In this context, she argues, tensions around the need for clear and explicit writing guidance and for accommodating diverse writing practices are particularly exposed. She frames this as a "clear practical dilemma" for Academic Literacies of finding a workable "third way" that avoids the pitfalls of both overly implicit and obscure and excessively prescriptive and normative approaches to teaching writing. Drawing on interviews with lecturers and students, the author points to the importance of student agency, teachers' preparedness to question their own assumptions and room for negotiation and consciousness-raising in order to create more constructive and transformative learning opportunities for both students and teachers.

The last three chapters in this section focus on the meaning-making practices of teachers and the unique resources and perspectives they bring to the teaching relationship. Jackie Tuck's chapter is concerned with an exploration of the meanings of writing and the teaching of writing that disciplinary lecturers bring to and extract from their teaching practice. Drawing on empirical ethnographic data from interviews, assessment materials and audio-recordings of marking sessions from participants working in different universities and disciplines in the United Kingdom, she argues that transformative pedagogic design can only flourish where the lived experiences and perspectives of both teachers and students are taken into account. In her study she found that meaningful engagement, such as the feeling of making a positive difference to student writing, was as important as pragmatic considerations, such as time and available resources, in providing an incentive for teachers to transform their practices beyond often unproductive routines. She also shows the ways in which transformation of students' engagement with academic writing is inseparably bound up with teachers' own transformations. Her findings suggest that what counts as a positive change needs to be negotiated and seen as worthwhile for both students and teachers, and she argues that nurturing the conditions for teacher transformation is as crucial for effecting positive change as is providing incentives for students to engage meaningfully with their writing. Kevin Roozen, Paul Prior, Rebecca Woodard and Sonia Kline consider teachers' developing practices and identities. They argue that in the same way that students' histories and experiences of literacy can enrich learning in the classroom, so can teachers' histories and literate engagements beyond formal educational settings play a key role in transforming pedagogical practice and student learning. The authors present three vignettes of teachers working in school and university contexts in the United States, drawing variously on their experiences of a creative writing group, blogging and fan-fiction writing to enrich their classroom practices. The vignettes illustrate the opportunities for transformative pedagogy that can come from recognizing the rich complexity of teachers' identities and creatively linking them to classroom practice. The final chapter in this section by Jane Creaton investigates the way lecturers' written feedback practices both regulate and can be used to contest and transform norms of knowledge construction and student identity. The chapter looks in particular at the under-theorized area of professional doctorate writing and draws on an analysis of feedback comments to highlight the unique features of the student-supervisor relationship in the context of professional practice. Based on her findings, she suggests that programme-level discussion amongst colleagues can uncover tacit assumptions and normative practices that can be shared with students, and she offers an insightful feedback response to her own text that models both the goal and the challenges of transforming—and transformative—practice.

The two *Reflections* in this section offer perspectives from North American and French traditions of writing pedagogy and research to illuminate convergences and differences in how researcher-practitioners work with the concept of Academic Literacies in different cultural and institutional contexts. In conversation with Sally Mitchell, David Russell discusses the history of a critical approach within the Writing Across the Curriculum and Writing in the Disciplines movements in North America, suggesting that aspects of these traditions offer a critique of the normative/transformative continuum as conceptualized in Academic Literacies. At the same time he acknowledges the extent to which writing consultants accommodate disciplinary teachers' perspectives on writing conventions and epistemological practices, for both pragmatic and institutional reasons—but he also argues that there is potential for writing teachers' own transformation through interactions with a diversity of other perspectives. Isabelle Delcambre and Christiane Donahue consider areas of overlap and divergence in how transformation is understood and worked with across the different fields of Littéracies Universitaires in France, Composition Studies in the United States and Academic Literacies. Whilst University Literacies shares with Academic Literacies a notion of socially negotiated meanings between teachers and students, transformation in the former tradition concentrates on the writing knowledge and practices of students that need to evolve in order for them to participate fruitfully within new disciplinary communities of practice: unlike Academic Literacies, it does not adopt a critical stance towards the disciplinary writing practices themselves. By comparison, the tradition of Composition Studies in the United States is seen to share the critical transformative goal of Academic Literacies, with first-year composition courses providing sites of resistance, negotiation and transformation of practice which value the inherently dynamic and open-ended process of learning—and in this sense are to be distinguished from a more integrative approach to norms and conventions found in disciplinary writing practice and teaching.

CHAPTER 9

OPENING UP THE CURRICULUM: MOVING FROM THE NORMATIVE TO THE TRANSFORMATIVE IN TEACHERS' UNDERSTANDINGS OF DISCIPLINARY LITERACY PRACTICES

Cecilia Jacobs

This chapter covers what Theresa Lillis (2009) refers to as "living the normative, transformative space" through the experiences of a group of academics at a South African university of technology. Four dominant institutional discourses framed the way academic literacies were understood at the institution: "knowledge as something to be imparted, and the curriculum as a body of content to be learned"; "academic literacies as a list of skills (related to writing and reading and often studying) that could be taught separately in decontextualized ways and then transferred unproblematically to disciplines of study"; "academic literacy teaching as something that was needed by English Second Language students who were not proficient in English (the medium of instruction)"; and "the framing of students, particularly second language speakers of English, in a deficit mode." These institutional discourses typically saw students as the "problem" and the reason for poor academic performance, while it also absolved lecturers from critically reflecting on their practice, and the institution from critically reflecting on its systems. These institutional discourses gave rise to dominant institutional practices such as academic literacy teaching through add-on, autonomous modules/subjects/courses, which were marginal to the mainstream curriculum. Referred to as "service subjects," these courses were taught by academic literacy (language) lecturers who straddled academic departments, faculties and campuses, were itinerant and marginal to the day-to-day functioning of departments, and often hourly paid temporary appointments or contract positions. Given these institutional discourses and practices, alternative forms of responsiveness were explored through an academic literacies initiative with a deliberate shift of focus from students and their language proficiency to lecturers and their pedagogy. The purpose of this initiative was to challenge the above-mentioned institutional discourses by transforming academic literacy teaching at the university *from* the prevailing separate, generic, skills-based courses taught by academic literacies lecturers, *to* an integrated approach where academic literacies (AL) and disciplinary lecturers worked collaboratively to integrate academic literacy teaching into various disciplines.

DESCRIPTION OF THE ACADEMIC LITERACIES INITIATIVE

The initiative, detailed elsewhere (Cecilia Jacobs, 2008), was implemented as a three-year institutional project that brought together ten partnerships between AL and disciplinary lecturers. The partnerships worked collaboratively on developing linguistically inclusive, integrated mainstream curricula. The emphasis was thus not on add-on approaches or "patching up" perceived language deficits but on engaging both AL and disciplinary lecturers in new ways of teaching disciplinary literacy practices, which I have termed "collaborative pedagogy." These ten partnerships in turn formed a transdisciplinary collective of twenty academics, which was the institutional platform that networked the discipline-based partnerships between AL and disciplinary lecturers. The partnerships became the vehicle for integrating academic literacies into the respective disciplines by exploring the discursive practices of those disciplines, while the institutional project team provided a transdisciplinary space for those academics to explore their professional roles as tertiary educators. The collaborative processes, occurring in the ten partnerships as well as the transdisciplinary collective, appeared to enable the explicit teaching of disciplinary literacy practices through unlocking the tacit knowledge that the disciplinary lecturers had of these literacy practices.

So instead of AL lecturers teaching separate courses, they worked collaboratively with disciplinary lecturers on unpacking what the literacy practices of the discipline of study are (tacit knowledge for disciplinary lecturers) and then developing joint classroom activities to make these practices explicit to students. Some partnerships moved beyond just making these practices explicit and inducting students into the literacy practices of the discipline (the normative), to opening up curriculum spaces where the literacy practices of disciplines might be critiqued and contested by their students (the transformative). The partnerships also involved team teaching, where AL and disciplinary lecturers collaboratively taught in ways that embedded reading and writing within the ways that their particular academic disciplines used language in practice.

Without a roadmap for how this process might unfold, these partnerships engaged in collaborative teaching practices as a meaning-making exercise. It was through collaboratively planning their lessons, jointly developing the teaching materials, the actual practice of team teaching and then co-researching their practice that some of these lecturers developed alternative understandings and practices regarding academic literacies to those understandings and practices that had dominated institutional discourses. This initiative was undertaken as an institutionally organized pedagogical project, and involved AL and disciplinary partnerships across a range of disciplines and academic departments, including science, radiography, architecture, mechanical engineering, electrical engineering, law, marketing, human resource management, business administration, and public administration. The initiative aimed to shift lecturers' "ways of thinking" about academic literacies from the "normative" towards the "transformative" (Theresa Lillis & Mary Scott, 2007).

CONCEPTUAL FRAMING

I have drawn on theoretical frameworks and empirical research from the broad field of academic literacies research (James Gee, 1990, 1998, 2003; Mary Lea & Barry Stierer, 2000; Mary Lea & Brian Street, 2006; Theresa Lillis, 2001, 2003; Brian Street, 1999, 2003). My work was informed by early theoretical models emanating from the New Literacy Studies, such as the "ideological and autonomous models" of literacy (Street, 1984), as well as more recent constructs emerging from the UK perspective on academic literacies research, such as the normative (identify and induct) and transformative (situate and contest) approaches to academic literacies research and practice (Lillis & Scott, 2007). Twenty years down the line, the autonomous model of literacy and normative approaches still appear to dominate understandings of academic literacies teaching at the institution where my research was located. This would suggest that there is a need for ongoing research into the practice of academic literacies teaching in higher education and the understandings that underpin these practices.

The literature suggests that a transformative pedagogy requires lecturers to move beyond the normative "academic socialization approach" which seeks to enculturate students into disciplinary literacy practices, to the teaching of Academic Literacies. A transformative pedagogy would require lecturers to open up curriculum spaces where the literacy practices of disciplines might be critiqued and contested. This chapter briefly reports on the findings from an initiative which engaged a group of partnered AL and disciplinary lecturers (from a range of disciplines) in collaborative teaching practices with a view to shifting from a normative towards a transformative pedagogy. The chapter will explore the range of understandings that these lecturers brought to their collaborative practices, and analyse how some of these understandings shifted over time.

I have used the three theoretical orientations to the teaching of academic literacies (skills, socialization and literacies), offered by Lea & Street (2006), as a tool for analyzing how participants in my study understood their teaching of academic literacies. The findings are drawn from an analysis of the transcripts of narrative interviews and focus group sessions, in which the twenty AL and disciplinary lecturers participated. My data revealed that all three of the orientations to the teaching of academic literacies discussed in the conceptual framing above were evident in the understandings that these lecturers brought to their approach to the teaching of academic literacies, as I illustrate with some excerpts from my data set.

ACADEMIC SKILLS UNDERSTANDING

> I can see they don't do well, maybe not because they don't know, it's because they can't express themselves. So I picked that up really, that it really is a language barrier, nothing else. Nothing else.

> If students can't speak English properly then you must take students with a higher level of English. They must be put on support programmes to improve their language. What else do you want? I mean that's enough. The (institution) is doing that. It's doing enough. You don't need to do more.

These participants understood academic literacies teaching as being about promoting general language proficiency, enabling students to understand English as a medium of instruction and using grammatically correct English. This understanding is underpinned by the notion that the barrier to students' success in their disciplines of study is the medium of instruction, and this academic literacies pedagogy is firmly located within the autonomous, add-on support model. The classroom activities tended to focus on semantics and vocabulary, rather than on literacy practices. This understanding was expressed in teaching materials that made content knowledge accessible to students by simplifying the disciplinary language of authentic academic texts of the disciplines, including substituting technical terminology with common-sense terms wherever possible (see Street et al. Reflections 5 this volume).

ACADEMIC SOCIALIZATION UNDERSTANDING

> Nowadays I would look at it much more in terms of the less tangible skills that you actually impart to your students which then helps them in the learning in the classroom, and helps them access the language. The glossary … was very tangible, and crossword puzzles and annotating text and things like that. Whereas now, I think I'm far more open to how you get the students' pathways through learning, how to assert your subject, as well as learning the language of the subject and the language they need to write it academically. There's a whole underground layer, under learning, which depends upon it. Sort of a bedrock

layer of basic tools that allows the learner to access the different
languages. And possibly, I think (at the start of the project) I
was also still looking at language more in terms of medium of
instruction.

This participant understood academic literacies teaching as being about uncritically inducting students into the literacy practices of the disciplines. However what is interesting in this excerpt is that she appears to have shifted in her thinking. She describes her initial understanding of academic literacies pedagogy as being about "tangible skills" and refers to classroom activities involving glossaries, crossword puzzles and annotated text. This would point to an academic skills understanding with a focus on language per se rather than practices. She then goes on to describe her emerging understanding of academic literacies pedagogy as involving "learning the language of the subject and the language they need to write it academically." She then refers to a process of inducting her learners into the "basic tools" that allow the learner to access the disciplinary languages. This understanding was expressed in teaching materials that sought to make explicit to students the rules underpinning the literacy practices of her discipline.

ACADEMIC LITERACIES UNDERSTANDING

Initially one could have said you only need to know the words
and the meanings to understand (the discipline) better. But
you need to do more than that. What I'm saying is you need to
be able to place the term where it comes from, what it means,
what the implications are, how just one word changes the whole
meaning, how language sets up relationships of power, how
it sets up relationships of equality or inequality. So it's getting
deeper into conceptual understanding of these things. And I
think it's not only a matter of having certain language proficiency, it's more than that …. It's because words ultimately operate in
a context, but it doesn't only operate in the context of a passage
or in the context of a book. It operates in the context of a reality,
of a life; it operates in the context of your experience.

This participant understood academic literacies teaching as being about making visible for students the ways in which their discipline operated as a site of discourse and power. His pedagogy went beyond just giving students access to the workings of disciplinary discourses, to include how these discourses might be contested. This understanding was expressed in teaching materials that sought to make explicit the relationships of power within the discourses of the discipline and its literacy practices.

The participants in my study had worked in collaborative partnerships over a period of three years. Through their collaborative pedagogy they not only developed and shared understandings of academic literacies teaching, but also shifted from their initial understandings. These shifts seemed to move along a continuum of understandings, from an academic skills understanding at the outset (and some participants never managed to shift from this understanding), to an academic socialization understanding (in the case of a number of the participants), to an academic literacies understanding (in a few cases).

I have found it useful in my data analysis to represent these shifts as points along a continuum of understandings of the teaching of academic literacies (see Figure 9.1).

There were many factors influencing why some partnerships were more successful in shifting than others, such as similar age, compatible personalities, shared life experiences, common educational vision, comparable levels of commitment, previous collaborative engagement, disciplinary expertise and disciplinary status (Jacobs, 2010). While one would expect that text-based disciplines would be more open to the academic literacies approach than disciplines that grant status to knowledge which is empirically constructed, this did not emerge in the data. This was partly because most disciplines at a university of technology are of the "empirically constructed" kind. Interestingly the disciplinary lecturers who shifted most towards the academic literacies approach were from the disciplines of architecture and radiography, neither of which would be regarded as text-based. For those partnerships who shifted from their initial understandings of academic literacies teaching, it was about both parties sharing their different perspectives about what it means to be literate in the discipline, with the AL lecturers bringing outsider knowledge of the teaching and learning of literacies, and the disciplinary lecturers bringing insider knowledge of the discursive practices of their particular disciplines. The following excerpts, from two different disciplinary lecturers, illustrate how the collaborative pedagogy led to shifts in their approaches and perspectives:

> We needed someone from the outside to be able to see because
> once you are inside, you're the player, you don't see everything.

Figure 9.1: Continuum of understandings of the teaching of academic literacies.

But the person (AL lecturer), the spectator so to speak, can see the whole game as it were, and that perspective is important. Just to bring you back and say, "Look this is what I can see," and maybe you can't because you're so focussed, you just see your own role and not how it fits into the broader picture.

Just working with a language person (AL lecturer) you suddenly realize that you're veering way into the discipline, like talking out from the discipline rather than bringing people in with you, into it, that's always sort of hard when you're in something … you're very familiar with all these things and this other person can't actually see it … they can hear you but they really aren't sure what you're actually meaning. And it's only when you move outside it like that, that is where I found the language person helped a lot … the language lecturer saying to you, "Sorry, it is not really very clear at all," that I found very, very helpful.

In both excerpts from the data the disciplinary lecturers describe themselves as insiders to the discipline who found it difficult to "see" explicitly the discursive practices of their disciplines and they describe the AL lecturers as having an outsider perspective which they found useful in helping them make explicit their tacit insider knowledge. This type of collaborative engagement, in the planning of their joint teaching materials and team taught lessons, led to pedagogies that sought to make this tacit knowledge explicit for their students.

DISCUSSION

How the participants in the study understood the teaching of academic literacies was linked to their collaborative pedagogy. In revealing the nature of disciplinary literacy practices and disciplines as sites of discourse and power, lecturers needed to make these often invisible processes explicit for students, and teach them the literacy "rules of the game." Few of the partnerships reached this level of understanding, and this was evident in their jointly developed teaching materials and in the actual practice of their team-taught lessons. An example of teaching materials demonstrating this level of understanding is illustrated in Table 9.1:

Table 9.1 illustrates for students the progression of a professional term as it moves through different contexts, from the classroom (immobilization device) to practical demonstrations simulating the real world of radiography practice (impression and cast), to the clinical environment with real patients (mask). It demonstrates to students that in radiography practice there are specific forms of language usage for interacting with patients, for interacting with fellow professionals and for use in an academic environment. It also demonstrates that within the multidisciplinary team of professionals there are more formal terms (impression) and more informal terms (cast) used. The purpose of the pedagogy would be to make explicit to students not only which terms are suitable for which contexts, but also why. For example in the simulated clinical context it would be acceptable for fellow radiography students to use the informal term (cast) when talking to each other, but in communication between the practitioner and the students, it would be more acceptable to use the more formal term (impression). Although the environment remains the same here, the power differential invokes a more formal term in the latter case. So students learn the appropriate terms, as well as how these terms are used by different hierarchies of experts both within the discipline of radiography and its practice in the real world. This opens up a space in the curriculum where such hierarchies might be critiqued and contested.

Table 9.1 Progression of a professional term through different contexts

MASK	CAST	IMPRESSION	IMMOBILIZATION DEVICE
Layman's term	Informal (jargon)	Formal (technical term)	Formal (academic term)
Patient	Colleagues	Colleagues	Presentation and writing
Real clinical context	Simulated clinical context		University context

Adapted from: Bridget Wyrley-Birch, 2010.

For lecturers to teach in this way, they needed to make the conceptual shift from a normative towards a transformative pedagogy. My research has shown that such shifts in the conceptualizations of lecturers was enhanced by a collaborative pedagogy, and it was in the doing (planning for and engaging in this collaborative pedagogy) that both the literacy and disciplinary lecturers were able to re-shape their "ways of thinking" about their literacy teaching practices, and ultimately transform their classroom practices. The "ways of doing" these collaborative partnerships involved the following:

- Collaborative development of teaching materials that attempted to make explicit for students the workings of their disciplinary discourses.
- Team teaching, where literacy and disciplinary lecturers shared the same classroom space.
- Joint design and assessment of tasks focussing on disciplinary literacy practices.
- Co-researching this "new" collaborative approach to the teaching of academic literacies.

The "ways of thinking" and the re-shaping of their conceptualizations of the teaching of academic literacies happened in the discursive spaces where this collaborative engagement took place (e.g., the workshops, the planning sessions for their team taught lessons, and in the process of designing their teaching materials and assessment tasks and in researching their practices). Through these activities they confronted issues of disciplinarity, transgressed their disciplinary boundaries, and in a process of shared meaning-making they came to understand what it meant to teach literacy as a social practice, reveal the rhetorical nature of texts and make explicit the ways in which disciplinary discourses function in powerful practices. The *outsider* position of the AL lecturer in relation to the discipline complemented the *insider* position of the disciplinary lecturer. The outsiders, through a process of interrogation and negotiation, helped shift the disciplinary lecturers to more explicit understandings of the workings of disciplinary discourses and the rules underpinning the literacy practices of their disciplines, and from this perspective they were better able to understand how to make this explicit for their novice students (Jacobs, 2007). This shift of perspective appeared to be a key factor in moving lecturers towards a transformative pedagogy. The collaborative engagement with an outsider enabled disciplinary lecturers to have some critical distance from the disciplinary discourses in which they were so immersed and in some cases this translated into transformative pedagogy which sought to go beyond simply identifying and inducting students into dominant disciplinary conventions, by making explicit in their teaching the contested nature of the knowledge shaping their disciplines. The collaborating partnerships drew on a range of pedagogical strategies which helped shift their teaching towards a more transformative pedagogy, such as developing learning materials which interrogate not only the words, symbols, diagrams and formulas through which their disciplines communicate meaning, but also the actions and practices underpinning these expressions of discourse; and using texts that demonstrate the practice of disciplines and illustrate how a discipline "reads and writes" itself in the real world.

The reality for most partnerships though, was that they taught within that grey area between the "normative" and "transformative," as they shifted uneasily along a continuum of understandings (Figure 9.1), experiencing moments of "insider/ outsiderness" (Theresa Lillis & Lucy Rai, 2011) in their collaborative engagement. While psycho-social and disciplinary factors influenced to some extent whether lecturers shifted or not, it was in the interplay of these factors and how they impacted on the balance of power within the collaborative partnerships that movement beyond the grey area between the "normative" and "transformative" occurred or did not. However, the process of bringing disciplinary lecturers' tacit insider knowledge to more explicit awareness requires time for interrogation and negotiation between AL and disciplinary lecturers. When such time is not invested, these collaborations tend to have unproductive consequences and set up patterns of inequality. To maintain relationships based on equality, the collaborative space needs to be free of disciplinary alignment, and both AL and disciplinary lecturers need to occupy a central position in the partnerships, with neither feeling peripheral to the process.

My findings seem to suggest that it was the process of shared meaning-making through collaborative engagement that facilitated movement towards transformative pedagogy. To sustain such collaborative engagement, institutions of higher education need to create discursive spaces where academic literacies and disciplinary lecturers could work across departmental and disciplinary boundaries. Such discursive spaces need to transcend the silo-nature of universities and address issues such as how to develop classroom materials that highlight the complex (often hidden) social practices that determine the principles and patterns through which disciplines communicate meaning, and then how to mediate such materials in a collaborative pedagogy.

A transformative pedagogy, which requires lecturers to move beyond simply identifying and inducting students into dominant disciplinary conventions, would require lecturers to open up curriculum spaces where the literacy practices of disciplines might be critiqued and contested. But in order to critique and contest such practices, lecturers would need to interrogate the "ways of knowing" in their disciplines, as well as the "modes" and "tools" that their disciplines draw on to create disciplinary ways of knowing. The insights from such interrogation then need to be translated into explicit pedagogy. This is the challenge confronting all academics and one in which academic developers, particularly AL practitioners, could play a more progressive role than they are currently playing in the context of higher education institutions in South Africa.

REFERENCES

Gee, J. P. (1990). *Social linguistics and literacies: Ideology in discourses*. London: Falmer.

Gee, J. P. (1998). *The new literacy studies and the social turn*. Mimeograph handout University of Wisconsin-Madison, Department of Curriculum and Instruction, Madison, WI.

Gee, J. P. (2003). *What video games have to teach us about learning and literacy*. New York: Palgrave Macmillan Publishing.

Jacobs, C. (2007). Mainstreaming academic literacy teaching: Implications for how AD understands its work in HE. *South African Journal of Higher Education, 21*(7), 868-879.

Jacobs, C. (2008). In search of discursive spaces in higher education. In E. Weber (Ed.), *Educational change in South Africa: Reflections on local realities, practices and reforms* (pp. 247-266). Rotterdam: Sense Publishers.

Jacobs, C. (2010). Collaboration as pedagogy: Consequences and implications for partnerships between communication and disciplinary specialists. *Southern Af-*

rican Linguistics and Applied Language Studies, 28(3), 227-237.

Lea, M., & Stierer, B. (Eds.). (2000). *Student writing in higher education: New contexts.* Buckingham, UK: Open University Press.

Lea, M. R., & Street, B. V. (2006). The "academic literacies" model: Theory and applications. *Theory Into Practice, 45*(4), 368-377.

Lillis, T. (2001). *Student writing. Access, regulation, desire.* London: Routledge.

Lillis, T. (2003). An "academic literacies" approach to student writing in higher education: Drawing on Bakhtin to move from critique to design. *Language and Education, 17*(3), 192-207.

Lillis, T. (2009, September). *Academic literacies as a transformative project? Exploring research interests and intervention possibilities.* Seminar presentation at Stellenbosch University, South Africa.

Lillis, T., & Rai, L. (2011). A case study of a research-based collaboration around writing in social work. *Across the Disciplines, 8*(3). Retrieved from http://wac.colostate.edu/atd/clil/lillis-rai.cfm

Lillis, T., & Scott, M. (2007). Defining academic literacies research: Issues of epistemology, ideology and strategy. *Journal of Applied Linguistics, 4*(1), 5-32.

Street, B. V. (1984). *Literacy in theory and practice.* Cambridge, UK: Cambridge University Press.

Street, B. V. (1999). New literacies in theory and practice: What are the implications for language in education? *Linguistics and Education, 10*(1), 1-24.

Street, B. V. (2003). What's "new" in new literacy studies? Critical approaches to literacy in theory and practice. *Current Issues in Comparative Education, 5*(2). Retrieved from http://www.tc.columbia.edu/cice/

Wyrley-Birch, B. (2010). "Talking technical": Learning how to communicate as a healthcare professional. *Southern African Linguistics and Applied Language Studies, 28*(3), 209-218.

CHAPTER 10

WRITING DEVELOPMENT, CO-TEACHING AND ACADEMIC LITERACIES: EXPLORING THE CONNECTIONS

Julian Ingle and Nadya Yakovchuk

Writing can be a means of knowing and being in the world. That kind of writing requires self-examination, self-awareness, consciousness of the process of writing and reading.

– John Edgar Wideman, Preface to the 2nd edition of *Brothers and Keepers*.

ENTERING THE SPACE

Following the signs, trying to navigate the sections and subsections of the Mile End hospital, a collection of workaday modernist and Victorian sanatorium architectures, I find the back stairs to the Sports Medicine Clinical Assessment Service. At the end of a blue and magnolia corridor of closed doors, each with nameplate and title, are two large notice boards with rows of journal articles pinned up in

Figure 10.1: Photo 1. © J. Ingle, 2012

plastic pockets, five across, three down. On one side a lectern facing the wall holds a thick file of journal articles. Flicking through, the thud of each article and weight of research and publication.

Figure 10.2: Photo 2. © J. Ingle, 2012

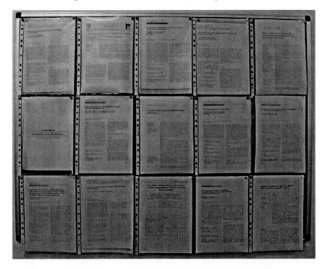

Figure 10.3: Photo 3. © J. Ingle, 2012

A doorway leads into a large open area in drab NHS (National Health Service) colors. Along the walls are treatment beds covered in industrial blue plastic, head-shaped holes where the pillow would normally go. Femurs and fragments of skeletons lie on the bed, the disjecta membra of the medical subject ready for treatment and learning. The theme continues in the classroom, a disarticulated skeleton without limbs asleep on the desk, a loose foot lying by its head, with painted markings, caveman-like. The skull lies with its cheek on the desk, the cranium to one side, a vanitas without clock or book.

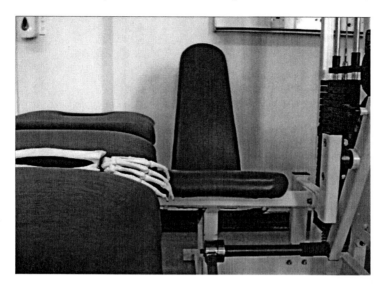

Figure 10.4: Photo 4. © J. Ingle, 2012

Figure 10.5: Photo 5. © J. Ingle, 2012

This is a familiar environment to medical students: by their third or fourth year they will have spent plenty of time in and around hospitals and clinics. To the outsider it is striking: traces of authority, impersonal fragments of human anatomy …

Figure 10.6: Photo 6. © J. Ingle, 2012

IDENTIFYING THE SPACE

Each year more than twenty Bachelor of Medicine students from the Barts and The London School of Medicine and Dentistry (Queen Mary University of London) and elsewhere choose to intercalate (insert) an extra year of study in the field of Sports and Exercise Medicine to qualify for a BSc (Hons). This chapter discusses the work of designing and co-teaching a series of writing workshops that prepare students to write a 6,000-word research project. The project is their most significant piece of assessed coursework, and is intended (with guidance from the Centre for Sports and Exercise Medicine (CSEM) tutors) to reach a standard suitable for publication in the British Journal of Sports Medicine (BJSM) or as a conference paper.

If disciplinary writing is bound to the social practices in which it is realized (Romy Clark & Roz Ivanič, 1997; Theresa Lillis & Mary Scott, 2007), then to begin to grasp the ways power and identity inform and maintain such practices may help us discover more about the character of writers and their writing. Our question in designing the workshops was whether exploring aspects of the ways power and identity are manifest within the sports and exercise medicine discipline would help students to position themselves more effectively as researchers and writers. Our response drew on the critical frame of Academic Literacies (Mary Lea & Brian Street, 1998; Lillis & Scott, 2007), in particular its "emphasis on dialogic methodologies" (Lillis & Scott, 2007, p. 11) and "a transformative stance" (ibid., p. 12). What we set out to develop was a small scale exploratory case study in which co-teaching, reflections and discussions fed into subsequent teaching and reflections. In putting together the workshops we designed a number of activities to open up dialogue and to foreground questions of disciplinary knowledge construction, identity and power that would perhaps enable students and teachers to explore, and in some cases question, some of the conventions and practices around research writing in medicine.

SHARING THE SPACE

Our collaboration with the CSEM began in 2006, in response to concerns raised by staff and external examiners about a marked disparity between the ability of the students to articulate ideas orally and in writing. From the outset, the Intercalated BSc (iBSc) Course Lead was closely involved in the design of the syllabus, workshops and materials, and keen to co-teach the sessions. The four writing workshops are now co-taught by the Research Supervisor[1] (henceforth referred to as RS) from the CSEM and a member of Thinking Writing, a staff-facing curriculum and writing development initiative at Queen Mary University of London (http://www.thinkingwriting.qmul.ac.uk/). There has been an increasing commitment by CSEM to this work: the workshops are now fully integrated into the module design and its assessment structure, whereas for the first five years of our collaboration they were additional to its core content. In addition, a three day semi-structured writing retreat that we piloted and co-facilitated in 2010 has now been permanently incorporated into the programme, as a further point of transition for those students who are keen to publish their projects.

What we hope the presence of a disciplinary tutor working with a writing specialist signals to students is that research writing is not a prosthesis (Elainne Showalter & Anne Griffin, 2000) or "skill" they can attach to themselves, but is inseparable from the ways in which knowledge is constructed and represented in a discipline (Charles Bazerman, 1981; Mary Lea, 2004; Jonathan Monroe, 2003). As such, this work is loosely grounded in the Writing in the Disciplines approaches to writing development (Monroe, 2003, 2007; David Russell, 2002). More broadly, it reflects a growing consensus within areas of the work around writing in higher education about the "need for writing development, wherever possible, to be embedded within disciplinary teaching, and taught and supported by disciplinary teachers, precisely because of a recognition that writing and thinking are, or should be, integral processes" (Sally Mitchell, 2010, p. 136).

The outlines and syllabus Julian was working with could be characterized as encompassing a range of approaches and methodologies from Roz Ivanič's "Discourses of Writing" framework for describing writing in higher education (2004, p.

255). The activities included, for example, student reflections on their writing and reading processes (a process approach), and, following John Swales and Christine Feak (2004), looking at the moves, features and language in systematic reviews and research papers from the BJSM (a genre approach). Many of the activities used could be broadly characterized as falling within the domain of "academic socialization" (Lea & Street, 1998; Lillis, 2001). And while there was no problem with the course, since the potential for publication was very important to students and the CSEM, we began to feel it was worth trying to shift the approach and broaden the range of activities in order to help students negotiate and understand better their transition into research publication, thus enabling a more "comprehensive approach to the teaching of writing" (Ivanič, 2004, p. 241). Our co-teaching approach enabled disciplinary staff and writing tutors to open up a dialogue, bringing their specific understandings *in situ* to the tasks being written, a dialogue the students were very much at the centre of. Simply put, we wanted to "make space for talk" (Lillis, 2001, p. 133).

The co-authors occupied the space in different ways: Julian, from Thinking Writing, had the coordinating role and co-taught the sessions with the CSEM RS, but he also had the benefit of preparing and reflecting on the sessions with Nadya, also a member of the Thinking Writing team at the time, which helped re-articulate the teaching and brought an external voice when interviewing the tutors retrospectively.

TRANSFORMING THE SPACE

To explore more general questions about writing and knowledge construction, and to expand the range of writing students might use, freewriting activities were designed that would prompt discussions about broader aspects of the discipline. One example was a slightly contentious statement as a prompt: "Most medical research, and therefore writing, is about confirming and enlarging existing beliefs, not in developing new ones."

Here are extracts from two freewrites:

> To an extent, medical research is about confirming existing
> beliefs, but if this were the case, no truly groundbreaking dis-
> coveries would be made. A lot of great scientific writing flies [?]
> against the current dogma. I feel this is the case because to con-
> firm what is already known is futile and, in some regard, a vanity
> project. But to write of something truly new, that falls outside
> our belief system but happens to be true, is where real progress is
> made within the discipline.

> … ethics and money/finance define modern medicine esp in the
> UK and with the NHS. Research will usually take place in fields

> where finance is available. eg. A previous project on this course
> was looking at hamstring activation + EMG. [My] the person
> doing the study first wanted to look at kicking in taekwondo,
> but then was told by his supervisor to look at running/football
> because that's where the money is.

Although each student had their own take on the statement, most showed a concern with how this disciplinary community operates. In the second extract, the implication is that what gets research funding often has to conform to internal and external pressures; while at the same time it illustrates a "consciousness [of] the social context of writing [and] the nature of the discourse community they are working in ..." (Clark & Ivanič, 1997, p. 233). What also came out of the discussions after the freewriting was how clinical practice changes in response to new insights derived from research, and the significance of this nexus of research, writing and practice.

For students as emergent researchers, we considered that it was particularly relevant to make more visible "the centrality of identity and identification" and "the impact of power relations on student writing," following Lillis and Scott (2007, p. 12). Through discussion and reflection, we hoped to explore the multiple identities of these students (novice academic writers, novice researchers trying to achieve "legitimate peripheral participation" (Eitienne Wenger, 2008, p. 100), supervisees, future medical practitioners, possibly future academics, etc.) and how these identities may shape the way in which students engage with their writing.

> There is no room to breathe or express yourself. You could say
> this is typical of medicine as a whole subject, not just research.
> (A student's freewrite).

This extract demonstrates the tension between the desire for self-expression and the disciplinary and institutional constraints that one has to negotiate. A further example of how such tensions and power relations manifest themselves emerged from a discussion about author order in a journal article the students had been reading—they were keen to question the status of each author and what their position in the list might mean. In response, the RS explained that in medical sciences, the author order is not linear: first and last authors carry most weight; usually, the first has done most of the work and the last is the most important in terms of status, funding grants, and publications (but may often contribute very little to the actual writing apart from signing it off). How work was allocated and who came next in the pecking order of second and third authors were questions of debate and often compromise.

Although initially unaware of the hierarchy of author order, the students already had some sense of their identity as researchers and the difficulties of negotiating their status within this research community. There was a discussion of their concerns about the role of student researcher being abused, for example, that they could be used as free (and unacknowledged) labour on research projects. The RS explained that they had to "earn their spurs" or "serve their time" in the research community in order to move towards the status of last author. Interestingly, both metaphors come from two tightly structured and very hierarchical institutions—the army and the prison system.

Once the students' awareness of the significance of author order had been raised, the presence of a struggle with their place in the research community was evident in subsequent aspects of the course. In a presentation by a journal editor, one of the students followed up a point about lack of recognition of their role because of being shifted to third author in the research project. What emerged was a conflict of interests between the students, who needed to be first or second authors to get extra points in their Foundation Programme process,[2] which would improve their chances of employment, and their supervisors, who also needed to be in poll position to maintain their academic careers as researchers and ensure they met appraisal and national evaluation requirements for sufficient publications (for the system used in UK context see http://www.ref.ac.uk).

MAKING "SPACE FOR TALK"

By opening up their classroom, there was in one sense a break with the tradition of writing and researcher instruction in the CSEM. Rather than an "add on" approach or the induction from within the discipline itself, the co-teaching explicitly set out to open up and maintain dialogue among all participants, thus transforming the teaching space itself and making the students more open to talk and engage.

> NY: Did you notice anything specific about how students reacted to two tutors teaching them?
>
> JI: To me, certainly at university level, it seems to unsettle that normal dynamic—in a good way.
>
> RS: It makes it a bit less formal I think, which is important as well. Rather than just being talked at, they are more likely to engage if there's two people at the front talking. They are more likely to also talk themselves, as opposed to if there's just one they don't want to be the second person talking. ... That drew a lot of interaction from them.
>
> JI: That's right, I think it pulls them in.

In feedback, students commented on the value of having a different perspective on writing, perhaps because it may help them position their own disciplinary writing as one of many types of research writing and made the mystery around academic writing less mysterious (Lillis, 2001).

There was also a visible transformation for the tutors involved. The RS had previously learned the disciplinary conventions of research writing though "osmosis" (Lillis, 2001, p. 54) and the complex socialization that takes place in writing one's doctorate. While academics tend to have a tacit understanding of how knowledge is articulated in their discipline, they do not always "know that they have this rhetorical knowledge and cannot readily explain this to others" (Joan Turner, 2011, p. 434). The writing sessions helped the RS to make this tacit knowledge explicit to himself and the students. The writing tutor, in turn, gained considerable insight into not just the way scientific knowledge is represented in writing, but also the nature of the discipline and science in general. In response to Nadya's question about the benefits of co-teaching, the following exchange exemplifies some of the insights for both co-tutors:

> RS: A lot of the writing processes you go through and all the writing aspects … although I may have had some of the skills I wasn't aware of the skills I did have, so in terms of transferring that to teaching I didn't know what I'd needed to try and teach, but having Julian come in from a completely different world had helped to put perspective on that for me …

> JI: For me what it's been is the process of learning about scientific writing, or writing for this very specific journal actually … but also a little bit about the broader discipline and how research methods are used, and how you go about analyzing data and things like that …. It has undermined illusions or preconceptions that I had about science writing ….

> NY: Could you elaborate on that?

> JI: [For me] … science is always something that was set in stone, and couldn't be questioned, and is utterly rigorous … but what was happening was very exploratory and tentative and … this is the best possible hypothesis for this particular context, so I saw it as much more context-bound …. There wasn't nearly as much certainty that I assumed existed in the sciences and that was purely my preconception of scientific thinking.

These shifts in the thinking of the tutors also became manifest in their teaching practices. There was a trajectory along which tutors inched into each other's disciplinary spaces as a result of sharing the space. Through these dialogic encounters, they became briefly at home in each other's disciplinary languages. For example, Julian felt more able to join in critiques of experimental methodologies when looking at systematic reviews of specialist areas of sports medicine, while the RS felt comfortable discussing linguistic features such as redundant language when, in a whole class activity, the students applied it to one of the RS's published abstracts.

LEAVING THE SPACE

Do the practices, insights and changes described reflect Lillis and Scott's claim for "the explicit transformational interest that is at the core of academic literacies work" (2007, p. 23)? For these students, the fact of participating in these writing workshops may have led to a transformation in their understanding in its most basic sense of learning something they did not know, which may be no different from other learning situations. One could argue, therefore, that what we have done has less to do with the "transformational approach" (ibid., p. 13) of Academic Literacies but more about the transformative nature of learning. Similarly, the insights gained by the co-teachers from the shared experience of teaching the students were perhaps no different from those of any practitioner given the opportunity to reflect on their teaching.

While these reservations may be valid, we maintain that aspects of this work are more than this and go part of the way towards a transformative approach by locating the conventions of medical science in relation to contested traditions of knowledge making. We would therefore suggest that the "complex insider knowledge" (Ivanič, 1998, p. 344) that is required of these students to negotiate the two very different social practices of writing for assessment versus writing for publication is fostered through this approach to co-teaching. Our discussions and the small-scale but overt focus on power, identity and epistemology may have helped clarify and make explicit some of the "values, beliefs and practices" (ibid.) within this sub-discipline. Expanding the range of textual practices (and, possibly, ways of making meaning (Lillis & Scott, 2007)) that students engaged in has, we hope, helped them refine their understanding of the discipline and their positions within it. Through discussing the opportunities for our pedagogical practice that an Academic Literacies framework offers, and by reflecting on some of its limitations, we have hoped to make a contribution to current debates on the relationship between Academic Literacies theory and practice. In particular, co-curricular design, the use of co-teaching and the potentially transformative nature of the discussions that took place are areas that offer some directions in further exploration of the "design" potential of Academic Literacies.

RE-ENTERING THE SPACE

The writing work described here started from the premise that opening up and foregrounding questions about knowledge, meaning making, power, and identity would lead to insight for both teachers and students, allowing them to position themselves as writers and researchers in a more conscious way, and to become more aware of how their discipline works and how their current and emergent identities may be mapped onto the disciplinary canvas.

We hope that this work will allow those involved (students, disciplinary teachers and writing developers) to re-enter and locate themselves in the disciplinary (and also institutional/departmental/academic) spaces in a slightly different way—with enriched insight and deepened understanding of the complexity and multifaceted nature of "knowing and being" in the academic world. Returning to Wideman's quote in the epigraph to this chapter, then, we could perhaps transform and extend it to writing in academia in the following way:

> Academic writing can be a means of acquiring, developing and demonstrating disciplinary knowledge, as well as experiencing and having presence in the academic world. This kind of writing requires examination of the multiple identities that one has to negotiate in the process of producing a piece of academic writing, awareness of how these identities interact with wider structures and relations existing in academia and beyond, and consciousness of the processes and practices surrounding the production, transmission and use of academic texts.

ACKNOWLEDGEMENTS

We would like to thank Dylan Morrissey, Christian Barton and the staff from the Centre for Sports and Exercise Medicine, for the warmth of their welcome and the insights and expertise they have shared. We would also like to thank Sally Mitchell (without whom this work would not have been possible) for her thoughtful, patient readings and discussions.

NOTES

1. It should be noted that the Research Supervisor post in CSEM is usually a six-month, fixed-term contract aimed at a practicing physiotherapist who has recently completed his or her PhD. This, therefore, entails forming a new collaboration each year with the appointed co-teacher(s).

2. As Foundation Doctors in the final two years of their medical degree, students can accrue points for research publications.

REFERENCES

Bazerman, C. (1981). What written knowledge does: Three examples of academic discourse. *Philosophy of Social Sciences, 11*(3), 361-387.

Clark, R., & Ivanič, R. (1997). *The politics of writing.* Abingdon, UK: Routledge.

Ivanič, R. (1998). *Writing and identity: The discoursal construction of identity in academic writing.* Amsterdam: John Benjamins Publishing Company.

Ivanič, R. (2004). Discourses of writing and learning to write. *Language and Education, 18*(3), 220-245.

Lea, M. (2004). Academic literacies: A pedagogy for course design. *Studies in Higher Education, 29*(6), 739-756.

Lea, M. R., & Street, B. V. (1998). Student writing in higher education: An academic literacies approach. *Studies in Higher Education, 23*(2), 157-170.

Lillis, T. (2001) *Student writing: Access, regulation, desire.* London: Routledge.

Lillis, T., & Scott, M. (2007). Defining academic literacies research: Issues of epistemology, ideology and strategy. *Journal of Applied Linguistics, 4*(1), 5-32.

Mitchell, S. (2010). Now you don't see it; now you do: Writing made visible in the university. *Arts and Humanities in Higher Education, 9*(2), 133-148.

Monroe, J. (2003). Writing and the disciplines. *Peer Review, 1,* 4-7.

Monroe, J. (2007). Writing, assessment, and the authority of the disciplines. *Educational Studies in language and Literature, 8*(2), 59-88.

Russell, D. R. (2002). *Writing in the academic disciplines: A curricular history* (2nd ed.). Carbondale, IL: Southern Illinois University Press.

Showalter E., & Griffin A. (2000). Teaching medical students how to write well. *Medical Education, 34*(3), 165.

Swales, J. M., & Feak, C. B. (2004). *Academic writing for graduate students: Essential tasks and skills* (2nd ed.). Ann Arbor, MI: University of Michigan Press.

Turner, J. (2011). Rewriting writing in higher education: The contested spaces of proofreading. *Studies in Higher Education, 36*(4), 427-440.

Wenger, E. (2008). *Communities of practice.* Cambridge, UK: Cambridge University Press.

Wideman, J. E. (2005). *Brothers and keepers.* New York: Mariner Books.

CHAPTER 11

TRANSFORMATIVE AND NORMATIVE? IMPLICATIONS FOR ACADEMIC LITERACIES RESEARCH IN QUANTITATIVE DISCIPLINES

Moragh Paxton and Vera Frith

MEANINGS OF TRANSFORMATION IN SOUTH AFRICAN HIGHER EDUCATION

SOCIAL TRANSFORMATION

Transformation can mean many things but it has very specific implications in the South African higher education context. Although there has been a marked improvement in equity of access to higher education in South Africa since 1994, equity in completion rates remains racially skewed and disappointing (Ian Scott, Nan Yeld & Jane Hendry, 2007). Transformation, at the formerly white and privileged institution of the University of Cape Town, therefore involves reappraisal and reorganization of teaching and learning in the university in order to cater to a growing black student population, many of whom are second language speakers of English from poor, rural, or urban working class backgrounds. It is a priority to ensure that completion rates are increased, reflecting that higher education and students' experience of it are *transformed* (see Thesen Reflections 6 this volume).

PEDAGOGIC TRANSFORMATION

Academic developers teaching in foundation courses and extended curricular programmes such as the one discussed in this chapter have a very clear mission, which is to focus on preparing students for epistemological access, defined by Wally Morrow (2009, p. 77) as "learning how to become a successful participant in an academic practice." We recognize that there is a mismatch between teaching approaches and student experience at our institution, mostly because staff come from very different backgrounds from those of the students. Therefore we work with the staff helping them to understand students' prior and existing knowledge-making practices and to critically explore the way students' prior knowledge and practices may enable or present barriers in the learning and teaching of new, unfamiliar, or what we think of as "mistakenly familiar" conventions (as we illustrate below), discourses, and concepts. We see our role as change agents in the broader university, improving the effectiveness of teaching and learning in the interests of both equity and development.

ACADEMIC LITERACIES AS TRANSFORMATION

In the context of science and maths education at the university level, we find the tension highlighted by Theresa Lillis and Mary Scott (2007) between normative and transformative approaches to language and literacy particularly heightened. Lillis and Scott (2007, p. 13) have highlighted the transformative role of academic literacies research as being interested in discovering alternative ways of meaning making by considering the resources that students bring as "legitimate tools for meaning making." They have contrasted this with the normative understanding of academic literacy which tends more towards "identifying" disciplinary conventions and "inducting" the students into correct ways of thinking and writing. In our particular context we are acutely aware that—given the history of apartheid and the ongoing crisis in South African schooling including the lack of resources and breakdown of a culture of learning and teaching in the schools—normative approaches that involve inducting students into existing and available discourses are essential. Where we locate the transformative dimension to our work is in the following two key elements: 1) a rejection of a deficit position on students and the semiotic and linguistic resources they draw on and enact in higher education; and 2) a commitment to understanding and uncovering existing and prior practices that may enhance or present barriers to learning and teaching. We will illustrate this argument by discussing some of the data from an academic literacies research project in a foundation course in the Biological, Earth, and Environmental Sciences (BEES) at the University of Cape Town.

THE CASE STUDY

Through researching a collaborative initiative aimed at integrating academic literacies in this course, we have developed a three-way conversation between the academic literacy, numeracy studies and science specialists, which has informed the curricular design. Most of the students, in a class which averages around 50 students, came from educationally disadvantaged backgrounds and many of them were speakers of English as an additional language.

In 2010 and 2011 students in the BEES course were required to write a scientific research report which acted as a central focus for formative assessment. Numeracy and academic literacy specialists offered teaching and learning activities throughout the year to prepare students for the writing of the report. Assessments explicitly addressed these activities and built incrementally towards the final scientific report. After a series of lectures and Excel-based tutorials on the analysis and interpretation of data, they were given data and a series of directed questions which guided them through its analysis. These were presented in the form of a structured Excel spreadsheet, on which the students could perform the statistical analysis, create the charts and graphs and write the descriptions of the results. This data analysis was carried forward into the results section of the final scientific report. In doing this project students were engaging in a very diverse range of modes integrating verbal, graphic, pictorial and mathematical representations in order to make meaning in the natural sciences.

In 2011 we developed a collaborative action research project between the academic literacy, numeracy studies and science specialists aimed at further development of the pedagogy and curriculum for this course. Our research project follows the typical action research spiral: Plan, Act, Observe, Reflect (Stephen Kemmis & Robin McTaggart, 1982). A key finding emerging from this phase of the project was that a much greater degree of collaboration between the people teaching students about writing the research report was needed in order to integrate the different aspects taught and hence allow students to produce a more integrated product. In 2012 we moved into the second action research cycle as we designed and planned changes to the course on the basis of our early findings.

We used Academic Literacies research methods to gain insights into the practices and assumptions students drew on as they learned to write about quantitative information in science. This involved adopting an ethnographic stance, orienting both to texts and to writers' perspectives: we analyzed early drafts of student writing and then interviewed students about their writing. Instead of assuming that the student is cognitively unable to grasp the concepts, we recognize the socially situated nature of literacy (Mary Lea, 2004; Mary Lea & Brian Street, 2000; Lillis & Scott, 2007; Street, 2005) and that if we are to appropriately address students' needs and help them to become successful participants in the science disciplines, it is crucial for us to understand and build on what students know and to uncover prior practices and conceptions that may enhance or present barriers to further learning.

In the following sections we illustrate how we have worked with students to uncover prior practices and assumptions. We describe the ways in which students were understanding quantitative concepts (Theme 1) and highlight some of the prior schooling practices that may be impacting the way students write in the natural sciences (Theme 2). Finally, we outline some implications of these findings for teaching, curriculum and staff development.

THEME 1: CONCEPTS IN NUMERACY

Quantitative information and concepts are conveyed through language, often using precise terminology and discipline-specific forms of expression which are associated with specific quantitative ideas. Writing about quantitative information involves using terms and phrases that often include everyday words, but which have specific meanings, and which convey a richness of conceptual meaning. An example is the word "rate," which has an everyday meaning (speed) but in more technical contexts is used more broadly to describe ratios of various kinds, not only those that express changes with respect to time. Understanding the term "rate" in a given context involves understanding the significance of describing a quantity not in absolute terms, but relative to some other quantity, which is for most students not a trivial concept. Learning to use terms and phrases of this kind correctly (and with a proper understanding of the concepts to which they refer) is fundamental to quantitative literacy and is essential for a science student.

In their writing of a scientific report many of the students used quantitative terms and phrases inappropriately, often in a manner that was grammatically correct, but conceptually incorrect, revealing that they either did not understand the specific contextual meanings of the terms they were using or that they did not understand the concepts the terms refer to, or both. One example of a phrase applied incorrectly is "is proportional to"[1] as illustrated in Figure 11.1.

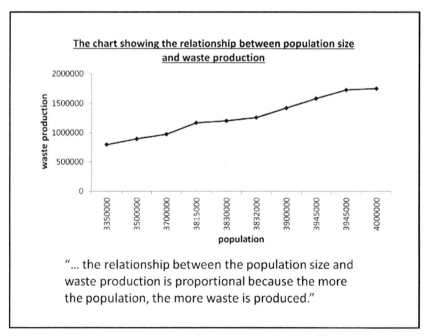

Figure 11.1: Graph and description from student's report.

We will discuss this example to illustrate how the ethnographic approach helped us to gain a better understanding of what the students were signifying by their use of this term and of the origins of this usage. We will then suggest how this insight helps us to teach the use of quantitative language more effectively.

Because many students had used "is proportional to" to describe relationships that were not proportional (that is, where the two variables were not in a constant ratio with each other), in the interviews we asked, "What does it mean when you say one thing is proportional to another?" All but one student expressed their understanding in a manner similar to this: "… if the other one increases the other one which is proportional to it also increases …." Further questioning revealed that all these students believed that this was a sufficient condition for proportionality; or in other words, that "is proportional to" defines any relationship where an increase in one variable is associated with an increase in the other. So for example, when shown a sketch of a graph showing an exponential growth situation, students confirmed that they understood this to be a case of proportionality.

When asked where they first encountered the use of a phrase like "A is proportional to B," all students said their first encounter with the term was in physics lessons at school. For example, a student sketched a formula of the form "$V \alpha p$" and said "mostly in physics … for formulas where you are maybe told the volume of something is directly proportional to this … as this increases the other increases the change in this, if this changes it affects the other one"; whilst saying "this," she pointed to the p in the formula, and when saying "the other one" to the V. In school physics it is common to use the symbol 'α' to represent "is proportional to" in a formula. This disguises the fact that the relationship being represented is of the form $V = kp$, where k is the constant of proportionality (that is, the constant ratio). In explaining that if V is proportional to p, then as p increases so will V, a physics teacher is making a true statement, but it seems that in many cases teachers have not prevented students from concluding that the converse is true. It is easy to see how if whenever a student hears the phrase "is proportional to" it is in the context of noticing how one variable is associated with an increase in the other variable, they will conclude that this is what the expression means.

In reading students' written reports we might have been tempted to discount the incorrect statements about proportional relationships as "poor English" but through questioning students about their writing we gained rich insights into an unexpected realm of their experience. From the point of view of what many of the students apparently learned in physics classes, their use of the phrase "is proportional to" was a correct description of the relationship they were describing, so simply correcting the language would have been merely confusing to them. For us, the realization that students' incorrect use of this phrase is not a superficial slip, but rather an expression of an entrenched conceptual misunderstanding, has been very useful. It helps us to appreciate that if we want to teach students to use quantitative words and phrases appropriately in context, we must first make sure they properly understand the concepts to which the words refer before attempting to teach the conventional ways of expressing those concepts. It is through talking to students about the understanding underlying their choices of expression that we can find out which concepts we should give attention to. The insights gained in this way will (and already have) changed the nature and emphasis of our teaching in this course.

THEME 2: STUDENTS' PRIOR PRACTICES IN WRITING FOR SCIENCE

There has been extensive research indicating that the transition from school to university is complex and that students have difficulty trying to reconcile the discursive identities of home, school and university (Ken Hyland, 2002; Roz Ivanič, 1997; Moragh Paxton, 2003, 2007a, 2007b; Lucia Thesen & Ermien van Pletzen, 2006). However we had not realized that local schools had recently started teaching academic literacy practices such as report writing and "referencing" and that the way these were taught conflicted quite markedly with university academic literacy practices.

Students spoke about their experience of writing school assignments for life sciences and geography as being very "free." They reported having had freedom to use any form they liked:

> In geography you could do anything, there were no rules or
> anything you just wrote like you were writing your own diary …
> point form, flow chart and mind map …

They were required to write scientific reports at school, but it seemed—from students' accounts—that this involved collecting information from the World Wide Web and cutting and pasting it into the text. Students also reported that in school writing opinions or claims unsupported by evidence were also acceptable. The students were surprised at the fairly rigid genre and discourse of the university research report in the natural sciences and that their lecturers had expected them to "write only facts" and use supporting evidence drawn from the readings or their own graphical and numerical results. The students believed they had been taught to reference at school, yet they had found university referencing practices very different and very rigorous:

> (At school) you didn't have to all the time do in-text referencing,
> you just had to do like something of a bibliography, we were
> used to that … like writing which book it comes from.

At school, referencing often meant simply pasting URLs into a bibliography, and there was no need to acknowledge explicitly those whose ideas and words the students were drawing on. In fact, the idea of acknowledging outside sources **in the text** was quite foreign to them.

This research has been transformative for us because it has made us aware of new school-based digital literacy practices and made us more sensitive to the precise challenges facing the students. We recognize that the transition from school to university literacy practices demands new self-understandings and the development of new identities around authorship. The experience of interviewing the students not only made us aware of conceptual difficulties they experience (and their origins), but also gave us a great deal more insight into students' lived experience of schooling and of being new university students, which we believe has made us into more empathetic teachers.

CONCLUSION

The action research project has been important for teaching and curriculum development, and significant changes were incorporated into the curriculum based on the findings of the first action research cycle. We have found that it has been critical to understand the way students are constructing understanding and to get to know their prior practices and discourses so that we can address these in our teaching of concepts and of university literacy practices. Based on the research findings which show that students are confused about some of the quantitative concepts, we have incorporated fuller explanations of these concepts and pointed students to the reasons for their confusion. In addition, the research has highlighted changes in school literacy practices that we were not aware of. It has given us the opportunity, as we assist students in taking on new scientific identities, not only to signal distinctions between school and university discourses, but also to note that the disciplines of mathematics and science call for a particularly rigorous approach to use of language and genre. This is perhaps particularly true in our country which is itself in the process of change and where we, as teachers, have to respond regularly to changing structures and changing discourses.

Thus the collaborative research project has been very useful in informing the on-going development of the curriculum, but has also contributed to our own academic development. The science discipline specialist, through participating in the academic literacy and numeracy workshops, has realized that she needs to embed the teaching of these literacies and concepts in her own teaching throughout her course (which for us would represent the best-practice scenario): she has changed and developed her curriculum accordingly. The science discipline and numeracy specialists have learned the importance of the language they use in conveying conceptual information, while the language development specialist has gained insight into the role played by numeracy in a broader conception of academic literacy.

NOTE

1. We say "a" is proportional to "b" when the variables "a" and "b" are in a constant ratio

with each other. So if the value of "a" is doubled then the value of "b" will be doubled, etc.

REFERENCES

Hyland, K. (2002). Authority and invisibility: Authorial identity in academic writing. *Journal of Pragmatics, 34,* 1091-1112.

Ivanič, R. (1997). *Writing and identity: The discoursal construction of identity in academic writing.* Amsterdam: John Benjamins Publishing Company.

Kemmis, S., & McTaggart, R. (1982). *The action research planner.* Victoria, AU: Deakin University.

Lea, M. (2004). Academic literacies: A pedagogy for course design. *Studies in Higher Education, 29*(6), 739-756.

Lea, M., & Street, B. (2000). Student writing and staff feedback in higher education: An academic literacies approach. In M. Lea & B. Stierer (Eds.), *Student writing in higher education: New Contexts* (pp. 32-46). Buckingham, UK: Open University Press.

Lillis, T., & Scott, M. (2007). Defining academic literacies research: Issues of epistemology, ideology and strategy. *Journal of Applied Linguistics, 4*(1), 5-32.

Morrow, W. (2009). *Bounds of democracy: Epistemological access to higher education.* Pretoria: HSRC Press. Retrieved from http://www.hsrcpress.ac.za/product. php?productid=2254&freedownload=1

Paxton, M. (2003). Ways in which students gain access to university discourses: The intersection of the academic curriculum with student voices. In C. Prichard & P. Trowler (Eds.), *Realizing qualitative research into higher education* (pp. 21-39). Aldershot, UK: Ashgate Publishers.

Paxton, M. (2007a). Students' interim literacies as a dynamic resource for teaching and transformation. *Southern African Linguistics and Applied Language Studies, 25*(1), 45-55.

Paxton, M. (2007b). Tensions between textbook pedagogy and the literacy practices of the disciplinary community: A study of writing in first year economics. *Journal of English for Academic Purposes, 6*(2), 1-14.

Scott, I., Yeld, N., & Hendry, J. (2007). *Higher education monitor no. 6: A case for improving teaching and learning in South African higher education.* Pretoria: The Council on Higher Education. Retrieved from http://www.che.ac.za/ media_and_publications/higher-education-monitor/higher-education-monitor-6-case-improving-teaching

Street, B. (2005). Applying new literacy studies to numeracy as social practice. In A. Rogers (Ed.), *Urban literacy: Communication, identity and learning in development contexts* (pp. 87-96). Hamburg: UNESCO Institute for Education.

Thesen, L., & van Pletzen, E. (Eds.). (2006). *Academic literacy and the languages of change.* London: Continuum International Publishing Group.

CHAPTER 12

LEARNING FROM LECTURERS: WHAT DISCIPLINARY PRACTICE CAN TEACH US ABOUT "GOOD" STUDENT WRITING

Maria Leedham

This study brings together the methodology of corpus linguistics and the framing of academic literacies in an exploration of Chinese and British students' undergraduate assignments in UK universities. I consider how student writing, particularly that of non-native speakers (NNSs),[1] is traditionally framed as deficient writing within corpus linguistics, and discuss how an academic literacies approach challenges this assumption.

One finding revealed through the analysis is the Chinese students' significantly higher use of tables, figures, images (collectively termed "visuals"), formulae and writing in lists, in comparison with the British students' writing, and the chapter provides data on this from Economics, Biology, and Engineering. Detailed exploration of individual assignments in Engineering together with interview data from lecturers in the three disciplines suggests that high use of visuals, formulae, and lists rather than writing mainly in connected prose is a different, yet equally acceptable, means of producing successful assignments. This is in marked contrast to the usual focus within English for Academic Purposes (EAP) classes on traditional essays written in continuous prose. In this paper I argue that writing teachers could usefully draw on an academic literacies approach as a way to expand their ideas of what constitutes "good" student writing and to transform their pedagogical practice in a way that recognizes student diversity rather than deficit.

UNDERGRADUATE WRITING IN UK UNIVERSITIES

Many researchers have emphasized how university students have to learn to write in ways prescribed by their discipline in order to have their voices heard (e.g., Nigel Harwood & Gregory Hadley, 2004; Ann Hewings, 1999; Ken Hyland, 2008; Sarah North, 2005), and this point is central to scholars within academic literacies (e.g. Mary Lea & Brian Street, 1998; Theresa Lillis, 2001). Despite the growing recognition of disciplinary difference and the importance of student voice, most EAP classes comprise students from a broad range of subject areas through practical necessity. At postgraduate level, students are likely to be familiar with the conventions of their discipline, and to be writing within familiar genres such as a research report or dissertation. At undergraduate level, however, students are still learning how to write in their discipline(s) and additionally have to contend with the recent "unprecedented amount of innovation in assessment" (Graham Gibbs, 2006, p. 20). This plethora of new genres at undergraduate level includes e-posters, websites and reflective journals and represents a move away from the traditional undergraduate essay (Lisa Ganobcsik-Williams, 2004; Maria Leedham, 2009; Hilary Nesi & Sheena Gardner, 2006).

While students may look to writing tutors for guidance in coping with writing in a new discipline and new genres, most applied linguists (and by implication most EAP and writing tutors) are "trained in the humanities, where words are central to disciplinary values and argumentation" (Ann Johns, 1998, p. 183). Tutors may thus "find themselves relying on disciplinary norms they are familiar with" (Sheena Gardner & Jasper Holmes, 2009, p. 251) and it is likely that these norms will include a concentration on "linear text" (Johns, 1998, p. 183) rather than on the interaction of visuals, formulae and lists with prose. The use of EAP textbooks does not resolve this problem since, as Chris Tribble points out, "the majority of the writing coursebooks ... focus on developing essayist literacy" (2009, p. 416).

EXPLORING STUDENT WRITING
THROUGH CORPUS LINGUISTICS

The dataset in this study is first approached through corpus linguistics, a rapidly-growing field involving the investigation of language use through organized, electronically-stored collections of texts (or "corpora"). Common methodological procedures include counting the frequency of textual features, comparing one corpus with a larger "reference" corpus and extracting contiguous word sequences (see Stefan Gries, 2009, for a readable introduction). Findings from these procedures are supported in this study by qualitative analysis of selected texts and data from lecturer interviews.

The majority of corpus linguistic studies of student writing, particularly NNS writing, adopt a deficit approach in which NNS writing is compared to either NS student or professional academic writing and seen to fall short of these "norms." The language used to report these studies is thus couched in terms of a deficit discourse rather than one of variational "difference." For example Gaëtanelle Gilquin and Magali Paquot (2008, p. 58) suggest that "remedial materials" are required to help NNSs "overcome register-related problems," and Yu-Hua Chen and Paul Baker (2010, p. 34) discuss "immature student academic writing … [across] three groups of different writing proficiency levels" in their corpora of NNS student, NS student and expert academic writing. Thus a linguistic proficiency cline is often visualised from low to high-level NNSs followed by NSs and culminating in the language of professional academic writers, at which point the NS/NNS distinction ceases to be noteworthy. In contrast, the academic literacies perspective adopted here does not dichotomize NS and NNS students but instead views all undergraduates as learners of writing within the academy, while acknowledging the additional challenges faced by L2 English writers (see Ramona Tang, 2012b, for studies on this theme).

DATA AND METHODS

The dataset for this study is a subset of the British Academic Written English[2] (BAWE) corpus (Nesi & Gardner, 2012) (see BAWE site for details of corpus holdings) with a small number of additionally-collected assignments from Chinese undergraduates, and comprises texts from 12 disciplines and across three years of undergraduate study. All assignments achieved a minimum score of 60% from discipline lecturers (a First [distinction] or Upper Second [merit] in the United Kingdom) and can thus be said to represent "proficient" student writing since they met marking expectations to a sufficiently high extent (cf. Gardner & Holmes, 2009). Alongside the compilation of the BAWE corpus, interviews with 58 lecturers were conducted to provide an emic perspective on what this proficiency entails and on valued and "disliked" features of undergraduate assignments (Nesi & Gardner, 2006).

An initial search was carried out on the datasets to compare the frequency of single words and contiguous word sequences in the 279,000-word Chinese corpus with those in the 1.3 million word reference corpus of British students' writing in the same 12 disciplines to uncover items used statistically more frequently in the former. The resulting "keywords" include numbers, formulae and references to data items (e.g., according to the + figure/appendix/equation, refer to (the) + figure/table + [number]), suggesting that the Chinese students make greater use of formulae, visuals and numbered lists than the British students (see Leedham, 2012 for a fuller account of the keyword process).

To determine the usage of these items, the number of disciplines was narrowed to three (Biology, Economics and Engineering), chosen as they offered a range of texts across student corpora and year groups (see Table 12.1).

As several keywords refer to tables, figures and formulae, or appear to be part of numbered lists, automatic counts were conducted of these textual features (see Table 12.2).

Table 12.1 Discipline subcorpora

	L1 Chinese		L1 English	
Discipline	No. texts	No. words	No. texts	No. words
Biology	18	33,633	83	173,412
Economics	20	38,086	22	52,158
Engineering	20	35,627	97	203,782

Table 12.2 Textual features per 10,000 words

	Tables	Figures	Lists	Listlikes	Formulae
Chi-Biology	15****	25****	1	4	17****
Eng-Biology	5	13	2	6	8
Chi-Economics	1	14****	2*	25****	42****
Eng-Economics	0	12	1	3	30
Chi-Engineering	10*	21	7	53****	106****
Eng-Engineering	7	21	10	24	67

*(Statistical differences are shown between student groups within each discipline, using log likelihood, * p<.05; ****p<.0001).*

In the BAWE corpus, a "table" is a graphic containing rows and columns while a "figure" covers any graph, diagram or image. A distinction is made between "lists" and "listlikes," both of which contain bulleted or numbered items, in that the former comprise lists of words or noun/verb phrases, and the latter comprise items in complete sentences and displayed in list format.

Table 12.2 suggests that both disciplinary differences and student group differences exist. Texts in Biology contain the most tables and figures, while Engineering texts contain the most listlikes and formulae. Within the student groups, the majority of categories in the Chinese corpora show significantly greater use of each textual feature than the English corpora. Disciplinary variations in these features are to be expected, since, for example, Biology entails the use of images of natural phenomena and Economics may involve reports with writing in lists, but it is less clear why the student groups should also differ in their usage.

The next stage was to look at these items in the context of whole assignments. Due to limited space, I confine discussion to a pair of assignments by an L1 Chinese student and an L1 British student within Engineering (see Table 12.3). This assignment pair was selected as the texts answer the same question within the same year 2 module at one university, though the spread of textual features appears typical of those across Chi-Engineering and Eng-Engineering.

Table 12.3 Comparison of two Engineering assignments

Textual feature	L1 Chinese, 0254g	L1 British, 0329e
No. of pages excluding references	11	5.5
No. of words	1,432	2,064
No. of tables	1	0
No. of figures	1	0
No. of formulae	34	10
No. of lists	2	2
No. of listlikes	9	0

Note: The number of formulae for the English text has been altered from the three given in BAWE data to ten, to correct a disparity in tagging.

Each assignment is entitled "centrifugal pump experiment," and is divided into sections with self-explanatory headings such as "introduction" and "apparatus and methods." While the Chinese writer begins each section on a new page, the British student simply uses a line break before a new section, resulting in the Chinese writer's assignment containing double the number of pages yet only two-thirds the word count of the British student's assignment (Table 12. 3).

The differing quantities of formulae and prose are illustrated by page extracts in Figure 12.1. Whereas the Chinese student's discussion weaves together formulae and prose, the British student's response is given as a series of short paragraphs.

Throughout the assignment, the Chinese student employs lists to both present data and make substantive points whereas the British student uses discursive prose (Figure 12.2).

The top box of Figure 12.2 shows the Chinese student's bulleted conclusion, given in complete sentences and stating the bald facts of the experiment:

The experiment yielded the following conclusions:

- The efficiency of a single stage centrifugal pump at high pump speed (3000 RPM) is better than …
- The input power with high pump speed increases …
  (Extract from Conclusion, 0254g).

In contrast, the British student's conclusion is more discursive, introducing the results and relating these to the experiments:

In this investigation into the performance characteristics of a centrifugal pump at different speeds many things were realized. Firstly, it was seen that at the two different speeds the character-

Analysis and Discussion of Results

Figure 1 in the Appendix 2 showed the performance characteristics of the centrifugal pump. Firstly, the total head of the pump decreased as the discharge increased, whatever the pump frequency was 2000 RPM or 3000 RPM. The curves of the relationship between total head and discharge were identical between 2000 RPM and 3000 RPM, but the total head of 3000 RPM was much higher than the one with 2000 RPM. Secondly, the efficiency was fluctuant as the discharge increased. Whereas, the efficiency was direct proportional to the discharge for both speed settings when the discharge was less than *0.5 l/s*. And for the pump speed of 2000 RPM, the efficiency peaked when the discharge was about *1 l/s*, for the pump speed of 3000 RPM, the efficiency peaked when the discharge was about *0.9 l/s*. The highest value of efficiency for 3000 RPM was *64%*, and the peak efficiency for 2000 RPM was *18* percentages less, which was *46%*. Overall, the higher speed pump worked more efficient than lower speed pump. Thirdly, input power was direct proportional to the discharge for both speed settings, but the gradient of the relationship with 3000 RPM was greater than the one with 2000 RPM, it indicated that the input power increased faster with higher pump speed.

Figure 2 in the Appendix 2 showed the relationship among the non-dimensional groups. Firstly, the non-dimensional group $\frac{Q}{f_p D^3}$ was inverse proportional to the non-dimensional group $\frac{\Delta P}{\rho f_p^2 D^2}$ for both speed settings, and those two linear lines were parallel, but the one with 3000 RPM was 5 units greater than the one with 2000 RPM. Secondly, the non-dimensional group $\frac{T}{\rho f_p^2 D^5}$ decreased as the non-dimensional group $\frac{\Delta P}{\rho f_p^2 D^2}$ increased, the relationship was a curve, those two curves of 3000 RPM and 2000 RPM were identical, but the non-dimensional group $\frac{T}{\rho f_p^2 D^5}$ was greater with higher pump speed.

0254g (L1 Chinese)

These three graphs are shown in Appendices 2, 3, and 4 respectively.

Evaluation of Results

When the pump is running at 2000rpm the performance characteristics, as displayed by Graph 1, are as follows. Efficiency is a parabolic curve in which the maximum value of around 23.5% efficiency occurs at 0.9 litres sec-1 flow rate. Total head decreases at a constant rate as discharge increases, until discharge reaches 0.9 litres sec-1, at which point the total head starts decreasing at an increasing rate. Input power increases at a constant rate almost throughout.

When the pump is running at 3000rpm the performance characteristics, as displayed by Graph 2, are as follows. Efficiency is a parabolic curve in which the maximum value of around 31.5% efficiency occurs at 1.2 litres sec-1 flow rate. Total head decreases at an increasing rate. However, it is fairly linear between 0 litres sec-1 and 0.9 litres sec-1 flow rate. Input power increases at a constant rate almost throughout.

It is now possible to compare performance characteristics for when the pump is running at the two different speeds. At speeds of 3000rpm the pump has a maximum efficiency of 8% more than when it is running at 2000rpm. However, efficiencies are the same as each other for flow speeds of up to 0.4 litres sec-1. The total head decreases at the same rate at each speed when compared to the range of the flow rate. For example, if you stretched out the curve for 2000rpm, it would look like 3000rpm to quite a high extent. This suggests that if you tested another speed then its total head would also act in the same way as compared to its range of flow rate. Input power at 3000rpm increases at a faster rate than for 2000rpm. This means that for the same increase in flow rate, a greater power input increase is needed for higher speeds.

In order to analyse Graph 3, which displays the 'Non-dimensional results', we can consider that the non-dimensional results represent coefficients of the variables within them, and therefore the non-dimensional results change in proportion to the variables, as discussed below.

decreases at an almost constant rate. This is because delivery pressure is the variable that is changed at a constant rate during the experiment. The only other variable in the equation, which forms ?P, is the suction pressure. The suction pressure also changes at a constant rate. This non-dimensional will therefore change at a constant rate because ?P changes at a constant rate.

increases at a decreasing rate. This is because discharge, Q, increases at a decreasing rate.

increases at a decreasing rate. This is because force increases at a decreasing rate, which means that torque, T, increases at a decreasing rate.

It can be seen from Graph 3 that for 3000rpm is larger than for 2000rpm. However, for 3000rpm is smaller than for 2000rpm. This indicates, due to the layout of the graph axes that as the speed increases the values of the non-dimensional numbers and will move closer together. However, the speed would have to increase by a very significant amount for them to have the same value.

There are some possible sources of random error in this experiment, which may account for any anomalies within the data. Firstly, due to the fact that

0329e (L1 English)
Figure 12.1: Discussion sections.

Conclusions

The experiment yielded the following conclusions:
- The efficiency of a single stage centrifugal pump at high pump speed (3000 RPM) is better than it at low pump speed (2000 RPM).
- The input power with high pump speed increases faster than the one with low pump speed as discharge increases.
- The relationship between total head and discharge is not affected by pump speed, but higher pump speed provides higher total head.

0254g (L1 Chinese)

```
Conclusions

    In this investigation into the performance characteristics of a centrifugal
pump at different speeds many things were realised.  Firstly, it was seen that
at the two different speeds the characteristics were very similar.  They were
similar due to the forms and gradients of the graphs being very close to one
another.  However, small differences still existed such as the spread of the
results and slight variations in gradient, such as with input power in Graphs 1
and 2, where for Graph 2 it has a slightly steeper gradient than in Graph 1.  It
was also discovered that the pump would run up to 8% more efficiently at 3000rpm
than at 2000rpm.

    Secondly, it was seen that in Graph 3, for the non-dimensional results, if
speed were to be increased then  and  would theoretically move closer together.

    It can be seen that this sort of investigation into centrifugal pump
performance characteristics is extremely useful in analysing how well a pump
will work in certain situations.  The graphs derived would be invaluable in a
situation where you had to pick a pump to be used in a system.  For example, you
could use them to determine what speed and power intake you would need in order
to get a  particular discharge.  Overall, the techniques used in this
investigation and their results are a versatile tool in analysing the
performance of pumps.
```

0329e (L1 English)
Figure 12.2: Conclusions

istics were very similar. They were similar due to the … (Extract from Conclusion, 0329j)

Since both texts have been judged as proficient by the discipline lecturers, (i.e., awarded at least a merit), it seems reasonable to conclude that different combinations and proportions of textual features are acceptable. Similar studies of assignment pairs in Biology and Economics revealed wide variation of the use of images and lengthy captions in the former and of lists and listlikes in the latter (Leedham, 2015) (see also work by Arlene Archer, 2006, on South African students of Engineering using both visual and textual semiotic resources).

It is difficult to speculate, however, as to the preferred characteristics of student writing in particular disciplines, and the next section draws on discipline lecturers' views of valued features.

INTERVIEWS WITH LECTURERS

Overall, the interviews conducted for the BAWE project indicate that "proficiency" in writing for discipline lecturers relates to a range of criteria, including (but not limited to) linguistic proficiency, understanding of content, presentation, clarity, concision, integration of graphics and careful referencing. While a broad consensus may be agreed on at university, discipline or department level, an academic literacies perspective entails recognition that the precise balance of acceptable features may in fact differ from lecturer to lecturer and even from one assignment to another. Part of the task of the student writer is thus attempting "to unpack the ground rules of writing in any particular context" (Lea, 2004).

The rest of this section briefly examines interview comments relating to brevity, use of visuals, and lists in Biology, Economics and Engineering interviews (n=11).

- *Being concise:* In Biology, a lecturer commented that "there's never been a penalty for an essay that's too short"; similarly, in Economics one lecturer outlined their preference for "precision, incision, concision." Engineering lecturers valued the ability to be "clear and concise," "succinct," and point to a dislike of "verbosity." The integration of formulae and prose in discussion and the bulleted conclusion of the Chinese student's text clearly adhere to these values (Figures 12.1 and 12.2).

- *Employing visuals:* In Biology, it was suggested that a lab report of five or six pages should include diagrams, highlighting the visual nature of the discipline (e.g., John Dinolfo, Barbara Heifferon, & Lesly Temesvari, 2007). A "typical" essay in Economics was said to contain both diagrams and formulae "as the spine of the essay." In Engineering, meanwhile, marks for presentation may include the assessment of diagrams, tables and overall layout. The corpus data presented in Table 12.2 points to a greater use of visual features by Chinese students in the three disciplines.

- *Writing in lists:* Few lecturers mentioned list writing, since the interviews were conducted without reference to individual student texts. One Economics lecturer stated a dislike of written work containing "just diagrams and incomplete notes" rather than complete sentences. An Engineering lecturer similarly remarked that he disliked the use of bullet points as a space-saving feature, perhaps viewing these as a way of circumventing the occasional setting of page (as well as word) limits. However, in the assignment pair considered earlier, the list is a bulleted "listlike" (i.e., contains complete sentences) so may be more positively viewed as an aid to concision and clarity in the writing rather than a means of meeting word limits.

IMPLICATIONS FOR PRACTICE

This chapter has argued that, for the disciplines investigated, it is acceptable for students to integrate visuals, formulae and lists in addition to or instead of limiting responses to connected prose. While studies such as this one can explore the range of textual features used in successful undergraduate assessed writing, it is not possible to give highly specific guidance since lecturers in different contexts are likely to vary in their views on the nature of good writing in particular assignments (Lea & Street, 1998). Given that EAP tutors frequently have a background in the more discursive subjects within Arts and Humanities and may be unfamiliar with writing practices in other disciplines, this section offers suggestions as to how tutors can increase their awareness of the diversity of undergraduate student writing, and thus assist students in becoming more effective writers.

Concrete means of establishing the range of acceptability in a discipline include exploring corpora (such as BAWE) and analyzing assignment exemplars of the genres their students are asked to produce. Stronger links with the local context would also enable EAP tutors to better understand discipline lecturers' expectations. However, more fundamental to any transformation in EAP tutors' views are reflexivity in exploring the "taken-for-granted" procedures and practices (Lillis, 2012, p. 245) and a flexible attitude in considering what might be acceptable within unfamiliar disciplines and genres. This open-mindedness moves beyond lexicogrammatical considerations (e.g., the acceptability of "I" or the choice of passive/active voice) to exploring assignments holistically and multimodally (Is it ok to use a table to display results? Can the conclusion be presented as a bulleted list?). Breadth of vision allows tutors to recognize different ways of achieving the same end goal in writing, as with the two Engineering texts, and to embrace the different cultural backgrounds L2 English students bring to their studies.

Possibilities for transformation occur at all levels, from student to professional, covering linguistic aspects and beyond: in her report on an interview study of L2 English scholars, Tang (2012a, p. 210) discusses the potential of university scholars from diverse linguistic and cultural backgrounds to "enrich the discussions in their disciplines." While recognizing that L2 English writers have to learn the rules of the writing "game" (Christine Casanave, 2002), Tang proposes that increasing participation of these scholars may "result in an opening up of the community mindset to allow for different kinds of norms to be deemed viable" (p. 224-225). Thus aspects of the writing in a community are "likely to shape the future practices of that community" (p. 225).

Discipline tutors can assist in the process of change by continuing to embrace different ways of carrying out the same task, rather than adhering to a UK NS "normative pedagogic imperative" (Lillis, 2012, p. 240) and by recognizing that both NS and NNS undergraduate students need help in understanding what is expected in assignments. This guidance could take the form of exemplars and accompanying commentary to illustrate possible assignment responses, and allowing dedicated time within lectures for discussion of their expectations. Discipline lecturers could also work with EAP tutors to jointly understand the needs of all students and to more precisely articulate the difficulties which different groups may face.

This chapter has challenged the common approach within corpus linguistics research of NNS student writing as in some way deficient when compared to NS or to "expert" writing, arguing that the Chinese students' significantly higher use of visuals, formulae and lists function as different, yet equally valued, ways of achieving success at undergraduate level. A more rounded perspective than can be found through corpus studies alone has been obtained through the combination of corpus linguistics with close study of textual features in two assignments and the emic perspective offered by lecturers. An Academic Literacies approach has much to offer since this views learning how to write in the preferred ways of a specific situational context (e.g., a particular assignment set by an individual lecturer within their university department at one point in time) as a challenge for both NNS and NS university students, and recognizes that this may be accomplished in varying ways (Archer, 2006; Lillis, 2012) (see also Ute Römer's 2009 discussion of how both NS and NNS have to develop their competence in academic writing). For both EAP tutors and discipline lecturers, then, a transformation within teaching can come about through recognizing the importance of our own academic and cultural backgrounds in shaping beliefs, and through questioning our assumptions as to the nature of "good" student writing. Academic Literacies can assist here in providing the theorization behind such a transformation and in guiding us towards more diverse ways of viewing good writing, with the result that NNS writers are viewed not in terms of deficit but in terms of what they can bring to the academy (Tang, 2012a).

NOTES

1. In this paper I have, for convenience and brevity, used the terms "NS" and "NNS" while recognizing that these are contentious (see Leung, Harris & Rampton, 1997). The "L1 Chinese" group refers to students who speak any dialect of Chinese and who lived in a Chinese-speaking environment for all or most of their secondary education. "L1 English" denotes students whose self-proclaimed L1 is English and who lived in the United Kingdom for all or most of their secondary schooling.

2. The data in this study come from the British Academic Written English (BAWE) corpus, which was developed at the Universities of Warwick, Reading and Oxford Brookes under the directorship of Hilary Nesi and Sheena Gardner (formerly of the Centre for Applied Linguistics [previously called CELTE], Warwick), Paul Thompson (formerly of the Department of Applied Linguistics, Reading) and Paul Wickens (Westminster Institute of Education, Oxford Brookes), with funding from the ESRC (RES-000-23-0800).

REFERENCES

Archer, A. (2006). A multimodal approach to academic "Literacies": Problematising the visual/verbal divide. *Language and Education, 20*(6), 449-462.

Casanave, C. P. (2002). *Writing games: Multicultural case studies of academic literacy practices in higher education.* Mahwah, NJ: Lawrence Erlbaum Associates.

Chen, Y.-H., & Baker, P. (2010). Lexical bundles in L1 and L2 academic writing. *Language Learning and Technology, 14*(2), 30-49.

Dinolfo, J., Heifferon, B., & Temesvari, L. A. (2007). Seeing cells: Teaching the visual/verbal rhetoric of biology. *Journal of Technical Writing and Communication, 37*(4), 395-417.

Ganobcsik-Williams, L. (2004). *A report on the teaching of academic writing in UK Higher Education.* London: Royal Literary Fund.

Gardner, S., & Holmes, J. (2009). Can I use headings in my essay? Section headings, macrostructures and genre families in the BAWE corpus of student writing. In M. Charles, D. Pecorari, & S. Hunston (Eds). *Academic writing: At the interface of corpus and discourse* (pp: 251-271). London: Continuum.

Gibbs, G. (2006). Why assessment is changing. In C. Bryan & K. Clegg (Eds.), *Innovative assessment in higher education* (pp. 11-22). New York: Routledge.

Gilquin, G., & Paquot, M. (2008). Too chatty: Learner academic writing and register variation. *English Text Construction, 1*, 41-61.

Gries, S. T. (2009). What is corpus linguistics? *Language and Linguistics Compass, 3*, 1-17.

Harwood, N., & Hadley, G. (2004). Demystifying institutional practices: Critical pragmatism and the teaching of academic writing. *English for Specific Purposes, 23*(4), 355-377.

Hewings, A. (1999). *Disciplinary engagement in undergraduate writing: An investigation of clause-initial elements in geography essays.* (Unpublished doctoral thesis). University of Birmingham, Birmingham, UK.

Hyland, K. (2008). As can be seen: Lexical bundles and disciplinary variation. *English for Specific Purposes, 27*(1), 4-21.

Johns, A. M. (1998). The visual and the verbal: A case study in macroeconomics. *English for Specific Purposes, 17*(2), 183-197.

Lea, M. R. (2004). Academic literacies: A pedagogy for course design. *Studies in Higher Education, 29*(6), 739-756.

Lea, M. R., & Street, B. V. (1998). Student writing in higher education: An academic literacies approach. *Studies in Higher Education, 23*(2), 157-172.

Leedham, M. (2009). From traditional essay to "ready steady cook" presentation: Reasons for innovative changes in assignments. *Active Learning in Higher Education, 10*(2), 191-206.

Leedham, M. (2012). Writing in tables and lists: A study of Chinese students' undergraduate assignments in UK universities. In R. Tang (Ed.), *Academic writing in a second or foreign language: Issues and challenges facing ESL/EFL academic writers in higher education contexts*. London.

Leedham, M. (2015). *Chinese students' writing in English: Implications from a corpus-driven study*. Abingdon, UK: Routledge.

Leung, C., Harris, R., & Rampton, B. (1997). The idealized native speaker, reified ethnicities, and classroom realities. *TESOL Quarterly, 31*(3), 543-560.

Lillis, T. (2001). *Student writing: Access, regulation, desire*. London: Routledge.

Lillis, T. (2012). English medium writing for academic purposes: Foundational categories, certainty and contingency. In R. Tang (Ed.), *Academic writing in a second or foreign language: Issues and challenges facing ESL/EFL academic writers in higher education Contexts* (pp. 235-247). London.

Nesi, H., & Gardner, S. (2006). Variation in disciplinary culture: University tutors' views on assessed writing tasks. In R. Kiely, G. Clibbon, P. Rea-Dickins, & H. Woodfield (Eds.), *Language, culture and identity in applied linguistics (Vol. British Studies in Applied Linguistics)*. (pp. 99-107). London: Equinox Publishing.

Nesi, H., & Gardner, S. (2012). *Genres across the Disciplines: Student writing in higher education*. Cambridge, UK: Cambridge University Press.

North, S. (2005). Disciplinary variation in the use of theme in undergraduate essays. *Applied Linguistics, 26*(3), 431-452.

Römer, U. (2009). English in Academia: Does Nativeness Matter? Anglistik: *International Journal of English Studies, 20*(2), 89-100.

Tang, R. (2012a). Two sides of the same coin: Challenges and opportunities for scholars from EFL backgrounds. In R. Tang (Ed.), *Academic writing in a second or foreign language: Issues and challenges facing ESL/EFL academic writers in higher education contexts* (pp. 204-232). London.

Tang, R. (Ed.). (2012b). *Academic writing in a second or foreign language: Issues and challenges facing ESL/EFL Academic writers in higher education contexts*. London.

Tribble, C. (2009). Writing academic English: A survey review of current published resources. *English Language Teaching Journal, 63*(4), 400-417.

THINKING CRITICALLY
AND NEGOTIATING PRACTICES
IN THE DISCIPLINES

David Russell in conversation with Sally Mitchell

David Russell, Professor of English at Iowa State University, researches writing in the disciplines and professions, consults on writing in HE, and teaches in a PhD programme in Rhetoric and Professional Communication. He spent three months in 2005 working alongside Sally Mitchell on "Thinking Writing,", an institutional initiative at Queen Mary University of London which is influenced by US thinking and practice around "Writing across the Curriculum" and "Writing in the Disciplines" and which also draws on aspects of "Academic Literacies."

Sally: To ground our discussion I'm going to start with Mary Lea and Brian Street's much cited 1998 paper in which they set out a heuristic for looking at data gathered in UK universities in terms of approaches to student writing: a study skills approach/frame; a socialization approach/frame; an academic literacies approach/frame. I want to notice that it's not fully clear in the way the paper is often referred to, whether the three-part distinction is an approach or a frame. In my own thinking I don't want to commit to either, but prefer to preserve both terms; the first suggesting pedagogical practices, the second a conceptualization or stance. In her book on student writing, Theresa Lillis (2001) visited these distinctions again, adding to them "creative self-expression" as an approach and differentiating between socialization as "implicit induction into established discourse practices" and socialization involving "explicit teaching of features of academic genres." I found that further distinction useful especially in terms of thinking about how disciplinary teachers (rather than writing teachers) teach writing. She viewed the approaches to student writing as ranged along a continuum that indexed a vision of higher education as at one end "homogeneous," with "practices oriented to the reproduction of official discourses" and at the other 'heterogeneous"—and by association, "oppositional." Pedagogical practices at this end she glossed as "oriented to making visible/challenging/playing with official and unofficial discourse practices" (2001).

In our experiences, in our respective institutional contexts, which—importantly—are mainly "teacher-facing" rather than "student-facing," it seems to me we are often involved in interrogating this continuum in terms both of pedagogical approach and conceptual stance: what do we do? How do we conceive of what it is we do? And why? Just as the interplay between practice and stance is complex, so, we find, is the naming of these as either "normative" or "transformative," "assimilationist" or "resisting."

David: It's crucial to begin with the institutional context—and the role played within the institution. In Thinking Writing at QMUL and in North American Writing In the Disciplines programmes (WID), we do not teach language courses. In the day-to-day work of supporting writing in the disciplines (and thus thinking and learning and development more broadly), staff with expertise in academic writing/literacies (like you and me) play primarily a consulting or staff development role with faculties and departments and teachers. We try to listen carefully, understand how literacy operates in the field, department, classroom; how the teachers and students use and understand it, and we then engage them in reflecting on it. There's a lot of contact with people in other disciplines than our own (rhetoric, academic writing, applied linguistics, are some of the names on our hats). And a lot of meetings, workshops, classroom visits—perhaps to run a workshop for students with the teacher present or in collaboration with the teacher.

Working in a unit that is outside any department, with an institution-wide brief for making change (as is usually the case with WID programmes), provides a good place to think about difference and what it means to be critical, because students spend most of their time in the disciplines, not in language/writing courses (see Horner and Lillis this volume, Reflections 4). And there is automatically a great deal of "heterogeneity," because we have all those disciplines (and sub- and inter-disciplines, not to mention the professions often linked to them). When we worked together in 2005, we discussed the challenges of talking to academic staff about their goals for developing critical thinking in their courses or in the wording of their assignments; for example, "When you say you want your students to 'be critical' *what kind of critical* do you mean?" And teachers and departments may well ask us that too.

Sally: In thinking about the work we do in education and writing development, teacher-facing practice certainly complicates what being transformative at, or near, the oppositional end of Lillis's continuum might mean. Being critical can imply a challenge to the forms and functions of authoritative discourse (academic, disciplinary, neo-liberal marketization), making these the object of study and interrogation, rather than taking them as unquestioned givens in the making and communication of knowledge. An example of an oppositional stance would be to challenge the "container metaphor" of language or the neo-liberal separation of skills from knowledge that enables institutions to separate out "content courses" from "language courses" and to place one in the service of the other (see Neculai this volume, chapter 30). A strongly critical response might then involve us declining a department's request to provide a stand-alone "study skills" course, or lead to a refusal to provide help "grading the writing" of a particular assignment while the disciplinary teacher "grades the content."

David: To pick up the example you used—refusing to serve, or service, a department or curriculum or teacher by "grading the writing" is usually tempered, in North American WID programmes at least, by the offer of different kinds of engagement: reformulating assignments, introducing peer review, collaborative teaching or research, and so on. In time (and sometimes very rapidly—because many academic teachers are creative and curious), working together on these areas can lead to critical and transformative practices—the introduction of peer assessment for example, or popular genres, or debates (John Bean, 2011). Norms then may begin to shift, to transform, both on the part of the teachers/departments and the writing/literacies staff. After all, writing/literacies experts also belong to a discipline (or proto-sub-discipline, however marginal), which can be critiqued by teachers in other disciplines.

Sally: The question of where the norm is located is also an interesting one. A shift in norms we've been talking about at work recently is the notion of "student as producer or co-producer"—of resources, curriculum and assessment. It's gaining what feels like increasing momentum in the United Kingdom—and as a contrast to "student as consumer," it feels exciting and radical. But as "student as producer" becomes a newer "norm," it is already becoming assimilated to other more pervasive, powerful agendas in the sector ("employability" is one). This doesn't mean however that a classroom or programme in which "the student as producer" becomes the new ethos isn't in some way, at some level, transformative of what had previously held sway. It's just that the promised radicalism is held in check by larger ideological frames. And, of course, even the limited radicalism driving the idea will need to be tested in practice and scrutinized through research. What does "student as producer" look like as/in practice?; what is it like for students to be socialized into this apparently new way of doing things?; what are the new warrants that will open up the new practice to criticism and resistance? Looked at this way you can't really fit any developing practices onto a single point on Lillis's continuum—they'll always be shifting about over time.

David: Yes, and indeed the very theoretical concept of a continuum at times may melt down in the crucible of teacher-facing practice, into something resembling a multi-party negotiation, as engagements with teachers and the professionals beyond them (mutual learning and mutual transformation of practices) might occur.

Very early on, in the late 1980s, a few critics of WAC, like Daniel Mahala (1991) argued that WAC should offer a highly political, hard-edged critique of the discourse of disciplines and professions. In practice, in teacher-facing practice (redundancy intended) it is necessary to develop allies—and there are some in every discipline and university who are critical in various ways—without alienating potential allies. Writing consultants unfortunately don't have the power to make others listen to our expertise (as some language/writing teachers have the power to do with their students). Consultant experts must offer something of value to engage them in an ongoing dialog. Teachers in the disciplines who take a critical view of their own or their discipline's pedagogical practice and want to transform it often show up at our WID workshops. We consult with them or even do long range teaching change and/or research projects. It's slow work, often.

Sally: So how far did Mahala have a point, in your view? I guess I'm unsettled by the idea that writing people don't have power (though I concede you're probably right in some significant ways). But I think we can take power for ourselves too, and one way is through having some conceptual framework that articulates the assumptions on which options for practice are based. To have this gives you power—and it's also a responsibility—to know how your practice is positioned, and what assumptions (e.g., about language, knowledge, permission) it rests on. It enables you to be critical and reflexive—and to be open to challenge and change. I think the AcLits framework is useful in this regard—as a critical and reflective tool. But it shouldn't be taken as a given or an endpoint. New articulations always need to be made—one I encountered recently that I found very refreshing of my own practice was by Magnus Gustafsson and Cecilia Jacobs (2013). And Mahala's critique wasn't over once he'd voiced it, was it? From papers you've pointed me to, the strand of critical questioning and response has continued in WAC and WID—and this is a good thing.

David: I simply mean that writing *teachers*—like most university teachers—have been granted the power of the grade, the mark, by the institution, the students, and the wider society. As teachers we also have much power to determine what we teach and how. Teachers can require students to write differently or be critical (or pretend to—as some controversial ethnographic research has shown (David Seitz, 2004)). But as writing *consultants* we have not been granted the institutional or social power to remake curriculums in our critical ways—yet. We must gain that rhetorically, by persuasion, which is one reason why theories of how power operates institutionally have been important in WID research—Bruno Latour, Pierre Bourdieu, Anthony Giddens. So I very much agree that our power will come from having something intellectually valuable to offer to teachers in other disciplines—but valuable in terms of their values as well as those our own discipline(s).

The question of how oppositional and transformative practice is, and what those terms mean, and how to frame arguments for outsiders, has indeed had a long and thoughtful airing in the United States, dating back to the late 1980s, when WID programmes were first becoming numerous (and some felt—wrongly it turned out—that they would supplant required first-year composition courses). That debate often pointed to a central tension, between writing as an uncritical/un-problematic tool in the development of disciplinary and professional thinking and practice (so normative, assimilationist and with an apparently "clear mission"), and the need to contest writing as an agent in the inscription of disciplinary subjects (so resisting and critical, with a more contested mission). This debate maps onto critical approaches to academic writing elsewhere (AcLits, clearly, but also some work in SFL (systemic functional linguistics), LAP, Brazilian/Swiss pedagogical sequences, etc. (Anis Bawarshi & Mary JoReiff, 2010)), and there's longstanding and on-going debate in WID about how and how much it is and should be critical (see Charles Bazerman et al. 2005, Chapter 8 for a summary).

But North American WID approaches are also characterized, since their beginnings in the 1980s, by a different kind of critical analysis, one that grows out of research into the rhetoric of disciplines and professions and workplaces that students will enter. It seemed presumptuous to many North Americans doing WID work to be critical of the disciplines' discursive practices—or to teach their students to be literate, much less critically so—without having studied in some detail their discursive practices: what is important to them, how they go about their work, including (but not only) the literacy part. A historical and ethnographic research tradition has ensued, which investigates how knowledge and power are produced and circulate in the documentary networks of institutions in their practices *over time* (as both historical and long-term ethnographic methods make time central). (For reviews see Bazerman, 2008; Bazerman et al. 2005, Chapters 6 and 7; David Russell, 2001, 2007, 2008).

The goal here is to inform a critical approach to supporting writing in the disciplines that takes into account *both* the affordances *and* constraints of disciplinary and professional discourse. By looking carefully at how discourses work it is possible to formulate not only a backward looking critique of how disciplinary discourses limit students, but also a forward looking critique to discern the potential in disciplinary discourses for students to develop knowledge and power—and eventually transform institutions (and their discourse) in positive ways, as the students become professionals with power. Dorothy Smith's study of the documentary organization of medical practice, for example, reveals its deep sexism, but it also shows how it saves lives, through organizing care (checklists for the surgical procedures, etc.) (see Dorothy Smith & Catherine Schryer, 2008 for an overview of these studies). Dorothy Winsor's study of textual power negotiations in engineering practice (2003) shows deep class exploitation, but it also shows how exploited workers exercise agency textually. Anthony Paré's study of Inuit social workers (2002) reveals the racism of the Canadian social work profession but also the ways native social workers negotiate the circulation of knowledge to enhance the power and autonomy of their communities. Theresa Lillis and Mary Jane Curry's study of professionals doing academic research outside the Anglophone centers of power (2010) is consonant with WID research in significant ways, as it exposes not only the hegemonic practices and their effects but also the textual dynamics of that power and the agentive and resistance potentials for the future.

This is why cultural-historical activity theory and Carolyn Miller's theory of genre as social action (1984) have been important in this tradition. They emphasize the historical and dynamic quality of academic/professional discourses, and their ties to changing practices (see Charles Bazerman & James Paradis, Eds., 1985, and for research methods used see Charles Bazerman & Paul Prior, 2004).

Historical and ethnographic—especially longitudinal—studies of writing in HE, as well as in the professions beyond HE, provide insight into what I call forward looking critique. Again, as the metaphor suggests, time is key. Writing/language teachers typically have students only one or two terms (unless they are preparing writing/language teachers or researchers). But staff in the disciplines often have them for three or more years, and the department's reputation is at stake in their preparation, as well as the future of the profession they prepare them for—as are people's and society's safety, health, and so on, in the case of many disciplines/professions. So the time scale is different in the disciplines, as are the stakes.

Encountering teachers and departments in a range of disciplines other than one's own (e.g., writing studies) suggests ways to reframe the assimilation/transformation dichotomy. Every future professional must "assimilate" to the extent of assuming the identity of a professional in that field (otherwise she will not be able to participate or exert agency or, indeed, write in the discipline/profession). For students—especially those from marginalized groups—entering a profession is transformative in terms of their lives, and in terms of their potential agency, their chances in life and their chance to make a difference. And in a collective sense, every discipline/profession/institution will be transformed, in ways large and small, by the changing conditions of its practice and the agency of its practitioners—or it will become obsolete. Transformation, like assimilation, is inevitable, and the two go hand in hand—but on different time scales. The question then is what sorts of assimilation and what sorts of transformation occur, not only within individuals, but also within broader social formations/institutions? And what is the role of the writing/literacies expert in shaping those things?

Sally: For me that last question goes back to the position taken by the literacies expert—how strongly critical they want or are able to be. I go along with Miller's understanding of genre as in a sense having transformation built in (as she says, "genres change, evolve and decay"), but I think sometimes in our work with disciplines we can influence, critically and creatively, the way genres, particularly the genres that carry teaching and learning along, change and evolve. I like your point about historical and ethnographic studies. The value of ethnography that includes observations of classrooms etc. is that it tends to work against the hardening of categories. Ethnography encourages "a willingness to accept (and run with) the fact that … experience has ways of boiling over and making us correct our current formulas" (W. James, 1978, in Ben Rampton et al., 2004, quoted in Lillis, 2008, p. 376). I'm quite interested in how the Lea and Street categories (derived from an ethnographic type study, of course) have given rise to some anxiety that they are mutually exclusive, that you're in one camp or the other—assimilationist or transforming. It seems a curious reaction to the heuristic.

David: We in North America have certainly seen these kinds of categories complicated, at times transmuted, in the crucible of practice, as I have suggested. Context again is absolutely key. The ethnographic turn in rhetoric and composition studies came in the 1980s in North America, with the proliferation of WAC/WID programmes. Much of that research was practitioner-based, as writing consultants collaborated with teachers in the disciplines. McCarthy's seminal 1987 article, "A Stranger in Strange Lands" gave us a first window on a student struggling to cope with writing in multiple disciplines. There followed a large number of ethnographic studies including eleven longitudinal studies of undergraduates—some following students from the first year of HE into several years of professional practice—involving sustained engagement between researcher and participants and drawing on multiple methods in addition to talk around texts. A recent major review of these studies of student writing at university (Paul Rogers, 2008), as well as research reviews of qualitative studies (Russell, 2001) and studies in technical communication (Russell, 2007), suggest that the WID work has much in common with AcLits research—including a lively debate over the meaning of "critical" in ethnography and the ethical representation of the "other," especially in relation to teaching practice (Russell et al., 2009; Jerry Stinnett, 2012).

Indeed, in my view, the most useful recent large scale study of writing in the disciplines is by Roz Ivanič and her team (2009) in Scotland and England. This was the product of two years of collaborative research with teachers in three disciplines in further education colleges, what we call community colleges in the United States. It involved their multi-modal text production in and outside of class, their motives—assimilationist and beyond—as well as interventions the teachers developed and made, in consultation with the writing experts, and their reactions to them.

Ivanič et al. are quite aware that having a critique is not enough; one has to have a pedagogy to enact and develop that critique. And as part of that, I would argue, students must learn the (discourse) practices of their disciplines and professions, as I mentioned before, or they will fail their courses—and will have far less agency for transforming professional practices or discourses. WID has a variety of common pedagogical strategies centered around encouraging critical thinking through writing awareness (Bean, 2011) and around encouraging critique of the disciplines by viewing genres as dynamic and linked to practices—often by having students do ethnographic investigations in one way or another (Bawarshi & Reiff, 2010, Chapter 11). Many disciplines now have a literature on writing in that discipline. Few of these have an explicit goal to challenge the dominant discourses. But in practice, they may be taken up in ways that do that.

Sally: Certainly I've found that disciplinary teachers can be innovative and playful in taking their students towards the disciplinary thinking and forms that they value. If the conditions are right they are creative and relaxed about setting "divergent" writing tasks (dialogues, questions, postcards …) that can give rise to startling articulations of sharp disciplinary thinking. The writing tasks are perhaps unusual (transformative of the default pedagogy, perhaps you could say?) but far from "oppositional": the concern is to socialize—to make the students better students and graduates of whatever discipline; and for themselves, the concern is to become better teachers of students in their discipline (which seems to me to be generally more accurate and richer than simply saying "better teachers of their discipline").

David: I like your formulation "teachers of students in their discipline," which puts the emphasis on students—without forgetting the discipline. I might add "teachers of students in and for their discipline," as the students hopefully leave HE to enter specialized forms of work and knowledge-making.

Sally: Assimilation, then, or transformation?!

David: Well, both certainly, and many things in between and around the dichotomy or continuum or negotiation. Writing in the Disciplines, since its origin in the massification of North American HE in the 1970s, has tried more or less successfully to position itself as an *educational reform movement*. In 1989, Sue McLeod described WID Programs as doing "transformational" work, in the sense that they explicitly push for ways of viewing writing that go beyond the dominant remedial, deficit model and move towards writing as a way of supporting critical thinking, learning development and "academic success,"—by which HE generally means graduation and a job in one's chosen field. One goal of having a WAC/WID programme at one's university is to call attention to the invisible practices of writing and teaching and learning and to make the institution aware of them. As a result, WAC/WID has encountered a great deal of ongoing resistance—but at the same time it has managed currently to be a feature of over half of all HE and of 65% of PhD degree-granting institutions in the United States (Chris Thaiss & Tara Porter, 2010).

Quite a degree of success, but of course there's still work to be done. One area is in addressing some of the issues around race, class, gender and language background that have been the subject of research and discussion within the more confined and controllable spaces of Composition. As we've been discussing, this is less straightforward for WID consultants who must form and maintain alliances in institutional spaces where these issues may have relatively lower priority than in English departments. It'll be interesting—and important—to see how the recent critique of WID in this regard is developed and responded to (Anne Herrington & Charles Moran, 2006).

REFERENCES

Bawarshi, A. S., & Reiff, M. J. (2010). *Genre: An introduction to history, theory, research, and pedagogy.* West Lafayette, IN: Parlor Press/The WAC Clearinghouse. Retrieved from http://wac.colostate.edu/books/bawarshi_reiff/

Bazerman, C., & Paradis, J. G. (1991). *Textual dynamics of the professions: Historical and contemporary studies of writing in professional communities.* Madison, WI: University of Wisconsin Press.

Bazerman, C., Bethel, L., Chavkin, T., Fouquette, D., & Garufis, J. (2005.). *Reference guide to writing across the curriculum.* West Lafayette, IN: Parlor Press/The WAC Clearinghouse. Retrieved from http://wac.colostate.edu/books/bazerman_wac/

Bazerman, C. (2007). *Handbook of research on writing: History, society, school, individual, text.* New York: Routledge.

Bazerman, C. (2008). Theories of the middle range in historical studies of writing practice. *Written Communication, 25*(3), 298-318.

Bazerman, C. & Prior, P. A. (2004). *What writing does and how it does it: An introduction to analyzing texts and textual practices.* New York: Routledge.

Bean, J. C. (2011). *Engaging ideas: The professor's guide to integrating writing, critical thinking, and active learning in the classroom.* San Francisco: Jossey-Bass.

Gustafsson, M., & Jacobs, C. (2013). Editorial: Student learning and ICLHE—Frameworks and contexts. *Journal of Academic Writing, 3*(1), ii-xii.

Herrington, A., & Moran, C. (2006). Writing across the curriculum: The Power of an idea: IWAC 2006: Keynote Address. Retrieved from http://wac.colostate.edu/proceedings/iwac2006/keynote.cfm

Ivanic, R., Edwards, R., Barton, D., Martin-Jones, M., Fowler, Z., Hughes, B., and Smith, J. (2009). *Improving learning in college: Rethinking literacies across the curriculum.* London: Routledge.

Lea, M. R., & Street, B. V. (1998). Student writing in higher education: An academic literacies approach. *Studies in Higher Education, 23*(2), 157-172.

Lillis, T., & Curry, M. J. (2010). *Academic writing in a global context: The poli-*

tics and practices of publishing in English. Retrieved from http://www.aelfe.org/documents/12_22_Mezek.pdf

Lillis, T. M. (2001). *Student writing: access, regulation and desire*. London: Routledge.

Lillis, T. (2008). Ethnography as method, methodology and "deep theorizing": Closing the gap between text and context in academic writing research. *Written Communication, 25*, 353-388.

Mahala, D. (1991). Writing utopias: Writing across the curriculum and the promise of reform. *College English, 53*(7), 773-89.

McCarthy, L. P. (1987). A stranger in strange lands: A college student writing across the curriculum. *Research in the Teaching of English*, 233-265.

Miller, C. (1984). Genre as social action. *Quarterly Journal of Speech, 70*.

Paré, A. (2002). Genre and identity: Individuals, institutions, and ideology. In R. Coe, L. Lingard, & T. Teslenko (Eds.), *The rhetoric and ideology of genre* (pp. 57-71). Creskill, NJ: Hampton.

Rogers, P. M. (2008). *The development of writers and writing abilities: A longitudinal study across and beyond the college-span*. Ann Arbor, MI: ProQuest.

Russell, D. R., Lea, M., Parker, J., Street, B., & Donahue, T. (2009). Exploring notions of genre in "academic literacies" and "writing across the curriculum": Approaches across countries and contexts. In C. Bazerman, A. Bonini, & D. Figueiredo (Eds.), *Genre in a changing world* (pp. 395-423). Fort Collins, CO: The WAC Clearinghouse/Parlor Press. Retrieved from http://wac.colostate.edu/books/genre/

Russell, D. R. (2001). Where do the naturalistic studies of WAC/WID point? A research review. In S. H. McLeod, E. Miraglia, & M. Soven (Eds.), *WAC for the new millennium: Strategies for continuing writing-across-the-curriculum programs* (pp. 259-298). Urbana, IL: National Council of Teachers of English.

Russell, D. R. (2007). Rethinking the articulation between business and technical communication and writing in the disciplines. Useful avenues for teaching and research. *Journal of Business and Technical Communication, 21*(3), 248-277.

Seitz, D. (2004). *Who can afford critical consciousness?: Practicing a pedagogy of humility*. New York: Hampton Press.

Smith, D. E., & Schryer, C. F. (2008). On documentary society. In C. Bazerman (Ed.), *Handbook of research on writing: History, society, school, individual, text* (pp. 113-127). New York: Routledge.

Stinnett, J. (2012). Emerging voices: Resituating expertise—An activity theory perspective on representation in critical ethnography. *College English, 75*(2), 129-149.

Thaiss, C., & Porter, T. (2010). The state of WAC/WID in 2010: Methods and results of the US survey of the international WAC/WID mapping project. *College Composition and Communication, 61*(3), 534-570.

Winsor, D. A. (2003). *Writing power: Communication in an engineering center*. Albany, NY: SUNY Press.

CHAPTER 13

ACADEMIC WRITING IN AN ELF ENVIRONMENT: STANDARDIZATION, ACCOMMODATION—OR TRANSFORMATION?

Laura McCambridge

THE CONTEXT

Academic Literacies scholars in past years have identified and criticized two main approaches to academic writing. On the one hand, many instructors in UK higher education have been said to treat academic writing as an autonomous cognitive skill rather than a social practice. This, Theresa Lillis (2001, p. 58) argues, has led to an "institutional practice of mystery" where expectations for writing are vague, leaving "non-traditional" students who have not long been inducted into elite writing practices at a clear disadvantage. On the other hand, Academic Literacies has also criticized what is termed an "academic socialization approach" (Mary Lea & Brian Street, 1998, p. 158) in which students are explicitly taught or socialized into the dominant practices of an academic discourse community. This approach has been said to be overly prescriptive, uncritically reinforcing power relations and both oversimplifying and essentializing community norms. Having thus criticized both sides of this apparent dichotomy, Academic Literacies research is left with a clear practical dilemma: If an implicit approach is too vague and an explicit approach too prescriptive, what can teachers actually do? How can teachers help students understand and actively negotiate the writing expectations they face without prescribing an explicit, standard set of norms? In applying its theoretical perspective to pedagogical design and practice, academic literacies must find a third way.

In attempting to identify such a "third way," this paper focuses on writing practices and experiences on an international master's degree programme at a university in Finland. "International" programmes such as these, which are becoming increasingly common in Europe, expose the dilemma of vague versus prescriptive teaching yet more intensely. These programmes can often be described as "super-diverse" (see

Steven Vertovec, 2007); their temporary communities consist of highly mobile students with very varied linguistic, cultural and academic backgrounds, and they are often explicitly oriented towards a global scale of academia while still clearly situated in local institutional contexts. Moreover, the programmes typically use English as a Lingua Franca (ELF), i.e., removed from the local sociolinguistic traditions of English native speaking communities. The issue of whether and how to integrate students into a standard set of writing norms in English becomes even more complex in this context—the most obvious question being whose norms to consider the standard? In an ELF context, assuming that there is a set of normative standards that should be taught runs the risk not only of foreclosing students' agency in their writing, but also of reinforcing a global academia in which perceived Anglophone-centre writing practices are idealized. On the other hand, if expectations for writing are left vague, students in this super-diverse setting may find themselves with an even more obscure mystery to solve than those studying in L1 Anglophone dominant contexts.

Tensions concerning the need for clearer, more explicit writing norms versus the need to accommodate diverse writing practices arose repeatedly during a longitudinal ethnographic investigation into this context. This paper will overview each of these two needs in turn, drawing from both teachers' and students' perspectives, before suggesting possible solutions in the conclusion. It suggests that the potential for a transformative approach in this context – for students and teachers – lies in moving away from "in English" as an authoritative rationale in EAP writing pedagogy, cultivating students' agency in their writing choices, and encouraging critical negotiation of practices and expectations.

The master's degree programme in question is located in a medium-sized university in Finland and is conducted entirely through English. Its subject is multidisciplinary, within the field of culture studies. The programme officially lasts two years, but students are able to complete their final research projects (i.e., the master's thesis) part-time.

For this concise paper, the following data was used:

- Four sets of semi-structured interviews with three students over two years concerning six of their written assignments. See Table 13.1 (pseudonyms are used).
- Interviews with four teachers concerning their experiences with writing on the programme and their evaluation of these students' texts. See Table 13.2 (pseudonyms are used).
- Teachers' instructional materials for written assignments.
- Feedback sessions between Megan (one teacher participant) and the students.

The "writing norms" discussed in this paper include any practice or convention that the participants refer to in regards to how a text should be written and what it should include. Isolating one particular type of norm—e.g., lexico-grammatical, discourse structure, topic, content, purpose, process—would have been unnecessarily limiting; these various levels are clearly intertwined and together contribute to the completion and evaluation of a text.

Table 13.1 Student participants

Mei	29-year-old female student from China, first language Chinese. Completed her BA in English Translation in China through Chinese and English.
Stephanie	26-year-old female student from Germany, first language German. Completed her BA in British and American Studies in Germany through English. Spent 6 months in Finland as an exchange student during her BA. Lived in Ireland for 2 years working as an au pair.
Kimiko	30-year-old female student from Japan/first language Japanese. Completed her BA in the United States through English. Studied photography for one year in Turkey through Turkish.

Table 13.2. Teacher participants

Antti	Male professor and head of the programme. From Finland, first language Finnish.
Mikko	Male lecturer on the programme. From Finland, first language Finnish.
Matti	Male professor from Finland, first language Finnish. Completed his PhD in the United States through English.
Anita	Female rofessor from Finland, first language Swedish.
Megan	Female lecturer for the university's language centre. From the United States, first language English. Language centres in Finnish universities provide compulsory and optional language courses for students, often divided according to discipline. Megan teaches a compulsory course on English academic writing/presenting for first year students on the programme.

THE NEED FOR EXPLICIT, STANDARD NORMS

From the teachers' perspectives, more standardized norms were needed due to the difficulties that students' diverse writing practices often created for evaluation. They explained that students' varied linguistic, cultural and academic backgrounds sometimes led to such differences in their texts that they were difficult to understand let alone evaluate. As Antti put it simply, "it is difficult to evaluate those texts where you don't understand the meaning."

Interestingly, although students' texts tended to be different in terms of language use and rhetorical style, difficulty in understanding also resulted from differences in addressivity, i.e., assumptions concerning the imagined reader. Matti, for example, explained that he had to invite an Iranian student to discuss his essay as a result of such misunderstandings:

> He came to me to talk about it because I couldn't make out
> what he was actually meaning so we had a long very interesting
> discussion his argument was kind of too compressed that was the
> problem because I don't know the background of Iranian reli-
> gious history quite simply so it was very difficult for me but very
> interesting and important subject and the writer knows what he's
> writing you can kind of conclude it from the text.

Here, Matti acknowledges that the problem was due to the writer's expectations of the reader's knowledge; he assumed that he could address either an Iranian reader or a global reader aware of Iranian religious conflict in his text. In this case, Matti nevertheless allowed for negotiation of meaning, eventually giving the student a very good grade after all.

For the American English teacher, Megan, who was employed to teach the "conventions of research reporting and academic writing" (as stated in the course description), the diversity of students' texts and lack of standard norms was particularly problematic. The main pressure seemed to stem from the responsibility she felt to even out students' differences and bring them into conventional English academic writing practices, particularly perceived British or American practices. From the subject teachers' perspectives too, the responsibility seemed to fall to Megan as a native English-speaking language teacher to make the students' writing fit for an external reader, primarily in terms of grammar and vocabulary. Several teachers expressed a lack of authority as non-native speakers in focusing on students' English language uses themselves; Mikko put it rhetorically, "who am I to judge their language?"

This responsibility to an imagined external, implicitly native, reader was felt particularly in regards to the master's thesis. Individual course essays were viewed as *local*, for local teachers' eyes only and therefore subject to their flexible preferences. The thesis on the other hand was viewed as a *public* research document, as Antti put it, "a window into what is done on the programme," and therefore subject to strict English language norms.

From the students' perspective, the need for more explicit norms arose particularly during the first year of the programme. They all mentioned that the instructions for written assignments tended to be very general and flexible on many levels (e.g., topic, structure, register) and students were expected to be independent. Often at the end of courses, students were simply asked to write a paper on a topic of their choice related to the course content. The students felt that they had no idea where to start with this freedom, especially since the subject areas were sometimes new and searching through source material was slow work in a second language. They appreciated when a teacher did give more specific instructions.

Students particularly expressed frustration at not understanding the content, structure and linguistic expectations for assignment types that were new to them, such as summaries, diaries and research proposals. For example, on one course the students were asked to write reflective summaries of a series of books. When asked how she found this assignment, Mei showed clear signs of confusion:

> I think it's kind of I don't know it's quite like I said completely
> new for me so I'm just like trying I don't like I said I don't know
> what they want that's what I cannot give them I mean so I would
> just try to use what I can.

All of the students mentioned that they would search for example texts either online or from fellow students in order to "imitate" some of their features. They seemed to do this not only because the text structures were unfamiliar but also because of their heightened need as second language users to acquire more language in order to mimic the voice they are expected to adopt. However, further frustration was expressed with the difficulty of finding examples that were actually suitable models for the specific papers they were asked to write. Mei, for example, noticed the difficulty of trying to transfer what are assumed to be objective, universal genre norms into her own work, remarking "maybe what we find on the internet maybe belong to other countries you know maybe other areas so it's not maybe not what she expects." Moreover, Stephanie mentioned that she found it difficult to tell from the examples she found which features would be considered strengths or flaws by evaluators. The implication here was that not only did these students crave examples, but they craved examples that were specific to the assignment given and explicitly deconstructed by the teacher.

THE NEED TO ACCOMMODATE DIVERSE PRACTICES

Despite these frustrations, a discourse of accepting or encouraging diversity and flexibility in writing expectations also arose over this two-year period. For example, just after expressing concerns regarding students' very varied written English, Mikko nevertheless stated:

> But the global markets that we are collecting our students cul-
> turally its richness we actually need to think positively about the
> people's academic backgrounds when we make a selection.

In defence of the freedom allowed in written assignments, teachers explained that it was in order for students to pursue their own interests on the programme, especially in relation to the master's thesis. This was actually seen as a strategy for coping with students' diverse content knowledge in particular. If students could relate the course materials to their own interests and discover sources that would be useful for their theses, this could only be constructive.

Although the students struggled with this freedom at first, they eventually appreciated it during their second year. Stephanie, for example, had previously studied under strict requirements in Germany, where she took many obligatory courses on English writing in order to learn, in her words, "don't do this and don't do that and be aware." During her second year, she claimed that she had benefited from the more flexible system:

> Stephanie: I think that the thing that helped me to improve a lot was that it's like free you can do whatever you want to so you can actually like write about those things you enjoy writing.
>
> Laura: Is that what made you more ambitious?
>
> Stephanie: Yeah I think I enjoy it much more it's well I actually enjoy writing nowadays and that's the biggest difference.

It seems that for Stephanie the freedom to choose the content and to some extent the style of her texts entailed a freedom to personalize her academic writing and integrate it into her identity. Mei reiterated this point almost exactly, explaining that in China she had to follow very detailed instructions, whereas on the programme she has much more freedom. Although it frightened her at first, she eventually began to enjoy finding ways to relate theory to her own interests. She too seemed to integrate this process of writing into her identity (and vice-versa):

> Mei: Now if you give me any topic, give me certain time, I can write, somehow it helps you. I mean that's how the people who study culture and literature and everything see the world when they look carefully enough, they can see something behind.

Importantly, Mei feels she is beginning to "see the world" as a scholar and writer in her field. She contrasted this enthusiasm with her earlier experiences of simply trying to "deal with the teacher."

When Anita, one of the subject professors, was asked specifically whether she would like students to be taught a particular set of norms for writing their papers, she replied that definitely not. Referring mostly to text structure, but also touching on lexical norms, she explained, "it would be very boring if everyone wrote in a kind of strict what is for me an Anglo-American analytic ideal." Instead, Anita hoped that teaching on writing would make students aware of options, the underlying logic behind those options, and their underlying ideologies. She explained that students should be made aware of how various practices might help them in writing, but should nevertheless be expected to make their own choices, using their own judgment.

It was also clear that applying a simplistic "one size fits all" set of writing norms within a clearly diverse sociolinguistic context would not necessarily address individual students' writing difficulties. It was difficult for teachers to tell whether a feature of a student's text they found "weak" was due to disciplinary background, home culture, language level, lack of effort or something else entirely. For example in giving feedback, the English teacher, Megan, tended to generalize a student's writing issues as being due to clear-cut cultural or register differences in writing practice. In one instance, Mei began a paper by writing an introduction of nearly a page with long sentences and no paragraph divisions. In a feedback session with Megan, she was told that although in China long sentences and paragraphs may be acceptable, it "doesn't work well in English." Mei later told me that she was actually used in China to using shorter sentences and had been trying instead to lengthen her English sentences in order to seem less "childish" and to imitate what she thought was an English norm. In regards to the paragraph length, she explained:

> Mei: I found some examples of research plan on the internet and they are doing this …. I know of course in the body of the essay you will separate, but I don't know if you can do this in the introduction it's not like it's very long … but of course you know when we were kids in primary school we always have this kind of exam about like doing the paragraph thing.
>
> Laura: So you don't think it's true that in China they …
>
> Mei: No, no, no, no.

In exotifying and essentializing the student's cultural background, the teacher positions herself as an ambassador of new cultural practices into which the student must be socialized. She thus misses an opportunity for more meaningful negotiation with the student over the logic behind her choices and her actual dilemmas in writing.

CONCLUSION

The frustrations expressed by students in this data over vague or confusing expectations for writing mirror observations in previous academic literacies research in the United Kingdom (see e.g., Lea & Street, 1998; Lillis, 2001). On the other hand, the problems associated with prescribing standard norms are amplified in this super-diverse community. This paper set out to identify a third way to approach academic writing pedagogy. In my view, the data points to two themes that might characterize this third way: namely, agency and negotiation.

Firstly, the students themselves found that the process of improving as writers was a process of acquiring agency in their writing choices and in turn forming identities as writers in their discipline. This agency and identity could be encouraged by an approach that helps students to connect writing practices to disciplinary purposes. Kate Chanock (2001, p. 8) put it well that the problem is not with having criteria, but rather with the only rationale behind the criteria being "because I say so." I would add to this the rationale "in English, this is how we do it," which is the equivalent in EFL teaching on writing. Teachers are often themselves unaware that conflicting practices exist which vary according to discipline, methodology, culture, text-type and so on. If the sole evaluation criterion for students' writing is its ability to match one imagined Anglo-American set of norms, both the writing and its evaluation lose their pedagogical value. Instead, I would reiterate Anita's suggestion that students (and teachers) become aware of various options in academic writing, their functions and underlying ideologies.

This approach to connecting form, function and ideology would in turn benefit from collaborative methods in writing pedagogy where emphasis is on negotiation and consciousness-raising rather than prescription. This would mean, for instance, including those examples/models/templates that students seem so much to crave and enabling them to become researchers of their discipline's writing practices. Examples that are close to the text types students are actually expected to produce and close to what they can themselves achieve are particularly useful. Again, however, it is important that options are given. The danger in giving only one example which the teacher alone deconstructs as an ideal text is that the students' aim will simply be to copy its features. Instead, various examples could be used in order to provoke negotiation in which both students and teacher can justify their preferences. Nigel Harwood and Gregory Hadley (2004, pp. 366-374) similarly argue for a "corpus-based critical pragmatic approach," in which teachers and students investigate their discipline's discourse norms using corpus data.

It is important to emphasize that accommodating diversity and promoting student agency does not mean *laissez-faire*. The point is not to leave students to struggle and then evaluate whether their work meets a particular teacher's ideals. As Claudio Baraldi (2006, p. 60) puts it, "conflicts between cultural forms must be managed, not avoided." One way to manage these conflicts might be found in the example of Matti's experience with the Iranian student's writing. In evaluating a text that he did not understand due to the student's very different background, Matti was prepared to negotiate with the student and actually came to appreciate his perspective. If teachers allow students space to explain their choices and are even prepared to question their own assumptions, teacher-student interactions are more likely to become genuinely dialogic and transformative, and ultimately more constructive learning opportunities for students—and in fact for teachers themselves.

REFERENCES

Baraldi, C. (2006). New forms of intercultural communication in a globalized world. *The International Communication Gazette, 68*(1), 53-69.

Chanock, K. (2001). From mystery to mastery. In B. James, A. Percy, J. Skillen, & N. Trivett (Eds.), *Changing identities: Proceedings of the language and academic skills (LAS) conference.* University of Wollongong.

Harwood, N., & Hadley, G. (2004). Demystifying institutional practices: Critical pragmatism and the teaching of academic writing. *English for Specific Purposes, 23*(4), 355-377.

Lea, M. R., & Street, B. V. (1998). Student writing in higher education: An academic literacies approach. *Studies in Higher Education, 23*(2), 157-172.

Lillis, T. M. (2001). *Student writing. Access, regulation, desire.* London: Routledge.

Vertovec, S. (2007). Super-diversity and its implications. *Ethnic and Racial Studies, 30*(6), 1024-1054.

CHAPTER 14

"DOING SOMETHING THAT'S REALLY IMPORTANT": MEANINGFUL ENGAGEMENT AS A RESOURCE FOR TEACHERS' TRANSFORMATIVE WORK WITH STUDENT WRITERS IN THE DISCIPLINES

Jackie Tuck

A number of studies drawing on academic literacies have focused on the perspectives of academics as writers (e.g., Lesley Gourlay, 2011; Mary Lea & Barry Stierer, 2009; Theresa Lillis & Mary Jane Curry, 2010). However, academics' pedagogic practices around student writing have generally been investigated with an emphasis on learners' point of view (e.g., Roz Ivanič, 1998; Roz Ivanič, Romy Clark & Rachel Rimmershaw, 2000; Theresa Lillis, 2001), though with some exceptions (Richard Bailey & Mark Garner, 2010; Brenda Gay et al., 1999; Mary Lea & Brian Street, 1999). This has resulted in a powerful critique of prevailing practice, without blaming individual teachers (Lea & Stierer, 2000). Much work in the field over the past decade has also addressed the need for a "design frame" (Gunther Kress, 1998, 2000, cited in Lillis, 2003) "which can actively contribute to student writing pedagogy as both theory and practice" (p. 192). Thus pedagogies around writing are present in academic literacies research as a frequent source of difficulty for students but also as having "transformative" potential (Theresa Lillis & Mary Scott, 2007). Here, I broadly adopt Theresa Lillis and Mary Scott's framing of "transformative" approaches to student writing as contrasting with a more "normative" stance resting on a number of educational myths (Kress, 2007) including "the unidirectionality of the teacher-student relation" (Lillis & Scott, 2007, p. 13). One of the key constitutive elements of this transformative approach is an interest in eliciting the (often undervalued) perspectives of student writers and in valuing the resources they bring to meaning-making in the academy.

However, numerous empirical studies have shown that academic writers' textual practices are frequently embodied in complex chains of events, in which a number of different actors play a range of roles in shaping the text, as co-writers, feedback-givers, proof-readers, etc. (e.g., Nigel Harwood et al., 2009; Lillis & Curry, 2010). It is therefore impossible to draw neat boundaries between student writers' practices and those of other social actors such as their academic teachers. I argue therefore that "transformative" pedagogic design around student writing can only flourish where "the lived experience of teaching and learning from **both** student and tutor perspectives" (Roz Ivanič & Mary Lea, 2006 p. 7; my emphasis) is taken into account. This helps to ensure that one form of "unidirectionality" is not replaced by another, and acknowledges that pedagogical relations are open to contestation and change. It also recognizes that a "transformative interest in meaning-making" (Lillis & Scott, 2007, p. 13) legitimately encompasses the meanings teachers bring to and derive from their practices around student writing (see also Roozen et al., Chapter 15 this volume).

The study I draw on in this paper therefore used ethnographically-oriented methodologies (Judith Green & David Bloome, 1997; Lillis, 2008) to focus on the less extensively researched experiences and perspectives of disciplinary academic teachers, framing pedagogies around writing as a dimension of academic literacies to be empirically explored, without "making prior assumptions as to which [practices] are either appropriate or effective" (Lea & Street, 1998, p. 158). Thus my approach was to highlight participants' understandings of what was satisfactory, generative and meaningful, or otherwise, in their practice around student writing as an indication of what might be "transformative" in their contexts.

THE EMPIRICAL STUDY

The project involved fourteen academic teacher participants, in six diverse UK universities and a range of disciplines. Initial, semi-structured interviews were followed up with text-focused interviews, based for example around marked assignments, or moderation paperwork, generating "talk around text" (Lillis, 2008, 2009). Other data were collected, such as guidance and assessment materials, audio-recordings of observed face-to-face sessions, or made by participants while marking assignments. The analytical approach was to weave a detailed picture by moving back and forth between different sources of data, using individual case studies as "vertical" warp threads running through the analysis, connected by the weft of "horizontal" thematic analysis across the study (David Barton & Mary Hamilton, 1998). I was interested in participants' experience of their disciplinary writing work with students, in their perceptions of its success and what it meant to them. I therefore paid attention to ways in which participants' practices and wordings might invoke broader "discourses of writing and of learning to write" (Ivanič, 2004) in the academy. This approach showed clearly that individual teachers actively configured contexts for writing work with students, and positioned themselves within—rather than simply responding to—their institutional contexts through practice around student writing. Here I present two (pseudonymous) miniature case studies which convey something of the complexity of disciplinary writing work with students, and of how it is experienced, valued and understood by academic teachers.

MINIATURE CASE STUDY 1: MIKE, GEOGRAPHY

Mike works in a small, relatively new "teaching-led"[1] university. He describes himself as an "enthusiastic teacher of Geography" and in a departmental website video declares a commitment to professional teaching in the subject. A contrast emerges between Mike's practice on an "innovative" third year module and his routines elsewhere, for example on a second-year urban landscapes module. The latter is assessed through an assignment which Mike describes as a:

> conventional essay … where students do have to jump through
> the hoops otherwise there's no foundation.

He collects the anonymized scripts from a locked box after the deadline "and then they lurk" in piles in his office until he has time to tackle them. Mike's marking involves a range of specific practices, including scanning for relevant academic references and key words, and ticking when he finds them:

> ok they've got the basic points about geometry, cleanliness …
> they get a tick for that.

He writes marginal comments and finishes with a feedback summary. However, he believes that these "carefully crafted" messages often go unheeded by students:

> they see 62 and then they put it back on the pile and then they
> go home.

In his third year feminist geography module, Mike has introduced a new assessed "guided learning log" which cannot be anonymized. He gives a detailed description in the module handbook, holds an assignment-specific workshop, provides guidance and feedback for each diary entry, as well as a final summative assessment. Mike describes how taking on this module proved to be a key moment in his development as an academic teacher:

> It's almost like an epiphany—that if you understood the material
> that I was teaching properly you wouldn't assess it in traditional
> ways.

He explains that the new learning log is a hybrid genre of academic writing in which students must be "personal" and at the same time "scholarly"; through writing they are coming to grips with "ways of knowing" in this branch of the discipline, engaging in "feminist critiques of science." Mike's practice around this assignment involves collaboration with a writing support specialist in his institution to set up tailored group support sessions. Their work together begins with a chance conversation in a pub, which Mike believes partly accounts for the success of the collaboration:

> Because J and I knew each other and I'd had a good relaxed conversation with her perhaps ... she knew exactly what I was trying to achieve with this work.

MINIATURE CASE STUDY 2: EMMA, COMPUTER SCIENCE

Emma works in a prestigious Russell Group university. She is personally interested in teaching, but believes that the work around student writing she talks about is "worth zero" in institutions like hers where "research ... is what counts." Like Mike, Emma adopts contrasting approaches to student writing in different modules. In one second year module, students produce some computer code and write a descriptive report: guidelines and brief assessment criteria are provided on the Virtual Learning Environment (VLE). Emma marks half the one hundred scripts, describing marking fifty assignments on the same topic as "horrendous"; she also expresses doubt about its effectiveness:

> I'm not sure that the student, by getting it wrong and then by getting short remarks on it which tell him that's not good, actually can really improve to be honest.

Students also dislike the module and the assessment; however, Emma doubts whether anything will change in future, because although she has offered her "take" on the assignment to the unit leader, she explains that feeling comfortable enough to pursue such matters depends on relationships with colleagues, and that "essentially [she has] none with this guy."

Emma is unit leader responsible for a third/fourth year specialist module. Soon after arriving in post, she changed the assessment, introducing a very different working process. Instead of an individual essay on a set theme, students choose their own topic in small groups, do some initial research and write an "extended abstract." Groups then meet with both course lecturers to receive feedback, ask questions and set out plans for completing the project in the form of a "proper scientific paper." At every stage, students are supported by face-to-face contact:

> We really try to get them to understand that they are not alone in this ... we really encourage them to come, and we are not making fun of them or ... seeing this as ... just a trivial thing, just a student's problem.

Emma contrasts the experience of reading completed scripts with the second year assignment:

> This is **way** more interesting to read … there were fifteen groups
> and all of them have had different topics … [Emma's emphasis]

This enthusiasm is echoed in observed group meetings in which Emma and her colleague make plain their enjoyment of student writing which does not cover too-familiar territory. For example, to one group Emma says she is really pleased with their topic, because it will mean "good added value for me and the other students." To another, she remarks positively on the "added value for you writing and for me reading." The idea of "value added" seems to be closely aligned during these sessions with the level of personal interest and potential for learning which each assignment topic presents for tutors. In one session, Emma remarks that students have chosen a nice topic and "you're lucky that I don't know so much about [x], lucky you." This appears to reverse the usual tutor/student hierarchies around writing: Emma is openly hoping that students will choose topics which are new to her, positioning herself as someone who is still learning and curious about her subject, and students as having something to offer. This message is echoed in VLE guidance which explains to students that the assignment provides an opportunity to "try out being the lecturer for a small part of the course."

Another good reason in Emma's view for introducing this new assignment is that master's students who also take the module, often from overseas, benefit greatly from the chance to practice this sort of research-oriented writing in English in a UK setting. Although time consuming for tutors, the benefits come later, when they are supporting their dissertation work. Emma thinks it would be even better

> If we could get the language people … drag them somehow into
> our courses where there is writing done … but there is no inter-
> action in this way, it just doesn't happen.

Another key benefit she sees in this way of working is that it emphasizes a process which will be very valuable for students as engineers in the future.

STEPPING OUT OF ROUTINE PRACTICES

These brief accounts illustrate some themes recurring across the study. Both Mike and Emma are engaged in routine practices around student writing, which have negative associations for them as tedious and dreaded tasks with questionable impact on students (Jackie Tuck, 2012). However, along with other study participants, both experienced much more satisfying moments in which it seemed possible to make a worthwhile difference to students' writing practices. These were often characterized by an opportunity to interact face-to-face with students during the writing process, either where disciplinary contact time was allocated for the purpose, or where there was a conscious decision to make time available informally, for example when Emma and her colleague "really try to get [students] to understand they're not alone." These opportunities enabled academic teachers to work iteratively and formatively with students' texts, rather than in a one-off engagement at the point of summative assessment.

Emma's case illustrates another characteristic of the more satisfying and productive moments in participants' disciplinary writing work: the opportunity to disrupt, even if only briefly, the hierarchies usually associated with student writing for assessment. For example, Emma's group assignment encourages students "to try out being the lecturer," she emphasizes to them their future role as engineers, and that staff will not "make fun" or trivialize their concerns. These moments also often involved opportunities to collaborate closely with disciplinary colleagues or with language specialists, often building on existing informal alliances—for example, Mike's chance conversation in a pub with a writing support specialist. Where these informal opportunities were absent, as in Emma's case where she has no "relationship" with the second year unit leader, or "interaction" with the "language people," participants seemed less likely to step out of routine practices, however unsatisfactory. A thread running through these examples is that pedagogic practices which participants felt were making a positive difference to student writing also entailed transformations in relationships with students and colleagues, emphasising dialogue and mutual exchange. These opportunities did not simply arise, but had to be actively carved out through creative trade-offs between what was desirable and what was possible at different times.

INVESTING IN DISCIPLINARY WRITING WORK

These findings raise a further question: what made the investment involved in finding space, time and energy for productive disciplinary writing work "worthwhile"? Again, both Mike's and Emma's cases reflect broader patterns in the study as a whole. Emma offers an interesting critical reflection:

> Writing is called a transferable skill but I'm not sure that it actu-
> ally is so much, because quite often you only learn when you're
> doing something that's really important.

Just as students' academic writing may only really develop when they are doing "something really important" to them, teacher-participants needed good reasons to step out of the usual routines around student writing. There were pragmatic and strategic benefits which encouraged them to invest time and effort in productive disciplinary writing work, for example, where personal reputation within or beyond the organization was perceived to be at stake, or where time spent now saved time later. However, equally important was the opportunity for meaningful engagement, for example, where Emma and her colleague on the specialist module can learn something new about their subject.

These cases also point to factors which seemed to discourage academic teachers in the study from moving beyond unproductive routine practices. Again, questions of meaningful engagement were as important as pragmatic considerations such as time or reputation. In some participants' institutions, anonymized assessment regimes precluded the type of mutually satisfying formative engagement with students' texts illustrated in the cases discussed here, except in situations where an exception could be made, as in Mike's learning log.

DISCOURSES OF LEARNING AND WRITING

The study also brought to light the ways in which academic teachers' practices were bound up with discourses of learning and of writing. For example, the investment Mike makes in an alternative approach to writing on his third year module is a profoundly epistemological one: sudden insight leads him to make a connection between students' disciplinary thinking and what they *do* in writing. What is striking here is that this epistemological approach seems to contrast with Mike's experience on other modules where students just "tell you what they think you need to know" and "jump through the hoops." Similarly, while Emma sees her work with students on the third year module as helping them understand "what scientific means in terms of writing," she has no equivalent sense of disciplinary purpose in her work with the second year students' reports, commenting that "you wonder why you're doing it." These examples suggest that an approach which downplays disciplinary meaning-making for student writers is frequently experienced by academic teachers as rather meaningless and pointless in pedagogic terms.

This separation in discourse and practice between disciplinary learning on one hand, and learning to write on the other, where the latter is cast as the content-free acquisition of skills and mastery of conventions, surfaced repeatedly across the study in different types of data, including texts (echoing Lea & Street, 1999). However, as these miniature case studies show, at particular moments and in specific contexts, a perceived link between writing and learning for students was mirrored in a more epistemological approach to writing pedagogy. Albeit briefly in some cases, disciplinary learning/teaching and the learning/teaching of writing were one and the same.

IMPLICATIONS

The study described here brought to light a number of ways in which academic teachers were finding productive—and potentially transformative—ways to work with their students on writing in the disciplines, where there was sufficient perceived incentive for the teacher in doing so. One clear implication for practice is that it is important to find ways of developing disciplinary writing work by nurturing academic teachers' sense of personal investment in initiatives which help them move away from less productive routine practices (see Bailey & Garner, 2010). "Value-added" can take a number of pragmatic forms (e.g., enhanced reputation, time saved later) but also key was meaningful engagement: the rewards of mutual learning and the pleasures of collaboration. These case studies show that what might be transformative for students in terms of academic writing is inseparable from teachers' own transformation, for example Mike's "epiphany" when he realizes he can devise an assessment which connects epistemologically with the subject, or Emma's more incremental realization in the light of experience that writing may not be an easily transferable skill.

Academic literacies research has brought to light the importance of a "transformative interest" in student-writer meanings and perspectives as the foundation for transformative pedagogies, acknowledging a commitment to helping students to be successful writers in their own terms. The findings of this study refine this picture, suggesting that what counts as making a positive difference has to be negotiated: both students and teachers need to see the point, and to feel that the investment of time, reputation and other resources is "worthwhile." It is arguably therefore just as important to nurture the conditions for teacher transformation as it is to provide incentives for students to engage at more than a superficial level with academic writing. Although participants in this study were not explicitly drawing on an academic literacies framework in their disciplinary work with student writers, these findings suggest that an academic literacies approach has the potential to support the development of such conditions.

One way to work towards this may be to remind academic teachers of what many already instinctively know when they engage in their own writing for the discipline: that thinking, learning and knowledge-making are inseparable from representation, and that writing is therefore profoundly relevant to learning and so to teaching in the disciplines. Institutions must support both timetabled and informal provision if this integration is to be realized. Other challenges must be addressed at institutional level. It is difficult not to reduce large-cohort written assessments to "hoop-jumping exercises" with little meaning for staff or students. This is particularly so where students are writing in traditional academic genres such as the essay which lend themselves to standardized assessment predicated on the assumption of a single (anonymous) author. Perhaps one way to approach this problem would be to accept the need in the current context for assessments in which students demonstrate that they have the "foundation" (Mike), but to dissociate this sort of assessed outcome more often from the process of academic text production. For example, more use could be made of multiple choice or short answer assessment in order to free up time for more dialogic and collaborative pedagogies which are the *sine qua non* of transformative practice around student writing.

NOTE

1. Study participants often used the terminology of the UK sector in defining their institutions as either "research-led" such as those in the Russell Group, or "teaching-led," for example Mike's institution, a small university specializing mainly in Arts subjects, established within the past fifteen years. The Russell Group is a large, long-established, elite grouping of "top" UK research-intensive universities.

REFERENCES

Bailey, R., & Garner, M. (2010). Is the feedback in higher education assessment worth the paper it is written on? *Teaching in Higher Education, 15*(2), 187-198.

Barton, D., & Hamilton, M. (1998). *Local literacies: Reading and writing in one community.* London: Routledge.

Gay, B., Jones, C., & Jones, J. (1999). Writing assignments on a PGCE (secondary) course: Two case studies. In C. Jones, J. Turner, & B. Street (Eds.), *Students writing in the university; Cultural and epistemological issues* (pp. 81-102). Amsterdam: John Benjamins Publishing Company.

Gourlay, L. (2011). New lecturers and the myth of communities of practice. *Studies in Continuing Education, 33*(1), 67-77.

Green, J., & Bloome, D. (1997). Ethnography and ethnographers of and in education: A situated persepctive. In J. Flood, S. B. Heath & D. Lapp (Eds.), *Handbook of research on teaching literacy through the communicative and visual Arts* (pp. 181-202). New York: Macmillan.

Harwood, N., Austin, L., & Macaulay, R. (2009). Proofreading in UK university: Proofreaders' beliefs and experiences. *Journal of Second Language Writing, 18*(3), 166-190.

Ivanič, R. (2004). Discourses of writing and learning to write. *Language and Education, 18*(3), 220-245.

Ivanič, R. (1998). *Writing and identity: The discoursal construction of identity in academic writing.* Amsterdam: John Benjamins Publishing Company.

Ivanič, R., Clark, R., & Rimmershaw, R. (2000). "What am I supposed to make of this?" The messages conveyed to students by tutors' written comments. In M. R. Lea & B. Stierer (Eds.), *Student writing in higher education: New contexts* (pp. 48-63). Buckingham, UK: Society for Research into Higher Education and Open University.

Ivanič, R., & Lea, M. R. (2006). New contexts, new challenges: The teaching of writing in UK higher education. In L. Ganobcsik-Williams (Ed.), *Teaching ac-*

ademic writing in UK higher education (pp. 6-15). Basingstoke, UK: Palgrave Macmillan Publishing.

Kress, G. (1998). Visual and verbal modes of representation in electronically mediated communication: The potentials of new forms of text. In I. Snyder (Ed.), *Page to Screen* (pp. 55-80). London: Routledge.

Kress, G. (2000). Multimodality. In B. Cope & M. Kalantzis (Eds.), *Multiliteracies. Literacy, learning and the design of social futures* (pp. 182-202). London: Routledge.

Kress, G. (2007). Thinking about meaning and learning in a world of instability and multiplicity. *Pedagogies: An International Journal, 1*, 19-34.

Lea, M., & Stierer, B. (Eds.). (2000). *Student writing in higher education: New contexts.* Buckingham, UK: Society for Research into Higher Education.

Lea, M. R., & Stierer, B. (2009). Lecturers' everyday writing as professional practice in the university as workplace: New insights into academic identities. *Studies in Higher Education, 34*(4), 417-428.

Lea, M., & Street, B. (1999). Writing as academic literacies: Understanding textual practices in higher education. In C. Candlin & K. Hyland (Eds.), *Writing: Texts, processes and practices* (pp. 62-81). London: Addison Wesley Longman.

Lea, M. R., & Street, B. V. (1998). Student writing in higher education: An academic literacies approach. *Studies in Higher Education, 23*(2), 157-172.

Lillis, T. (2001). *Student writing: Access, regulation and desire.* London: Routledge.

Lillis, T. (2003). Student writing as "academic literacies": Drawing on Bakhtin to move from critique to design. *Language and Education, 17*(3), 192-207.

Lillis, T. (2008). Ethnography as method, methodology and deep theorising: Closing the gap between text and context in academic writing research. *Written Communication, 25*(3), 353-388.

Lillis, T. (2009). Bringing writers' voices to writing research: Talk around text. In A. Carter, T. Lillis, & S. Parkin (Eds.), *Why writing matters: Issues of access and identity in writing research and pedagogy* (pp. 169-187). Amsterdam: John Benjamins Publishing Company.

Lillis, T., & Curry, M. J. (2010). *Academic writing in a global context: The politics and practices of publishing in English.* London: Routledge.

Lillis, T., & Scott, M. (2007). Defining academic literacies research: Issues of epistemology, ideology and strategy. *Journal of Applied Linguistics, 4*(1), 5-32.

Tuck, J. (2012). Feedback-giving as social practice: Academic teachers' perspectives on feedback as institutional requirement work and dialogue. *Teaching in Higher Education, 17*(2), 209-221.

CHAPTER 15

THE TRANSFORMATIVE POTENTIAL OF LAMINATING TRAJECTORIES: THREE TEACHERS' DEVELOPING PEDAGOGICAL PRACTICES AND IDENTITIES

Kevin Roozen, Rebecca Woodard, Sonia Kline and Paul Prior

In its efforts to develop a richer, more complex analysis of what it means to be academically literate, Academic Literacies scholarship has illuminated alternative ways of being and meaning-making that animate and complicate academic settings, activities, and identities (Roz Ivanič, 2009; Roz Ivanič & Candice Satchwell, 2007; Mary Lea & Brian Street, 1998; Theresa Lillis & Mary Scott, 2007). Research (e.g., Amy Burgess & Roz Ivanič, 2010; Roz Ivanič, 1998; Theresa Lillis, 2001; Kate Pahl, 2008) has primarily focused on students as agents with significant lives outside of school, highlighting that the heterogeneous resources and social identities that students bring to schooling are critical grounds for transforming learning, contesting dominant classroom ideologies and practices, and forging productive linkages between the often disparate worlds of school and everyday life. Teachers' practices and identities, in contrast, have received limited attention, and the histories they bring to the classroom have been configured largely in terms of their participation with institutional spaces and roles (Gail Richmond, Mary Juzwick & Michael Steele, 2011). In response to Mary Lea and Brian Street's (1998) argument that "[i]n order to understand the nature of academic learning, it is important to investigate the understandings of both academic staff and students about their own literacy practices without making prior assumptions as to which practices are either appropriate or effective" (p. 158), we present here three vignettes drawn from larger case studies of three teachers: Lisa (eighth grade English Language Arts), Dave (ninth and twelfth grade science) and Kate (university-level composition). Rebecca's case study of Lisa focuses on how her participation in a creative writing group outside of school influenced her instruction, Sonia's case study of Dave looks at his participation in digital literacies and the National Writing Project, and Kevin's case study of Kate seeks to understand how her participation in fan-fiction writing relates to her other literate engagements (Kevin Roozen, 2009, 2011). Each of these cases exploring teachers' identities as literate persons in the world suggests the importance of locating teachers as well as students in the laminated trajectories of their sociocultural lives (see also Tuck Chapter 14 this volume).

We draw from a body of work that understands the construction of identity as an ongoing process of weaving together multiple streams of activity over time. Drawing on Erving Goffman's (1974, 1981) work on framing and footings, we understand the interweaving of multiple historical streams as a pervasive process of lamination of activities, artifacts, and identities (Paul Prior, 1998; Paul Prior & Jody Shipka, 2003). In this sense, identity is located not within and determined by a particular social setting, but rather along trajectories of participation that stretch across, and thus draw together, multiple sites of engagement (Ole Drier, 1999; Dorothy Holland, William Lachicotte, Debra Skinner & Carole Cain, 1998; Ron Scollon, 2001; JohnVan Mannen, 1984; Etienne Wenger, 1998; Stanton Wortham, 2006). Although it is not common, some teacher educators and researchers have recognized the laminated nature of teachers' identities and practices (e.g., Janet Alsup, 2006; Deborah Britzman, 1991; Christine Casanave & Xiaoming Li, 2008; Mank Varghese, Brian Morgan, Bill Johnson & Kimberly Johnson, 2005). For example, Deborah Britzman (1991) describes teaching

> as a struggle for voice and discursive practices amid a cacoph-
> ony of past and present voices, lived experiences, and available
> practices. The tensions among what has preceded, what is con-
> fronted, and what one desires shape the contradictory realities of
> learning to teach. (p. 31)

Educators' reflections on and negotiations among those resources can transform or disrupt their classroom identities and practices (Alsup, 2006). In this chapter, we argue for including laminated identities among the available tools in teachers' repertoires. Beyond mapping the laminated trajectories of teachers' identities and practices, then, we suggest that—much as students' histories with literacy beyond school can enrich classroom learning—teachers' histories can likewise play a crucial role in shaping pedagogical practices in ways that can reconfigure student learning.

By tracing the trajectories of teachers' situated practices across settings, we attempt to better describe how fundamentally laminated teachers' identities and practices are, and to begin exploring how lamination may (or may not) lead to transformative teaching practices. Informed by Academic Literacies and sociocultural approaches that emphasize the ways people and practices develop by tying together seemingly disparate activities across a range of representational media (e.g., Burgess & Ivanič, 2010; Pierre Bourdieu, 1990; Bruno Latour, 2005; Jay Lemke, 2000; Prior, 1998; Paul Prior & Julie Hengst, 2010; Scollon, 2001, 2005), our analysis aims to make visible how three teachers at different educational levels and in diverse disciplinary fields in the United States weave together everyday and professional worlds and identities, transforming in at least some key ways their teaching practices.

Lisa: "A Teacher Who Also Is Working Towards Becoming a Writer"

Lisa, in her seventh year as a middle school English Language Arts teacher in New York City, wrote extensively outside of her classroom—meeting with her creative writing instructor and/or writing group on a weekly basis, yet she hesitated to identify herself as a writer: "I'm someone who writes but I think a writer is someone who publishes things …. For the most part I'd say I'm a teacher who also is working towards becoming a writer." Although Lisa drew a sharp distinction between her rights to call herself a teacher and a writer, as I (Rebecca) looked closely at her actions and talk, I concluded that they tell a somewhat different story—one where Lisa's literate activities across sites are complexly laminated. For example, in my observations of both her writing classroom and creative writing experiences, Lisa used the specialized discourses of creative writing to represent the routine practices of creative writers (e.g., writers "bury" obvious parts of their writings, writers constantly pay attention to their lives to get ideas).

Transcripts of discussions between Lisa and her writing instructor, Will, and Lisa and her eighth grade student, Esmerelda, demonstrate Lisa's focus on "brave" writerly practices. At a coffee shop in downtown New York City, Lisa and Will began their meeting by discussing Joan Didion's (1976) essay *Why I Write*, which Will had asked Lisa to read beforehand. Lisa told Will that she was particularly struck by a part where Didion said that she sometimes "sits on [an idea] for several years" before writing about it. Lisa thought this "was pretty brave" of Didion, and said that she tried to do this, but often felt that she needed to develop her ideas quickly. Will told her that a "notebook can be really helpful" for saving ideas for a later time, and that writers often keep ideas around for a long time because "sometimes you're not ready to write that scene" yet. The next day, Esmerelda, one of Lisa's students, began a classroom writing conference by telling Lisa that she had worked on her weekend assignment to make "radical revisions" to her historical fiction story. Esmerelda had decided that she had too much going on in her story, and was going to get rid of an extraneous character, revising or cutting all the parts related to that character. Lisa praised Esmerelda for making such significant cuts in her story, telling her that "we have a brave writer right here." They read through Esmerelda's story together, and Lisa gave Esmerelda strategies to help make her story flow after deleting the character.

Later, Lisa explained how asking students to make radical revisions, especially right before a project was due, "used to scare me, but now I think they [students] are better for it." After Lisa began writing outside of school herself, she regularly encouraged students to cut large parts of their drafts. Both Will and Lisa tried to name writerly practices and make them visible to their students, and Lisa's developing understandings of "brave" writers appeared in both settings. In her classroom, Lisa used her authenticity as a writer who really does "live this" and "believe in" the writing process to share the writerly world with her students. She said, "[I want to give] students certain tools and strategies. For example, here's how you can get ideas for this, here's how you can plan out a story ... you need to understand how it's done." My observations confirmed the parallels in Lisa's representations of writing and writers across sites, and supported Lisa's own report that working as a creative writer was transforming the way she represented writing and the kinds of writerly roles she invited students to take. Across settings, her words and practices undoubtedly "taste[d] of the context and contexts in which[they had] lived" (Mikhail Bakhtin, 1981, p. 293).

However, such transformations were not complete. For example, Lisa struggled to implement some of her own creative writing practices, like peer feedback, in her classroom. Although she said that getting the students to do "authentic partner critiquing" was a big goal for her and she even videotaped part of her own peer-writing discussion for her students, in my multiple classroom observations peers only spent about 6% of total class time talking about their writing (a sharp contrast to the 35% of the time Lisa talked with Will about her own writing). In her classroom, Lisa had to designate significantly more time to direct instruction, independent writing, and general management than in her own writing practice.

Moreover, we can return to the initial contradiction. Despite Lisa's rich writing experiences and prominent calls for broadening notions of writing and writers (e.g., Kathleen Yancey, 2009), Lisa struggled with her own writerly authority and identity. Her struggles highlight the need to further explore how deeply rooted cultural conceptions of writing (where print literacies are often valued over digital and networked literacies) and authorship (where sponsored publication often links tightly to identity) inform—and disrupt—teachers' identity work and classroom practices.

DAVE: "THE ACCIDENTAL BLOGGER"

A high school biology teacher, scientist, computer buff, and photographer, Dave has hosted for almost two years a blog—Things Biological: Insects, Macrophotography, Teaching, Life (http://www.nwp.org/)—that ties tightly together his practices and identities. Although he calls himself "the accidental blogger," his blogging is anything but accidental. The genesis, trajectories, and interconnections of Dave's identities are visible in his blog space, conversations, after-school club and classroom. Unlike Lisa, Dave does not appear to perceive sharp boundaries between his multiple identities and practices. By discussing his blog, which in name and nature serves as a key link of his varied engagements, I (Sonia) aim to explore how this weaving together of Dave's laminated identities and practices transformed his pedagogical work.

Dave's blog posts usually include at least one recently captured photograph accompanied by text providing background information about the subject (see example in Figure 15.1). When Dave knows his Internet access may be restricted (during a vacation trip, for instance), he uploads posts early and pre-sets them to publish in his absence. He is the first to admit he is a little obsessed. However, in a video he created in 2010 during a National Writing Project (NWP) summer institute for teachers, Dave narrated: "I have to admit that I have never been a fan of blogs …. Life is short. There are so many other things to do that are more important than devoting a significant part of your life to writing to an unknown (or entirely absent) audience."

Wolf spider (Hogna sp.) added to the classroom
December 24, 2011 by allthingsbiological

Female wolf spider (*Hogna sp.*) shows me the *Tenbrio molitor* pupa I had just given her. How thoughtful! Click/double click to enlarge.

This individual was brought to me by one of my students (thanks, Wyatt!) whose father found it in their workplace. It had to go, so it is now in my possession. Because it's too cold to release, the spider will stay in my classroom until spring.

These quick, agile hunters are solitary, tackling and rapidly consuming prey approaching their own size. This individual is certainly a much more aggressive feeder than either of the desert-originating Mexican red knee tarantulas (*Brachypelma smithi*), though the native wolf spiders live on a much more rapid timescale than the slow-growing, multi-decade surviving red knee tarantulas.

Like all wolf spiders, two of her eight eyes are large and prominent, distinguishing her from nursery web spiders whose eyes are all of approximately equal size.

Important insect control agents, these spiders may bite if harassed, though the bite is medically insignificant.

Figure 15.1: Example of a post from Dave's blog.

What then motivated Dave to begin blogging? On a number of occasions he posed this question and offered answers. For instance, in his very first blog post he described two separate catalysts: attending a nature photographer's presentation and then following the man's blog and previewing blogs from other NWP teachers during that summer institute. At another time Dave mentioned that his interest in macrophotography was fuelled when a group of students in one of his extracurricular groups gave him a macro (close-up) lens for his camera as a thank-you gift. He also described attending a presentation by a retiring photographer, after which he asked him what he would do with his enormous collection of images. On hearing that they would be placed in boxes for storage, Dave was dismayed. His decision to begin a blog, as he retold, was in part an alternative way of storing, organizing and sharing his photographs. Finally, another classroom event came into play. One of his students brought to class a gravid praying mantis that produced several egg cases. This mantis, the egg cases, and the resulting offspring became the focus of the students' attention and Dave's photographic efforts for several weeks.

Grounded in these heterogeneous experiences, Dave's blog work has transformed some of his teaching and his students' practices. Now students regularly share arthropods with Dave, and some follow or comment on his posts. On field trips his students seek out potential photographic subjects, and Dave credits them on his blog for their assistance. He talks to them about what makes a good scientific photograph and shows them how to use field guides and the Internet to learn more. He uses his own photographs for teaching, and freely encourages educational use of his images. His stock of photographs is now so large that he has enough material to create his own field guide, which he hopes to share with other teachers and students. Dave's blog has also helped to connect him with a wider community of scientists, photographers and arthropod enthusiasts. As the only biology teacher in the school, this connection is really important for Dave: "I now feel more part of scientific community … and more up-to-date … than I ever did, even as a graduate student." Dave appeared to translate his deep enthusiasm for understanding nature into a range of practices that aimed to instil a spirit of exploration in his students.

This account of Dave's practices has centered on his blog, but such blending of his out-of-school and in-school identities and practices was also evident across other settings and times—for instance, in relation to his active participation in the local National Writing Project site and to his after-school club. Dave's identities and practices as biology teacher, scientist, computer buff, and blogger are so intensely intertwined that to separate them seems futile. Significantly, however, Dave teaches in a selective admission public university laboratory high school whose mission to be "a catalyst for educational innovation" allows, perhaps encourages, such blurring. This is not the reality for many teachers—at what loss, one wonders, for their students?

KATE: "SHOWING THE STUDENTS THAT I'M A FAN"

Kate is a full-time composition instructor at a four-year university in the south-eastern United States. When I (Kevin) asked her during one of our interviews what excited her the most about her teaching, she immediately commented, "showing the students that I'm a fan." Kate's use of the term "fan" here signals her membership in a community Henry Jenkins (1992) describes as enthusiasts of popular video games, anime, movies, novels or other cultural texts who use a particular text as a source "from which to generate a wide range of media related stories … stretching its boundaries to incorporate their concerns, remoulding its character to better suit their desires" (p. 156). In previous publications (Roozen, 2009, 2011), I analyzed the ways Kate's deep involvement with fan fiction and fan art profoundly laminated her engagement with English Studies as a student in high school English, as an undergraduate English major and in her MA programme in Writing Studies. Here I extend my tracing of this laminated trajectory beyond Kate's MA work to address how her involvement as a "fan" textures and transforms her activities as a professional teacher.

Working on her fan fiction over the past thirteen years, Kate has published online multiple novels, dozens of short stories and poems and a variety of other prose pieces from the popular texts at the centercentre of the more than fifty "fandoms" she participates in, including those dedicated to movies, comics, videogames and a wide range of novels, anime, cartoons and television shows. In addition, her novels, stories and poems are frequently supplemented by the many forms of fan art she creates. According to Kate, "I have such a vivid picture of them [the characters and scenes depicted in her fan fiction] in my mind, I just wanted people to really see what they look like. I can describe them in words, but I think people can understand them better if they can see them." Kate's fan art includes pencil, crayon, and digital drawings; cartoons; music videos; costumes and clothing; dolls; stuffed animals; and jewellery based on characters and scenes from the cultural texts at the center of her fandoms. David Barton and Mary Hamilton (1998) noted that "being a fan involved a range of literacy activities spanning reading and writing and incorporating other media" (p. 249). For Kate, being a "fan" clearly involves engagement with a wide range of textual and semiotic practices.

The fan fiction and fan art featured on the wiki Kate created for Sonic Wings, a Japanese video game, offers a good sense of Kate's engagement as a fan. In addition to the dozen or so short stories she's written based on the characters of Sonic Wings, Kate's wiki also features two fan novels based on two different versions of the game, one of which is currently thirteen chapters in length. The wiki also showcases dozens of drawings that Kate has made based on events and scenes from Sonic Wings, including "profiles" Kate created for the game's major and minor characters, each profile containing a representative drawing and key information about the character.

Evidencing the lamination of her identity as a fan and her developing identity as a composition teacher, Kate discussed in one interview her plans for developing composition courses:

> I'll be teaching the themed, research-based comp[osition] II
> course next semester, and I'm really looking for the opportunity
> to incorporate fan fiction. I want to do it with a theme of anima-
> tion. That means I'll get to show the students a lot of movies and
> cartoons I'm a fan of. I haven't fully planned the course yet, but I
> already have ideas of what I want to show.

One of the follow-up questions I emailed a few weeks later invited Kate to say more about the connection she saw between her fan activities and the aims of the composition course she was planning. Kate responded by writing, "the research areas [of the university's] new curriculum covers—evaluation, comparison, synthesis, and argument—are all a part of what fan fiction authors (good ones, anyway!) do." As the semester approached, Kate drew upon her engagement as a fan, and in particular her experience with anime, to develop two different versions of the composition II course, one based on the topic of animation and the second based on the subject of the South in the United States (a regional categorization still rooted in the Civil War). Briefly describing these courses in an email interview during the semester, Kate wrote, "I'm using Squidbillies [an animated cartoon based on squid-like characters living in the southern United States] in composition II, both in the animation class and in the south one."

Kate's emerging professional practices and identities have been shaped by her broad array of literate activities; what might appear to be stable and homogeneous professional practices and identities are actually woven from an amalgam of literate engagements, some of which come from their encounters with formal education and formal professional development, and some of which come from her "other" literate engagements as a fan. My sense is that these laminated trajectories have not only transformed Kate's developing identity as an educator, but also stand to transform how her students encounter and engage with the university's composition instruction and with writing and literate activity more broadly.

CONCLUSION

Informed by theoretical perspectives that emphasize the profoundly dialogic and hybrid nature of literate action (Ivanič, 2009; Ivanič & Satchwell, 2007; Lea & Street, 1998; Lillis & Scott, 2007), Academic Literacies theories have argued that the heterogeneous resources and social identities that students bring to schooling serve as fertile grounds for constructing and reconstructing new identities, disrupting dominant power relationships, illuminating the affordances and constraints of various forms of discourse, and, ultimately, transforming classroom spaces and practices. As a result, Academic Literacies has productively critiqued conventional approaches to student writing that are oriented towards the monologic reproduction of privileged academic discourses and has called for pedagogical practices and perspectives that foreground the dialogic interplay of official and unofficial discourse practices. Based on our case studies of Lisa, Dave, and Kate, we argue that the laminated trajectories of practices and identities that teachers bring to school also deserve close attention and can become a key resource for pedagogies that create classroom spaces in which students are invited and encouraged to weave together multiple, seemingly disparate voices, selves, and practices from their own repertoires. In other words, we suggest that the pedagogical practices that emerge when Lisa, Dave, and Kate work to blend their laminated trajectories into their teaching offer one way of putting Academic Literacy theory into practice. When we trace these teachers' trajectories of practices and identities, much as when research has examined students' literate lives and selves, a complicated picture of laminated pedagogical practices emerges. Our case studies suggest that Lisa, Dave, and Kate's blending of everyday and school literacies (in the latter cases promoted by disciplinary interventions like the National Writing Project and graduate courses in Writing Studies) have transformed the way they teach. We also imagine that Lisa, Dave, and Kate's laminated trajectories of pedagogical practice have the potential to transform the way their students encounter and engage with school literacy practices. Lisa's interweaving of discourses from her creative writing experiences as she conferences with her middle school students, for example, can enrich their strategies for revision and broaden their representations of literate activity. The interconnections Dave forges among his blog space, after-school club, and his classroom seem to be encouraging his students to create and maintain similar kinds of linkages and enriching their understanding of the multimodal dimension of literate action. Kate's use of her experiences with fan-fiction as grounds for her university writing syllabi and tasks can productively complicate her students' understanding of the distinctions between and hierarchies among vernacular and school-based literacies. Of course, Lisa, Dave, and Kate drew from some aspects of their everyday literate and semiotic resources to transform their teaching, but did not draw from everything or transform all dimensions of school life. Nevertheless, these case studies, in our view, argue for increased attention to the way linking teachers' pedagogical practices to their everyday literate engagements can open up opportunities for transformation, as well as critique, of classroom practice, and for more fully recognizing, valuing, and promoting such linkages as a key element in the production of pedagogical practice.

REFERENCES

Alsup, J. (2006). *Teacher identity discourses: Negotiating personal and professional spaces*. Mahwah, NJ: Lawrence Erlbaum Associates/National Council of Teachers of English.

Bakhtin, M. (1981). *The dialogic imagination* (C. Emerson & M. Holquist, Trans.). Austin, TX: University of Texas Press.

Barton, D., & Hamilton, M. (1998). *Local literacies: Reading and writing in one community.* London: Routledge.

Bourdieu, P. (1990). *The logic of practice.* Stanford, CA: Stanford University Press.

Britzman, D. P. (1991). *Practice makes practice: A critical study of learning to teach.* Albany: SUNY Press.

Burgess, A., & Ivanič, R. (2010). Writing and being written: Issues of identity across timescales. *Written Communication, (27),* 228-255.

Casanave, C., & Li, X. (2008). *Learning the literacy practices of graduate school: Insiders' reflections on academic enculturation.* Ann Arbor, MI: University of Michigan Press.

Didion, J. (1976, December 5). Why I write. *The New York Times Book Review,* pp. 98-99.

Drier, O. (1999). Personal trajectories of participation across contexts of social practice. *Outlines, 1,* 5-32.

Goffman, E. (1974). *Frame analysis: An essay on the organization of experience.* Boston: Northeastern University Press.

Goffman, E. (1981). *Forms of talk.* Philadelphia: University of Pennsylvania Press.

Holland, D., Lachicotte, W., Skinner, D., & Cain, C. (1998). *Identity and agency in cultural worlds.* Cambridge, MA: Harvard University Press.

Ivanič, R. (1998). *Writing and identity: The discoursal construction of identity in academic writing.* Amsterdam: John Benjamins Publishing Company.

Ivanič, R. (2009). Bringing literacy studies into research on learning across the curriculum. In M. Baynham & M. Prinsloo (Eds.), *The future of literacy studies* (pp. 100-122). Basingstoke, UK: Palgrave Macmillan Publishing.

Ivanič, R., & Satchwell, C. (2007). Boundary crossing: Networking and transforming literacies in research processes and college courses. *Journal of Applied Linguistics, 4,* 101-124.

Jenkins, H. (1992). *Textual poachers: Television fans and participatory culture.* New York: Routledge.

Latour, B. (2005). *Reassembling the social: An introduction to actor network theory.* Oxford, UK: Oxford University Press.

Lea, M., & Street, B. (1998). Student writing in higher education: An academic literacies approach. *Studies in Higher Education, 23,* 157-172.

Lemke, J. (2000). Across the scales of time: Artifacts, activities, and meanings in ecosocial systems. *Mind, Culture, and Activity, 7,* 273-290.

Lillis, T. (2001). *Student writing: access, regulation, desire.* London: Routledge.

Lillis, T., & Scott, M. (2007). Defining academic literacies research: Issues of epistemology, ideology and strategy. *Journal of Applied Linguistics, 4,* 5-32.

Pahl, K. (2008). Habitus in children's multimodal text-making: A discussion. In

M. Prinsloo & M. Baynham (Eds.), *Literacies, local and global.* Amsterdam: Johns Benjamins Publishing Company.

Prior, P. (1998). *Writing/disciplinarity: A sociohistoric account of literate activity in the academy.* Mahwah, NJ: Lawrence Erlbaum Associates.

Prior, P., & Hengst, J. (Eds.). (2010). *Exploring semiotic remediation as discourse practice.* New York: Palgrave Macmillan Publishing.

Prior, P., & Shipka, J. (2003). Chronotopic lamination: Tracing the contours of literate activity. In C. Bazerman & D. Russell (Eds.), *Writing selves, writing societies* (pp. 180-238). Fort Collins, CO: The WAC Clearinghouse/Parlor Press. Retrieved from http://wac.colostate.edu/books/selves_societies/

Richmond, G., Juzwick, M., & Steele, M. (2011). Trajectories of teacher identity development across institutional contexts: Constructing a narrative approach. *Teachers College Record, 113,* 1863-1905.

Roozen, K. (2009). "Fan fic-ing" English studies: A case study exploring the interplay of vernacular literacies and disciplinary engagement. *Research in the Teaching of English, 44,* 136-169.

Roozen, K. (2011). Polyliterate orientations: Mapping meshings of textual practice. In V. Young & A. Martinez (Eds.), *Code meshing as world English* (pp. 203-230). Urbana, IL: National Council of Teachers of English.

Scollon, R. (2001). *Mediated discourse: The nexus of practice.* London: Routledge.

Scollon, R. (2005). The rhythmic integration of action and discourse: Work, the body, and the earth. In S. Norris & R. H. Jones (Eds.), *Discourse in action: Introducing mediated discourse analysis* (pp. 20-31). London: Routledge.

Van Mannen, J. (1984). Doing new things in old ways: The chains of socialization. In J. Bess (Ed.), *College and university organization: Insights from the behavioural sciences* (pp. 211-247). New York: New York University Press.

Varghese, M., Morgan, B., Johnston, B., & Johnson, K. (2005). Theorizing language teacher identity: Three perspectives and beyond. *Journal of Language, Identity, and Education, 4,* 21-44.

Wenger, E. (1998). *Communities of practice: Learning, meaning, and identity.* Cambridge, UK: Cambridge University Press.

Wortham, S. (2006). *Learning identity: The joint emergence of social identification and academic learning.* Cambridge, UK: Cambridge University Press.

Yancey, K. (2009). *Writing in the 21st century: A report from the National Council of Teachers of English.* Urbana, IL: National Council of Teachers of English.

CHAPTER 16

MARKING THE BOUNDARIES: KNOWLEDGE AND IDENTITY IN PROFESSIONAL DOCTORATES

Jane Creaton

Writing is a central feature of all aspects of the doctoral process. Students are engaged in textual activities such as the taking of notes, the keeping of research diaries, the analysis of interview data and the preparation of reports and conference papers well before they write their thesis. Hence Barbara Kamler and Pat Thomson (2006, p. 4) conceptualize doctoral research as a continuous process of inquiry through writing, and for David Scott and Robin Usher (1996, p. 43) research is "writing and the production of a text." However, despite the dominance of writing in the process of knowledge production, the area of doctoral writing remains relatively under-theorized as a social practice. While there is a profusion of self-help and advice books on the market, most take a skills-based approach in which deficits in writing can be addressed through learning a set of decontextualized tips and techniques (Kamler & Thomson, 2004). This "study skills" model (Mary Lea & Brian Street, 1998) treats writing as a set of technical transferable skills, failing to recognize how academic writing practices are situated in wider social and institutional contexts. Although there are guides for supervisors (Kamler & Thomson, 2006) and students (Rowena Murray, 2011) which do acknowledge writing as a social practice, Claire Aitchison et al. (2012, p. 2) conclude that relatively little is known about "how doctoral students actually learn research writing, how supervisors 'teach' or develop the writing of their students and what happens to students and supervisors during this process."

In researching students' and supervisors' perspectives on doctoral writing, Aitchison, et al. (2012) found that both parties identified feedback as the primary mechanism through which students learned how to write. The nature and content of this feedback was crucial to the relationship between supervisor and student and to the development of the student's doctoral identity. In this chapter, the role of feedback in constructing doctoral writing practices is explored through an analysis of the written feedback given to doctoral students. Interviews with students and supervisors can provide some insight into the perceptions of, and attitudes to, feedback. However, previous research has identified an interesting disjuncture between what lecturers *did* and what they *said they did* in relation to marking and feedback (Barbara Read, Becky Francis & Jocelyn Robson, 2004; Frank Webster, David Pepper & Alan Jenkins, 2000). Furthermore, written feedback on student work is a specific genre of writing, which can itself be seen a social practice. It is therefore a productive site for the study of the educational discourses which staff engage with in making and justifying their responses to student writing.

This study is part of an ongoing practice-based project relating to the written feedback that is given to students in higher education. An earlier phase of the research analyzed samples of feedback from a range of units in an undergraduate criminology programme to consider how the feedback given to students were shaped by the departmental, disciplinary and institutional contexts (Creaton, 2011). This phase of the project analyzes feedback from a very different type of programme—a professional doctorate—which raises different, but equally interesting issues about the discourses which underpin marking and feedback. The chapter begins with an overview of the professional doctorate and then analyzes some of the key themes that emerge from an analysis of the written feedback that was given to students on the first stage of the programme. It then goes on to consider the implications of these findings for enhancing feedback practice and concludes with a discussion on the value of the academic literacies approach as a tool for pedagogical enhancement (see also Kaufhold Chapter 6 and Badenhorst et al. Chapter 7 this volume).

THE PROFESSIONAL DOCTORATE

The feedback analyzed for this study came from a professional doctorate in Criminal Justice (DCrimJ) programme offered by the Institute of Criminal Justice Studies at the University of Portsmouth. The Framework for Higher Education Qualifications does not distinguish between the PhD and the professional doctorate: both are awarded for "the creation and interpretation of new knowledge, through original research or other advanced scholarship, of a quality to satisfy peer review, extend the forefront of the discipline, and merit publication" (Quality Assurance Agency for Higher Education, 2008). However, there are some differences in the structure, delivery and ethos of the awards. Professional doctorate programmes usually include a series of taught modules as a precursor to the research phase and in the DCrimJ, students study four taught doctoral level units (Professional Review and Development, Advanced Research Techniques, Publication and Dissemination, Research Proposal) followed by a research project which culminates in a 50,000 word thesis. Students are required to be engaged in a relevant field of professional activity and in this programme, a wide range of criminal justice sector backgrounds are represented, including the police, probation, social work and the law. The teaching of the units is embedded in the criminal justice context and students link their assignments to their specific field of professional activity.

A professional doctorate programme was chosen partly for practical reasons—unlike the largely bilateral and private nature of feedback that is given by a PhD supervisor, the feedback that is given to professional doctorate students on the taught phase of programme is agreed between a first and second marker, scrutinized by an external examiner and retained for audit purposes. There was, therefore, an accessible source of naturally occurring data through which the conventions around academic and professional discourse could be interrogated. However, the professional doctorate is, in any event, a rich source of data for the investigation of discursive practices. David Boud and Mark Tennant (2006) note that the informal, situated and contingent knowledge generated through professional practice (Michael Eraut, 1994, 2000) can present some challenges for academic staff inducted in more formal disciplinary-based knowledge of the academy (Tony Becher & Paul Trowler, 2001). Whilst dispositional knowledge generated through reflection and reflective practice is well established in educational and health disciplines, it may be viewed with suspicion in disciplines located within a more positivist tradition. The multidisciplinary nature of criminology means that students and staff come to the DCrimJ with a range of different epistemological, theoretical and methodological perspectives. These are reflected in the written texts that are produced for assessment, and it is these texts and the responses to them, which are the subject of this chapter.

The sample comprised 63 assignments which were submitted by students in 2007-2011 for the Professional Review and Development module. This module is the first one that students take on entry to the programme and includes a critical review of the concepts of professionalism, professional practice and professional knowledge; reflective practice and an introduction to the philosophical underpinnings of research. Students are assessed through a three-part assignment which requires them to critique an academic journal article from the perspective of their professional practice; to provide a reflective account of their personal and professional journey to the professional doctorate and an assessment of their learning and development needs; and to critically analyze the concepts of professionalism, professional practice and professional knowledge within their own field.

The feedback that had been given on these assessments was uploaded to NVivo for coding and analysis. The first phase of coding was concerned with analyzing the comments at what Theresa Lillis (2008) terms the transparent/referential level. These included comments that staff made about student writing, particularly in relation to surface level features of the text. The second phase of coding focussed on the discursive/indexical level, looking at the linguistic features of the feedback indexing wider discourses. This chapter discusses two key themes which emerged from the analysis of the data: the relationship between professional and academic knowledge and the negotiation of doctoral identity.

KNOWLEDGE

Markers made a range of comments about aspects of students' writing, such as structure and referencing, which also featured in the undergraduate feedback from the first phase of the project. The most significant difference between the two samples was the markers' attitude to language which explicitly positioned the student within the text. In traditional undergraduate essays, markers strongly disapproved of students using the first person or making reference to their personal or professional knowledge or experience. From an academic literacies perspective, these conventions can be seen as having an ideological function beyond a simply stylistic preference. The exclusion of personal experience, the absence of the author in the text, the use of objective prose are all features of a dominant "essayist literacy," which privileges the discursive practices of particular social groups. Lillis (2001, p. 115), for example, found that the "institutional rejection" of personal experience was a particular issue for the student writers in her study, who felt marginalized by the lack of opportunities for drawing on their own lived experiences as a resource for meaning making within higher education.

However, aspects of the professional doctorate assignment required students to explicitly engage with their personal and professional perspectives. Markers also made it clear that, even in relation to the more conventionally academic aspects of the assignment, it was critical to position themselves as a practitioner:

> I think it would have added value to position yourself at the outset. As a police officer you would presumably take a particular view of this.

> ... although you allude to your profession right at the end, you have not explicitly stated why this article is of interest to you in your particular professional role/context.

Elizabeth Chiseri-Strater (1996, p. 127) suggests that locating oneself assertively and deliberately within a text reflects ethical, rhetorical and theoretical choices on the part of the researcher. However, for students, these choices are often determined by wider disciplinary and institutional constraints. In the case of the professional doctorate, the deliberate foregrounding of both the personal and the professional can be seen as disrupting some of the traditional epistemological and disciplinary boundaries and practices which have applied in dominant academic writing contexts. Acknowledging the legitimacy of professional and personal knowledge requires a reconsideration of the academic writing practices which are entwined with the particular type of disciplinary knowledge generated in the academy. It can also make explicit the function that writing and feedback practices serve in reinforcing power relationships and existing patterns of knowledge construction.

IDENTITY

A second key theme which emerged from the analysis of the feedback was how tutors positioned themselves in relation to the students through the feedback that they gave. Markers often addressed the students by name and made extensive use of the second person to frame their comments. A more intimate relationship between the marker and the student was also established through the use of other metadiscoursal features. The use of hedges and tentative language was prominent, with markers using phrases such as "would have liked," "wondered if," or "possibly" when discussing areas of possible omission or further discussion. Even where there were areas of disagreement, phrases such as "I'm not sure that I agree," or "I'm not entirely convinced" were used. The feedback was also noticeable for the extent of personal engagement that markers had with the text. There were examples of markers responding to points in the student essays with anecdotes from their own professional experience, drawing on examples from their current research or sharing their perspectives on the doctoral journey. There were also numerous expressions of pleasure and enjoyment in reading the students' work and in the prospect of working with the student in the future.

The pedagogical discourses employed by members of staff on this course are in significant contrast to those at undergraduate level, where feedback was written in a largely impersonal tone, was more authoritative in nature and disclosed little about the marker's own position. These differences suggest a renegotiation of the identities of students and markers at doctorate level. At undergraduate level, there is usually a very clear difference in status and expertise between the staff and student, which is reinforced through the form and language of the feedback genre. However, professional doctoral students often occupy senior positions within the criminal justice sector and have embarked on the programme with the intention of becoming "researching professionals" rather than "professional researchers." The student may be seeking academic recognition of their existing professional knowledge and experience rather than an apprenticeship to the academy. The language used in the feedback reflects the different nature of the relationship in which knowledge is exchanged rather than simply validated.

IMPLICATIONS FOR PRACTICE

Mary Lea & Brian Street (2006) argue that the academic literacies approach has both theoretical and practical value—as a heuristic model for understanding literacy practices and as a framework for curriculum development, training programmes and personal reflection and development. How then can the evidence from this research project inform current practice in approaches to marking and feedback more generally?

Firstly, a close analysis of the feedback that staff give to students can provide useful evidence to monitor and inform assessment practices. Royce Sadler (2005, p. 192) argues that the focus on making assessment criteria transparent is misplaced, because the difficulties in defining terms precisely simply "sets up new verbal terms that in turn call for more elaboration, and so on in infinite regress." A more productive approach, he suggests, is to identify the norms of the assessment community through a close examination of the nature of, and reasons for, the actual marking decisions made by tutors. Through this inductive process it should be possible to identify and convey to students the standards which are embedded in the tacit knowledge of a particular localised assessment community.

Arguably, however, these strategies may simply reinforce existing patterns of knowledge construction and representation within the academy. A central criticism of the communities of practice approach is that issues of power, authority, and structure tend to be unacknowledged and under-theorized. The approach does not account for how particular groups of students may be excluded or marginalized from the process of legitimate peripheral participation (Romy Clark & Roz Ivanic, 1997; Lillis, 2001) or how dominant literacy practices may serve as a barrier to engagement rather than as a shared resource (Lea, 2005). The development of a more coherent set of shared standards may make for fairer assessment practices, but does not challenge the role of the university in defining and reifying particular forms of literacy practices.

Thus, Lillis (2003) argues for a more radical transformation of pedagogical practice. She uses Mikhail Bakhtin's work as a theoretical framework through which to argue for a shift away from monologic approaches that privilege the single authoritative voice of the tutor and towards dialogic approaches which include a range of discourses and voices. Practical examples of this approach include: "talkback" rather than feedback on students' written texts, opening up disciplinary content to a wider range of external interests and influences, and opening up academic writing conventions to new and different ways of knowing. This, she argues, is the crucial step through which an academic literacies approach can shift from a theoretical frame to a pedagogical frame.

A second practical implication of this research relates to staff development. A starting point would be to have course-level or programme-level discussions in relation to establishing what views are in relation to acceptable forms of knowledge and representation practices within the discipline. What sources of knowledge are acceptable within the discipline and is there a preferred hierarchy? For example, should students be looking for theoretical support or to empirical evidence in the first instance? When looking for sources of evidence, are particular types ruled in or out, for example internet sources, or newspapers? This exercise is not necessarily expected to result in a consensus which can apply across all units and disciplines—

it is a rare discipline indeed where a course team would be able to agree on all of these issues. However, it provides the basis upon which to share some of this tacit knowledge with students and to highlight or flag up areas where there might be lack of consensus or certainty.

Another strategy for explicating some of this tacit knowledge would be the analysis of written feedback that is given to students within a particular unit or course. Discourse and/or conversation analysis provides a useful way to identify underlying assumptions and conventions in particular contexts. It provides an opportunity for questioning hegemonic or conventional practices within the discipline and for showing how taken-for-granted practices can be explored and made visible. It also has the advantage of enabling discussions about shared aims and tacit assumptions to be had without identifying or singling out particular members of staff. These practical strategies to uncover some of the tacit knowledge underpinning judgements about marking and feedback might provide valuable information about the norms, conventions and practices of the discipline that can then be shared with students. Alternatively Ann Johns' (1997) work on "students as researchers" suggests a way of getting students to investigate the academic setting in which they are writing and the values and expectations which underlie the texts they are being asked to produce.

In the context of the professional doctorate, the application of the academic literacies approach suggests a number of ways in which feedback and assessment practices could be reviewed. There is evidence of markers encouraging students to reconsider their academic writing practices and in developing different types of feedback relationships. However, the giving of feedback remains a largely private and monologic process and the final assessment—a thesis and viva—is the same as for the traditional doctorate. This might be seen as evidence of what David Scott, Andrew Brown, Ingrid Lunt and Lucy Thorne (2004) see as evidence of a "colonization" model in which dominant academic modes of representing knowledge take precedence over other methods of communication and dissemination. Tom Maxwell (2003) suggests that this is characteristic of "first generation" professional doctorates, which tend to conform to existing institutional doctoral practices. However, as professional doctorates become more established, he suggests that "second generation" doctorates offer a more radical potential to reshape the academic and professional partnerships. This might be reflected in the development of alternative forms of feedback, for example, dialogic feedback within the professional doctorate cohort as a whole; alternative forms of written representations, for example, practice based reports; and alternative forms of assessment, for example, a portfolio of evidence.

CONCLUSION

The example of the professional doctorate shows how an academic literacies approach can connect academic writing and feedback to wider discourses around knowledge and identity. The analysis of the feedback given on professional doctorates suggests that feedback practices are epistemological, in that they involve judgements about what counts as valid knowledge in the department, discipline or the academy. They are also ideological, in that they are implicated in reinforcing existing patterns of power and privilege. Given the crucial gatekeeping function of marking and feedback, an understanding of how academic staff construct the boundaries of appropriate knowledge and identities and the extent to which they may allow them to be contested, is key to an effective theorization and teaching of academic writing.

CODA: FEEDBACK TO THE AUTHOR FROM THE AUTHOR

Dear Jane,

This was an interesting and enjoyable read. However, it was interesting to note that, despite the implied critique of traditional academic writing conventions, this piece was written largely in accordance with those very conventions. So for example, it is written in the third person and you have avoided positioning yourself explicitly in the text. However, your own experience does seem very relevant—you are a member of the course team for the programme which is the focus of the research study and you even wrote some of the feedback that you analyzed as part of the project! I think it might also have been worth mentioning that you completed a professional doctorate yourself and encountered some of the same difficulties in negotiating the boundaries between the professional and the academic with which these students are grappling. Isn't it the case that your identities as course team member, marker and (ex)student will give you a particular perspective on these issues?

The fact that you have found it difficult to write outside the genre (despite the active encouragement of the editors of this volume to do so) illustrates the problems that are likely to be encountered in encouraging changes to deep-seated academic writing practices. A first step may be to set tasks which involve a standard written assignment but which encourage students to provide some interaction of commentary on the text (for example, asking students to write a couple of feedback paragraphs on an assignment; using the comment function to provide commentaries on the text). This allows students to produce conventional academic text but which also enables some engagement with and critique of the processes through which it is produced. Maybe you should consider something similar with this chapter?

REFERENCES

Aitchison, C., Catterall, J., Ross, P., & Burgin, S. (2012). "Tough love and tears": Learning doctoral writing in the sciences. *Higher Education Research & Development*, 1-13.

Becher, T., & Trowler, P. (2001). *Academic tribes and territories.* Buckingham, UK: Society for Research into Higher Education.

Boud, D., & Tennant, M. (2006). Putting doctoral education to work: Challenges to academic practice. *Higher Education Research & Development, 25*(3), 293-306.

Chiseri-Strater, E. (1996). Turning in upon ourselves: Positionality, subjectivity, and reflexivity in case study and ethnographic research. *Ethics and representation in qualitative studies of literacy,* 115-133.

Clark, R., & Ivanic, R. (1997). *The politics of writing.* London: Routledge.

Creaton, J. (2011). *Policing the boundaries: The writing, representation and regulation of criminology.* (Doctoral thesis).University of Sussex, Brighton, UK.

Eraut, M. (1994). *Developing Professional Knowledge and Competence.* London: Falmer Press.

Eraut, M. (2000). Non-formal learning and tacit knowledge in professional work. *British Journal of Educational Psychology, 70*(1), 113-136.

Johns, A. (1997). *Text, role and context.* Cambridge, UK: Cambridge University Press.

Kamler, B., & Thomson, P. (2004). Driven to abstraction: Doctoral supervision and writing pedagogies. *Teaching in Higher Education, 9*(2), 195-209.

Kamler, B., & Thomson, P. (2006). *Helping doctoral students write: Pedagogies for supervision.* London: Routledge.

Lea, M. (2005). Communities of practice in higher education: Useful heuristic or educational model. In D. Barton & K. Tusting (Eds.), *Beyond communities of practice* (pp. 180-197). Cambridge, UK: Cambridge University Press.

Lea, M., & Street, B. (1998). Student writing in higher education: An academic literacies approach. *Studies in Higher Education, 23*(2), 157-172.

Lea, M., & Street, B. (2006). The "academic literacies" model: Theory and applications. *Theory into Practice, 45*(4), 368-377.

Lillis, T. (2001). *Student writing: Access, regulation, desire.* London: Routledge.

Lillis, T. (2003). Student writing as "academic literacies": Drawing on Bakhtin to move from critique to design. *Language and Education, 17*(3), 192-207.

Lillis, T. (2008). Ethnography as method, methodology, and "deep theorizing": Closing The gap between text and context in academic writing research. *Written Communication, 25*(3), 353.

Maxwell, T. (2003). From first to second generation professional doctorate. *Studies in Higher Education, 28*(3), 279-291.

Murray, R. (2011). *How to write a thesis* (3rd ed.). Buckingham, UK: Open University Press.

Quality Assurance Agency for Higher Education. (2008). *The framework for higher education qualifications in England, Wales, and Northern Ireland.* Gloucester, UK: The Quality Assurance Agency for Higher Education.

Read, B., Francis, B., & Robson, J. (2004). Re-viewing undergraduate writing:

tutors' perceptions of essay qualities according to gender. *Research in Post-Compulsory Education, 9*(2), 217-238.

Sadler, R. (2005). Interpretations of criteria-based assessment and grading in higher education. *Assessment & Evaluation in Higher Education, 30*(2), 175-194.

Scott, D., & Usher, R. (1996). *Understanding educational research*. London: Routledge.

Scott, D., Brown, A., Lunt, I., & Thorne, L. (2004). *Professional doctorates: integrating professional and academic knowledge*. Maidenhead: McGrawHill Education.

Webster, F., Pepper, D. & Alan Jenkins (2000). Assessing the Undergraduate Dissertation. *Assessment & Evaluation in Higher Education, 25*(1), 71-80.

REFLECTIONS 3
WHAT'S AT STAKE
IN DIFFERENT TRADITIONS?
LES LITTÉRACIES UNIVERSITAIRES
AND ACADEMIC LITERACIES

Isabelle Delcambre in conversation with Christiane Donahue

Isabelle Delcambre is Professor Emeritus at the Université de Lille, France and a member of the Théodile-CIREL laboratory. Christiane Donahue is Associate Professor of Linguistics, Director of the Institute for Writing and Rhetoric, Dartmouth College, US, and a member of the Théodile-CIREL laboratory. Isabelle and Christiane have worked together, exploring university writing in France and the United States via exchanges and shared projects, and have been learning about writing research and teaching in each others' contexts for some twelve years. They have published together and separately on these topics, in particular as the result of a three-year study of French university student writing across disciplines, led by Isabelle.

Christiane: You have been at the forefront of research about writing in secondary and postsecondary education in France for decades (e.g., Delcambre 1997). What is the current status of post-secondary writing research and teaching in France?

Isabelle: Many research fields study *university practices*—this question is within that context. Aspects that have long been studied include the role of meta-cognition in university success, and sociological studies (e.g., Pierre Bourdieu & Jean-Claude Passeron, 1964) about students' trajectories and socialization, their failure in the first years, their modes of living and studying, etc. Studies of writing at university, the genres produced there and the forms of continued learning of writing in university contexts have contributed to establishing this larger area of university practices as a field, *la pédagogie universitaire*. In particular, the focus has been on supporting students' entry into a "writing universe." Not all college writing is in the form of exams for evaluation. We have asked ourselves, who are students? Future professionals? Future academics seeking knowledge? Who are faculty? Teachers or researchers?

This diversity of purposes for writing indicates a diversity of practices. Possibly, a student who writes as a future professional encounters different genres and difficulties from those encountered by a future academic seeking knowledge; the same is true for faculty. Descriptions of academic genres in a rhetorical or functional vein dominated in the 1990s in France. Yves Reuter (1998) was the first to theorize the question of student writers and their difficult relationship to academic writing. The question of the author's identity, or the enunciative perspective on writing appears much later in our research discussions (see the work on "writerly images," Isabelle Delcambre & Yves Reuter, 2002). The current focus on authorship from an enunciative standpoint is the focus of other research groups in France, most notably the Grenoble group (cf. Françoise Boch & Fanny Rinck, 2010).

Christiane: Tell me about your first encounter with "Academic Literacies"?

Isabelle: I discovered the debates between Jack Goody (e.g., 1977, 1986) and Brian Street (e.g., 1995) in the 1990s. I was first influenced by Goody's theory about writing and the construction of thinking that writing provides; and then I heard of Brian Street's work, incidentally, and I was somewhat astonished that Goody's theories could be challenged. That shows the intellectual domination of Goody's theories in France at that time for researchers, who were not so well informed about research abroad. Later, during a major research project funded by the French government, I met many colleagues from AcLits, and read their essays, discussed with them, and so on …

Christiane: What points of shared interest did you find in these discussions?

Isabelle: I was first astonished (and a bit envious) when I encountered the well-established importance of university writing research in AcLits. In those years in France, very few people were interested in such questions, apart from those who developed a "technical skills" point of view on students' difficulties (less frequent nowadays, with the development of "pédagogie universitaire"). The AcLits search for explanations of students' difficulties by the means of concepts such as social practices, identity, power, empowerment and transformation met, in my opinion, our didactic points of view on attitudes towards writing ("rapport à l'écriture"), representations (of writing, of the self as a writer, of knowledge, etc.) and disciplinary awareness (for all these concepts, see Yves Reuter et al., 2013).

But some of these concepts do not receive quite the same definition. For example, *social practices* seem to be, for didacticians, more a range of determinations (historical, cultural and personal) and less a high-stakes object of negotiation, power or struggle. In the same way, when we talk about *representation* there have always been questions about what was intended. In fact, in Educational Sciences, this term, borrowed from social psychology, is quite ordinary, referring to the ideas that people construct about writing processes, writing's functions, its objectives and so on.

In addition, it seems that for AcLits *social practices* applies to social contexts as well as to academic contexts, with the same reference to power and domination (see Street et al., Reflections 5 this volume). In didactics, too, practices are understood both at the university level and in the social world, but I think that didacticians have focused on the influence or relationship between the social and the school world, even in the most ordinary practices of writing. The concept of "pratiques sociales de référence" (referential social practices) proposed by Jean Louis Martinand (1986), a didactician of technology, is often used to understand the distance between school genres and socially grounded genres when accounting for the difficulties students may encounter when trying to fulfill school expectations. Many conflicts or tensions could happen between these different kinds of practices.

Christiane: The term you have developed in French research is littéracies universitaires—university literacies; what are the roots of that term?

Isabelle: This field brings together two long-term research traditions, didactics and linguistics, to describe practices and written genres in university contexts (though certainly other fields come into play—psychology, cognition, ethnography …). "Literacy" emphasizes the contextual, social and cultural aspects of reading and writing.

The intellectual history of the term "literacy" in France includes: Goody (1977, 1986) as a point of departure (thus shared in some ways with UK developments); Françoise Boch et al. (2004) offered attention to university writing in a sustained way, both theoretically and in terms of practices, but not yet using the term "literacy"; Jean Marie Privat and Mohamed Kara in 2006 published "La littéracie," reflecting on the anglo-saxon tradition of the term; Kara developed "Les écrits de savoir" in 2009, reflecting on the heuristic functions of writing in research disciplines.

In a different vein, Béatrice Fraenkel and Aïssatou Mbodj (2010) developed the social and cultural senses of literacy extensively, introducing in France the New Literacy Studies work, translating foundational pieces such as Sylvia Scribner and Michael Cole (1981) and focusing primarily on the ethnological dimensions of New Literacy Studies.

A new name was needed for this new research field with its particular data, its multidisciplinarity, its methods and concepts. "Littéracies" allows an echo of "academic literacies" given the shared ground and objects of attention; it allows at the same time attention to what is different. It also allows an essential connection to disciplinary and institutional contexts in the elaboration of practices, but avoids the link to "académique," seen in French as negative, pretentious, formal; "university literacies" is an institutional sphere of discourse production.

Christiane: Why not just "didactics of university French"? Why "literacies"?

Isabelle: "Didactics of French" generally refers to the analysis of teaching and learning French as a language, or to remedial practices; it does not generally take up the epistemological and discursive activities of writing. A "didactics of writing" would be meaningless in a French university, in contrast to what US composition theory had to create when it separated from/opposed English literature as a university department and discipline. Because the discipline "French" does not exist in universities (neither for teaching nor for research), references to a "didactics of university French" would seem rather to be linked to French as a school subject.

Why do you think didactics has not developed as a field in Anglo-Saxon traditions? What are (if there are) the specificities of didactics from your point of view? To what extent is it possible to link them in the American panorama? Or maybe it is impossible?

Christiane: This is complex. "Didactics" as a field does not indeed seem to exist in at least US Anglo-Saxon traditions. We have Education and we have research in pedagogy, directly informing our teaching. Didactics seems, to me, to fit the research tradition that resists "applicationism" (by which I mean applying research results immediately to pedagogical contexts seeking practical applications) in favor of research that is more detached from the direct realities of teaching. Thus, didactics of, say, science, focuses on the theory of science teaching and learning as a research discipline. This gets complicated for writing; if we discuss a "didactics of writing" we are positing writing as a discipline. And so, here is a strong link to Composition Studies or Writing Studies in the United States, which takes as its object the teaching and learning of university writing as a discipline. Where does "Ac Lits" fit within these framings I wonder?

Isabelle: Unlike "university literacies," whose emergence is linked more to the extension into university levels of the research questions and themes that had been constructed for secondary and primary education writing research (didactics of French), from my point of view, AcLits came about as a specific area of New Literacy Studies, in order to describe non traditional students' literacies or literacies associated with new practices (distance learning, new media), and with a critical vision with respect to the implicit norms and ways of working of the traditional university. As I understand it, AcLits seeks to understand the specific terrain of the university; it studies relationships to writing; non-native speakers' encounters with UK university writing; transformation of practices of writing linked to digital environments; distance learning and writing; relationships between personal and university writing; scholars' writing practices. It supports thinking about university writing as mobilizing relationships of power and forms of identity construction in which students' writing practices are caught; it develops, in response, a critique of academic writing conventions and attends to different disciplinary contexts. How do you generally understand AcLits in relation to your US domain?

Christiane: For me, US-style "first-year composition" has many of the features that AcLits has developed in terms of writing in the university at large, in the disciplines and beyond. That is, in the United States we have tended to think of the first year of college writing as the site of negotiation and resistance. In the theorizing and analysis of this work, we have sought to understand transformative practices in these contexts. The domain of disciplinary writing has settled far more squarely into an integrative model with a sense of norms and conventions, even as it has argued for writing as transforming the knowledge of the discipline (see also discussion in Russell and Mitchell Reflections 2 this volume). One of the recent trends in US writing scholarship, the "writing knowledge transfer" research, is relevant here in a lateral way. The idea of writing knowledge "transfer" was initially focused on what students learn that can be re-used in subsequent tasks and contexts. What's interesting is that the goal of integration is more appropriate for the "transfer" model, while knowledge "transformation," given the dynamic nature of learning and growth, works with appropriation, negotiation, resistance, critical reflection, metacognitive reshaping.

Isabelle: I'm thinking now about the connections and differences between what we refer to as "university literacies" and "Ac Lits." University literacies does not focus on multimodal or new media literacies, at least not yet. To date, university literacies has remained a research field without engaging much with pedagogical practice, while AcLits has engaged both with teaching practices and broader institutional practices. This is perhaps due to the structure of French universities (where faculty are more professors and lecturers than "simple" teachers) and to the dominant contempt for pedagogy (due to faculty evaluation models, which do not give credit for pedagogical activities).

Perhaps most important: AcLits analyzes students' resistance to university acculturation, reflects on questions of power relations and authority in writing practices, and seeks perhaps even to encourage these resistances; university literacies' point of departure is not ideological but descriptive (the descriptive analysis of university discourses and students'/teachers' representations).

Transformation in the sense of challenging or resisting dominant conventions is not the goal of university literacies, at least not to date. Transformation at whatever level—i.e., opening up debate about what kinds of language/s, conventions, semiotic resources can be used at university, is not important to university literacies. University literacies does not have a critical stance towards practices of writing or evaluation, unlike French didactics in secondary school in the 1980s, which deconstructed traditional writing exercises and was highly critical of the practices underlying these exercises (see Jean-François Halté, 1992, for example). University literacies is far too underdeveloped, far too institutionally "weak" to be transformative in this way. That said, French didactics took 15 years to transform secondary school writing practices, and even today, traditional practices resurface periodically in some contexts.

Christiane: So, transforming the university itself and its writing practices is not within the current goals of university literacies. But perhaps university literacies seeks to transform the students' experiences of entering a universe that is in many ways foreign to what they have known until now? To listen to and understand those experiences? To unseat the dominant view of "writing" as "micro-linguistic competencies," especially in light of the changing international nature of language demands? Doesn't "university literacies" seek to transform, in a way, the French university?

Isabelle: Yes, for sure. University Literacies is grounded in the idea that students get to the university with writing knowledge and practices that must transform in order to enter into the disciplinary writing practices that they will progressively discover throughout the curriculum. And also in the idea that it is the responsibility of faculty to accompany students in these discoveries, rather than to hope that someday such accompanying will no longer be needed. The ANR research project (e.g. Delcambre and Donahue, 2010, 2012; Isabelle Delcambre & Dominique Lahanier -Reuter, 2010) showed how much the transition from the undergraduate level to the master's level profoundly transforms students' conceptions. They talk at length about the new writing challenges they find as they write their master's theses. University Literacies supports the idea that learning writing is an ongoing task. In that sense, we can say that University Literacies has a transformative approach, based on empirical research that allows descriptions of students' and teachers' representations and creates an understanding of the conditions needed for fruitful dialogue between these two groups.

Christiane: I'm also thinking that critical discourse analysis—used in Ac Lits and all about power and authority—has specific, deep roots in French theory?

Isabelle: Yes, but the French theory (Pierre Bourdieu and Jean Passeron, 1964; Bourdieu 1998; Michel Foucault, 1971), which is the roots of CDA and used in Ac Lits is not discussed in the French university contexts from where "littéracies universitaires" emerges (as you showed in your paper with Cinthia Gannett, John Brereton, Theresa Lillis and Mary Scott—see Donahue et al., 2009). Even if, in France, Bourdieu is central in sociology, and Foucault in philosophy and literature, the fields of didactics, linguistics and even sociolinguistics are not really influenced by Foucault and Bourdieu …

However French university literacies does include attention to social context and status, student success, etc.: Bourdieu and Passeron, for example (with their extensive focus on social selection, social reproduction), are always on the horizon of studies of university students' writing. As an effect of the disciplinary organization of the French university, a current rule is not to trespass on others' research domain. Thus, sociological studies are used as contributions to didactics inquiry ("disciplines contributoires," Reuter et al., 2013), not as main references. Yves Reuter does theorize the notion of "tension" as a distinctive feature of writing practices—and this notion can be seen as not so far away from notions of resistance and negotiation. However, tensions in writing are often presented as a way to understand students' difficulties and to help them to resolve these tensions, to modify their attitude towards texts and academic writing. In my opinion, they are not presented as an occasion to modify the academic world or conventions, or only in a very "light touch" and individual way.

There are shared interests between Ac Lits and Univ Lits in the attention given to making visible the implicit expectations of university work, crystallized in a set of rules; it is a complex adaptation for students moving into the postsecondary world; students must "affiliate" with the world of the university, and secondary education cannot prepare them—given the decoding they must do. Seeing it this way means students are not "missing" something but are in a social negotiation. Teachers' and students' representations aren't compatible.

But there are differences between Univ Lits and Ac Lits: university literacies currently focuses on the need to describe textual objects generally practiced in university fields and studies; to identify their specificities (especially those with which students have difficulty) to facilitate learning and appropriation; to deal with difficulties often associated with new genres, new practices, and the distance between students' written culture and university written culture.

Christiane: How might the plural "literacies" be important to both Ac Lits and University Literacies?

Isabelle: It signifies the multiple social and cultural practices in play. It challenges the idea that literacy is an individual (isolated) cognitive act, as Lea and Street noted in 1998. It allows us to signal that literacy is always linked to social and cultural practices of reading and writing in particular contexts (disciplines too).

Christiane: What questions do you have for the future of University Literacies and of Academic Literacies?

Isabelle: Currently, the creation of the "ESPE" (Ecoles supérieures du professorat et de l'éducation), which take the place of the former teacher-training institutions inside the universities, is an opportunity for many university structures to think about writing programmes, first for the teachers-to-be, and then, I hope, for all the students …. There are also some universities that are thinking about writing support programmes aimed at PhD students who are "moniteurs," as it was a tradition in the former CIES (Centres d'initiation à l'enseignement supérieur). These "monitors" were, from 1989 to 2009, doctoral students who were paid to learn to become university professors and received a particular training while they covered the small-group work sessions of university courses. Currently doctoral candidates do this work, but they are no longer trained in a consistent way: what individual universities do depends on the political decisions made in each university.

Will we see a didactics of university disciplines taking shape, as scholars like Francis Grossmann and Yves Reuter have suggested in a 2012 issue of *Pratiques*? If it does, it is likely that a deeper reflection on epistemological dimensions of university writing practices will develop. In the same way that didactics of disciplines in secondary school thought through their uses of writing and the specific issues with writing (not just in French but in the sciences, history, mathematics), university disciplines need to elucidate their uses of writing and their textual practices, beyond the narrow level of linguistic micro-skills.

As far as AcLits is concerned, we are very intrigued in France by the questions it asks. The French context does not yet seem ready for some of these questions. But the University Literacies aspects I've just mentioned seem in some ways quite shared with AcLits: deeper reflection on epistemological dimensions of university writing, for example, or deeper understanding of the fluid nature of genres that are adopted and adapted by different university populations.

REFERENCES

Boch, F., Laborde-Milaa, I., & Reuter, Y. (Eds.). (2004). *Pratiques*, n°121-122, *Les écrits universitaires*.

Boch, F., & Rinck, F. (Eds.). (2010). Issue: Énonciation et rhétorique dans l'écrit scientifique. *LIDIL, 41*.

Bourdieu, P., & Passeron, J. C. (1964). *Les héritiers*. Paris: Editions du Minuit.

Bourdieu, P. (1998). *State nobility: Elite schools in the field of power*. Cambridge, UK: Polity.

Delcambre I. (1997). *L'exemplification dans les dissertations. Etude didactique des difficultés des élèves*. Villeneuve d'Ascq, FR: Presses Universitaires du Septentrion.

Delcambre I. & Lahanier-Reuter D. (2010). Les littéracies universitaires: Influence des disciplines et du niveau d'étude dans les pratiques de l'écrit, *Diptyque* n° 18, *L'appropriation des discours universitaires*, Namur, BE: Presses Universitaires de Namur, p. 11-42. Retrieved from http://www.forumlecture.ch/sysModules/obxLeseforum/Artikel/431/Les-litteracies-universitaires.pdf

Delcambre, I., & Donahue, C. (2011). University literacies: French students at a disciplinary "threshold"? *Journal of Academic Writing, 1*(1), 13-28. Retrieved from http://e-learning.coventry.ac.uk/ojs/index.php/joaw/article/view/6/47

Delcambre, I., & Donahue, C. (2012). Academic writing activity: Student writing in transition. In M. Castelló & C. Donahue (Eds.), *Studies in Writing:Vol. 24.University writing: Selves and texts in academic societies.* (pp. 129-149). Bingley, UK: Emerald Group Publishing.

Delcambre, I., & Lahanier-Reuter, D. (Eds.). (2012). *Pratiques 153-154, Littéracies universitaires: nouvelles perspectives.*

Delcambre I., & Reuter, Y. (Eds.). (2002). *Pratiques,* n° 113-114*, Images du scripteur et rapport à l'écriture.*

Delcambre I. & Reuter, Y. (2010). The French didactics approach to writing, from elementary school to university. In C. Bazerman et al. (Eds.), *Traditions of writing research* (pp. 17-30). New York and London: Routledge, Taylor & Francis.

Donahue, C., Brereton, J., Gannett, C., Lillis, T., & Scott, M. (2009). La circulation de perspectives socioculturelles états-uniennes et britanniques: Traitements de l'écrit dans le supérieur? In B. Daunay, I. Delcambre, & Y. Reuter (Eds.) *Didactique du Français: Le socioculturel en question.* Villeneuve d'Ascq, FR: Presses Universitaires du Septentrion.

Foucault, M. (1966). *Les mots et les choses—une archéologie des sciences humaines* Paris: Gallimard.

Foucault, M. (1971). *L'ordre du discours.* Paris: Gallimard.

Fraenkel, B., & Mbodj, A. (2010). Introduction. Les new literacy studies, jalons historiques et perspectives actuelles. *Langage et société, 133,* 7-24.

Goody, J. (1977). *The domestication of the savage mind.* Cambridge, UK: Cambridge University Press.

Goody, J. (1986). *The logic of writing and the organization of society.* Cambridge, UK: Cambridge University Press.

Grossman, F. (2012). Pourquoi et comment cela change? Standardization et variation dans le champ des discours scientifiques. *Pratiques 153-154,* 141-160.

Halté, J. F. (1992). *La didactique du Français.* Paris: Presses Universitaires de France.

Kara, M. (Ed.). (2009). *Pratiques, 143-144, Ecrits de savoir*

Martinand, J. L. (1986). *Connaître et transformer la matière.* Bern, CH: Peter Lang Publishing Group.

Privat, J. M., & Kara, M. (Eds.). (2006). *Pratiques, 131-132, La littéracie. Autour de Jack Goody.*

Reuter, Y. (1998). De quelques obstacles à l'écriture de recherche. *Lidil, 17,* 11-23.

Reuter, Y. (2012). Les didactiques et la question des literacies universitaires. *Pratiques,* 153-154, 161-176.

Reuter, Y., Cohen-Azria C., Daunay B., Delcambre I., & Lahanier-Reuter D. (Eds.). (2013) *Dictionnaire des concepts fondamentaux des didactiques.* Bruxelles: De Boeck, 3rd edition.

Scribner, S., & Cole, M. (1981). *The psychology of literacy.* Cambridge, MA: Harvard University Press.

Street, B. V. (1995). *Social literacies: Critical approaches to literacy in development, ethnography and education*. London: Longman.

SECTION 3
TRANSFORMING RESOURCES, GENRES AND SEMIOTIC PRACTICES

INTRODUCTION TO SECTION 3

This section of the book picks up the central concerns of the volume both in providing exemplars of how the transformative approach is being instantiated in practice and in foregrounding how Academic Literacies can engage generatively with other theories which inform approaches to writing. It focuses in particular on the "semiotic stuff" of writing for knowledge making with an emphasis on changing textual and semiotic practices in society more widely and the implications of these for text creation and meaning making. Although the contributions in this section range widely in terms of both approach and contexts, they all point to the transformative possibilities in the work they describe. Whilst some focus upon the theoretical underpinnings necessary for understanding emergent textual configurations, challenging our taken-for-granted assumptions about what we value, others provide detailed accounts and/or personal reflections of practice around supporting student writers. In three of the contributions the "digital" offers an organizing frame with regard to the changing status of knowledge and the potential for engaging in transformative practices for both readers and writers. All offer a window onto everyday work that we hope will inspire readers to scrutinize and rethink some of their/our own practices.

Fiona English takes a close lens to the notion of genre, arguing that we need to move on from identifying the features of genres and teaching these to students. Her research indicates that our concern should be with what genres can actually *do* and how they come to shape our thinking and our knowledge production. Her interest is in how a transformative academic literacies perspective can underpin both classroom activity and theory with respect to genre pedagogy. For English, genre is no longer merely a pedagogic goal but becomes a pedagogic resource. Illustrating this move, she offers examples of what she calls "regenring" and explains what happened when her students reworked their essays using a range of different genres. This not only made visible how genres work but impacted on student's disciplinary knowledge, engagement and understanding. English's approach shows how an academic literacies perspective can actively engage with other theoretical traditions to transform how we might think about writing work. As she points out, genre work in writing pedagogy is drawn from a range of theoretical traditions but there is a danger that when these become translated into practice the focus for students is on the reproduction of genres and, therefore, of knowledge. In contrast, "regenring" draws in the academic literacies frame, theoretically and methodologically, and helps student to engage at the level of epistemology (thus revealing the transformative nature of what she proposes), so that students can become producers of knowledge.

Lynn Coleman also extends the theoretical lens in offering a further illustration of how academic literacies can engage generatively with other traditions. She does this through a detailed exploration of the semiotic practices that emerge when sets of practices drawn from the contrasting contexts of industry and academia are brought together in a graphic design course. Her interest is in broader structuring processes and how texts come to be within the curriculum, arguing that combining academic literacies research and Bernsteinian perspectives can help us to understand how curricula, subjects and assessment practices are constructed. In this respect she explores "scamping," a term used in graphic design which refers to the process of making ideas visible through creating a drawing or sketch. She highlights the literacy practices that support scamping and uses Bernstein's concept of recontextualization to illuminate how these practices emerge from bringing together those from both professional and academic domains. She argues that we can track the privileging of particular literacy practices as professional-based practices intersect with and become transformed by academic-informed values and practices.

The transformative possibilities of visual representation are at the heart of Fay Stevens' chapter as she explores the value of collaborative journal writing in relation to issues of self and identity. Her concern is with the potential of collaborative journals for both individual and collective transformation. She contrasts students' expression of loss of identity and lack of creativity in their assessed academic writing with their experience of contributing to a collective journal and being able to represent who they felt they were or wanted to be. Stevens provides examples of the richness, diversity and combination of text type and image in this collaborative, social and creative space. Although contrasting strongly with the academic writing tasks with which they are more familiar, contributing to the journal appears to have enabled the students to develop an awareness of self, both in relation to being at university more generally and being a writer in a particular discipline. The entries created by the students suggest that image is central to this process of transformation and meaning making. In addition, Stevens draws on a range of theoretical perspectives—which broaden what we might traditionally see as those associated with academic literacies—to develop her argument that the journal is a method of inquiry rather than merely a space for writing.

Claire Penketh and Tasleem Shakur's concern is with a collaborative blog as an emergent textual practice. They outline how they used blogging in order to help make visible both students' and tutors' reading and writing practices. The blog was introduced on a course in human geography as a way of helping students to explore their understanding of key texts and make connections between these and their broader experiences. They did this by encouraging students to combine words with "found" images in their postings to the blog. Although the authors acknowledge that the reading of postmodern texts—a prerequisite for this course—was both challenging and difficult for students, the blog provided a shared space where students were able to explore what it meant to read and write differently in this context using the combination of word and image. Penketh and Shakur believe that this gave their students the freedom to read in unpredictable ways, rather than always expecting the text they were reading to be transparent. The blog was not only potentially transformative for students, in relation to their reading practices, but also for the teachers as authors, who found themselves rethinking the role of writing in enhancing reading, which, they suggest transformed their own practices.

A transformative approach to meaning making is a key orientation to the work of Gillian Lazar and Beverley Barnaby. They consider the meaning and value of grammar outside of a prescriptive agenda and how working with grammar can relate to an academic literacies approach that scrutinizes the dominant values, norms and institutional practices around academic writing. Working with both university lecturers and students on the thorny issue of "poor grammar," they ask whether an academic literacies perspective can usefully incorporate a specific focus on grammar, when on the face of it this might signal a "study skills" approach. In tackling this conundrum, they offer worked through examples of the activities they introduced to students to help them reflect upon the relationship between choices of grammatical forms with aspects of their own identity. The authors explore some of the tensions that emerged between students' desire to "learn the rules" and the exploratory approach that they were asking students to engage with, which met with some resistance. They also examine their experiences of working with academic staff and moving away from surface level notions of grammar towards considerations of meaning making. They conclude that the role of the writing specialist is always to provide spaces for questioning and exploration in order to enable both students and their teachers to recognize the power of genuinely transformative attitudes towards grammar and its relationship to meaning making.

Diane Rushton, Cathy Malone, and Andrew Middleton's interest is with the integration of digital technologies into writing work with students. In attempting to open up possibilities for transformation, they consider the relationship between the spoken and the written word. In their chapter they report on the use of Digital Posters, which they have found offer students a different kind of space for them to experiment with their own academic voice. The authors argue that this contrasts with what is possible when students are working on their own academic writing. The screen capture technology they use relies on visual prompts from just one power point slide. Key to its success is that it requires students to respond verbally and spontaneously and that creating their own Digital Posters helps them to engage in their chosen topic in ways they are then able to take forward into their own academic writing.

Helen Bowstead's call for transformation goes out to academic literacies researchers and practitioners themselves, who, she believes, should be transgressing and challenging normative texts in their own work if the field is going to have a lasting impact on what we expect from our students. She develops this position through a personal account of reflection and her dissatisfaction with the way in which, she argues, we attempt to impose one voice on our students, despite the diversity of an international student body. Her interest is in working with personal narrative and textual forms that embrace student heterogeneity, and in doing so she brings some complementary theoretical perspectives to sit alongside the academic literacies literature. Bowstead examines and questions her own complicity in imposing rules and norms around writing that the academy sanctions, which she suggests serve to make invisible issues of personhood for her students who are bringing rich experiences from outside the academy. She concludes that although academic literacies has opened up spaces for the exploration of meaning making, identity and power it is perhaps the case that those working in the field are not doing enough to actually challenge the institutional practices which are implicit in the kinds of texts they/we produce.

In the final chapter of this section, Colleen McKenna raises important questions about the spaces the digital offers for the transformation of writing practices. Through an expansion of Lea and Street's original framework, she demonstrates the dialogic and oppositional potential of some forms of digital academic writing. Her interest here is in the possibilities that online writing offers to be transformative for readers and writers, academics and students. Drawing on examples of digital texts from both these groups, she introduces the term "intertext" in order to capture the ways in which online texts are much more than a translation from one text type to another. She argues that digital intertexts always bring dimensions that are highly significant in the processes of meaning making and can disrupt the ways in which we build academic arguments and subvert the taken for granted conventions of academic writing. Although design always has rhetorical requirements that are central to meaning, McKenna illustrates how digital academic texts are offering new possibilities for reader-writer relationships, text production and distribution. Her contribution reminds us of the dominance and power of historical academic writing practices but at the same time also points to the slow uptake in valuing digital textual forms. The latter, she argues, have a transformative potential both in disrupting institutional regulation and offer different ways and opportunities for building scholarly identities.

This section closes with a conversation between Bruce Horner and Theresa Lillis who seek to understand each other's positions on the link between "difference" and transformation in the academy. At the centre of their conversation is the question of what is understood by "difference" and in particular what difference looks like in semiotic or textual terms. Horner cautions against valuing "different" textual forms (for example the mixing or meshing of languages) as necessarily indicating a challenging of dominant conventions, or of assuming that texts which use semiotic practices that differ from conventional academic writing necessarily signal greater authorial agency than texts which seem to simply enact dominant conventions.

Lillis agrees that there is a danger of reifying or fetishizing any specific semiotic form but also argues that there is an urgent need for the academy to recognize and value a greater range of linguistic and semiotic forms and practices than is currently the case within dominant assessment regimes. Horner argues that a way out of any potential impasse is to adopt what he calls a "spatiotemporal framework" and, drawing in particular on the work of Lu (e.g., 1994), emphasizes that a pedagogic goal must always be to explore with student writers the significance of their choices, whether these be, as Horner states "to iterate conventional discursive forms" or to make "ostensible breaks" with these forms.

CHAPTER 17

GENRE AS A PEDAGOGICAL RESOURCE AT UNIVERSITY

Fiona English

In this chapter I want to consider genre as a dynamic and transformative resource in the learning and teaching portfolio. I argue that conventional approaches to genre tend to be both limited and limiting with their emphasis on what genres look like and what they are for and argue instead that it is more helpful to explore what genres actually do, how they shape our thinking and the knowledge we produce. Using examples taken from a larger study (Fiona English, 2011), the discussion shows how such an approach can enable students to develop not only a meaningful genre awareness but also a deeper understanding of their disciplinary knowledge.

GENRE AND ACADEMIC LITERACIES

Genre has been an important category in writing pedagogy for many years but has taken different forms depending on different theoretical frames of reference. In the United States it has been firmly based within the long standing rhetoric and composition tradition whereas in the United Kingdom, for example, it has been more linguistically oriented following Michael Halliday and Ruqaiya Hasan (e.g., 1989) whereby genres are seen as social processes that enable us to shape texts in particular ways to achieve particular goals (e.g., Jim Martin, 1993). This approach with its strong focus on the features, or elements, (grammatical structures, lexical configurations and organizational strategies) that typify a given genre has been very influential in the teaching of writing at school (e.g., Tom Gorman et al., 1990) and at university (e.g., Ken Hyland, 2007).

However, with the increasing drive for quick "solutions" to the "problem" of student writing in the climate of a "skills" over knowledge (Ron Barnett, 2009), emphasis has been placed on a "how to" approach and much genre-based writing pedagogy has come to concentrate on producing *genres* rather than on producing *knowledge*. A genre becomes simplified into little more than a template (a report, an essay etc.) and so long as the "elements" are in place, an appropriate a successful text, it is supposed, will emerge. As Gunther Kress (1994) warns, "Effective teaching of genres can make the individual into an efficiently intuitive, and unreflecting, user of the genre …. The genre will construct the world for its proficient user. Is that what we want?" (p. 126).

This divorce between content and form ignores the reality of the writing experience and the many different kinds of *work* involved and writing comes to be viewed as technique, a means of displaying knowledge. It is here that an academic literacies perspective can intervene by offering a critique to such thinking, foregrounding writing as knowledge *making* instead of transmission (e.g., Theresa Lillis, 2003) and in so doing, offer a thicker description of what it means to write at university or school both in the context of research and pedagogy (e.g. Mary Lea, 2004).

DOING ACADEMIC LITERACIES

The work I discuss here presents an example of how academic literacies can work in both pedagogy, in underpinning classroom activity, and theory, in encouraging new thinking about taken-for-granted literacy practices such as genre. It also confirms that academic literacies, far from being a methodology, as it is sometimes taken to be, is more an epistemology, a way of thinking about literacy as negotiated and contested practices (Lea & Brian Street, 1998) within the specific and complex communicative landscape (English, 2011) of the educational institution.

The example I use emerged from a credit-bearing first year module option that I developed whilst working as an academic literacies practitioner at a specialist university in London. The module was institutionally understood as "study skills" but as I had been given free rein over the content, I was able to develop a programme around practices rather than skills, oriented towards learning at the level of analysis and critique so as to encourage students to reflect their own textual interactions. Genre was obviously a key topic, but rather than adopting the kind of modelling approach that typifies study skills courses, we problematized such fixed-form concepts and explored instead how genres developed out of specific practices and why. Following on from this, the final assignment involved students reworking an essay that they had already submitted for their major studies (e.g., politics, social anthropology, linguistics, economics) using any genre they liked, a process I now call "regenring." I asked them to also submit the original essay alongside the new version as a point of reference for me.

The students chose to rework their essays using a range of different genres including journalistic (a tabloidesque report on a time travellers conference on political systems), pedagogic (an "information" booklet for 11 year-olds on the use of loan words), and, most popularly, dramatic (e.g., a simulated radio debate and phone-in with Freidman and Keynes; a play in eight scenes enacting an ethnographic study of the "built environment"). What the students produced far exceeded any expectations I had, not just in terms of the quality of the writing and the evidence of their genre awareness, but, more importantly, on the impact that this work had had on their disciplinary understanding and engagement. They were more "alive" than the essays and the students seemed to have enjoyed writing them, something that was commented on in interview:

> It wasn't so much having to reproduce facts and saying the right thing to get the marks, it was more of an exercise in doing it the way you wanted to. (Peter)

Whatever the genre used, it quickly became clear that there had been a profound shift, not only in terms of what I might once have thought of as generic "shape" but in the materiality of the work itself. Regenring involved far more than simply relocating material from one "frame" into another. It had had a profound impact on the students' knowledge and understanding as well as on their own sense of involvement. As Dan, one of the group pointed out, commenting on his play:

> And I felt that by using the characters … I found myself free or freer to express my opinions or my ideas of my feelings toward the subject in a way that the purely conventional way of writing didn't or wouldn't allow me. (Dan)

CASE STUDY

For the purposes of showing the effects of regenring, I have chosen to discuss "Sonia's" work. She was taking a degree in African Studies and had completed the first term of the course but was already disaffected with her studies. She commented on this when talking about her reasons for choosing the regenring assignment.

> Since I've started university I've felt myself struggling with the academic work and yearning to do something creative. This assignment seemed like a good opportunity. (Sonia)

The following extracts come from different parts of an essay written in response to the following instruction, *Give an account of the origin and present day function of one African lingua franca,* and reflect the tone of the whole essay.

Extract One

[-1-] The word "Swahili" is Arabic in origin and means coast. Swahili is spoken on the East coast of Africa by many as a first language and has spread into the interior as far as the Congo as a lingua franca. Though Swahili uses words adopted from Arabic, English and Portuguese, it has the definite structure of a Bantu language and is written in the Latin script.

> [-2-] Swahili is presumed to have started its life in the region of the Tana River estuary and to have spread further when Arabs and Persians settled in the area due to trading, thus spreading the language along their trading roots. In 975 Ali Ben Sultan al Hassan Ben Ali bought the island of Kilwa in exchange for a few bales of textiles and it became an important trading centre encouraging the use of Swahili along the coast south of the Zambezi River.

> [-3-] There are a very large number of Swahili dialects that have derived from specific social situations, some of which are dying out because of a change in social circumstances. Due to the function of some of these dialects, such as the mode of common communication in the army and work force the dialect has undergone considerable simplification and lost much of its structure until it can only be called a pidgin.

The first thing that strikes us about these extracts is that Sonia has adopted a literal approach to the task. The extracts typify the whole essay in their encyclopaedic exposition of the topic and the assertiveness with which the information is presented seems at odds with the "struggle" that Sonia refers to above. There is a textbook type quality about the discourse which, as Bruno Latour and Steven Woolgar (1986) point out in their discussion of "statement" types (pp. 75-88), tends to present information as uncontroversial fact, using unhedged assertions in contrast to "authentic" professional disciplinary debates and arguments. In Sonia's essay there is no commentary on the information presented, nor is any indication given of its sources apart from the list of four references at the end. In fact, although it is obvious that Sonia has been able to identify relevant information and use certain linguistic terms of reference it is not clear whether she has understood the relevant body of knowledge or whether she has simply located it.

In contrast to the essay, the regenred work offers a very different take on the topic. Her alternative title, *Culturally Confused*, indicates a different kind of understanding of the topic compared to the original essay. It problematizes the idea of a "lingua franca" by locating it in the context of culture and identity. The new version is produced as a dramatised scenario of a father telling a bedtime "story" to his two children aged eight or nine and in the process becomes grounded in a "real world" context. Extract Two is a good illustration of this.

The demands of the genre, characterisation and setting and the to-ing and fro-ing of dialogue between the children and the parent, force Sonia to shape the information differently. The "facts" of the essay are now represented as dialogue which means they are discussed rather than presented, argued over rather than accepted. Despite the factual exaggeration regarding the number of languages spoken in Africa, this version introduces new dimensions to the work, not least of which is a "critical perspective," that most elusive, but desired, aspect of student academic performance. Ultimately, in the new version, Sonia has laid claim to the disciplinary material and instead of merely displaying a series of "facts," as in her essay, she provides a *view* on the topic.

A further aspect of Sonia's regenred work is the provision of detailed supplementary notes. These include contextual notes, which explain why she designed the new version as she did, and stage management notes, which explain the physical and interpersonal contexts of the play. In this way Sonia uses both the physical environment, as discussed in Carey Jewitt (2005), and the interpersonal histories of the participants as semiotic resources. The contextual notes demonstrate the strength of agency that Sonia has in relation to the new work and the confidence with which she can creatively combine "*imagination as well as the intellect*," something she feels unable to do in conventional academic work. Extract Three is an example of this.

Extract Two

> Parent:
> At this point seated in the armchair addressing the children.
> "Can you remember what our bedtime story was about yesterday?"
>
> Child 1:
> "Yessssssssss! It was about …
> [six more exchanges]
>
> Parent:
> "OK, anyway, today I thought I could tell you the story about how Swahili came to be such an important language in East Africa. People always talk about the importance of English as a world language but they rarely consider that there exist many other important non-European languages all over the world. People need to learn one of these important languages so they can talk to people who have different first languages to themselves."
>
> Child 1:
> "Umm … Why would they be speaking to people with a different language?"
>
> Parent:
> "That's a good question you bright little spark! Now in the situation of Africa there are two hundred thousand different languages spoken. It's not like in England. In Africa if you go from one village to the next you are likely to find a different language …."

Extract Three

> *The set … must be minimal and modern with two single beds and an armchair to the left. Perhaps the beds could have patchwork quilts on them and the wooden floor a Moroccan rug. A giant world map can be stuck to the walls behind the beds, with pins, scribbles and highlighter indicating places they have been, want to go, or various important and trivial facts the children have learnt. Some of the visible toys should serve an education function and not be associated with popular culture. It is clearly a conscientious household striving to create a corner of individuality and safety in a contrary, consumer world. … Through the window should be a view of an intimidating grey city, harsh and cold against the bedroom warmth. The city serves as a contrast to the African world the parent talks about ….*

Such information has no place in an essay because essays orient away from "everyday" experienced knowledge towards academic "articulated knowledge" (Diana

Laurillard, 1993) problematized in Lea (1998). However, these stage management notes do something that essays also do; that is they provide authorial guidance. Successful essays do this by choosing specific textual materials such as discourse links or expressions of modality that indicate how the reader is supposed to understand the writer's intentions, as has been widely discussed (Maggi Charles, 2006, English, 1999, Susan Hunston & Geoff Thompson, 2000). Writers of plays use stage management instead and Sonia has made good use of this resource in asserting this authorial control.

There is a further dimension to Sonia's new version, that of reflection on being a student, something that is almost always invisible in conventional essays but which other students using dramatic genres also found themselves doing. In the present case, it is represented by the children themselves who both guide, through questioning, and subvert, through challenge and distraction, the father's "story." Their interventions are intended to shift the discussion away from what *he* wants to talk about to what *they* want to talk about. As his contributions become longer and longer there is a gradual shift from initial enthusiasm on the part of the children towards a growing boredom which echoes, it is tempting to say, Sonia's own experiences at the time.

Extract Four

> Parent:
> [after a lengthy phase of expounding on the topic of Swahili] "Sorry, I can see you're getting bored now—but I just want to tell you one more thing!"
> [he proceeds to tell it …]
>
> Child 2:
> "If you lived in Africa people would put sellotape over your mouth or everyone would always be asleep!"

The opportunity to give voice to such feelings would be considered out of place in a student essay, but here it is made possible by the construction of the plot and the characters who "perform" it. In fact, the humour of the child's remark in Extract Four reflects an attitude, not of despair but rather of exasperation, an attitude confirmed by Sonia's eventual re-engagement with academia.

THE ORIENTATION OF GENRES— A FRAMEWORK FOR ANALYSIS

To understand what was going on with this work, I developed an analytic framework (see Figure 17.1) that could be sufficiently flexible yet theoretically robust enough to explain how genre choice affected both disciplinary content and student experience which were the two key aspects that the students reported during interview. The concept of "orientation" allows for a focus on these elements by separating them out into two main categories (the social and the material) and then subdividing them into the more specific analytical categories: *contextual orientation,* associated with the circumstances and purposes surrounding the production, *discursive orientation,* associated with authorial identity and agency, *thematic orientation,* concerning choice of topics and organization and *semiotic orientation,* associated with choice of mode (e.g., writing, speaking, performance) and what I call textual resources (e.g., grammatical structures, vocabulary, gestures).

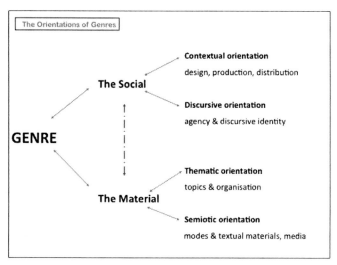

Figure 17.1: The social orientations of genres.

Working with Sonia's two versions, Tables 17.1 and 17.2 demonstrate how the framework can be used to reveal the effects of the different genres. It is possible to consider each category separately by reading across and down each table but it is also possible to see how the two tables interact by considering how the material resources that are used (thematic and semiotic) reflect and promote particular social effects (contextual and discursive). Because of the constraints of space, I can only offer the tables as exemplification. A full explanation can be found in English (2011).

Table 17.1 focuses on the context in which Sonia produced her work and how that context positioned her. Setting out the differences using the categories in this way demonstrates more clearly the affordances of the different genres in relation to the orientations established above.

Table 17.2 summarizes key differences in the material orientation of the genres. It considers how each version is organized, the themes they include and the modes and textual materials they use in their production.

Taking both tables together it is possible to see how the social is reflected in and promoted by the material (thematic and semiotic), and the material in turn, reflects and promotes the social (contextual and discursive). Using the analytical tool of orientation highlights, the ways in which genre choice affords different ways of knowing, different ways representing and different ways of experiencing.

CONCLUSION

In this discussion I have argued for a new direction in genre pedagogy using the

Table 17.1—Social orientations of genres

	THE SOCIAL	
	Essay	**Interactive Bedtime "Story"**
	Contextual Orientation	
Design	Responding to client's design	Designing for client
Production	Essayist (student essay)	Dramatic, didactic "conversation"
Distribution	For institutional assessment. Normative practice, reproduction of … Evaluation against normative implicit disciplinary (and institutionalised) criteria and/ or values	For institutional assessment Alternative practice, experiment, reconfiguration of … Interpretive effect—for assessment/ evaluation against non-normative disciplinary criteria and/or values
	Discursive Orientation	
Purpose	Display knowledge of client's design Display learning	Experiment with learning/ writing Tell (teach) about Inform Entertain
Process	Acquire Reflect Reproduce Replicate	Reflect (on disciplinary materials) Reflect (on experience) Synthesize Recontextualize Create Inform Contend/Evaluate
Identity	Novice as though expert	Expert as if parent (Unwilling) pupils (as if) young children
Role	Performer	Informer (parent) Dissenter (children)
Agency	Mediated Disguised/ unidentifiable Intertextual	Unmediated Visible Interpersonal

insights provided by academic literacies. Rather than seeing genre as a pedagogical goal, I have shown how it can be used as a pedagogical resource. Of particular relevance to the present book is the clear evidence from the example used here

Table 17.2—Material orientations of genres

	Essay	Interactive Bedtime "Story"
THE MATERIAL		
Thematic Orientation		
Organization	Essay management (introduction, "body," conclusion i.e., sequence of information/ideas) Descriptions, examples	Narrative & stage management (sequence of events) Story telling Interactions between characters, dialogues
Topics & specific characteristics	Disciplinary topics Linguistic terms of reference Swahili as a lingua franca Examples of history and uses presented as list	Disciplinary topics "Everyday" terms of reference Swahili as a lingua franca presented as political act, linked to discussion on linguistic terminology Didactic parent and argumentative, assertive children.
Semiotic Orientation		
Modes	Writing (writtenness)	Written speech/scripted speech (spokenness) Characters, props, stage management
Textual Materials	Impersonal forms (e.g., "it" fronted, nominalizations, passive constructions) Clause complexity/ density of expression Disciplinary terminology—unexplained Formal (writing-like) expression (e.g., full forms, subordination) Topically organized with no explicit threading Absence of interpersonal resources (i.e., no cohesive directives, lack of attitudinal markers, no links between topics) Explicitness as asserted fact—encyclopaedic information (e.g., no hedges)	Personal forms—subject fronted, personal pronouns + impersonal forms where "father" is "recounting" the essayist information Clause intricacy + clause complexity during "recount" sections Disciplinary terminology explained + colloquial terms Colloquial (speech) expression Topically organized but strongly mediated by dialogic interactions (e.g., responses to questions, challenges, recapitulations) Frequent use of interpersonal resources, interruptions, agreements/ disagreements Explicitness—pedagogized information—didactic, directives (e.g., People need to learn …), approbation (e.g., That's a good question) hedges (e.g., Perhaps it's to do with …)

of how this approach to genre enables students to engage at the epistemological level that academic literacies argues for, as has been well documented in Lea and Street (1998), Carys Jones et al. (1999) and more recently in Lillis and Mary Scott (2007). The analytical framework, which draws on social semiotics (e.g., Kress, 2010), serves to reveal the transformative nature of the regenring activity offering insights not only into the nature of academic knowledge and the close association between the genres used and the knowledge produced, akin to Basil Bernstein's (2000) vertical and horizontal discourses, but also into the experiences of students in their attempts to interact with the disciplines they have chosen. Working with students in this way also encourages the critique that academic literacies thinking promotes and provides the opportunity for students to position themselves as producers of knowledge rather than as merely receivers.

The discussion also raises questions about the genres that typify university education and the ways that they constrain how disciplines can be understood. I am not arguing for the abandonment of essays, nor am I suggesting that they are a poor way of helping students reflect on their disciplinary material. What I am suggesting is that we incorporate a wider range of genres into the learning and teaching repertoire, even including tasks such as the regenring activity described here. In this way it may be possible to encourage *"new ways of looking at old questions,"* as one of my lecturer informants put it when asked what they hoped to see in their students' assignments. However, this will only be achieved if we develop new ways of asking those questions and offering students new ways to explore them.

REFERENCES

Barnett, R. (2009). Knowing and becoming. *The Higher Education Curriculum Studies in Higher Education, 34*(4), 429-440.

Bernstein, B. (2000). Pedagogy, symbolic control and identity. (Revised ed.). Oxford, UK: Rowman and Littlefield.

Charles, M. (2006). Revealing and obscuring writer's identity. In R. Keily, P. Rea-Dickens, H. Woodfield, & G. Clibban (Eds.), *Language, culture and identity in applied linguistics* (pp. 147-161). London. BAAL/Equinox.

English, F. (2011). *Student writing and genre: Reconfiguring academic knowledge.* London. Bloomsbury Academic.

English, F. (1999). What do students really say? In C. Jones, J. Turner, & B. Street (Eds.),*Students writing in the university: Cultural and epistemological issues* (pp. 17-36) Amsterdam: John Benjamins Publishing Company.

Gorman, T. P., White, J., Brooks, G., & English, F. (1990). *Language for learning. Schools examinations and assessments council.* London: Department for Education and Science.

Halliday, M. A. K., & Hasan, R. (1989). *Language, context and text: Aspects of language in a social-semiotic perspective* (2nd ed.). Oxford: Oxford University Press.

Hunston, S., & Thompson, G. (Eds.). (2000). *Evaluation in text: Authorial stance and the construction of discourse.* Oxford: Oxford University Press.

Hyland, K. (2007). Genre pedagogy: Language, literacy and L2 writing instruction. *Journal of Second Language Writing, 16*(3), 148-164.

Jewitt, C. (2005). Classrooms and the design of pedagogic discourse: A multimodal approach. *Culture and Psychology, 11*(3), 309-320.

Jones, C., Turner, J., & Street, B., (Eds.). (1999). *Students writing in the university: cultural and epistemological issues.* Amsterdam: John Benjamins Publishing Company.

Kress, G. (2010). *Multimodality: A social semiotic approach to contemporary communication.* London: Routledge.

Kress, G. (1994). *Learning to write* (2nd ed.). London: Routledge.

Latour, B., & Woolgar, S. (1986). *Laboratory life: The social construction of scientific facts* (S2nd ed.). Princeton, NJ: Princetown University Press.

Lea, M., (2004). Academic literacies: A pedagogy for course design. *Studies in Higher Education, 29*(6), 739-796.

Lea, M. R. (1999). Academic literacies and learning in higher education: Constructing knowledge through texts and experiences. In C. Jones, J. Turner, & B. V. Street (Eds.), *Student writing in the university: cultural and epistemological issues* (pp. 103-142). Amsterdam: John Benjamins Publishing Company.

Lea, M., & Street, B. (1998). Student writing and faculty feedback in higher education: An academic literacies approach. *Studies in Higher Education, 23*(2), 157-172.

Lillis, T., (2003). Student writing as "academic literacies": Drawing on Bakhtin to move from critique to design. *Language and Education*, 17(3), 192-207.

Lillis, T., & Scott, M. (2007). Introduction: New directions in academic literacies research. *Journal of Applied Linguistics, 4*(1), 5-32.

Martin, J. R., (1993). A contextual theory of language. In B. Cope & M. Kalantizis (Eds.), *The powers of literacy.* London: Falmer Press.

CHAPTER 18

HOW DRAWING IS USED TO CONCEPTUALIZE AND COMMUNICATE DESIGN IDEAS IN GRAPHIC DESIGN: EXPLORING SCAMPING THROUGH A LITERACY PRACTICE LENS

Lynn Coleman

Most students in higher education are typically required to demonstrate their learning and thinking through the production of some form of written text, often an essay. However, in course environments where knowledge forms and practices are constituted visually or rely heavily on other semiotic resources for meaning-making, this is frequently not the case. Students in such academic contexts demonstrate their learning and give expression to their thinking in predominantly non-written and visual ways. This chapter draws on an aspect of a larger research study that used academic literacies as its theoretical and methodological framework. The study explored the literacy practices of students completing courses in visual art and media fields at a vocational higher education institution in South Africa. In these courses, students demonstrate their learning primarily through the production of visual, digital and print-based products such as film clips, posters, logos, photography, and three-dimensional (3D) product-packaging.

In this chapter I draw attention to students completing a graphic design (GD) diploma course and how they use drawings as the primary way of communicating their design ideas. Drawings that are used in this manner to visually articulate design ideas are called "scamps" and the process associated with creating such drawings is called "scamping." Scamping is also a valued practice in the professional context of GD where the designer is expected to translate information provided by a client and visually capture their concepts with scamps. I explore the process of scamping through a literacy practice lens but also subject this analysis to a further reading centred on how assumptions about knowledge in the academic and professional domains influence, guide and give value to the literacy practice itself. The discussion illustrates that a consideration of knowledge recontextualization pro-vides an explanation of how professional knowledge practices influence the literacy practices privileged in the academic domain. The exploration of scamping in this graphic design context provides a good example of the evolving semiotic practices in higher education that result when different sets of practices drawn from industry and academia are brought together. A further implication of this intersection of practices is the creation of a pedagogic space where the lecturer is able to act as a co-constructor in the creation of assignment texts alongside the student.

THEORETICAL FRAMING

Academic literacies as a field of research has typically focused on writing in higher education (HE) (Theresa Lillis & Mary Scott, 2007). However, a steady shift in this focus has seen the field's theorization being brought to bear on "new contexts" of vocational and professional studies (Mary Lea, 2012; Mary Lea & Barry Stierer, 2000; Candice Satchwell & Roz Ivanič, 2007), and the increasingly expansive range of communicative practices in the academy (Chris Abbott, 2002; Arlene Archer, 2006; Lucia Thesen, 2006). South African researchers have also explored the potential of visual communicative modes as an additional means whereby students can demonstrate their learning (Archer, 2006; Thesen, 2001). In recent research Mary Lea (2012) has argued that the nature of the texts students are required to produce for assessment purposes in HE are increasingly coming under the influence of a global shift from traditional discipline-based courses to professional programmes. She also proposes that an academic literacies lens can be generative for exploring the new assessment and learning spaces created as the inherent tensions between "professional practice-based knowledge and a theorized written assessment of that knowledge" jostle for position in HE (Lea, 2012, p. 94). My work is located along this new trajectory and explores meaning making and learning in vocational practice-based course environments where the construction of written texts is less prominent. In my research the concept of literacy practice is conceptualized in terms of epistemology (Lea, 1999, 2012). This understanding allows me to highlight the productive connection between curriculum theorization and the argument that literacy practices and knowledge in learning environments are embedded in each other.

CONSIDERING KNOWLEDGE IN THE CURRICULUM

Academic literacies has been valuable for exploring how students demonstrate their learning through their production of written and non-written texts. As a field of research however, it has been less helpful in providing the theoretical tools to explore the broader structuring processes implicated, but not directly visible, in the literacy practices that support the creation of assignment texts. Lea predicts that "as academic, disciplinary and professional boundaries shift and blur" academic literacies researchers will be required to focus not only on the "micro-practices" of text production but also cast their inquiry to broader institutional practices, like the curriculum, in order to fully understand the new learning spaces being created in the academy (2012, p. 109). Such a framework is already an imperative within in vocational HE as the impact and influence of the professional domain cannot be excluded from conceptualizing how curricula, subjects and assessment practices are constructed. Simply focusing on the literacy practices used by students to demonstrate their learning does not go far enough in explaining how such practices become privileged or the role the professional domain plays in structuring such practices. Basil Bernstein's (1996, 2000) notion of *knowledge recontextualization* offers a way of attending to this theoretical gap. Using recontextualization as an analytical lens provides a language of description for theorizing how professional practices and knowledge become implicated in the literacy practices associated with assignment production. Recontextualization describes the processes through which knowledge produced outside the educational context (in the disciplines or in the professional domains) becomes transformed, adapted and re-appropriated to constitute content subjects and the curriculum. Bernstein argues that as knowledge moves from its "original site to its new positioning, as pedagogic discourse, a transformation takes place" (2000, p. 32). This transformation occurs because as knowledge moves from one context to another, a space is created for ideology to play a role (Bernstein, 2000). The important outcome of this process is that knowledge associated with the curriculum, i.e., curriculum knowledge, is, therefore, different from what might be called disciplinary or workplace knowledge (Johan Muller, 2008). In its broadest sense, the main outcome of this recontextualization process is the curriculum (Suellen Shay, 2011). The curriculum is therefore influenced by ideologically mediated choices of key curriculum role players like lecturers or curriculum developers. The choices made by curriculum role players' about what knowledge to include in curricula is therefore also influenced by their assumptions about the purpose of education and their conceptualizations of learning and teaching or ideal graduate attributes. According to Bernstein, educational knowledge is de-contextualized or "abstracted from its social base, position and power relations" as a result of recontextualization (2000, p. 38).

WHAT IS SCAMPING?

Scamping is a term used in GD to refer to the process of making design ideas visible by creating a drawing or sketch. Scamping relies strongly on what graphic designers in education call hand skills, i.e., a suite of skills requiring the use of one's hands to cut, mount and manipulate a variety of materials, the foremost of these being the ability to sketch and draw. Hand skills are often contrasted with the use of technologies such as the computer or digital design tools when creating design products. Scamps are characteristically small drawings or sketches produced with pencils onto layout or photocopy paper. The materials used to produce scamps, that are cheap and easily erasable, function to give the scamping process a rehearsal quality, imbuing the scamps with a provisional or draft status. Multiple scamps are typically produced to explore a single idea and these are commonly drawn alongside each other. Unsuitable ideas are simply crossed out and newer iterations are drawn alongside the discarded drawings, as shown in Figures 18.1 and 18.2.

Figure 18.1: A series of scamps produced for a logo design project.

Because scamps are produced with impermanent and relatively cheap materials, the need to create a final, perfect design idea or concept is circumvented. Placing multiple draft ideas together on the same sheet of paper suggests that they all share the same status as potential "final" design concepts.

In the course, scamps are distinguished, on one level, from finished or final drawings on the basis of the "mark-making" materials used. Final drawings are commonly presented separately, can be mounted and are completed using gouache, paint, or copy markers on cartridge or bleed-proof paper; thus mark-making materials that are expensive and difficult to alter. In addition to being distinguished by their material qualities, scamps are also contrasted with other forms of drawing practiced in the course, specifically perceptual or naturalistic drawing associated with Fine Art:

> I'm saying it's drawing but it's different drawing … there's perceptual drawing which might be more what the Drawing subject does … scamping is drawing for design.

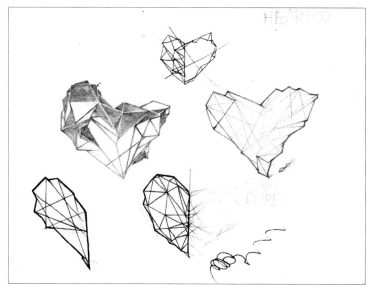

Figure 18.2: Scamps showing how a student experimented with a logo design idea.

In the interview extract above, Tessa, a course lecturer, alludes to the notion that the curriculum conceptualizes the act of drawing in different ways. The subject called Drawing, places focus on naturalistic and perceptual drawing commonly associated with the Fine Art discipline. The subject privileges personal expression using various observational and rendering techniques to create realistic images of, e.g., a landscape. When Tessa says "scamping is drawing for design" she is associating it with the activities of a designer who is more concerned with creating a visual message that meets a very specific purpose. Examples of this can be seen in images above of the logo scamps students produced for a Cape Town based organization. The scamps attempt to represent visually what such a logo might look like and show how the students experiment with image, text, typography, layout, composition and placement of their logo concept. In the course, lecturers talk about scamping as an image generating tool where one's conceptualization and thinking about a design product is visually expressed. This understanding is captured later by Tessa when she says "Scamping is really conceptual drawing"; suggesting that the primary semiotic purpose of scamping is the visualisation of conceptual ideas and the main way in which a creative or design concept becomes translated into a concrete and visual form.

SCAMPING AND ASSIGNMENT PRODUCTION

Scamping cannot be fully understood without relating it to the way assignments are completed in this course. Scamping is integral to the "Design Process"—a curriculum constructed procedure that guides and sequences the different tasks and activities students are required to undertake when completing a design-based assignment. A description of how assignments are meant to be produced is provided by this sequential six-stage process. Each stage is named and a description of the function the stage serves in the overall assignment construction process is provided. Scamping takes place at stage three of the process where students "put pencil to paper" and visually give meaning to their conceptual ideas. The design process is often directly incorporated into assignment briefs, with this practice especially evident at the 1st and 2nd year levels.

The design process aims to guide student assignment practices; however, it also provides direction for the role that lecturers are required to play as students construct their assignments. For example, the process explicitly requires students to "Show the lecturer what you are doing" and "Consult with [your] lecturer." Lecturers also need to "Sign off" or approve concepts before students are allowed to move onto the next stage of assignment construction. The process suggests that lecturers are continually involved in activities building up to the construction of the final assignment text. Additionally, periodic opportunities for lecturer-student interaction in the act of such text design and construction are also created. Helen, another lecturer in the course, highlights how this role is pedagogically constructed when she describes what happens when students show her their scamps.

> I look at the scamps ... and the student might say right these are the ones that I've come up with and then I'll say okay, "This looks promising or that doesn't because that's been re-done so many times" .... So I will give them guides saying this is a good potential option, this one not so much or that one, it's too, futuristic or it's too this or it's too that. So I will give them guidance. They'll be showing me their ideas on paper ... and then I'll say fine if you like it then maybe take that one further or show me more variations.

The lecturer's primary role is to comment on the quality of the work, and in the lower levels of the course this might involve approving or rejecting scamps. As Helen's description suggests, lecturers might propose alternative approaches and encourage students to be more exploratory and creative with a concept. These feedback moments provide opportunities for lecturers to offer guidance on how to overcome design related problems, while also checking that students are sticking to, or meeting, the requirements of the brief. In the course context, scamping and the production of assignments more generally also includes a prominent collaborative aspect. The lecturer is involved in providing continual feedback throughout the production of the assignment text, even though the creation of the text is undertaken primarily by the individual student.

SCAMPING IN THE PROFESSIONAL DOMAIN

In the discussion above I have shown that scamping is a fundamental semiotic practice that allows students to express and communicate their creative ideas and conceptualization through drawing. I have also suggested that the act of scamping is underpinned by conventions and rules, embedded and regulated by the curriculum and pedagogic practices that prescribe the material qualities of scamps and the function of scamping during assignment construction. These literacy practices support scamping as the key means of communicating design conceptualization. Scamping is, however, a practice rooted in the professional context. In the following extract, Helen explains how scamping is a fundamental aspect of the professional designer's practice.

> … as a designer you should be able to internalize what your client is giving you and be able to translate that information onto paper into a visual that the client can see …. So we're teaching them that, once they've got the research or once they've got their information they should be able to start translating that onto paper or into some sort of visual format for your client to see ….

Helen describes how, in industry, scamping as a practice is associated with translating "information into paper on to a visual that the client can see," suggesting that the designer is expected to visually represent their conceptualization of information provided by the client through scamps. She also recognizes that industry-referenced practices shift and change when incorporated into the academic domain. Helen's reference to "research," that is the first stage of the design process, signals that in the absence of a real client the creation of design products in the course has a different initiation point.

USING RECONTEXTUALIZATION TO UNDERSTAND SCAMPING

In this section I illustrate how subjecting the data on scamping to a further reading using recontextualization as an analytical lens helps to illuminate how the literacy practices that support scamping in this context are created through the bringing together of valued practices from both the professional and academic domains. The act of designing a logo in the professional context is largely dependent on several variables including the client, the designer(s), the purpose that the logo is meant to serve, the development timeframe and the budget. This means that in industry the design process of this logo can be a dynamic, quick and flexible process. However, when this process is recontextualized into the GD course it becomes the "design process"—a sequence of six steps usually carried out over six to ten days, in a classroom and/or computer lab environment where the pace, sequencing of selected tasks and the evaluation of such tasks are carefully constructed to adhere to the educational values and principles espoused by the course and its lecturers. In the process of creating the design process in the GD academic context, a translation occurs of what it means to undertake design work in industry. Typically, in industry, the design of any product is initiated by the client. The designer is tasked with interpreting the client's needs and as a first step visually representing their conceptualization with hand drawn scamps. Based on the data collected, the process of interpreting the client's needs happens quickly. The ability to draw scamps is prized as it allows the designer to visually express initial conceptualizations at the point of interaction with the client.

In the academic context, the design process, while attempting to capture and simulate professional design practices, is also a construction tailor-made to accommodate the contextual and educational demands and realities of the academic setting. Thus, the purpose of the design process, particularly as it is manifested in assignment briefs, is not simply to provide students with practical direction, for example, on how to construct a logo. It is also fundamentally about facilitating students' learning of a variety of conceptual principles about color theory, layout, and composition that are associated with various sub-disciplinary areas aligned to GD. The briefs therefore direct attention not only to the sequence and pace at which tasks need to be completed, often much slower than typically expected in industry, but they also include lecturer-facilitated explorations of conceptual and procedural knowledge to support the design work being completed.

In the academic context, stronger focus is placed on student learning and in this respect the design process foregrounds the lecturer's role in facilitating this learning. A simple reading of the assignment practices might suggest that the lecturer simply "stands in" for the client. However, the lecturer's role is deeply imbued with an educational function that accounts for a fundamental shift in how the design process is recontextualized in the academic context. The lecturer's feedback, that is structured to be continual and supportive, means that in certain instances there is a degree of co-construction of the assignment text as the lecturer helps the student refine and polish their ideas, and focus their efforts on meeting the requirements of the brief. The process of scamping and assignment construction, while mainly individual, always takes place in a communal, public and collaborative manner, and the draft quality of the produced text is as highly prized as the final assignment. This is in stark contrast to the construction of essays in HE, that is a highly individualistic and private activity that rarely accommodates the creation of draft or multiple versions of the same text for review. A conclusion could therefore be drawn that only the final essay product, rather than the process of its construction, is subjected to evaluation and the lecturer's role is primarily centred on the evaluation of the final text.

CONCLUDING COMMENTS

The purpose of this chapter has been twofold. Firstly, using a literacy practice lens it describes how students in a GD course use scamping as a way to visually express and communicate their design ideas and conceptualization. Secondly, I have presented an argument that illustrates the value of bringing a recontextualization analysis to the study of literacy practices. Using recontextualization as an analytical lens, I show how practices valued in the professional domain can come to inform the type of literacy practices students are required to use when completing assignments in their course. Furthermore, by paying attention to ideological process associated with choices about knowledge, recontextualization as an analytic lens offers a more nuanced understanding of how professional-based practices intersect with, and become transformed by, the academic-informed values and practices. In this way this provides insight into processes that give rise to privileged literacy practices. In the GD context, the literacy practices associated with scamping are forged as a result of the intersection between academia and industry, foregrounding the visual but also making provision for lecturers as co-constructors in the creation of visual assignments. Discussing scamping in GD through a literacy practice lens draws attention to the ways in which learning and thinking in HE are being continually mediated by an evolving range of semiotic resources.

REFERENCES

Abbott, C. (2002). Writing the visual. The use of graphic symbols in on screen text. In L. Snyder, (Ed.), *Silicon literacies* (pp. 31-46). London: Routledge.

Archer, A. (2006). Change as additive: Harnessing students' multimodal semiotic resources in an Engineering curriculum. In L. Thesen & E. van Pletzen, (Eds.), *Academic literacy and the languages of change* (pp. 130-150). London: Continuum International Publishing Group.

Bernstein, B., (1996). *Pedagogy, symbolic control and identity: Theory, research, critique.* London: Taylor & Francis.

Bernstein, B. (2000). *Pedagogy, symbolic control, and identity: Theory, research, cri-*

tique. (Revised ed.). Oxford, UK: Rowman & Littlefield Publishers.

Lea, M. R. (1999). Academic literacies and learning in higher education: Constructing knowledge through texts and experiences. In C. Jones, J. Turner, & B. V. Street (Eds.), *Student writing in the university: cultural and epistemological issues.* (pp. 103-142). Amsterdam: John Benjamins Publishing Company.

Lea, M. R. (2012). New genres in the academy: Issues of practice, meaning making and identity. In M. Castelló & C. Donahue, (Eds.), *University writing: Selves and texts in academic societies* (pp. 93-109). Bingley, UK: Emerald Group Publishing.

Lea, M. R., & Stierer, B. (2000). In M. R. Lea & B. Stierer, (Eds.), *Student writing in higher education. New contexts* (pp. 1-14) [Editors' introduction.]. Buckingham, UK: Society for Research into Higher Education/Open University Press.

Lillis, T., & Scott, M. (2007). Defining academic literacies research: Issues of epistemology, ideology and strategy. *Journal of Applied Linguistics, 4*(1), 5-32.

Muller, J. (2008). *In search of coherence: A conceptual guide to curriculum planning for comprehensive universities.* SANTED project, Parktown, ZA: Centre for Education Policy Development.

Satchwell, C., & Ivanič, I. (2007). The textuality of learning contexts in UK colleges [Special issue]. *Pedagogy, Culture and Society* on *Contexts, Networks and Communities; 15*(3), 303-316.

Shay, S. (2011). Curriculum formation: A case study from history. *Studies in Higher Education, 36*(3), 315-329.

Thesen, L. (2006). Who owns this image? Word, image and authority in the lecture. In L. Thesen & E. van Pletzen, (Eds.), *Academic literacy and the languages of change* (pp. 151-179). London: Continuum International Publishing Group.

Thesen, L. (2001). Modes, literacies and power: A university case study. *Language and Education, 15*(2-3), 132-145.

CHAPTER 19

"THERE IS A CAGE INSIDE MY HEAD AND I CANNOT LET THINGS OUT": AN EPISTEMOLOGY OF COLLABORATIVE JOURNAL WRITING

Fay Stevens

This chapter presents the outcomes of a journal project initially set-up in conjunction with cross-disciplinary courses in Academic Literacies (Writing in Academic Contexts, Writing Science), taught at The Centre for the Advancement of Learning and Teaching (CALT), from 2008 to 2011, as part of a Teaching Fellowship I held at that time. The project sets out to encourage journal writing and image making, consider issues of collaborative writing, social practice and identity and promote the transformative role collaborative journal writing can play within varying academic contexts.

In 2008, I encountered "The 1000 Journals Project," based around the global circulation of 1,000 journals: contributed to by those who encounter a journal (in a café, for example) and left for another person to stumble across. I was intrigued with the idea of the journal as mobile, independent, and as a particular kind of space for writing with its own emergent identity. I adapted the concept and introduced a collaborative journal into the academic literacies courses I was teaching. This project (The Journal Project), aimed to engage with the practice of contributing to a journal as a collaborative, interactive, academic, and transformative way of thinking and writing. It is a multi-authored method of communication and expression that can be shared within the community of writers participating in a writing-based course. A journal was circulated on a weekly basis and participants were invited to actively engage with the process of writing and image making in whatever way they felt pertinent to their writing, studies and life at university. The journal was presented as a medium through which students could further explore themes covered in the courses, in a space independent of written assessment. Participants were encouraged to be as creative, experimental, formal, academic, and exploratory as they wished. The outcomes are a collection of seven journals rich in discourse, imagery and ideas that encompass a wide-range of topics and issues central to an Academic Literacies approach to teaching, learning and writing.

I focus on the following themes: the journal as collaborative endeavour, putting "self" into the journal, image making and emergent textual practices. Theoretically, I concentrate on the journal as a method of inquiry via discussion on issues of identity and construction of "self." I argue that the journals have potential for transformation, both individually and collectively, within a group of course participants.

THE JOURNAL AS COLLABORATIVE ENDEAVOUR

Journals are often considered to function as particular spaces for writing (e.g., Phyllis Creme, 2008). Here, writing can be seen as an activity that always occurs in a social context, at both a more local, immediate level and at a broader social and cultural level. As such, there are different ways in which writing can be understood as a "social practice" (e.g. Roz Ivanič, 1998; Theresa Lillis, 2001). This might include, writing within specific academic and disciplinary communities (e.g. Elizabeth Sommerville & Phyllis Creme, 2005; Fay Stevens, 2009), as well as expressing personal and social identities. Yet, during class discussions, students expressed a loss of identity during the course of their studies and targeted academic writing as responsible for it. This loss was expressed as a stripping away of creativity and being made to write in a way that felt abstracted and not representative of who they "really are," or want to be.

All seven journals contrast in terms of coverage and content. It is interesting to see how the first journal entry shaped the focus and intention of following entries and how the journals took on an identity of their own. One journal, for example, set the scene with an opening that focused on gratitude. Following entries responded to this and as a consequence the journal has spiritual and therapeutic overtones. In contrast, another journal focused on the complex and composite identity of being a human scientist. Entries here, focused on the complex nature of the discipline and a writers' struggling sense of identity within it.

Collaboratively, all journals, in some way, focused on an individual/collective and writerly identity and the processes of transformation taking place. More often than not, this is expressed visually and textually as a process of struggle and negotiation. In general, journals engaged with fluidity, creativity, playfulness, and collectivity, particularly as a series of responses to previous entries. In many respects, the journals evolved into collaborative safe spaces in which participants developed a spirit of inquiry, knowledge and wisdom that was directly representative of the individual but written in collaboration with others.

PUTTING "SELF" INTO THE JOURNAL

Identity is a modern conceptual construct used in the social and behavioural sciences to refer to people's sense of themselves as distinct individuals in the context of community. At a basic level, identity could be said to refer to people's socially de-

termined sense of who they are—a kind of social statement of *who one is,* referring to a sense of "self" (aspects of the individual) that draws upon trends (representative of the collective), so as to present oneself simultaneously as part of a whole and as unique (Antonio Damasio, 2000). From a corporeal perspective, writing can been seen as a technique of the body (Marcel Mauss, 1973), a kind of dexterous, woven movement (Tim Ingold, 2000, p.403) and a sort of fiction created by language and all that we think of as being language (Jacques Derrida, 1967).

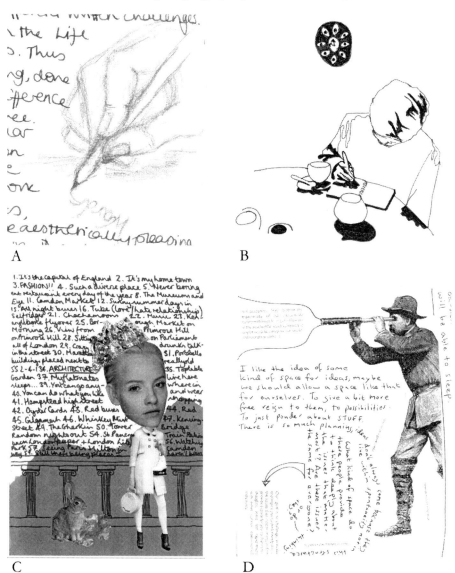

Figure 19.1: Visualising self in journal. .

Corporeal imagery features notably in the journals:

This includes an image of a hand in the process of writing "words" (Figure 19.1A), where the entry states that "writing can be exciting … frustrating … explorative … reassuring," while another image is of a figure writing in café (Figure 19.1B). The visual placing of the writer within the space of the journal includes an entry in which a collage figure bears a striking resemblance to the student who made the entry (Figure 19.1C) and an image of a person looking through a telescope (Figure 19.1D) and peering into the distance. Accompanying text states:

> I like the idea of some kind of space for ideas, maybe we should
> allow a space like that for ourselves.

"Self," in some instances, is visually present in other forms. In one example (Figure 19.2), the participant (human scientist) represents herself as a sequence of pie charts. Initially, her writing is expressed as two separate circles; what she refers to as "purely separate spheres of writing," where one chart represents "essay criteria academic assessed uni work" and the other "for me subjective personal journal diary." The following chart fuses the circles together. Here, she asks "do they overlap?", placing her "self" in the middle: a combination of the two spheres of writing. Finally, she states that "my writing is all part of the same thing, with different aspects that blend together," with an accompanying circle in which she places "myself as the writer" in the centre.

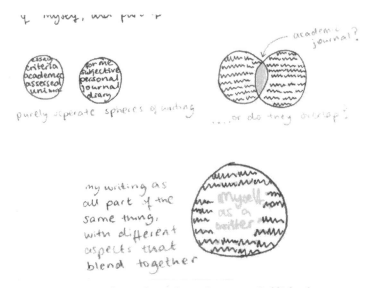

Figure 19.2: Visually working through putting "self" back into writing

Through the interplay of text and image, these particular journal entries explore the possibilities of connecting to and representing a "true" or "real" self, that has somehow become elusive to the writer. Participants demonstrate an awareness that their academic writing is not just about conveying an ideational content. It is also about the representation of "self" (e.g., Celia Hunt & Fiona Sampson, 2007; Ken Hyland, 2002) and expressing a sense of "self" (Peter Ashworth, 2004, p. 156; Phyllis Creme & Celia Hunt, 2008; Kristján Kristjànsson, 2008; Mary Lea & Brian Street, 1998). Moreover, that it is a social act that involves sharing work with peers (e.g. Maria Antoniou & Jessica Moriarty, 2008), as well as a set of processes which may contribute dynamically to knowledge making (cf. Graham Badley, 2009).

IMAGE MAKING

The concept of text comprises an infusion of words and pictures (e.g., Mike Sharples, 1999, p. 130) and an interweaving of text and graphic elements (cf. Ingold, 2007, p. 70). Writing, image and colour are said to lend themselves to doing different kinds of semiotic work, where each has its own distinct potential for meaning (Gunther Kress, 2010). We could even ask, "where does drawing end and writing begin?" (Ingold, 2007, p. 120-151).

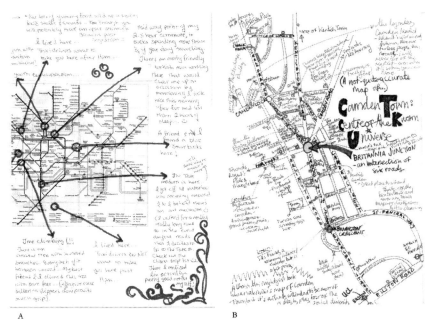

A   B

Figures 19.3A and 19.3B: "Mapping identity."

The interface of image and text is executed in a variety of ways in the journals: text written around images (Figures 19.1C, 19.1D, 19.5A), as well as images around and integrated with text (Figures, 19.3A, 19.3B, 19.5C). Moreover, varieties of maps de-

271

pict and describe spatial and conceptual journeys and places (Figure 19.3 [A-D]). Maps can function as a form of gesture (Barbara Belyea, 1996, p.11) or "self" (Rebecca Solnit, 2001) on the page, often with the purpose of providing directions so that others can follow along the same path (Alfred Gell, 1985; Ingold, 2000, p. 241).

A map of the world (Figure 19.3C), composed of text and a collage of cut out pieces of plastic bag (with varying designs and colours), includes the statement:

> Will this eventually lead to global citizenship, which is still an abstract idea, or even a global identity, or will nationalism and tradition come out on top. It is with that question that I will leave you, because no matter how much I speculate, the fact is; only time will tell.

C

D

Figures 19.3C and 19.3D: "Mapping identity.

Here, the participant is mapping out a concept, communicating directly to the reader as a visual and textual process that facilitates their own understanding of the topic, as well as an awareness of their thoughts and opinions on it; being both the writer and reader (writing to "self") of the entry.

A "Dissertation Map" (Figure 19.3D), is reminiscent of a pirate map that alludes to the dissertation as some kind of treacherous journey to get to "hidden treasure." References to London, include a tube-stop memoir (Figure 19.3A) that reveals an engagement with the collaborative free-sprit of the journal, stating the information might come in handy if the journal were ever lost and the finder "felt like roaming around London." Moreover, a map of "Camden Town: Centre of the Universe" (Figure 19.3B) presents a bricolage of information that includes social history and memories of previous visits, with a statement that identifies the map as "a play by play tour of social diversity."

These cartographical visuals act as evocative mediums for communicating a variety of information—corporeal, individual, composite, spatial and social—where the reader is required to engage concurrently with text and image and engage with the process of taking a journey as they "read" the map. Here, images can be seen to be much more than an adjunct to writing: they do not restate the data or reduce the need for prose, but offer a kind of separate or parallel "text" for reading and interpretation (see also Gimenez and Thomas Chapter 1, Good Chapter 3, Adams Chapter 4 this volume).

EMERGENT TEXTUAL PRACTICES

The journals demonstrate that when the opportunity arises, the process of experimentation is fully engaged with. Moreover, that emergent textual practices lead to a variety of methods and outcomes that engage with issues central to an academic literacies approach to writing.

Michel de Certeau (1984) imagined the modern writer as the isolated Cartesian subject, removed from the world and confronting the blank surface of a sheet of paper in much the same way as an urban planner confronts a wasteland or a conqueror confronts the surface of the earth (pp. 134-136). Being faced with the blank surface of a page is often expressed as one of the most worrying encounters a writer faces. Interestingly, a majority of entries in the journals subverted the linearity of the A4 page and presented an interplay of text and image. Figure 19.4, for example, is an entry of words and images that rotate around the page. Based around the theme of "A Night of Wanderings," the entry explores the "ping" of ideas as they pop into your head in the early hours of the morning and is playful in its approach to space, imagery, colour and text. Here, the reader not only engages with the content and visual impact of the entry, but also the gesture of reading, that involves moving the journal around in varying positions and shapes in order to read it and

Figure 19.4: Non linear writing.

engage with the materiality of the journal in a three-dimensional way. As such, the journal moves from being looked at/read to an object that has tactile multi-sensory qualities.

Thematic references to flying (Figures 19.5A, 19.5D) and containment (Figures 19.5B, 19.5C) are also present. The flying images are associated with text that tends to have a positive and spiritual quality and associated with a sense of realization and free-spiritedness. In direct contrast, images of containment seem to reflect constraint and frustration. In Figure 19.5C, containment is portrayed as a cage that sits within the mind of a human figure. The cage contains comments such as, "I don't want to be put into a category." "I am going to learn German." "Do I want to find a uniform way of expressing myself?" These are expressions of intention somehow constrained by the cage, but more specifically by the mind of the writer.

CONCLUSION

A fascinating aspect of this project is the resulting richness of the journal entries, with regard to the diversity of style of both text and images and the readiness of the participants to experiment with the process. I am touched by their willingness to engage with the journals and their candour when expressing their sense of self, identity and relationship with the written word and the visual image. Framed in this way (as

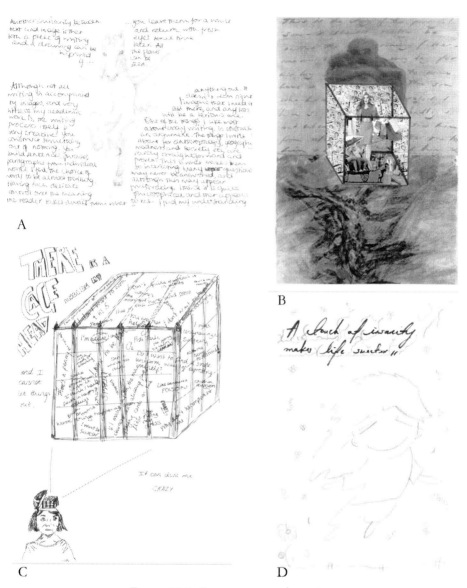

Figure 19.5: Emergent textual practices.
Images of flying (A & D) and containment (B & C).

collaborative, social, creative), the journals can be seen to be a powerful transformative tool for developing an awareness that identities are somehow being challenged and shaped as an outcome of being at university, breaking the bonds of perception of academic writing and how this is associated with their sense of "'self," both individually and collectively. Moreover, in this case, the journals facilitated a semiotic means of viewing self through the concept of being a writer in a particular discipline.

Writers gain opportunities to refine their judgment and decision making as to when and how they present information visually (cf. Robert Goldbort, 2006, p. 174-194) and these journals are associated with a "spirit of relaxation" associated with growth (cf. Elise Hancock, 2003, p. 28) and learning that may be fostered by providing participants with writing spaces that offer them freedom, but also an opportunity to re-make themselves (e.g., Phyllis Creme, 2008, p. 62, cf. Maggi Savin-Baden, 2008). Here, writing is a socially-situated set of meaning-making practices (cf. Lesley Gourlay, 2009, p. 182). As such, journaling can become a personal journey and tied in with a holistic vision of life (Clare Walker Leslie & Charles Roth, 2000, p. 93-100). There is a strong sense of desire and anticipation concerning a shift in a sense of "self" as a process of going to university and the journals appear to have become containers for an epistemological medium of expression, associated with a collective sense of "belonging" at university (cf. Mark Palmer, Paula O'Kane, & Martin Owens, 2009), an individual desire to not lose a sense of "self" during the process and an awareness that processes of transformation are taking place. As one participant articulates:

Academic writing feels like something I've produced that is separate to me and is passed on to the audience. In comparison journal entries feel more like an extension of me, and part of who I am.

REFERENCES

Antoniou, M., & Moriarty, J. (2008). What can academic writers learn from creative writers? Developing guidance and support for lecturers in higher education. *Teaching in Higher Education, 13*(2), 157-167.

Ashworth, P. (2004). Understanding as thetransformation of what is already known. *Teaching in Higher Education, 9*(2), 147-158.

Badley, G. (2009). Academic writing as shaping and re-shaping. *Teaching in Higher Education, 14*(2), 209-219.

Belyea, B. (1996). Inland journeys and native maps. *Cartographica, 33*, 1-16.

de Certeau, M. (1984). *The practice of everyday life* (S. Rendell, Trans.). Berkley,CA: University of California Press.

Creme, P. (2008). A space for academic play student learning journals as transitional writing. *Arts and Humanities in Higher Education, 7*, 49-64.

Creme, P., & Hunt, C. (2002). Creative participation in the essay writing process. *Arts and Humanities in Higher Education, 1*(2), 145-166.

Damasio, A. (2000). *The feeling of what happens: Body, emotion and the making of consciousness.* London: Vintage.

Derrida, J. (1967/1978). *Writing and difference* (A. Bass, Trans.). London: Routledge.

Gell, A. (1985). How to read a map: Remarks on the practical logic of navigation. *Man, 20*(2), 271-286.

Goldbort, R. (2006). *Writing for science.* New Haven, CT/London: Yale University Press.

Gourlay, L. (2009). Threshold practices: Becoming a student through academic literacies. *London Review of Education, 7*(2), 181-192.

Hancock, E. (2003). *Ideas into words. Mastering the craft of science writing.* Baltimore, MD: The John Hopkins University Press.

Hunt, C., & Sampson, F. (2007). *Writing: Self and reflexivity.* London: Palgrave Macmillan Publishing.

Hyland, K. (2002). Authority and invisibility: authorial identity in academic writing. *Journal of Pragmatics, 34*, 1091-1112.

Ingold, T. (2007). *Lines: A brief history.* London: Routledge.

Ingold, T. (2000). *The perception of the environment: Essays on livelihood, dwelling and skill.* London: Routledge.

Ivanič, R. (1998). *Writing and identity: The discoursal construction of identity in academic writing.* Amsterdam: John Benjamins Publishing Company.

Kress, G. (2010). *Multimodality. A social, semiotic approach to contemporary communication.* Oxon, UK: Routledge.

Kristjànsson, K. (2008). Education and self-change. *Cambridge Journal of Education, 38*(2), 217-230.

Lea, M., & Street, B. (1998). Student writing in higher education: An academic literacies approach. *Studies in Higher Education, 23*(2), 157-173.

Leslie, C. W., & Roth, C. E. (2000). Nature journaling with school groups. In C. McEwen & M. Statman (Eds.), *The alphabet of trees. A guide to nature writing* (pp. 93-100). New York: Teachers and Writers Collaborative.

Lillis, T. (2001). *Student writing. Access, regulation, desire*, London: Routledge.

Mauss, M. (1973). Techniques of the Body. *Economy and Society, 2*, 70-88.

Palmer, M., O'Kane, P., & Owens, M. (2009). Betwixt spaces: Student accounts of turning point experiences in the first year transition. *Studies in Higher Education, 34*(1), 37-54.

Savin-Baden, M. (2008). *Learning spaces. Creating opportunities for knowledge creation in academic life.* Berkshire, UK: Open University Press.

Sharples, M. (1999). *How we write. Writing as creative design.* London: Routledge.

Solnit, R. (2001). *Wanderlust: A history of walking.* London: Verso.

Sommerville, E. M., & Creme, P. (2005). Asking Pompeii questions: A co-operative approach to writing in the disciplines. *Teaching in Higher Education, 10*(1), 17-28.

Stevens, F. (2009). Articulating the bridge between theory and practice: A consideration of posters as genres of successful assessment in European prehistory. *Journal of Research in Archaeological Education, 1*(2), 41-57.

CHAPTER 20

BLOGGING TO CREATE MULTIMODAL READING AND WRITING EXPERIENCES IN POSTMODERN HUMAN GEOGRAPHIES

Claire Penketh and Tasleem Shakur

In this chapter we outline the creation of a "blog" as an emergent textual practice, designed to promote reading and writing for human geography students in their final year of undergraduate study. Aware that students on the "Postmodern Human Geographies" module were frequently challenged by the complexity of key readings, and, conscious that students appeared to read too little, we made significant changes to our practices in order to shift student conceptions of the role of reading and writing in this course. We introduced three strategies: a reduction in the reading expectation via the use of focused reading lists; the introduction of a blog where students were encouraged to respond by writing and contributing images and/or video links; and participation in a field trip to a contemporary art exhibition where the students, as readers, became observers of contemporary art work. This chapter will focus on the development of the blog as a means of encouraging students to develop their understanding of key texts by creating pieces of short writing and connecting these with found images. The creation of an explicit focus on reading and writing practices in this module offers a starting point for us to explore the transformative nature of the production of this collaborative online text for tutors and students.

EXPLORING READING AND LEARNING

There is a concern with encouraging students to "get their heads into their books" (see also Good, Chapter 3 this volume). The clear relationship between reading and writing practices is recognized in the development of academic literacies approaches (Lisa Ganobcsik-Williams, 2006, p. 102). Reading in the academy is acknowledged as a complex and creative process where the reader actively contributes to the making of meaning (Saranne Weller, 2010). There is an acknowledgement that attention should be paid to making the connections between reading, writing and thinking explicit to our students (John Bean, Virginia Chappell & Alice Gillam, 2011) and Bean (2011, p. 161) advises us that students "need to be taught to read powerfully," moving beyond reading for meaning to an understanding of how the text works. Such literacy based practices are recognized as forms of social enterprise where "spoken and written texts—do not exist in isolation but are bound up with what people do—practices in the material, social world" (Theresa Lillis, 2001, p. 34). In order to promote students' understanding of how a text works it therefore seems appropriate to encourage them to lift their heads occasionally in order to connect what they read and write with their experiences in the world. For us this has involved manufacturing a series of shifts between language, image and experience by encouraging students to combine, words with found images in response to their key readings in the form of a blog.

Before we go on to discuss the blog in more detail it is worth considering the connections between reading, writing and learning and the blog as a strategy to enhance our students' understanding. A central concern of this chapter is with the combination of word and image via the blog. We will now, therefore, explore the complexities of reading in the academy (Weller, 2010) by referring to two images; *Dusty Boots Line* by Richard Long (1988) and *City Drawings Series (London)* by Kathy Prendergast (1997).

Dusty Boots Line (Long, 1988) can be found at http://www.richardlong.org/Sculptures/2011sculpupgrades/dusty.html

Long's image, a photograph of a straight line in the landscape, is a simple scuff from A to B, from anywhere to nowhere. If we conceptualize reading as this "Dusty Boots Line" it is a means of moving from one point to another, a simple and clear line in an anonymous landscape. It would be a brief brisk walk, perhaps reading for information, moving through the text in a predetermined way. This might represent a simplistic and instrumental view of reading "as a means to an end" discussed by Weller (2010, p. 89) or "surface" reading (Roberts & Roberts, 2008).

City Drawings Series [London] (Prendergast, 1997) can be found at http://www.quodlibetica.com/wordpress/wp-content/files_flutter/1285879161CDLondon.jpg

The simplicity of walking a clear and unobstructed line contrasts with Kathy Prendergast's complex image, a hand-drawn map of a city with obliterated and erased lines. Although aspects of this landscape may be familiar (the River Thames in the London city map, for example) it is largely unclear and complicated. There are recognizable elements to which we might be drawn but some obscured pathways and a lack of clarity reminiscent of some of the tutor conceptions of reading identified by Weller (2010).

We argue here that reading for transparent objectives and predictable outcomes may not always be the most productive for promoting powerful reading and writing. The module "Postmodern human geographies: Space, Technology, and Culture" encourages students to read and apply the work of key postmodern theorists (e.g., Michel Foucault, Jean Baudrillard, Jean-François Lyotard) to their understanding of space, culture and technology. The material is acknowledged to be complex and students are encouraged to understand the contested nature of the relationship between technology, power, and knowledge in contemporary culture via their reading. Students acknowledged that attempting the reading for the course was problematic and had disrupted their understanding of what it meant to read effectively. In the initial sessions, students were introduced to readings from a key text, Michael Dear and Steven Flusty (2002), in order to enable them to make connections between postmodern theory and human geographies. They were asked to explore what they already knew about space, culture and technology and the relevance of this to human geography. We discussed the uncertainties of the topic and many students found the elusiveness of definitions of postmodernism disconcerting. One of our students commented on their initial experience of reading one of the key texts:

> Lee: I hated it [reading], the first couple of weeks—a lot of it was my misconceptions. It wasn't like your straight line oh this is the book, by the time I read this book I'll be able to sit down and write an assignment, it wasn't like that …
>
> A lot of it was very theoretical—on the whole the texts that you read for some of the modules it's black and white you know there's an end result there's an essay to write there's an assignment to do so I can read and I can copy and paste my way through.

Here Lee identifies a different kind of expectation in relation to his undergraduate reading, recognizing the differences in the type of material he was asked to read and his previous experiences of reading and writing at university. In describing his former experiences of writing he can track a clear and direct line between reading and writing. He describes a certainty in working to an end result that can be clearly defined. However, the reading expectation for "Postmodern Human Geographies" demanded that students work with uncertainty. Although potentially disconcerting for students, we recognize the possibilities of working with readings that might promote this different type of learning experience.

The work of Dennis Atkinson (2011) has been useful in exploring these ideas about uncertainty in the processes of learning and this has helped us to think about how we might encourage students to read and write with uncertainty. Drawing on the work of French philosopher Pierre Bourdieu, Atkinson describes real learning as an ontological shift involving the potential of a new state "that-which-is not-yet" (2011, p. 14).

Atkinson says:

> If we conceive of learning as a move into a new ontological

state, that is to say where learning opens up new possibilities, new ways of seeing things, new ways of making sense of what is presented to us in our different modes of existence, then this movement involves, "that which is not yet." Accepting such new states involves accepting new states of existence as learners. This idea would indicate a space of potential.

"Dusty boots line" represents "that-which-is" or that which is predetermined where the potential for real learning is closed down. Prendergast's map, in this context, represents "that-which-is-not-yet" where uncertainties about the nature of the text can offer "a space of potential." Uncertainty appears to offer potential for "real" learning but this can also be problematic. In previous iterations of the module there was an implicit expectation that students engage with complex reading but little work with students on the ways that they might do this. There was also no explicit reference made to the role that writing could play in enhancing students' understanding of the course. There appeared to be a mismatch between a module that embraced an engagement with complex reading yet offered no explicit teaching of strategies to do this effectively. We will now explore the blog as a strategy that offered an opportunity for students to open up a space for reading and writing in order to explore these uncertainties.

THE BLOG

The use of a blog, although new to us as a teaching and learning approach, is not particularly new or novel but part of an increasing range of technological approaches (Churchill, 2009; Will Richardson, 2006). The abbreviated "web-log" offers the potential for connectivity and collaboration via "micro-publishing" (Jeremy Williams & Joanne Jacobs, 2004) with the ability to share ideas and potentially reach a wide audience. This use of technology has strong associations with democracy and accessibility but this is off-set against concerns regarding a flood of low-level trivia. For us, the blog was an accessible platform where students could share their experiences of key texts via short pieces of exploratory writing. We considered these opportunities to write as particularly important since the module was assessed via spoken contributions to seminars and a final oral presentation. We were concerned that there were no formal opportunities for students to develop their thinking via writing about the texts and the blog provided a significant platform for the students to engage with "thinking-writing" (Sally Mitchell et al., 2006). The blog was created as an interpretative space where students could work with uncertainty via "low stakes" exploratory writing (Peter Elbow, 2001). We opted for a "closed blog" only accessible to our group of students and tutors to support this comparatively risk free approach.

Importantly, the blog emphasized visual as well as written contributions, and as tutors we aimed to encourage students to bring something to their emerging understanding of the text. We wanted to use the blog to support the students' understanding by their development of text/image combinations. For example, students were asked to consider the seemingly impossible task of defining postmodernism (Figures 20.1 & 20.2). They were able to draw on architecture, fashion, literature, and film in order to question difficulties of definition and express confusion at their first engagement with their reading. We designed the blog in order to promote a collaborative approach to understanding between students. In addition, tutors modelled their own thought processes via short pieces of writing and uploaded images that would resonate with key readings. Students were able to read each other's ideas and see images that others had connected to their readings. This next section explores the significance of the role that the image can play in deepening our understanding of language and outlines some of the key ideas that informed our practices in this respect.

VIOLENCE AND THE IMAGE

Figure 20.1: Initial Responses (1)—exploratory writing and image finding in response to defining postmodernism.

The essayist tradition as the dominant mode of teaching, learning, and assessment in higher education, prioritizes particular language-based practices. In designing the blog to visibly connect reading and writing, students constructed their own writing in response to the writing of others. Gunther Kress (2011, p. 206) discusses the centrality of language in learning and teaching where it is accepted as the "major route and vehicle for learning and knowing." He suggests that the routes we take through a word-based text can be "taken care of" by established traditions of interpreting reader or author meaning (Kress, 2003, p. 50). However, he encourages us to think about multimodal experiences, acknowledging that there are other vehicles or modes for learning, which can enrich the ways in which language is experienced. He suggests that the image, creates a reading path which is not "automatically given or readily recoverable." It is not only "difference" in mode but the "violence of the image" which "punctures" the language-based system (Jean-Luc Nancy, 2005). Nancy's description of violence as "a force that remains foreign to the dynamic or energetic system into which it intervenes" reinforces the significant differences between language and image based systems. It is possible that the use of a multimodal approach, combining images and observation within the reading process, could be employed to productively disrupt usual reading and writing practices.

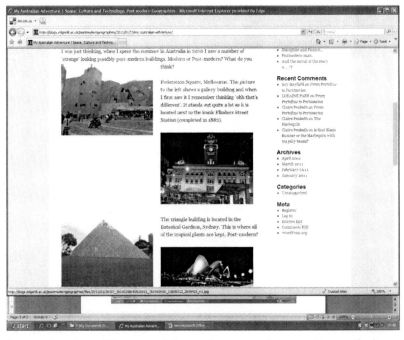

Figure 20.2: Initial Responses (2)—exploratory writing and image finding in response to defining postmodernism.

An emphasis in the module on the relationship between knowledge, power and technology encouraged us to draw on these resources in order to explore the creation of multimodal texts to promote learning. This could be described as the creation of a range of semiotic resources informed by Shirley Brice Heath's description of a web or ecology of learning environments (Brice Heath, 2000). Students engaged with their key reading and were encouraged to respond by introducing images and or video links that resonated with their understanding of their reading for that particular week. The inclusion of images was a deliberate attempt to create alternative spaces for interpretation and exploration, by resisting fixed responses (Elliott Eisner, 2004).

As a shared space, the blog was designed to be both democratic and accessible. Following the taught seminar sessions, students were able to use the blog to discuss various visionary and experiential geographies, uploading relevant postmodern architectural photographs, for example, and links to other literature, whilst making connections with the writing of peers, tutors and a guest lecturer. The blog appeared to be a useful space for creating multimodal texts as interpretive tools for making sense of the key readings. For example, one student uploaded an image from the film *Bladerunner* in response to a piece of science fiction that had been

Figure 20.3: A student's response made to "The Ticktockman" in Dear and Flusty, 2002.

set as a key reading (the "Ticktockman" shown in Figure 20.3). The posting of this image and the related comments prompted a later discussion between tutor and student via the blog. This took place outside the usual "face to face" teaching time and provided useful material for discussion with other students in the next session. It provided a useful extension of the face-to-face taught sessions and also prompted interaction with the key reading as students responded to their reading by bringing images and text to the blog.

SUMMARY

The use of the blog provided opportunities for regular short bursts of writing of comparatively informal texts with opportunities for student participation. Explicit connections were made between reading and writing from the outset and there appeared to be a greater level of interaction with key readings, evidenced, for example, in increased levels of participation in the seminar sessions. Students were active in their participation and contributed to written and visual resources for the module via the blog. We perceived a disruption to the reading paths experienced by this group in comparison to previous cohorts and we would attribute this to the ecology of reading and writing environments that were co-created via the blog. Importantly, students contributed to the production of these environments, rather than their consumption, and the responsibility for working towards some form of understanding was shared by tutor and student. The blog also created a space for writing to be reintroduced. Although there was no requirement to write for assessment, the blog created a forum where written and visual sources were valued for their contribution to collaborative meaning-making. In working with a new text form, and one that enabled creative combinations of text and image, the blog made us, as tutors, re-think the role and purpose of writing to enhance reading, transforming our own as well as students' practices in this respect.

There is an expectation that students in their final year of study will be confident in their understanding of academic practice. However, students are working with changing contexts and shifting expectations and there is value in making reading and writing practices visible for students at every point in their learning. In working with the blog as an emergent textual practice we were forced to revisit our own practices, making our own uncertainties visible to our students through image and text.

REFERENCES

Atkinson, D. (2011). *Art, equality and learning: Pedagogy against the state.* Rotterdam: Sense Publishers.

Bean, J. C. (2011). *Engaging ideas* (2nd ed.). San Francisco: Jossey-Bass.

Bean, J. C., Chappell, V. A., & Gilla, A. M. (2011). *Reading rhetorically*(3rd ed.). Boston/New York: Longman: Pearson Higher Education.

Brice-Heath, S. (2000). Seeing our way into learning. *Cambridge Journal of Education, 30*(1), 121-132.

Churchill, D. (2009). Educational applications of web 2.0: Using blogs to support teaching and learning. *British Journal of Educational Technology, 40*(1) 179-183.

Dear, M., & Flusty, S. (2002). *The spaces of postmodernity. Readings in human geography.* Oxford, UK: Wiley-Blackwell.

Dewey, J. (1910). *How we think.* Boston: D.C. Heath and Co.

Eisner, E. (2004). What can education learn from the arts about the practice of education. *International Journal of Education & the Arts 5*(4). Retrieved from http://ijea.org/articles.html

Elbow, P. (2001). *Everyone can write.* Oxford, UK: Oxford University Press.

Ganobcsik-Williams, A. (2006). Building an academic writing programme from within a discipline. In Ganobsick-Williams, L. (Ed.), *Teaching academic writing in UK higher education—Theories practice and models.* (pp. 98-105).Hampshire, UK/New York: Palgrave Macmillan Publishing.

Kress, G. (2011). Discourse analysis and education: A multimodal social semiotic approach. In Rogers, R. (Ed.), *Critical discourse analysis in education.* New York: Routledge.

Kress, G. (2003). *Literacy in the new media age.* London: Routledge.

Lillis, T. (2001). *Student writing. Access, regulation, desire.* London/New York: Routledge.

Long, R. (1988). *Dusty boots line.* Retrieved from http://www.independent.co.uk/arts-entertainment/art/features/richard-long-walks-on-the-wild-side-1694454.html?action=Gallery&ino=12

Nancy, J-L. (2005) *The ground of the image.* Bronx, NY: Fordham University Press.

Prendergast, K. (1997*). City drawings series. (London).* Retrieved from http://www.kerlin.ie/imagePopup.aspx?img=176

Richardson, W. (2006). *Blogs, wikis, podcasts and other powerful web tools for classrooms.* Thousand Oaks, CA: Corwin Press.

Roberts, J. C., & Roberts, K. A. (2008). Deep reading, cost/benefit, and the constructionof meaning: Enhancing reading and comprehension and deep learning in sociology courses. *Teaching Sociology, 36,* 125-140.

Weller, S. (2010). Comparing lecturer and student accounts of reading in the humanities. *Arts and Humanities in Higher Education 9*(1), 87-106.

Williams, J. B., & Jacobs, J. S. (2004). Exploring the use of blogs as learning spaces in the higher education sector. *Australasian Journal of Educational Technology, 20*(2), 232-247.

CHAPTER 21

WORKING WITH GRAMMAR AS A TOOL FOR MAKING MEANING

Gillian Lazar and Beverley Barnaby

Academic literacies has been described as an "overarching framework" (Joan Turner, 2012, p. 18) which aims to scrutinize critically the dominant values, norms and institutional practices relating to academic writing (Caroline Coffin & Jim Donoghue, 2012). One dominant value, often articulated by some academics and students, is that "correct grammar" at sentence-level is essential for good academic writing. However, this focus on sentence-level grammar is often associated with a top-down prescriptiveness in which "peremptory commands" about correct usage are linked with a negative evaluation of a person's speech or writing (Deborah Cameron, 2007, p. 1).

This chapter focuses on a small-scale project at a post-1992 university[1] in North London, in which a number of first-year "Education Studies and Early Years" students were referred to a writing specialist by an academic in order to improve their "poor grammar." The writing specialist had already collaborated closely with the academic and her colleagues in "Education Studies and Early Years" in developing three "embedded" sessions (Ursula Wingate, 2011) which were integrated within the students' modules, and were delivered during course time. The sessions were broadly informed by a "Writing in the Disciplines" approach, involving collaboration between academics and the writing specialist in terms of the design, content, and delivery of the sessions, and in encouraging students to engage from the outset with disciplinary discourse (Mary Deane & Peter O'Neill, 2011). These sessions aimed to make explicit to students the lecturers' tacit assumptions of what was required in academic writing assignments (Cecilia Jacobs, 2005) in relation to genre, argumentation, structure, academic style, and referencing. Nevertheless, even after the delivery of these sessions, a cohort of 23 students was identified by subject academics as still having significant problems with writing, primarily with "poor grammar." The academic who referred the students to the writing specialist was motivated by a strong commitment to provide appropriate support to these students, as weak grammar had been identified by academics teaching on the programme as the key difficulty which was preventing them from progressing in their studies.

The writing specialist was interested in unpacking the notion of "poor grammar" with both students and academic staff, since labelling students as having poor grammar seems to raise an important issue. To what extent can a focus on grammar form part of an academic literacies approach, since an emphasis on "surface features, grammar, and spelling" is often characteristic of the study skills approach, which attempts to "fix" students' problems with writing in a top-down, instrumentalist way (Mary Lea & Brian Street, 1998). Is a focus on sentence-level grammar compatible with the notion of exploring writing as a social practice, and its concomitant emphasis on issues of identity? The writing specialist was interested in investigating some of the views of academics with regards to grammar, particularly the ways that these manifested in the kinds of comments/annotations they wrote on student assignments. She was also interested in devising and delivering a series of classroom-based activities which might enable students to explore grammar in more transformative ways, for example, by investigating how grammar can be understood as a tool for making meaning, as well as the relationship between grammar, student identities and the complex power relationships both within the university and the wider geopolitical context. This chapter thus begins with a brief discussion of the overall context, and of a small-scale investigation of the views of three academics regarding "correct grammar" and the ways that these were instantiated in the kinds of annotations that they made on student assignments. Sample activities for classroom use are then provided, followed by students' reactions to these activities. We conclude with a brief discussion of some of the tensions and transformative possibilities arising from this project.

THE CONTEXT

The project involved working with a cohort of 23 students, identified by the academics marking their work as having "poor grammar" in an assignment in which students were required to outline and evaluate the contents of a chapter in a prescribed textbook. The cohort of students was linguistically extremely diverse. It included students who described themselves as native speakers of English, but who also used non-standard forms of grammar typical of local communities in London (Sian Preece, 2009). The cohort included bilingual or trilingual students who routinely used grammatical forms which may be considered acceptable in global varieties of English, such as Indian or Nigerian English, but which are generally considered wrong in standard British English (Andy Kirkpatrick, 2007). An example of such a form is pluralised uncountable nouns (e.g., *informations, knowledges, researches)*. A third group encompassed international students, who had learned some English at school in their own country. Finally, there was a category of multilingual students, often refugees, who spoke one language at home with their family, had been educated in a second or even third, and had then had to acquire English in informal settings when they arrived in the United Kingdom.

Given the constraints of timetabling, it was decided that four one-hour "grammar" sessions would be provided. Despite the efforts of academic staff to put a positive spin on the sessions, some of the students who were referred to the sessions may have felt stigmatized initially. In questionnaires devised by the academic following the delivery of the sessions, 69% of the students said that they appreciated the offer of help, while 31% said that it made them feel "uneasy," "uncomfortable," and "let down." Thus, it is clear that labelling students' work as grammatically deficient played into a very normative view of what constitutes acceptable academic writing. On the other hand, for many of the students involved, acquisition of sentence-level grammar in English was a largely unconscious process which had never been subjected to conscious analysis or reflection. This had two negative consequences. Firstly, students were limited in the ways that they could manipulate grammar to convey different meanings. Secondly, when students were asked to proofread their work by lecturers, many of them could not identify the ways in which their work departed from the grammatical norms that the lecturers were enforcing.

THE LECTURER PERSPECTIVE

Why did the academic staff involved in the project consider grammar to be important, and how did they signal this to their students? What types of grammar "errors" did they consider significant in student writing? In order to explore these questions, three lecturers who had marked student assignments on the course were interviewed. They were also asked to annotate chapter reviews from three students, bearing in mind the main areas of grammar which they felt should be pointed out to students.

The interviews with the lecturers revealed not only a strong consensus about why grammar was important, but a sense that grammar was not just a surface feature of writing, but a tool for communicating meaning:

> … in order to make sure they convey their ideas clearly, they
> need to learn basic grammar. (Lecturer 1, Interview 22/2/2012)

> Grammar is very important, because the meaning is lost if the
> grammar is incorrect. The clarity of expression and communica-
> tion is linked with grammar. (Lecturer 3, Interview 23/2/2012)

In addition to the interviews, the small sample of marked chapter reviews was analyzed, which revealed that lecturers had different approaches to marking grammar in assignments. One lecturer simply underlined errors, without providing any further information; another replaced the error with a "correct" version, while a third provided a "correct" version, but also wrote some explanatory comments in the margin. Overall, this approach to marking revealed a top-down prescriptiveness aligned to the 'study skills' approach to teaching writing (Lea & Street, 1998).

When the lecturers' annotations for the assignments were compared, it was clear that there was both a high level of agreement about which types of errors should be pointed out to students, as well as a high level of conformity to the norms of standard British English usage. In the interviews, grammatical areas which were mentioned as ones to point out to students included "faulty" sentence construction, incorrect punctuation, incorrect spelling, omission of "little" words such as definite articles, misuse of tenses, confusion between singulars and plurals (including pluralising uncountable nouns), and inappropriate word choice. It was significant that the list included the omission of definite articles and the pluralising of uncountable nouns, which are often features of non-British varieties of English (Eyamba Bokamba, 1992; Kirkpatrick, 2007). For students who are "native" speakers of these varieties in countries such as India and Nigeria, the "mistake" may only become evident in the context of British Standard English.

DEVELOPING CLASSROOM-BASED ACTIVITIES

In order to devise appropriate activities for the students, an analysis of common student "grammar errors" in the chapter reviews was undertaken. From the analysis, it was clear that, in addition to difficulties with grammar, some students had not understood the overall rhetorical purpose of the review, and had simply summarized the chapter contents. This suggests that "poor grammar" can sometimes be a blanket term that encompasses other aspects of "poor" writing. The assignments of other students revealed a good understanding of the purpose of a review, but were grammatically weak, often in the key areas identified by the lecturers. The question which then arose was how to develop students' grammatical competence in these areas in ways which emphasized the meaning-making potential of grammar, while also stimulating awareness of what Ann Johns (1997) calls a "socio-literate" perspective. This meant that the activities attempted to enable students to make connections between grammar and issues relating to identity and power relationships in writing. For example, if students routinely used grammar forms identified as "non-standard" in the British context, either with friends and family in the United Kingdom, or in more formal settings in their home country, then what kind of shifts of identity were required for them to use standard forms in their academic writing? An inventory of classroom activities was developed in response to this. The design of these activities was also informed by some of the evidence in research into second language acquisition that "form-focused" instruction (i.e., drawing students' attention explicitly to the form and meaning of a particular grammatical structure) is beneficial to their learning of grammar (Nina Spada, 2010). The working assumption was that form-focused instruction might benefit all students in the group, even if they were not second language speakers of English. In addition, the tasks incorporated a number of principles for promoting language awareness, including discussing the language analytically, employing learner-centred discovery activities and engaging students both affectively and cognitively (Simon Borg, 1994).

SOME SAMPLE ACTIVITIES

1. REFLECTION ON DIFFERENT VARIETIES OF GRAMMAR AND STUDENTS' IDENTITIES

The aim of these activities was to encourage students to reflect on how the grammatical forms they utilized might signal particular aspects of their identity, and to validate the complex hybridity of many student identities as expressed in the grammar they used. Suresh Canagarajah (1999) has pointed to the difficulties that students may experience in bridging the gap between the English they use in their vernacular, and the standard forms used in academic writing. Top-down feedback comments by academic staff underline the notion that there is only one "correct" form of grammar, thus potentially stigmatizing non-standard uses of grammar and the expressions of identity that go along with them.

   a. Students draw and discuss diagrams, detailing their own linguistic profile, including the different languages and varieties that they speak, with whom they are used and in what context.
   b. Students discuss sentences, contrasting sentences or paragraphs containing standard and non-standard grammatical forms, and explore when and by whom they might use them. For example, with family and friends versus in the university. How might shifting from one repertoire to another feel?
   c. Students discuss a series of statements relating to grammar:
      Do you agree or disagree with these statements. Why?
      • Using particular grammar makes you a member of a particular club.
      • Grammar can never be wrong; it can only be inappropriate.
      • Changing the grammar I use, changes the person I am.
   d. Students are asked to "think ethnographically" and note down examples of different grammatical forms they notice being used in their daily lives; these can then be discussed in class.

2. CONTRASTIVE ANALYSIS

The aim of these activities was to emphasize that the manipulation of different grammatical forms empowers writers to make meaning in different ways. For example, students compare a number of different sentences or paragraphs contextualized within academic texts, which illustrate contrastive uses of grammar, e.g., the active voice and the passive voice; or the use of the present simple and present perfect, versus the past simple when quoting. Do they reveal any differences about the writer's position in the text (Ken Hyland, 2002), or about the writer's attitude to the contemporary relevance of the quote (John Swales & Christine Feak, 2004)? How would students feel about using them and why?

3. Strategies for "Noticing" Different Grammatical Forms

The aim of these activities was to draw on some of the strategies commonly used in English Language Teaching to enable students to analyze the meanings encoded in specific grammatical forms. This might encourage students to engage cognitively with grammar, rather than slavishly accepting the "correct form" with no real understanding of why they might actively choose to use it.

a. Encouraging students to develop a series of "concept questions," which can help them to disambiguate grammatical meaning. For example, in relation to the sentence *The book is aimed at professional*, students could apply these questions: *Do you mean one, or more than one "professional?" Is this okay in the version of English spoken in your home country? In standard British English, how do you make it clear how many professionals there are?* Students are asked to apply these concept questions when proofreading.

b. Students are asked to compare a text with numerous grammar "mistakes," with a "reformulated text" (Scott Thornbury, 1997) with none. How significant are the mistakes in the original in terms of meaning? In what ways does the reformulated text change the meaning? In what ways does the reformulated text conform to standard usage? How important (or not) is this?

STUDENTS' RESPONSE TO THE ACTIVITIES

All of the activities above were used in the four sessions with the group. Initially, the intention was that the students should keep a reflective log of their reactions to the activities, but disappointingly, the responses to this were limited. When questioned, students mentioned that they were very short of time as they were working on assignments that counted towards their final grades, whereas the logs did not. However, some responses were received:

I found the activities useful, especially the activity that involved
us getting into pairs and discussing how our mother tongue

differs from English.

> From my point of view all the exercises we have in the lessons are useful but I have find(sic) that punctuation and the use of articles as one of the most important points to remember when we have to write an essay as it can change the meaning of what we are trying to say. It is also important to know when we should use singular and plural, as it might mean the opposite of what we are trying to explain.'

CONCLUSION

During the implementation of this project a number of tensions emerged. One surprising tension was that many of the students were initially keen to "learn rules" about grammar, and tended to classify any deviance from standard British English as "wrong." Discussions about the legitimacy and appropriacy of non-standard English became quite heated, with a few students vehemently insisting on the use of the standard form in all contexts. There was sometimes a slight impatience with discussions about the broader socio-politics of language, with students simply wanting to know what was "correct." This suggests that the views of students reflect the views about language held in the wider society, including the belief that prescriptive rules regarding correct usage are valid in all contexts. Thus, one of the tasks of the writing specialist is to encourage students to question and explore these in order to genuinely transform attitudes regarding grammar. Nevertheless, most students were very appreciative that the complexity of their linguistic identities was valued and seen as a resource, which may not always have been the case within the university context. This would suggest that the activities utilized in the sessions were genuinely transformative for some students in encouraging them to move from a view of grammar as simply "right or wrong," to one in which grammar is regarded as a tool that can be manipulated for expressing different aspects of identity in different contexts. The students thus appeared to develop an improved awareness of the kind of grammar considered appropriate in an academic context, while also feeling that their complex linguistic identities were being validated. For example, a number of students reported on feedback forms that the activities used in the sessions had changed their views about grammar and its relationship to meaning, and that they enjoyed the activities in which they were asked to draw on their own linguistic repertoires.

Another tension was between the academics' comments that grammar is a tool for making meaning, and the evidence from their annotations that standard forms need to be enforced, either by underlining these or providing the "correct" forms for the student. Theresa Lillis (2003) has called for a dialogue to be at the centre of an academic literacies approach, but lecturers' annotations about grammar generally communicate rather top-down prescriptiveness, with little space for encouraging critical engagement by students. Perhaps marking annotations could instead include "concept" questions relating to any ambiguities in meaning arising from the way a grammatical structure has been used in an assignment. Or perhaps annotations could encourage students to consider more deeply the issues of identity that may arise when they experiment with "new" forms of grammar. Overall, the collaboration between the writing specialist and academics has been transformative in initiating a dialogue about how marking methods could encourage a more dialogic relationship between staff and students, and in encouraging academic staff to consider how their marking practices can move from a "study skills" model of writing to one which is informed by an academic literacies approach. Such an approach enables academic staff to be more cognisant that the grammar used by students is not simply a surface level feature of text, but is often a complex manifestation of students' identities.

Joan Turner (2004, p. 108) has argued for "the constitutive importance of language in the academic context" to be better recognized. As sentence-level grammar is an essential part of this language, it will continue to generate both tensions, as well as creatively transformative responses, among those teaching and researching academic writing.

ACKNOWLEDGEMENTS

This project, and the writing about it, would not have come to fruition without the co-operation and support of our students and colleagues.

NOTE

1. The term "post 1992" universities in the United Kingdom refers to former polytechnics or colleges of higher education that were given university status through the Further and Higher Education Act 1992, and also sometimes to colleges that have been granted university status since then.

REFERENCES

Bokamba, E. (1992). The Africanization of English. In B. Kachru (Ed.), *The other tongue: English across cultures* (pp. 125-147). Urbana, IL/Chicago: University of Chicago Press.

Borg, S. (1994). Language awareness as methodology: Implications for teachers and teacher training. *Language Awareness, 3*(2), 611-71.

Cameron, D. (2007). *The teacher's guide to grammar.* Oxford, UK: Oxford University Press.

Canagarajah, S. (1999). *Resisting linguistic imperialism in English teaching.* Oxford, UK: Oxford University Press.

Coffin, C., & Donahue, J. P. (2012). Academic literacies and systemic functional linguistics: How do they relate? *Journal of English for Academic Purposes, 11*(1), 17-25.

Deane, M., & O'Neill, P. (Eds.). (2011). *Writing in the disciplines.* Basingstoke, UK: Palgrave Macmillan Publishing.

Hyland, K. (2002). Options of identity in academic writing. *ELT Journal, 56*/4, 351-358.

Jacobs, C. (2005). On being an insider on the outside: New spaces for integrating academic literacies. *Teaching in higher education, 10*(4), 475-487.

Johns, A. (1997). *Text, role and context: Developing academic literacies.* Cambridge, UK: Cambridge University Press.

Kirkpatrick, A. (2007). *World Englishes: Implications for international communication and English language teaching.* Cambridge, UK: Cambridge University Press.

Lea, M., & Street, B. (1998). Student writing in higher education, an academic literacies approach. *Studies in Higher Education, 23*(2), 157-172.

Lillis, T. (2003). Student writing as "academic literacies": Drawing on Bakhtin to move from critique to design. *Language and Education, 17*(3), 192-207.

Preece, S. (2009). *Posh talk: Language and identity in higher education.* London: Palgrave Macmillan Publishing.

Spada, N. (2010). Beyond form-focused instruction: Reflections on past, present and future research. *Language Teaching, 44*(2), 225-236.

Swales, J., & Feak, C. (2004). *Academic writing for graduate students: Essential tasks and skills* (2nd ed.). Ann Arbor, MI: University of Michigan Press.

Thornbury, S. (1997). Reformulation and reconstruction: Tasks that promote "noticing." *ELT Journal, 51*(4), 326-335.

Turner, J. (2004). Language as academic purpose. *Journal of English for Academic Purposes, 3*(2), 95-109.

Turner, J. (2012). Academic literacies: Providing a space for the socio-political dynamics of EAP. *Journal of English for Academic Purposes, 11*(1), 64-75.

Wingate, U. (2011). A comparison of "additional" and "embedded" approaches to teaching writing in the disciplines. In M. Deane & O'Neill, P. (Eds.), *Writing in the disciplines* (pp. 65-87). Basingstoke, UK: Palgrave Macmillan Publishing.

CHAPTER 22

DIGITAL POSTERS—TALKING CYCLES FOR ACADEMIC LITERACY

Diane Rushton, Cathy Malone and Andrew Middleton

This chapter explores an inter-disciplinary collaboration which set the written word to one side to explore the student voice in a space between speech and writing. It presents an emerging Digital Posters pedagogy in which student experimentation with the spoken word is designed to support their critical engagement with their subject and by extension their ability to produce the structures of academic writing. The method has been developed collaboratively over three years by the authors: an academic, a writing tutor and an educational developer. The approach has proved liberating for both staff and students and has provided a means of exploring conceptions of academic literacies as being about critical and constructive growth through the students' exploration of language and their representation of knowledge.

THE CHALLENGE

The massification of UK higher education and the growing diversity of the student body exacerbate the difficulty of establishing appropriate expectations for, and engagement with, academic writing. Diversity was central to the challenge in this case study, which involved students enrolled on two Sheffield Business School Level 5 (year 2) Business units: Managing in a Global Context (full-time degree, Erasmus, Chinese students, full-time Higher National Diploma (HND) students) and Globalization and Business (part-time degree/HND students). The primary challenge, stated simply, was how to engage these students in writing that promotes learning at degree level; a challenge further compounded by the teaching team's diverse understandings of the function of writing.

ADDRESSING THE CHALLENGE

Colin Bryson and Len Hand (2007, p. 360), in discussing learner engagement, reflect that "positive engagement … is unsurprisingly linked to [students] enjoying what they do" and as Karen Scouller (1998) argues, good performance in essay writing is linked to students developing and using deep learning strategies. We felt a fresh approach was required in engaging the students, one that was not likely to be perceived as addressing a technical deficit and one that developed within the subject itself. As a team we wanted to create a novel arena; one in which students could explore their own voices and, ultimately, re-engage with their own thinking and appreciation of writing as a space for exploring thinking.

DIGITAL POSTERS AND THE DIGITAL VOICE

The realization that a deeply engaging novel approach to embedding writing development was needed coincided with a university innovation project called Digital Voices. This initiative aimed to explore the value of the recorded voice to enhance learning and one of the methods being promoted in that work, Digital Posters, appeared to offer a new environment in which students could discover their academic voice. The Digital Voice project proposed that new, every-day technologies disrupt existing understandings of the "learning environment" and introduce diverse opportunities for using the recorded voice as a way to promote learning. At the same time, the Digital Voice project was intent on exploring usergenerated media as an integrated, pervasive phenomenon; not as something distinct and supplementary to existing teaching and learning concerns.

WHAT ARE DIGITAL POSTERS?

In this case, a Digital Poster is a video based on a single power point slide and produced by a student during a two hour workshop. Students are expected to record a five minute visually rich presentation with spoken commentary. They use screen capture technology, rather than a camera, to record their PC screen. The resultant recording is saved as a digital video file which can be played back immediately in the classroom or later online (see example: http://youtu.be/NitL1LqtG9c).

Technically, digital posters are made feasible by the simple production process which involves the use of familiar software (PowerPoint) and less familiar, yet reliable and highly accessible screencasting software (Camtasia Studio). Familiarity and usability are critical characteristics of the Digital Poster method, supporting the principle that, even though students will be required to work in a way that is new to them, the technical interface should not raise anxiety or otherwise disrupt the primary learning activity of talking about, listening to and reflecting on ideas and knowledge. It is important for the effective engagement of the students that the activity is straightforward, enjoyable and ultimately understood by them as being relevant and useful.

In this case study students used Digital Posters to report on the initial findings from their research into an agreed topic. Prior to attending the workshop, the students selected four or five images, representing their findings about the topic, which they were expected to organize on a single PowerPoint slide. It was explained to the students that they would need to use the images as "visual bullet-points" to support their commentary on their research topic. The students were required to work without written scripts and, instead, to depend on their visual cues as prompts. This was intended to create a structure while allowing them to explore different ways of explaining what they had discovered. The students were each given a headset and screencasting software to record their slide and talk. They were asked to begin by introducing their topic before addressing each of their selected images. To conclude, they were expected to identify any connections between the structural components. Once satisfied with their commentary, the students were able to add zoom and pan effects to their recording using other features in the software. This process resulted in the production of a visual and verbal journey around and then across their slide of images.

WORKSHOP DESIGN

The workshop is organized around four phases: modelling, presentation, production and reflection. The tutor begins by modelling the process in the PC Lab using a headset and the installed screencasting software. The methods are also explained on an illustrated handout which students follow later. The modelling intentionally highlights the difficulty of finding the right words and celebrates the hesitancy found in utterances such as "um" and "err," identifying them as being symbolic of the thinking required to construct an effective presentation of knowledge. This emphasizes that technical perfection is not an expected outcome of the exercise and that finding the right words requires some effort and experimentation.

It is important to stress here, as it is to the students, that the main value of the Digital Posters method is the formative process of making and thinking about the different ways they have to present their knowledge. It is the students' consideration of how they can best visually represent their chosen topic; explain their engagement with their topic and their knowledge of it, which is important at this early stage in their assignment. The students become involved in an electronically mediated, self-regulated, iterative process of talking about their study and rapidly reflecting on their presentation by making design decisions. The iterative cycle in the Digital Posters concept involves the student speaking and recording, replaying and reviewing, and then revising and re-recording their presentation until they are happy with it, or until the workshop moves from the presentation phase into its production phase. It provides an environment in which students can organize their thinking.

The structure of the workshop ensures that students are continuously engaged in making decisions within an ethos of "good enough" production quality, typical of user-generated digital media tasks (Martin Weller, 2011). Each presentation cycle takes about ten minutes depending on the extent of the revisions the student determines to be necessary. During the cycle students are asked to listen to the words they have used, the fluency with which they have used them, the suitability of the structure they have selected and how these factors enable or hinder them in making a coherent presentation. The intention, therefore, is not for students to get anything "right" but for them to explore the open-ended nature of an academic assignment, the need for them to manage this and to develop a suitable academic voice (Peter Elbow, 1995, p. xlvi). The task confirms the uncertain, emerging and fuzzy state of knowledge at this stage in their thinking. The forgiving nature of the spoken word and the inherent open-endedness of images contrast with the apparent finality of the written word at the heart of the student's anxiety. The spoken word gives the student room to navigate what they know and to find the appropriate structure and vocabulary they need. This multimodal view of literacy readily accommodates tentative and reflective expression and brings together the benefits of spatial logic through the visual elements and temporal logic in the use of words (Gunther Kress, 2003).

The production phase of the workshop provides some time for each student to develop their presentation using the software's zoom and pan tools. It allows the student producer to add visual emphasis and to make connections across the structure as well as creating a high level view of the topic in conclusion. The final review phase of the workshop takes the form of a ten minute plenary in which students reflect on the method and whether it helped them to explore their thinking and identify gaps in their knowledge. This metacognitive approach highlights the importance of language, structure and voice in representing knowledge. It is the academic equivalent to a warm down exercise in which students talk about their experience. The following section is largely based upon an analysis of transcripts from these plenary conversations.

REFLECTING ON THE WORKSHOPS

This section draws on our classroom observations of students making their digital posters and, in particular, on the workshop discussion. The data come from eight workshops conducted with approximately 40 students in the third year of this work.

It was immediately evident that students were intrigued by the technology and engaged positively with it. Beyond some initial shyness, the usual reticence of students to speak up disappeared as they began to record their reports. The challenge of recording a personal artefact appeared to absorb the students, immersing them in a private space, albeit within the public environment of a busy PC Lab (Figure 22.1). Students sat side-by-side in the lab, each speaking directly to their screens before playing back the recording. Not only did the use of technology appear to transform the public space into private space, but it also worked as an interactive mirror, creating a strong virtual audience for some students.

Figure 22.1: Students producing digital posters in a workshop.

The impersonality of the technology and the lack of social dynamic helped some students to focus on the task in hand:

> When you make eye contact with people [in presentations]
> you kind of think you're buying yourself a bit more time. It's
> just different when you're staring at a computer screen. It's like
> "Go"—that's it …

Others personified the computer as a listener; their partner in their dialogic exchange,

> You can kind of forget you're talking to a screen. You're talking to
> someone. So it's like they're listening and there's a connection there.

The novelty of the technology and the task was perceived positively as being "fun," "interesting," and "a good way to engage your attention," and contributed to a high sense of engagement and ownership:

> You learn a lot because you don't want to do it badly. Because it's your voice you want to get it right.

The Digital Poster method requires students to work without a written script or notes and many students remarked on how the use of images helped them to structure their thinking. This student's comment was echoed by many others:

> I think it is useful [to think about structure in terms of pictures] because you think about a picture in a lot more words than just writing. You get an image in your head and you create thoughts around the picture. I think it helps to open your mind about the topic.

As the concept of photo elicitation suggests (Douglas Harper, 2002), the students explained that while the pictures made room for thinking, they also created a focus:

> The pictures help you to concentrate. When you look at them your thoughts start to take shape and they help you to focus on your topics.

> It was easy to come up with words just by looking at the picture.

The technology enabled students to capture their words with spontaneity and then revisit and reflect on this as they mentally redrafted their digital poster. The interplay of "product" and "process" involving the rapid reversioning of artefacts seems to locate Digital Posters in a space between speech and writing. The process encouraged a metacognitive engagement among students alongside their focus on producing content. Because the method is modelled as an unusual, imperfect, and transitory media, it created a space for low-stakes, critical self-evaluation.

Due to the novelty of the medium, the students were not inhibited by preconceived ideas of perfection. The medium acted as a mirror:

> I spoke it initially, but when I listened back I realized I'd said it incorrectly ... it emphasizes the importance of having a good understanding of the subject you're talking about.

> It's good listening back to yourself because you can hear whether or not you know what you're talking about.

There was some evidence that the iterative process facilitated a shift in tone from a more personal to a more public, formal voice; one more suited to the academic context and task. The Digital Poster workshops were an isolated event for the students, but several suggested they might do something similar independently:

> I think it will definitely help a lot [to do more of this at home]. It's giving me a clearer view about what I'm doing.

> On future projects, if I'm not sure where I'm going, [using pictures to indicate structure] would help [me] to pick out what are the key points and elements which I need to use and which ones I need to research more on or change the ideas.

DIGITAL POSTER GALLERY

The students were given the option of uploading their posters to a "student gallery" in their Blackboard virtual learning environment. This created an audience for the products, allowing for peer review and comparison. The Digital Poster gallery also allowed the authors to reflect further on the approach. Having four pictures on one slide, rather than on a series of slides, meant the stronger students tended to make the connections between the visual elements, relating them back to an overarching idea or main point. This was echoed, but not replaced, by the use of the software's zoom and panning functionality to add emphasis.

The simple use of visual prompts encouraged students to engage in their topics in ways which could translate into their academic writing. For example, the relationship between carefully selected graphics and presentational clarity was a characteristic of the most successful posters. They created a coherent structure and organization; features that potentially make it easier for the "reader" to follow the presenter's train of thought, whether in speech or in writing. Feedback was given on the posters that had been uploaded to Blackboard. This provided an opportunity to deconstruct the best examples and begin to explore with the students how academic literacy develops, how abstractions such as critical analysis and the use of evidence and structure translate into language.

CONCLUSION

A major driver for this work was student disengagement with academic writing and their difficulty in valuing writing as anything other than a means of reporting their state of knowledge. Exploration of the Digital Posters method has not only helped to clarify to the students the significance of aspects of academic writing, but has been revelatory to us as developers of the method too. In particular the relationship of academic discourse to student selfregulation (Zimmerman, 1989), conceptualizations of multiple literacies and multimodality (Kress, 2003), and the benefits of reassessing digital media-enhanced learning environments have been influential in developing our own thinking.

The student production of Digital Posters created a useful framework with which to engage students as reflective and critical learners despite their reticence at being challenged. The novelty of the medium, the decision-making associated with designing the poster presentation, the clear communication required to represent the state of each student's grasp of their topic, and the immediate feedback coming through the iterative review, reflection and revision cycle, all contributed to creating a rich, immersive, intensive and engaging learning opportunity. For us, the shift from written media to the spoken word and the integration of audio-visual media seemed to recast the whole issue of student engagement in academic discourse and academic writing.

We found that the strongest indication of success in this study was in comparing the eagerness of the students to talk about their experience of constructing their Digital Posters, and their compulsion to produce "a good take," with their previous reticence to engage in discussions about academic writing. Looking to further developments, we are interested in exploring the intertextual and dialogic aspects (Mikhail Bakhtin, 1981) in the transfer of presented knowledge from one medium to another, which we hope might help us to engage students more critically with the relationship between their digital posters and their academic writing.

REFERENCES

Bakhtin, M. M. (M. Holquist,Ed.). (1981). *The dialogic imagination: Four essays.* Austin, TX: University of Texas Press.

Bryson, C., & Hand, L. (2007). The role of engagement in inspiring teaching and learning. *Innovations in Education and Teaching International, 44*(4), 349-362.

Elbow, P. (1995). *Landmark essays on voice and writing.* Mahwah, NJ: Lawrence Erlbaum Associates.

Elbow, P. (2007). *Enlisting speaking and spoken language for writing: The selected works of Peter Elbow.* Retrieved from http://works.bepress.com/peter_elbow/13

Harper, D. (2002). Talking about pictures: A case for photo elicitation. *Visual Studies, 17*(1). 13-26.

Kress, G. (2003). *Literacy in the new media age.* London/ New York: Routledge.

Lea, M., & Street, B. (1998). Student writing in higher education: An academic literacies approach. *Studies in Higher Education, 23*(2), pp. 157-72.

Scouller, K. (1998). The influence of assessment method on students' learning approaches: Multiple choice question examination versus assignment essay. *Higher Education, 35*, pp. 453-472.

Weller, M. (2011). *The digital scholar: How technology is changing academic practice.* London: Bloomsbury Academic.

Zimmerman, B. J. (1989). A social cognitive view of self-regulated academic learning. *Journal of Educational Psychology, 81*(3), 329-339.

CHAPTER 23

TELLING STORIES: INVESTIGATING THE CHALLENGES TO INTERNATIONAL STUDENTS' WRITING THROUGH PERSONAL NARRATIVE

Helen Bowstead

In an increasingly diverse educational context, the attempt to impose "one voice" and one "literacy" on the myriad of "voices" and "literacies" that now make up our student bodies seems ever more futile and ever less desirable. In this reflective piece, I suggest that in order to embrace this diversity, those who work in the field of academic literacies need to challenge and transgress the constraints inherent in "normative" texts in their own professional writing. By drawing on personal narrative and incorporating alternative textual forms, I hope to both argue and exemplify how those who work with student writers can, and should, be troubling dominant academic discourses.

Early responses to the massification of the British Higher Education system were very much informed by notions that many of the new type of university student were somehow lacking in the "skills" needed to succeed. Academic Literacies research has done much over the past 20 years to challenge this deficit model, yet, in my experience at least, the way the attributes and educational experiences of "international" students are conceptualized and described still very often perpetuate the perception that they are somehow "lacking" or "less."

> Discourses of internationalization often position Western and Asian education systems and scholarship in terms of binary opposites such as "deep/surface," "adversarial/harmonious," and "independent/dependent" and uncritically attribute these labels to whole populations and communities of practice. (Janette Ryan & Kam Louie, 2008, p. 65)

Within the binaries and generalizations commonly used to describe those who come from other cultural and educational backgrounds, there is little that does not reflect traditional Western notions of knowledge production or that encourages a positive engagement with the rich diversity an international student body brings to the HE context. In the same way that those students labelled "non-traditional" may struggle to learn the rules of the game and to participate successfully in higher education, so many international students have also found themselves excluded from academic discourse because the language skills and modes of knowledge production that have served them well until their arrival in the United Kingdom are suddenly deemed "deficient." Ursula Wingate and Christopher Tribble (2012, p. 484) argue that "all students, whether they are native or non-native speakers of English, or 'non-traditional,' or 'traditional' students, are novices when dealing with academic discourse in the disciplines" and will therefore need support with their academic writing. But if we accept the claim that all students are "novices," then this begs the question: Who are the experts? It would seem to me that one answer might be; those of us who write and publish academic texts. As Theresa Lillis and Mary Scott point out (2007, p. 18), "the high status academic journal article continues to serve as an implicit model for the texts students are expected to produce," and in almost every case that model closely follows the conventions of a "normative" text.

In my work I support both "home" and "international" students; my job is to help them improve their written language skills and to adapt to academic culture in the United Kingdom. I work closely with many students, often one on one, and while a student's language skills may be the focus of my work, often the personal and the political intervene:

> Angel came to see me because she wanted to practise her spoken English. What shall we talk about I ask her? She doesn't know. Well, tell me how you came to be in Plymouth, I say. Angel begins to talk. She speaks of life under Saddam Hussein. Of chemical warfare and the rising levels of infertility that are the terrible consequence. Of twelve nights in the basement of her house, hiding in the dark. She tells me how she had to battle with a hostile administrative system to be here. Of her determination to complete her PhD and take back something of value to her homeland. To help rebuild Iraq.

More and more in my work and in my research I find that I cannot help but respond to the individuals I engage with, and to what their story is telling me about them and about the world we live in (see Scott and Mitchell Reflections 1 this volume). There is a richness, a depth, a multi-layering in these narrative accounts that fascinate me and which I wish to capture in my writing. Van Maanen (1998, cited in Jaber Gubrium & James Holstein, 2003) says that how research is presented is at least as important as what is presented. Conventional academic writing is a powerful discourse that conceals and excludes; as Laurel Richardson argues, "*how* we are expected to write affects *what* we can write about; the form in which we write shapes the content" (cited in Gubrium & Holstein, 2003, p. 187). She argues that traditional modes of representation serve only to conceal the "lived, interactional context in which the text was co-produced" (Richardson, 1997, p. 139). And so, as I write about the individuals I meet and the way in which these encounters impact on my own writing practices, I try to embody these struggles in the shape and form and content of the text, and to "out" the personal in type (Ken Gale & Jonathan-Wyatt, 2009). I also write in the hope that this "story-telling" and "story-retelling" can help to break down some of the cultural, educational and emotional barriers that position students, and in particular "international" students, both as "other" and "deficient." Stories reflect the discourses that work upon us and therefore there is a need to subject personal narratives to a very "intense and focused" gaze in order to arrive at a better "understanding of the social, of the way individual subjectivities are created and maintained through specific kinds of discursive practices, within particular historical moments, in particular contexts" (Bronwyn Davies & Susan Gannon, 2006, p. 4). Davies and Gannon argue that it is only by recognizing the ways in which discourse works on us, and we on it, that we can begin to initiate some kind of change, to begin the vital process of "disturbing and destabilizing sedimented thinking" (2006, p. 147).

My work with Angel has spanned several years now. In her initial visits to me she wanted to develop her spoken English skills. She hadn't been in the United Kingdom much more than a year then, and had only recently begun work on her PhD. She struggled to convey quite basic information, both orally and in her writing, and gaining her doctorate seemed very far away, to both of us. We have been on a long and eventful journey, one that has revealed much to me about the nature of writing and the power of language. Angel is a university lecturer in Iraq. She is highly educated, and she is knowledgeable and passionate about her subject. Both academically and professionally I am her inferior, and yet because she has chosen to study in the United Kingdom, she is regarded as the one who is deficient. She has struggled to acculturise on a number of levels. Not just to the language of the academy and her discipline, but also to the myriad of other contexts and communities she must negotiate in order to "survive and succeed." Often her "lack" of language has been perceived as a "problem." Proof that she should not be here. An excuse to exclude and dismiss:

> Angel is having a difficult time. She is losing weight again and
> there is a blankness behind her eyes. She has been on placement
> in a local secondary school for the past few weeks so I haven't
> seen much of her. She thought she would be invited to teach, or
> perhaps share some of her expertise. But Angel has been treated
> very badly by some of the staff at the school. They ignore her in

the corridor and send her on menial errands.

"Miss, yes you Miss, I need some more lined paper."

Angel is disappointed in these English women and their behavior toward her. I am disappointed too. I have met those kinds of people before.

Discourses can have very real effects on people's lives. Failing to acknowledge the power discourses have to impact on the way we think and behave, or the way in which we are complicit in their construction and perpetration, is to become a prisoner of what Paulo Freire terms a "circle of certainty" (Freire, 2000, p. 39). If we believe that the world can be ordered and named, if we believe in absolute truths, then we lose the ability to "confront, to listen, to see the world unveiled" (Freire, 2000, p. 39). Freire argues that it is imperative that we engage in dialogues with our fellow men and women and to open ourselves up to what it is that is *really* being said. Working with Angel, listening to her stories and becoming her friend, has expanded my capacity to "know" and has helped me to begin to recognize and trouble the powerful discourses that are currently being constructed to define and maintain notions of the Muslim "other." It has also helped me to recognize the ways in which similar discourses impact on my engagement with all those who might just as easily be categorised as "not us." One of the things that drew me to write about (and with) Angel was the way her life and PhD work intertwined. In her research, she explores the communication barriers children who speak English as an Additional Language experience when they talk about pain and I know Angel and her family experienced the very same language and cultural barriers every day: Angel has lived the "real" experience of the EAL children she has chosen to research. Yet there is no evidence in Angel's professional writing of the painful and personal challenges and obstacles that she has overcome in its creation. For though there is nothing more personal than the work of the "lone scholar," traditional academic discourse encourages, even insists, that the writer must conceal herself and deny her subjective experience.

Angel has had an article published. She is pleased and proud.
She sends me a copy to read. I recognize her work immediately.
It is part of her thesis that we have spent many hours writing
and rewriting. I am intrigued by the smooth, professionalism
of the piece. It reads as a journal article "should." Gone are the
awkward sentences and faulty grammar. Her theoretical basis is
fluently and clearly expounded. The research relevant and appropriately referenced. Angel's work has been fully translated into
the "accepted" language of the academy. Although I am excited
for Angel, I am also saddened that she has been so successfully

"erased" from the text, that there is still no room for the personal or the subjective or the imperfect in the traditional "science story."

I am convinced that in order to challenge the powerful discourses of the "normative" text and to make way for a richer more varied, and more inclusive notion of what can constitute "academic" writing, there is an imperative for those of us who write professionally to reveal our subjectivities in both what we write and in the way we write. Lillis and Scott (2007) note the value of ethnographic research as a tool for addressing inequalities but also suggest that the often small-scale nature of such research projects may have inhibited empirical and theoretical developments in the field of academic literacies. But writers such as Ron Pelias argue that, conversely, it is vital that educators and researchers engage *more* and not less in what he terms "empathetic scholarship." The notion of a shared humanity is central to my research and my writing and I refuse to buy into the notion that ethnographic, even autoethnographic, practices are somehow lacking, less, or deficient. And so, like Pelias and others, I choose to position myself as a writer, and as a researcher who, "instead of hiding behind the illusion of objectivity, brings [herself] forward in the belief that an emotionally vulnerable, linguistically evocative, and sensuously poetic voice can place us closer to the subjects we wish to study" (Pelias, 2004, p. 1). I choose to produce texts that create spaces in which both the personal and the political can resonate and where linguistic norms and textual forms can be troubled (Helen Bowstead, 2011). Inspired by Laurel Richardson I have experimented with poetic transcription and in doing so I have experienced the evocative power of words liberated from the "bloodless prose" of the traditional academic text (Stoller, p. xv, cited in Pelias, 2004, p. 10). In exploring alternative textual forms, I have found I am able to write my way into a place where I can not only formulate a more meaningful response to the social, political and educational issues that I face in my work, but also give voice to those I work with in a way that both honours and empowers them (Richardson, 1997):

> Angel sits next to me while she writes. I try not to watch as her hand moves across the page. I think her hand will move right to left. Awkwardly, as my own would. But it dances across the page. There is nothing linear about the way she writes. When she is finished, I ask her to tell me what she has written. I write down her words but I am not sure I can capture in English what she has expressed in her own language. I decide not to try.

> Angel talks of the pity she sees in people's eyes, of how she feels "second-rate," inferior. But I do not pity her. I have only admiration. She has a lion's heart. I imagine how beautiful her PhD

would have been if she had been able to write it in her own language. How much more she would have been able to say and express. How she wouldn't have needed me, or her supervisors to correct her grammar and shape her prose. But even digitally Angel's language is denied her. Kurdish is not a language easily accessible in Microsoft word.

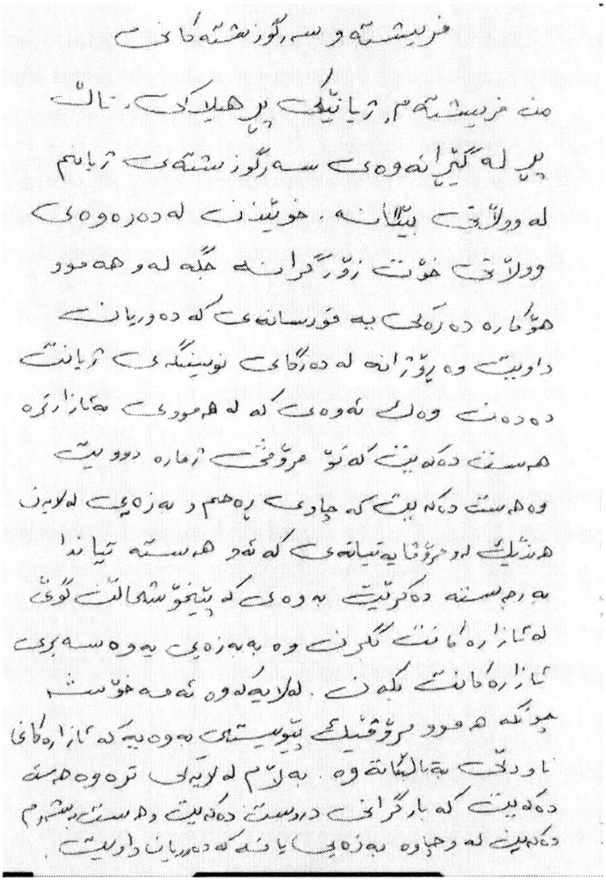

Figure 23.1: Angel and her painful stories.

As we move into a new era of funding regimes and shifting student populations, it is clear that, in many institutions at least, there is going to be a continued and potentially more aggressive push to recruit internationally. In this increasingly globalized higher education context, it seems to me there is an even more urgent need for a radical rethinking of "the ways writing is related to much deeper questions of epistemology and what counts as knowledge in the university" (Ivanič & Lea, 2006, p. 12). I have long felt complicit in something which troubles me greatly. I know for many students, including Angel, that they get through by following the rules, rules that I help impose. But even when they become more skilled players of the game, when they have become more familiar and more articulate in the language of their subject and of the institution, they often don't have the time, the energy, or the confidence to challenge and contest the dominant discourses that they find themselves writing to. Though the academic literacies model has opened up spaces for students to explore notions of meaning-making, identity and power, and though it has foregrounded "the variety and specificity of institutional practices and students' struggles to make sense of these" (Mary Lea & Brian Street, 2006, p. 376), perhaps what those who work in the field still do not do enough is to explicitly challenge those institutional practices in terms of the *kinds* of texts they themselves create and publish.

Westernized notions of coherence and cohesion are, like any discourse, are a construction and, if I can quote George Gershwin, "it ain't necessarily so." I believe that engaging with alternative writing practices, and by that I mean writing that is not bound by the "often impoverished perspective on language and literacy that is trumpeted in official and public discourses" (Lillis & Scott, 2007, p. 21), affords professional academic writers huge opportunities for engaging in the production of texts that embrace and promote forms of knowledge production that not only reflect and celebrate, but also *embody,* what it means to be part of the complex "new communicative order" that is emerging in our ever globalized world (Street, 2004, cited in Lillis & Scott, 2007). In her discussions with student writers, Theresa Lillis (2003, p. 205) often encountered "a desire to make meaning through logic and emotion, argument and poetry, impersonal and personal constructions of text," to create the kind of "hybrid" texts that are "pregnant with potential for new world views, with new 'internal forms' for perceiving the world in words" (Bakhtin, 1981, p. 36 cited in Lillis, 2003, p. 205). Yet, it is incredibly difficult for (novice) student writers to transform their writing practices unless they are exposed to (published) academic work that embodies this desire to trouble academic norms and to explore alternative textual forms. It is not that such texts do not exist, nor that they fail to meet the highest of academic standards. Writers such as John Danvers (2004), Ken Gale and Jonathan Wyatt (2009), Ron Pelias (2004), Laurel Richardson (1997,) Tammy Spry (2011) and Elizabeth St. Pierre (1997) have all published texts which, though they are often striking and personal, and sometimes challenging and difficult, easily meet the criteria that Richardson and St. Pierre (1994, p. 964) suggest can be used to measure texts produced through "creative analytical processes." That is to say that, as well as making a substantive contribution to our understanding of social life, these works demonstrate an aesthetic merit that is both complex and satisfying, and a deep reflexivity that clearly evidences the author's accountability to the people studied. And while it is important that "confounding expectations should not become a new orthodoxy" (Danvers, 2004, p. 171), these are all texts that have a significant emotional and intellectual impact on the reader (see also Horner and Lillis Reflections 4 this volume). Therefore, I am convinced that if we wish to develop a system of higher education "premised upon the explicit aims of inclusion and diversity" (Lillis, 2003, p. 192), then it behoves us as the writers in the field to seek out and produce textual forms that embody and embrace the heterogeneity of our student populations, texts which can act as models of the kinds of alternative modes of mean-making that our student writers can engage with, and aspire to.

REFERENCES

Bowstead, H. (2011). Coming to writing. *Journal of Learning Development in Higher Education,* (3), 8-25.

Danvers, J. (2004). Stuttering at the owl: Poetic displacements and emancipatory learning. In J. Satterthwaite, E. Atkinson, & W. Martin (Eds.), *Educational counter cultures: Confrontations, images, vision* (pp. 165-182).

Davies, B., & Gannon, S. (2006). *Doing collective biography.* Maidenhead, UK: Open University Press.

Freire, P. (2000). *Pedagogy of the oppressed* (30th ed.) (M. B. Ramos, Trans.). New York: Continuum International Publishing Group.

Gale, K., & Wyatt, J. (2009). *Between the two: A nomadic inquiry into collaborative writing and subjectivity.* Newcastle upon Tyne, UK: Cambridge Scholars Publishing.

Gubrium, J., & Holstein, J. (2003.) *Postmodern interviewing.* Thousand Oaks, CA: Sage Publications.

Ivanič, R., & Lea, M. (2006). New contexts, new challenges: The teaching of writing in UK higher education. In L. Ganobcsik-Williams (Ed.), *Teaching academic writing in UK higher education: Theories, practices and models* (pp. 6-14). Basingstoke, UK: Palgrave Macmillan Publishing.

Lea, M., & Street, B. (2006). The "academic literacies" Mmodel: Theory and applications. *Theory into Practice, 45*(4), 368-377.

Lillis, T. (2003). Student writing as "academic literacies": Drawing on Bakhtin to move from critique to design. *Language and Education, 17*(3), 192-206.

Lillis, T., & Scott, M. (2007). Defining academic literacies research: Issues of epistemology,i and strategy [Special issue]. New Directions in Academic Literacies. *Journal of Applied Linguistics 4*(1), 5-32.

Pelias, R. (2004). *A methodology of the heart.* Walnut Creek, CA: Altamira Press.

Richardson, L. (1997). *Fields of play: Constructing an academic life.* New Brunswick, NJ: Rutgers University Press.

Richardson, L., & St. Pierre, E. (1994). Writing: A method of inquiry. In N. Denzin & S. Lincoln (Eds.), *The handbook of qualitative research.* Thousand Oaks,

CA: Sage Publications.

Ryan, J., & Louie, K. (2008). False dichotomy? "Western" and "Confucian" concepts of scholarship and learning. In M. Mason (Ed.), *Critical thinking and learning*. Oxford, UK: Wiley-Blackwell Publishing.

Spry, T. (2011). Performative autoethnography: Critical embodiments and possibilities. In N. Denzin, N. & Y. Lincoln, (Eds.), *The Sage handbook of qualitative research* (pp. 497-511). London: Sage Publications.

St. Pierre, E. (1997). Methodology in the fold and the irruption of transgressive data. *Qualitative Studies in Education, 10*(2), 175-189.

Wingate, U., & Tribble, C. (2012). The best of both worlds? Towards an English for academic purposes/academic literacies writing pedagogy, *Studies in Higher Education, 37*(4), 481-495.

CHAPTER 24

DIGITAL WRITING AS TRANSFORMATIVE: INSTANTIATING ACADEMIC LITERACIES IN THEORY AND PRACTICE

Colleen McKenna

Online writing has the potential to be transformative both for readers and writers. Online texts can be distributed, disruptive, playful and multi-voiced, and they can challenge our assumptions about power, publication, argument, genre, and audience. Increasingly, researchers are exploring how academic work can be performed in digital spaces (Sian Bayne, 2010; Robin Goodfellow, 2011; Colleen McKenna, 2012; Colleen McKenna and & Claire McAvinia, 2011; Bronwyn Williams, 2009); however nearly all this work takes student writing as its focus and all of these cited texts are published in conventional formats (journal articles or book chapters). An exception is Theresa Lillis, 2011 who manipulates standard article formatting by juxtaposing texts on a page—but the piece is still subject to the constraints of a conventional, paper-based journal. Nonetheless, academics are increasingly turning to digital spaces to write about their work, and a body of online scholarship, that largely sits outside institutional quality and promotion structures, is growing up, almost in parallel to more conventional genres of articles, books and reports. Furthermore, online journals such as *Kairos*, which publishes only multimodal "webtexts," are promoting peer-reviewed, digital academic discourse.

In this piece I will consider some of the characteristics of digital writing (such as voice, modality, and spatial design) that are transforming practices of textual production and reading.[1] Building particularly on Lillis's work on dialogism in academic writing (2003, 2011), I will attempt to demonstrate how certain types of digital academic writing can be mapped onto her expanded version of Mary Lea and Brian Street's academic literacies framework, as dialogic, oppositional texts. I will argue that digital academic writing has a huge potential to represent academic literacies principles in practice as well as in theory. In terms of practices, I will draw on digital texts written by professional academics and students, as well as my experience of writing. I am regularly struck by the limitations of writing academic pieces about the digital in a paper-based format. So, part of the basis of this chapter is the development of a digital intertext which explores the ways in which online academic writing can instantiate aspects of academic literacies theory.

JOURNEYS INTO DIGITAL WRITING

In order to explore issues associated with doing academic work online, I have developed a digital intertext which can be found at the following site: http://prezi. com/ux2fxamh1uno/?utm_campaign=share&utm_medium=copy&rc=ex0share.

In this context, I am using the term "intertext," borrowed from poststructuralist literary criticism, to mean a text that is in conversation with another and which addresses similar, but not identical, material. "Intertext" seems more apt than "online version" because the movement between text types is not an act of translation: I am not just reproducing arguments expressed here in another space. Rather, while related concepts are being articulated, the digital environments demand and enable a range of different textual practices, particularly in terms of modality and spatial design. (For an example of a rich pair of digital intertexts, see Susan Delagrange's work on the digital *Wunderkammer*, Delagrange, 2009a, screen shot in Figure 24.1, and Delagrange, 2009b).

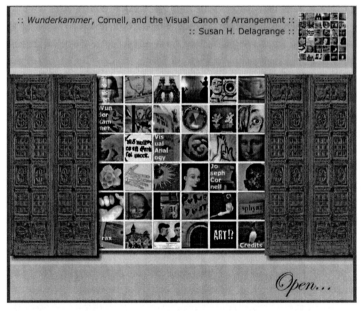

Figure 24.1: A screen shot from Delagrange (2009a).
Image by Susan Delagrange CC BY-NC, published originally in Kairos.

A particular challenge in my writing has been the selection of an apposite digital environment for the creation of the intertexts; "digital" writing can take many forms, and determining what genre, and thus what technical platform to use has been more difficult than anticipated. There were a number of issues to consider such as how far did I want to go back to first principles: for example, did I want to code the text in html? Did I want to build in opportunities for dialogue with readers? Did I mind using pre-formatted spaces? Is part of the purpose of this work to write within easily available and known genres such as blogs?

In terms of accessibility and familiarity of text type, a blog appeared to be an obvious choice. The affordances of blogs are that they allow for textual units or lexia of varying lengths, and they enable hypertextual, multimodal writing with inbuilt spaces for audiences to respond, so dialogism and hybridity are possible. There is also a tendency for the growing body of online academic writing referred to above to be published in this format. However, having initially written a blog on this topic, I ultimately found that the default organizing principle imposed too much of a linear, chronological arrangement of material.

So, after several false starts, I developed a Prezi.[2] Although Prezi is largely associated with presentations rather than texts to be read, there is no reason why it cannot be the source for text production. Indeed, the journal *Kairos* regularly publishes webtexts written using Prezi software. The advantages of Prezi texts (hereafter just Prezi) are that they offer a blank, "unbounded" space in which writing, images, audio, hyperlinks and video can be arranged. A chief affordance is the ease with which textual components can be positioned spatially and juxtaposed with one another; such visual organization is rather more constrained by mainstream blogging software. Furthermore, Prezis are technically easy to write and the author can offer multiple pathways through the text or none, leaving the reader to explore the digital space. The drawbacks with a Prezi are that the dialogic opportunities and practices associated with blogs are less evident and it is not really designed for extensive linking with other hypertexts.

Nevertheless, there is a certain writerly openness afforded by Prezi: there are no margins or pages—just screenspace. As Lillis (2011) drawing on Lipking suggests, in printed texts, there is a "danger of fixing the boundaries of our thinking to those of the published page ..." Digital academic texts have the potential to disrupt our ways of making arguments and describing ideas. They can foreground space and process, and they are often characterized by a lack of closure. They challenge what Lillis calls a textual "unity" and what David Kolb refers to as a "single ply" argument. Digital texts have the potential to bring dimensions including positioning, depth perception, alignment, juxtaposition, distance, and screen position, among others, to meaning making.

MODALITY—DISRUPTIVE AND TRANSFORMATIVE

As has been suggested elsewhere, one of the defining qualities of digital writing is the capacity to create multimodal texts (Bayne, 2010; McKenna, 2012; McKenna & McAvinia, 2011). Students have suggested that the ability to introduce images, audio and animation enables them to knowingly disrupt and playfully subvert the conventions of academic writing and to introduce humour, irony and shifts in voice that they otherwise would not have considered to be appropriate in academic texts (McKenna & McAvinia, 2011).

However, for some students, engaging in this type of work prompts fundamental questions about what constitutes academic texts and practices. (For example, do online texts have conclusions? Who is your audience?) Writing in digital spaces has the potential to throw into relief textual features and reading and writing practices that are largely invisible with more conventional essayistic work. As Gunther Kress (2010a) has observed, multimodality shows us the limitations and "boundedness of language." And beyond that, multimodality offers new and different opportunities for academic meaning making: "There are domains beyond the reach of language, where it is insufficient, where semiotic-conceptual work has to be and is done by means of other modes" (Kress, 2010a). The implication of this work and that of others, such as Lillis, is that digital texts may help "liberate" writers from the "structures of print" (Claire Lauer, 2012). Similarly, Delagrange (2009a) speaking of creating her digital *Wunderkammer* describes, how, in early iterations of the work, the written text literally and functionally "overwhelmed" the visual components of the work. The process of redesigning and rebalancing the work caused her to reconceptualize the topic, and she makes the point that, particularly when working with visual material, the very act of creating multimodal, digital texts creates a change in intellectual interpretation, argument and rhetorical approach.

SPACE, ORGANIZATION AND MAKING ARGUMENTS

A strong consideration when writing digital texts is the rhetorical function of spatial organization (and disorganization). In these texts, design is a mode: it is critical to meaning-making and has rhetorical requirements: layout, screen design, sizing; the positioning and presentation of elements all contribute to meaning making (Kress 2010b). Of course, this is not to say that design does not have a semantic role in conventional texts; however, I would argue that there are many fewer restrictions in digital writing, and much more scope to use spaces, gaps and other design elements. Additionally, digital texts enable multiple lines of argument or discussion to co-exist. Within individual sections of text or animation, a certain idea might be developed, but instead of an emphasis upon transitions sustaining a narrative line across an entire piece, a writer can represent the complexity of a web of ideas through a digital text, drawing on a mix of modes:

> It would be misleading to claim that all exposition and argument could and should be presented simply and clearly. Often that is the best way, but … sometimes complex hypertext presentations would increase self-awareness, make important contextual connections and present concepts and rhetorical gestures that refuse to be straightforward and single-ply. (David Kolb, 2008)

One such rhetorical gesture is juxtaposition. Digital texts enable juxtaposition of sections of writing, image, video (among other modes) on many levels: the positioning within the frame of a screen, through hyperlinks, through pop-up animation, to name a few. With a digital environment such as Prezi, the sense of juxtaposition can be extended with the simulation of a 3D space; a reader can zoom into the text to reveal items seemingly located underneath texts on a particular screen. Or, they can zoom out, revealing "super" layers of writing, imagery, animation that appears to sit above a portion of the text. Perspective, as well as positioning can therefore be a feature of juxtaposition. (In accordance with Kress's statement above about the boundedness of language, this rhetorical device is much better illustrated in the digital than on paper).

For Lillis (2011) juxtaposition is a transformative literacy practice that enables alternative ways of articulating academic knowledge including the enhancement of the single argumentative line with extra layers of "information, description and embedded argumentation." Additionally, juxtaposition introduces the potential for a multivocal approach to academic writing, with juxtaposed texts in dialogue with one another, thus enabling linguistic and modal variety (Lillis, 2011). Set out in this way, the practices and features of juxtaposition that Lillis values (plurality of genre, tone, mode and discourse) are frequently features afforded in digital text making. In earlier research (McKenna & McAvinia, 2011) we found that students, almost without exception, used juxtaposition and multimodality in this way when they were given the opportunity to write hypertext assignments.

More recently, Bayne has spoken of the liberating impact of offering her MSc students the option of writing "digital essays." The students use virtual worlds, blogs, video and hypertext to create digital texts which are experimental and unstable. She argues that through this work, students are able to interrogate the writing subject and that there is generally an enhanced awareness of the power relations between reader/writer. The texts are multimodal, disjointed, and often subversive, but they are sophisticated, provocative and stimulating (Bayne, 2012). Both the awareness of power as a feature of academic writing, as well as an awareness of the authorial self are prominent themes of the academic literacies research, particularly work by Mary Lea and Brian Street (1998), Roz Ivanič (1998) and Lillis (2001). Digital texts are useful in enacting these concepts in both practice and theory.

Additionally, Bayne's account suggests the transformative impact of engaging with multimodality and radically different opportunities for textual organization that digital texts have on authors: conventional literacy practices are defamiliarised and writers are potentially awakened to new possibilities for knowledge making. As one student writer told the author: "It [digital writing] does disturb the standard writing practices …. I definitely felt that in the hypertext I could not carry on writing like I did in the essay" (McKenna & McAvinia, 2011). We might ask whether a similar disruption is achieved through the publication of academics' digital scholarly work which disrupts the "normative stances towards meaning makings" (Lillis, 2011) that tend to operate in the academy. For example, Lauer (2011) citing Marshall McLuhan, writes about experiencing a "hybrid energy" when combining images and audio in a digital text, that enabled her to reflect more deeply and differently on her topic. Delagrange, too, observes that it is "impossible to overstate" the impact upon her argument and analysis of working in a digital space and attending to design, coding, screen organization and the integration (and dislocation) of different modes (2009a).

CONCLUSIONS: DIGITAL TEXTS AND ACADEMIC LITERACIES

Both digital texts (with their discontinuities and instabilities) and the associated practices (such as the dialogic interaction between reader and writer and the experimentation with new academic genres) are examples of academic literacies in action. Lillis suggests that the multivocal, dialogic academic text contests the primacy of the essayistic, monologic approach to writing that still is dominant in higher education. In her extension of the academic literacies framework (2003) she identifies dialogism as a literacy goal, and there is no doubt that digital texts and their related practices would sit comfortably in extended sections of her framework, particularly in the way that they make visible and challenge official and unofficial "discourse practices" (Lillis, 2003). Whereas Lillis asks "what are the implications for pedagogy?", this paper extends the question to ask what are the implications for professional academic writing?

Another component of the academic literacies framework foregrounded by digital writing is textual production. Textual production—in this case digital creation and publication—encompasses issues of power, modality, and writing as a social practice. Indeed a consideration of production highlights a potential point of fracture between institutional structures (publishers, universities) and writers. As many have observed, the academy is rooted in print literacy (Bayne, 2010; Goodfellow, 2011; Goodfellow & Lea, 2007; Colleen McKenna & JaneHughes, 2013), with its inherent and symbolic stability and fixity. Print-based texts are more easily controlled—both in terms of acceptance for publication and reader access—than digital ones are. The print "industry" supports a preservation of the status quo in terms of financial and quality models. And so, while I have been exploring the disruptive and potentially subversive features of digital writing from a rhetorical perspective, I feel they are also potentially disruptive from an institutional perspective: allowing scholars to cultivate an identity and readership that is much less easily regulated by a university, discipline or publisher. Beyond this, it is worth bearing in mind Delagrange's observation that the production of digital texts is a "powerful heuristic in its own right" (2009a).

As more academic texts are published in online spaces, pressure will build for institutions to acknowledge the merit of the digital, both for students and academics. That is not to say that I think that conventional essays/articles/books will be displaced, because as suggested above, these new texts are often doing different types of intellectual work. Rather, we will have a wider range of genres and readers as well as a richer understanding about how knowledge can be articulated and read. As suggested above, a notable journal in this regard is *Kairos* (http://kairos. technorhetoric.net/about.html) which publishes refereed "webtexts" (the journal's term) ranging from recognizable, "conventional" papers that have been formatted to enable easy navigation to more experimental forms including powerpoint, webpages, videos, and Prezi documents. *Kairos* is designed to be read online and a founding principle was that a discussion of new forms of writing ought to be conducted in the forms themselves: "As we are discovering the value of hypertextual and other online writing, it is not only important to have a forum for exploring this growing type of composition, but it is essential that we have a webbed forum within which to hold those conversations." (Mick Docherty, n.d.) Beyond such a forum, the value of digital discourse—which often displays a richness and diversity of resources that get flattened in the process of making monologic texts—should be acknowledged in the broader academic community.

Digital academic texts offer new opportunities for modality, spatial organization, reader-writer relationships and text production and distribution. Not only can academic literacies provide a useful frame through which to view such writing but, in return, such texts may help extend the literacies model. Beyond that, the social practices around production, distribution and reception of digital texts offer fertile ground for future academic literacies research.

NOTES

1. The "naming" of these sorts of texts is still relatively fluid (Lauer, 2012). In this paper, I am using the terms "digital writing" and "digital texts" to refer to academic work that is multimodal, created and distributed online, and which resists being easily "published in nondigital form" Delagrange (2009a).

2. For more information about Prezi software and texts, see www.prezi.com.

REFERENCES

Bayne, S. (2012, March). *Digital disaggregation: Accessing the uncanny posthumanism.* Paper presented at the *Society for Research into Higher Education Digital University Network Launch seminar*, London.

Bayne, S. (2010). Academetron, automaton, phantom: Uncanny digital pedagogies. *London Review of Education, 8*(1), 5-13.

Delagrange, S. (2009a). When revision is redesign: Key questions for digital scholarship. *Kairos: A journal of rhetoric, technology, and pedagogy, 14*(1). Retrieved from http://kairos.technorhetoric.net/14.1/inventio/delagrange/index.html

Delagrange, S. (2009b). Wunderkammer, Cornell, and the visual canon of arrangement. *Kairos: A journal of rhetoric, technology, and pedagogy, 13*(2). Retrieved from http://kairos.technorhetoric.net/13.2/topoi/delagrange/

Docherty, M. (n.d.). "What is Kairos?" Retrieved from http://kairos.technorhetoric.net/about.html#sections

Goodfellow, R. (2011). Literacy, literacies and the digital in higher education. *Teaching in Higher Education, 16*(1), 131-144.

Goodfellow, R., & Lea, M. (2007). *Challenging elearning in the university: A literacies perspective.* Maidenhead, UK: Open University Press.

Ivanič, R. (1998). *Writing and identity: The discoursal construction of identity in academic writing.* Amsterdam: John Benjamins Publishing Company.

Kolb, D. (n.d.). Hypertext as subversive. Retrieved from http://www.dkolb.org/ht/univ2.dkolb/Introduction_143.html

Kolb. D. (2008). The revenge of the page. Retrieved from http://www.dkolb.org/fp002.kolb.pdf

Kolb, D. (n.d.) Sprawling places. Retrieved from http://www.dkolb.org/sprawlingplaces/index.html

Kress, G. (2010a, February). *Social fragmentation and epistemological multiplicity: the doctoral thesis in an era of provisionality.* Keynote address The Doctoral Thesis in the Digital and Multimodal age, Institute of Education, London. Retrieved from http://newdoctorates.blogspot.co.uk/2010/02/doctoral-thesis-in-digital-and.html

Kress, G. (2010b). *Multimodality: A social semiotic approach to contemporary communication.* Abingdon,UK: Routledge.

Lauer, C. (2012). What's in a name? The anatomy of defining new/multi/modal/digital/media texts. *Kairos: A Journal of Rhetoric, Technology, and Pedagogy, 17*(1). Retrieved from http://kairos.technorhetoric.net/17.1/inventio/lauer/index.html

Lea, M., & Street, B. V. (1998). Student writing and staff feedback in higher education: An academic literacies approach. *Studies in Higher Education, 23*(2),

157-172.

Lillis, T. (2001). *Student writing: access, regulation, desire.* London: Routledge.

Lillis, T. (2003). Student writing as "academic literacies": Drawing on Bakhtin to move from critique to design. *Language and Education, 17*(3), 192-207.

Lillis, T. (2011) Legitimising dialogue as textual and ideological goal in academic writing for assessment and publication. *Arts and Humanities in Higher Education, 10*(4), 403-434.

McKenna, C. (2012). Digital texts and the construction of writerly spaces: Academic writing in hypertext. *Pratiques: Literacies Universitaires: Nouvelle Perspectives, 153-154,* 211-229.

McKenna, C., & Hughes, J. (2013). Values, digital texts and open practices—A changing scholarly landscape in higher education. In R. Goodfellow & M. Lea (Eds.), *Literacy in the digital university: Critical perspectives on learning, scholarship and technology.* London: Routledge.

McKenna, C., & McAvinia, C. (2011). Difference and discontinuity: Making meaning through hypertexts. In R. Land & S. Bayne (Eds.), *Digital difference: perspectives on online learning.* Rotterdam: Sense Publishers.

Williams, B. (2009). *Shimmering literacies: Popular culture and reading and writing online.* New York: Peter Laing

REFLECTIONS 4

LOOKING AT ACADEMIC LITER-ACIES FROM A COMPOSITION FRAME:
FROM SPATIAL TO SPATIO-TEMPO-RAL FRAMING OF DIFFERENCE

Bruce Horner in conversation with Theresa Lillis

Bruce Horner is a professor of rhetoric and composition at the University of Louisville. His work takes place within the context of US Composition. In this extract from a longer and ongoing conversation about connections between "Academic Literacies" and "Composition" and, in particular what is meant by transformation, Bruce explores what he sees as a key challenge—how to define and engage with the notion of "difference" in academic writing.

Bruce: A key challenge for us is how to engage with "difference." Scholars of "academic literacies" commonly conceive of difference in three ways: as a characteristic of its subject of inquiry—"academic literac-ies"; as a defining characteristic of the "new" students enrolling in higher education through programmes of massification; and as a goal—transformation (see Theresa Lillis & Mary Scott, 2007).

Theresa: When you say scholars of Academic literacies are you talking about "Academic literacies" as a specific field of work, linked mainly to the United Kingdom, or are you including work on writing from a range of contexts—like "basic writing"?[1]

Bruce: I use "academic literacies" to refer to a "critical field of inquiry with specific theoretical and ideological historical roots and interests" (Lillis & Scott 2007, p. 7), and more specifically an approach grounded in Brian Street's (1984) "ideological" model of literacy as social practice and as seeking to involve a "transformative" rather than "normative" stance towards existing academic literacy practices. But I would also include in "Academic Literacies," US work—mine too—that arises out of disciplinary traditions of literary study and cultural theory and in the United States context often located in the institutional and pedagogical site of "Composition."

In general, I think all of us working with academic writing—whatever the specific institutional or geopolitical location—need to be wary about slippages in how we think about difference. Such slippage may limit how we understand the goal of transformation and how that goal is to be achieved in the teaching of, or about, academic writing and literacy practices. In that slippage, differences among literacies, including academic literacies, come to be conflated with differences among students, and then these differences are identified with specific textual forms—often in terms of whether these are recognizably conventional or not.

Theresa: By "specific textual forms" would you for example mean specific uses of language? Specific languages? Specific levels of formality (or use of language often associated more with spoken language than written language)? Specific clusters of rhetorical conventions?

Bruce: The problem is complicated because any one of these levels of language—lexicon, syntax, register, organization—as well as notational practices more generally, can be claimed as nonconventional and that lack of conventionality identified with the (student) writer's social identity. While this is preferable to identifying such ostensible breaks with convention as evidence of cognitive lack or pathology, it assumes and reinforces a stability to what constitutes conventional academic writing while ignoring the role of the reader in producing a sense of conventionality or its obverse when reading, and likewise assumes a stability to the social and linguistic identity of the student writer that also ignores the mediating role of writing (and reading—Joseph Williams' 1981 essay on "The Phenomenology of Error is still one of the best accounts of this).

One recent version is where what are recognized, and known to be recognized, as instances of code-meshing—e.g., the insertion of representations of African American Vernacular English (AAVE) in academic essays whose lexicon and register are conventionally formal—are fetishized as in themselves doing transformative work. This shifts attention away from what might be said to assigning special status to specific techniques of saying. For example, Geneva Smitherman's (2000) insertion into her academic writing of features readers will identify as AAVE is hailed as in itself doing transformative work. This ignores the actual transformative import of what she is saying, and also overlooks the way in which her use of such features signals, primarily, her status as an established academic scholar—it is, after all, only those with low status who are expected to "watch their language."

Theresa: I understand the potential dangers and I'd probably have used the word reification rather than fetishization but think fetishization brings a useful nuance here. But I must say I am sympathetic to the attempt to disrupt strongly regulated production—and reception practices—and I think Smitherman's mixing or meshing actually adds power to the arguments she is making—in other words the form is not just for form's sake but has an epistemological purpose too. I also think scholars who try to illustrate how mixing might work in their own writings can be caught in a double bind here: if they try to play (for pleasure and fun as well as for serious academic purposes) with resources, they can be accused of using their status to get away with this; but if the same scholars encouraged students to play, without doing so in their own work, they'd be accused of making those with lesser power take responsibility for transforming the academy. I also think that you're overstating the power that scholarly status confers. As we know from our work on writing for publication (Theresa Lillis & Mary Jane & Curry, 2010), scholarly status—and how the language/s used—varies considerably within global scholarly hierarchies.

Bruce: I take your point about published scholarly writing. The danger for me, which you suggest, is in the tendency to argue for pedagogies that advocate "mixing" of forms as a goal in and of itself, which redirects our energies, and those of our students, in less useful directions: formal experimentation for formal experimentation's sake, outside and ignoring issues of context, including power relations, and purpose. More generally, I'm concerned about the slippage between people and forms. This slippage manifests in the use of a spatial framework whereby students, writing, and specific literacy practices are located in terms of relations of proximity, overlap, and hierarchy. Transformation is then understood in terms of resistance, challenges, or opposition to those relations: "importing" literacy practices belonging to one domain to another; challenging hierarchies among these practices by, say, granting legitimacy to those deemed subordinate or "vernacular"; multiplying writers' repertoire of practices, and identities; or deviating from the conventions and practices deemed "appropriate" to a given domain.

Theresa: I agree that there's always a danger of talking as if domains are hermetically sealed from each other—as if the "academic" domain were separate completely from the "home" domain (and I'd guess we'd need to carefully consider how we construct "home"). But I'm assuming that you aren't saying that we shouldn't question the dominant/conventionalized practices that have come to be defaults in specific domains, such as academia? I would be surprised if this were the case given what I know of your work—you challenge the institutional deficit positioning of students who are labeled as "basic writers" (Bruce Horner & Min Zhan Lu, 1999) and in your work on a translingual approach (Horner et al., 2011)) seem to be calling for us (teachers, readers, writers,) to rethink the ways in which we approach texts that look "different" in some way.

Bruce: That's right, though I'd put it somewhat differently now than I may have previously. What I think we most need to challenge, especially at the pedagogical level, is the stability itself of those dominant/conventionalized practices. We can and should teach these practices as historical rather than fixed. So whatever practices student writers (and everyone else) opt to participate in on a given occasion should be questioned, whether those practices are identified with the dominant or conventional or not. Many of us (especially those involved in basic writing) have been focused on rethinking practices identified as different from such dominant/ conventionalized ways, and often to defend the logic of these different practices, we've tended to engage in a peculiar textualism locating practices spatially but not temporally, hence as fixed rather than contingent in significance.

Min-Zhan Lu's chapter, "Professing Multiculturalism," in our book *Representing the "Other"* (1999) best exemplifies our position. The example discussed there of a student who first wrote "can able to" to express having both the ability and permission to do something, then revised this to "may be able to" shows a writer exhibiting agency in both instances. As Min argues, "can able to" should be probed for its logic rather than being dismissed as a simple grammatical error (though error is always a possibility). Writers can then consider whether to maintain that more idiosyncratic usage or a more conventional usage, aware that either decision carries risks and rewards.

For me there are two difficulties arising from adopting a spatial framework for understanding difference in academic (and other) literacies, students, and their literacy practices: first, such a framework appears to grant greater stability, internal uniformity, and a discrete character to the various kinds of literacies, literacy practices, and student identities than is warranted; and second, active writerly *agency* comes to be identified strictly with writers' recognizable deviations from these (thereby) stabilized practices. This poses a dilemma to teachers pursuing transformation of seeming to have to choose between either "inducting" students into dominant literacy practices—to allow for students' individual academic and economic survival—or encouraging students to resist the restrictions of these conventions, thereby putting their academic and economic futures at risk. The fact that requiring production of dominant writing conventions appears to align pedagogy with the (for many, discredited) ideology of the autonomous model of literacy (Brian Street, 1984), and the fact that the students concerned are likely to be from historically subordinated populations, and thus in most need of improvement to their economic situations, make this dilemma particularly acute.

Theresa: I agree that it would be irresponsible for teachers to tell students to resist conventions when using such conventions is central to success—to passing exams, to being recognized seriously as a student. But does anyone actually do this, particularly within disciplinary based spaces? Although I've argued—both implicitly and explicitly—that a wide range of textual forms (at the level of sentence level grammars, vocabulary, modes, languages) should be encouraged and debated in the academy, as a teacher, working with undergraduates and postgraduates in my field (applied and social linguistics), I make students aware of the rules of the game and the consequences of not using these. In some instances, there are opportunities for me to open up default conventions—for example when I'm setting and assessing assignments—but as often—and for writing teachers working at the edges of disciplinary spaces—this is often not possible.

Bruce: I think you're right that few teachers encourage students to avoid conventional academic conventions in their writing. But the terms for using these—often couched as "following conventions"—are often paltry and bleak: "do it to get by," to survive. That approach leaves the actual contingent nature of deploying specific forms unquestioned: curiously, again conventional language gets a pass, its significance treated as a given rather than subjected to genuine questioning. And our textualist bias leads to a conflation of notational difference with social or conceptual difference. Clearly there are times when breaks with conventional language are demanded insofar as that language stands in the way of conceptualization—neologisms like *translingualism* are a case in point. But I suspect that rejection of work on grounds of its breaks with conventional language is often a cover to reject that work because of the conceptual challenges it poses (as I think some of the cases in your 2010 book with Mary Jane Curry illustrate).

I guess what I'm saying is that we need to shift our metaphors or frameworks so that we don't get caught up in only ever recognizing transformation as something that is marked as different in the academy—or only ever recognizing value in *forms* our training leads us to recognize as "different." That would seem merely to flip, while reinforcing, binary oppositions of the conventional/unconventional while retaining an attribution of stable significance to form alone, treated in reified fashion. A US example of a scholar's efforts to grapple with the confines of the spatial framework in pursuing the goal of transformation is an essay by David Bartholomae, "The Tidy House: Basic Writing in the American Curriculum" (1993), frequently cited as calling for the abolition of a separate curricular space to teach students deemed "basic writers," i.e., those deemed unprepared to produce post-secondary-level writing. (see Horner, 1999a, pp. 192-193.) Bartholomae invokes Mary Louise Pratt's now well-known concept of the "contact zone" to counter what he sees as the tendency of basic writing programmes to "bridge AND preserve cultural difference, to enable students to enter the 'normal' curriculum but to insure, at the same time, that there are basic writers" (1993, p. 8). The problem, he sees, is that "the profession has not been able to think beyond an either/or formulation—either academic discourse or the discourse of the community; either argument or narrative; either imitation or expression" (Bartholomae, 1993, p. 324). To counter this, he calls for making "the contact between conventional and unconventional discourses the most interesting and productive moment for a writer or for a writing course" (Bartholomae, 1993, p. 19).

The focus on points of contact promises to allow for the possibility of inter-action among conflicting beliefs and practices. However, the spatial framework invoked (the "space" of the contact zone where, in Pratt's words, "cultures meet, clash, and grapple with one another" (Pratt, 1991) risks reinforcing, by assuming, the stability of the distinctions that Bartholomae aims to challenge: (basic/normal; conventional/unconventional; different/normal). Thus whereas his critique begins by complaining of difference as a product of the basic/normal framework, he ends up advocating a curriculum that retains the notion of students as different, but that adopts a strategy of their integration, rather than segregation. As critics have since complained, the interaction to be advanced is difficult to imagine.

If Bartholomae's work simply illustrates the continuing limitations a spatial framework imposes on thinking about differences and pedagogies of transforma-tion, another example, Roz Ivanič and colleagues' UK study *Improving Learning in College: Rethinking Literacies Across the Curriculum* (2009) directly addresses such limitations. Ivanič et al.'s study initially focused on the ways in which students' "everyday" literacy practices might interact with and support their learning of the literacies required in their college courses, and therefore explored the possible "in-terface" between and among these different literacies associated with different "'do-mains' of students" lives (2009, pp. 1-2), the "'border literacy practices' and 'border crossing' of literacy practices from the everyday to college" (pp. 22-23). However, Ivanič et al. ended up calling into question the "ways in which 'context,' 'domain,' 'site,' and 'setting' are conceptualized" (2009, p. 23) and, as well, the associated metaphors of "boundaries and borders, and of boundary zones, boundary objects and border-crossing" (pp. 23, 24). Ultimately, they concluded that such metaphors, "inscribed in the method we had used to collect the data" about literacy practices, led to a "static two-dimensionality about the Venn-diagram representations and mapped spaces which follow from talk of 'borders' and 'border-crossings,'" ren-dering "the concept of 'border literacies'" "untenable" (Ivanič et al., 2009, p. 172): "we had assumed a border space, but as we moved to bordering as a practice rather than identifying border literacy practices as entities, we saw that the relationship between domains and practices was more complex and messy: they co-emerge" (p. 172). As Ivanič (2009) has observed elsewhere, "'whole' literacy practices ... cannot be recontextualized wholesale into educational settings because the social domain changes the practice" (p. 114).

Theresa: I can see the problems with setting boundaried framings around lan-guage, writing, and semiotic practices, but isn't it also the case that the assessment of student writing in the various disciplines that make up the academy tends to be driven by quite rigid notions and ideologies about what counts as acceptable discourse which is monolithic and monologic in nature? In other words, quite rigid boundaries exist which student-writers (and teachers) constantly bump up against rather than being given opportunities to interact with. Isn't the writing space of "Composition" very different?

Bruce: Yes, you're right. One of the privileges of working in composition in the United States, at least for many of us, is that the composition course, even the required first-year composition course, for all its problems, remains a "special writing space," with instructors given significant say in assessment, as opposed to writing in other sites—one reason I oppose moves to abolish that course. I sense you're pointing to the need to direct our energies more to our colleagues outside writing studies (broadly conceived) and to the public. You've argued elsewhere (Lillis, 2013) that while we might rightly reject commonplace ways of valuing writing in terms of its ostensible "correctness," that does not absolve us of the responsibility for (and the inevitability of) arguing for some kind of valuation of writing. So we might direct our energies towards discussing these other ways of valuing writing: for example, its level of engagement, conceptual heft, accuracy, and so on. These are values that our academic colleagues, as well as the public, might well already share. Here I think I'm simply echoing your argument (Lillis, 2013) that we advocate for our own values in language use, as against prescriptivist grammar values invoked as ideologically neutral "standards."

Rethinking our metaphorical framings here, I think a temporal-spatial framework—rather than just a spatial one—might allow a conceptualization of difference and transformation that is both more readily within the reach of ourselves and our students, and at least potentially of greater consequence. It might help resolve the dilemma those pursuing transformation of academic literacies face of seeming to have to ask students to choose between submitting to dominant conventions in their writing or deviating from these at the risk of academic failure; and it radically challenges key features of the ideology of the autonomous model of literacy against which those taking an academic literacies approach are set. I attribute the fact that we typically do not recognize differences in temporality *as* differences, or as making a difference and accomplishing transformation, to the continuing operation of that ideology in our *dispositions* to language. I'm thinking of Pierre Bourdieu's caution that language ideology has "nothing in common with an explicitly professed, deliberate and revocable belief, or with an intentional act of accepting a 'norm.' It is inscribed, in a practical state, in dispositions which are impalpably inculcated, through a long and slow process of acquisition, by the sanctions of the linguistic market" (Bourdieu, 1991[1982], p. 51)

Theresa: I think the dichotomy may be overstated—I wouldn't see it as choosing between submitting to dominant conventions in writing or deviating from these at the risk of academic failure—I think it's more about focusing on the cracks between practices, allowing some of the forms to come through IF they enable writers to work at the kinds of knowledges that they want to work and towards what they want to mean. For me it's about increasing the range of discourses and semiotic resources that it's permissible to use in the academy. Obvious examples come to mind are the use of vernacular forms that you mentioned already—or I guess more precisely, the use of what have come to be defined as "vernacular" forms. But what does a focus on temporality get us? Or help us to avoid?

Bruce: My sense is that we should shift our emphasis from what is permitted or allowed in language (and media) to a focus on what we and our students might and should be attempting to work at in their compositional work (broadly construed). This focus on temporality gives us the ability to recognize students' agency as writers, and its deployment both when they iterate what seem to be conventional, "permitted" forms and when they deploy forms that are identified as breaking with convention. Pedagogically, that's a crucial advantage. This focus would certainly expand the range of discourses and semiotic resources under consideration, but I worry that framing the issue in terms of those resources in themselves, and which ones will be allowed, gets us sidetracked into 1) thinking about these as stable entities with inherent values, rather than focusing on what we might want to accomplish and why, and 2) mistaking dominant definitions of conventional resources and their meanings for all that has been, is, and might be accomplished in their guise. Of course, the material social conditions limiting access to and uses of particular resources would also come up for investigation. To bring it closer to home, in terms of languages, a translingual approach that my colleagues and I have argued for works against both conventional multilingualism and monolingualism: neither "English" as conventionally defined nor the usual proffered alternatives adequately represent what we have to work with. We are always instead writing "in translation," in Alastair Pennycook's terms (2010), even when appearing to write "in English."

To reiterate, a focus on temporality helps us to recognize the exercise of writerly agency even in iterations of what we are ideologically disposed to misrecognize as simply more of "the same," rather than identifying such agency only with what we are disposed to recognize as deviations from an ostensibly "same" practice. Musical iteration perhaps best illustrates this: a "repeat" of the same phrase in a melody (e.g., standard blues tunes) is both the same as what is repeated and, by virtue of following the first iteration of that phrase, different in temporal location and significance, which is why it is not typically heard as an unwitting mistake. From this perspective, difference is an inevitable characteristic of iteration rather than exceptional or alternative. Applied to writing, the question of difference and transformation is thus no longer whether to allow previously excluded difference to "enter" the academic sphere in order to achieve its transformation. Instead, it is a question of what kinds of difference and transformation to pursue, given their inevitability. From this perspective, such phenomena as hybridity and translation would be seen not as exceptions but part of the unacknowledged norm, as would the changes to practices arising from their re-location to "different" domains about which Ivanič remarked. With difference recognized as the norm, any apparent "sameness" would need to be accounted for as emerging products of practices. Iterations would be understood not as reproducing the "same" but, rather, as contributing to the ongoing sedimentation, or building up, over time, of language practices and the "context" of their iteration (Pennycook, 2010, p. 125). Context here would be understood as in co-constitutive relation to utterances and speaker identity, and, as in exchanges between colonizer and colonized, as creating new meanings and new relationships between meanings, with the potential to undermine the status and distinction of the dominant and transform the identities of all the participants (Homi Bhabha, 1985; Pennycook, 2010, p. 44; Pratt 1991).

Theresa: So, in pedagogical terms—what does it mean to adopt a spatio-temporal framework rather than just a spatial one? How would a shift in framework shape the work of a teacher of writing (in a separate writing space) or of a discipline in which students are doing writing?

Bruce: I think it would mean calling into genuine question (with one possible answer being to confirm) the aims and effects of any iteration. For example, what might iteration of an ostensible deviation from or reproduction of conventional discourse seem to accomplish for a writer and particular readers, how, and why, and so on. If we assume difference as an inevitability rather than an option, we change our question from one asking whether to allow difference in writing to asking what kind of difference to attempt to make in our writing, how and why. In posing such questions, teachers would in effect be assuming not their preference for a "contact zone" pedagogy or the need to introduce difference into the classroom but, rather, recognizing the classroom as always already a site of differences, "contact" or, better, relocalizing of practices: differences would be identifiable not as characteristics students (or their teachers) have brought to the classroom, or introduced there, but rather as always emerging products of specific reading and writing practices. Like the "errors" commonly, if mistakenly, seen as simply introduced by students "into" writing, differences are in fact "social achievements" resulting from interactions between readers and writers (see Horner 1999b, pp. 140-144). So, if students select to iterate conventional discursive forms, those can and should be put to question, just as iterations of ostensible breaks with these should be. And of course, given the contingent and interdependent relationship between context and discourse, these would be genuine questions for the students and the teacher.

NOTE

1. Basic writing' is a term used in the United States to identify the writing and courses in writing for adult students identified as unprepared to do college-level writing.

REFERENCES

Bartholomae, D. (1993). The tidy house: Basic writing in the American curriculum. *Journal of Basic Writing, 12.1*, 4-21.

Bhabha, H. (1985). Of mimicry and man: The ambivalence of colonial discourse. *October, 34,* 126-133.

Bourdieu, P. (1991[1982]). *Language and symbolic power* (J. B. Thompson, Ed.) (G. Raymond & M. Adamson, Trans.). Cambridge, MA: Harvard University Press.

Horner, B. (1999a). Some afterwords: Intersections and divergences. In B. Horner & M. Lu (Eds.), *Representing the "other": Basic writers and the teaching of basic writing* (pp. 191-205). Urbana, IL: National Council of Teachers of English.

Horner, B. (1999b). Rethinking the "sociality" of error: Teaching editing as negotiation. In B. Horner & M. Lu (Eds.), *Representing the "other": Basic writers and the teaching of basic writing* (pp. 139-165). Urbana, IL: National Council of Teachers of English.

Horner, B, & M. Lu, (1999) *Representing the "other": Basic writers and the teaching of basic writing*. Urbana, IL: National Council of Teachers of English

Horner, B., Lu, M. Z, Royster J., & Trimbur, J. (2011) Language difference in writing: Toward a translingual approach. *College English, 73*(3), 303-321.

Ivanič, R. (2009). Bringing literacy studies into research on learning across the curriculum. In M. Baynham & M. Prinsloo (Eds.), *The future of literacy studies* (pp. 100-122). London: Palgrave Macmillan Publishing.

Ivanič, R., Edwards, R., Barton, D., Martin-Jones, M., Fowler, Z., Hughes, B., … Smith, J. (2009). *Improving learning in college: Rethinking literacies across the curriculum*. Milton Park, UK: Routledge.

Lillis, T. (2013). *The sociolinguistics of writing*. Edinburgh, UK: Edinburgh University Press.

Lillis, T., & Curry, M. J. (2010) *Academic writing in a global context*. London: Routledge.

Lillis, T., & Scott, M. (2007). Defining academic literacies research: Issues of epistemology, ideology and strategy. *Journal of Applied Linguistics, 4,* 5-32.

Lu, M. (1999) Professing multiculturalism: the politics of style in the contact zone. In Horner, B. & Lu M. (Eds.), *Representing the "other": Basic Writers and the teaching of basic writing* (pp. 166-190-xx). Urbana, IL: National Council of Teachers of English.

Pennycook, A. (2010). *Language as a local practice.* New York: Routledge.

Pratt, M. (1991). Arts of the contact zone. *Profession,* 33-40.

Smitherman, G. (2000), *Talkin that talk. Language, culture and education in African America.* London/New York: Routledge

Street, B. (1984). *Literacy in theory and practice.* Cambridge, UK: Cambridge University Press.

Williams, J. (1981) The phenomenology of error. *College Composition and Communication, 32*(2), 152-168.

SECTION 4
TRANSFORMING INSTITUTIONAL
FRAMINGS OF ACADEMIC WRITING

INTRODUCTION TO SECTION 4

Many chapters in this book make reference to the ways in which literacy practices are shaped by institutional factors but in this section questions of transformative possibility within normative institutional frames are foregrounded. The chapters take a look at how particular institutional contexts shape and influence what can and cannot be said about—or count as—academic writing, what its purposes are seen to be, and how it is experienced by those who produce it. Whilst they point to practical and conceptual difficulties in challenging institutional norms and expectations around academic writing, the chapters also record instances of where successful outcomes—transformations—have been, or might become, possible.

Corinne Boz describes a project at the University of Cambridge, United Kingdom, which succeeded in shifting work to help bridge students' transition from school to university away from a focus on the skills of students and onto the pedagogical practices of tutors. In doing so the project sought to transform first the dominant institutional framing of writing as a problem of student underpreparedness, and second, the apprenticeship model of teaching in which questions of discourse are left under-articulated and assumed to be acquired largely through socialization alone. Boz observes that the project contributed to a new visibility in the institution for issues around teaching and student transition. Tutors who took part found themselves better equipped to discuss their expectations of disciplinary writing and at the same time experienced the benefits of engaging in dialogue around teaching—something hitherto not prevalent or valued in a system based on teaching through individual tutorials.

Another university initiative designed to make writing visible is described by Lawrence Cleary and Íde O'Sullivan, who were charged with setting up a Writing Centre at the University of Limerick, Ireland. To achieve this institutional transformation they drew on influences from Academic Literacies and New Rhetoric, creating the Centre as an institutional resource that would help students to recognize the situated nature of disciplinary language and to exercise their own critical agency as producers of various kinds of text. At the same time an emphasis on the "composing process" would offer the individual possibilities for "perpetual transformation" of meanings, values and the self. To show how these Writing Centre goals play out in practice, Cleary and O'Sullivan take us through a strand of teaching in first year Engineering that moves from close comparative and historical analyses of textual features to a discussion of language and rhetoric's role in creating authority and identity for the writer.

Cleary and O'Sullivan describe the setting up of their Centre as a "political act," that is, a principled intervention in the status quo based on certain choices. Other chapters describe similarly political moves. The Research Training Event series developed by the British Association for Lectures in English for Academic Purposes (BALEAP- currently also referred to as Global Forum for English for Academic Purposes Professionals), and described by Lia Blaj-Ward in her chapter, draws on Academic Literacies thinking to further the BALEAP goal of equipping and supporting EAP lecturers to become active researchers of their practice. The series is motivated by a recognition of the way in which the institutional positionings of EAP teachers' influence and limit the opportunities they have to conduct research, and it seeks to redress this. The rationale for the work contains a recognition that developing the status and self-awareness of EAP practitioners is a professional imperative if they are not simply to serve, but also to shape, global, governmental and institutional agendas around the international student experience.

The agency and institutional positioning of the writing teacher is the subject of Joan Turner's chapter also. While noting her institution's official claim to offer students a "transformative experience," her focus is on the "thornier" challenge of transforming institutional conceptions and expectations—here specifically in relation to proofreading. She reproduces a dialogue with a colleague that begins to nudge these understandings and expectations towards greater reflexivity and critique. Although she makes no claim to have fully achieved "transformation" through this encounter, Turner nevertheless contends that engaging in such dialogues within the institution should represent an important dimension of the work of the academic literacies practitioner.

How writing is framed institutionally is frequently a reflection of and response to wider agenda, national and international. In their chapter, Angels Oliva-Girbau and Marta Milian Gubern, explore the complex framings of what it means to write academically in a Catalan University that needs to comply with the Bologna process. They explain how they created an introductory course that aimed to equip students to write in genres of academic English and at the same time to exercise critical caution about such genres and the diminution and downgrading of expressions of knowing within their own Catalan language and culture. They reflect on the difficulty of maintaining these two aims at once, particularly the difficulty of engaging students in "contestation." They report that students were most likely to comply with a sense of English as the "language of prestige," and to embrace "Anglo-American academic genres as the solution to their communication issues," making their transformations as learners *towards* rather than away from the normative. The chapter sharply highlights what's at stake in such a process of assimilation from the perspective of a minority language.

The power of contextual framings and dominant ideologies is also looked at in Catalina Neculai's discussion of the possibilities for writing that are opened up and closed down by the neo-liberal agenda in UK Higher Education. She describes how the "calculative, market-driven spirit" of her modern university has created an employability curriculum which is instrumental in its motivations. At the same time, however, she argues that this curriculum provides spaces and visibility for more humanistically-inclined teaching of writing. So whilst the discourse of employability frames writing at an institutional—and arguably, sectoral—level, it is possible, she argues, for smaller groupings or individuals to exercise less compliant forms of agency. Further, Neculai argues that teaching academic writing as a discipline—"a functional field with its own meta-codes, discourses and community of practice"—is a way of transforming its status from "service" to "subject."

In contrast, perhaps, the "cautionary tale" which Kelly Peake and Sally Mitchell have to tell restates the difficulties of working meaningfully with writing where institutional framings identify it as a deficiency of skill that can be overcome. They describe their attempt to bridge sectoral boundaries by working with secondary schools on students' writing, detailing how, in order to access funding streams and institutional agendas, they had to work directly with students and with autonomous understandings of and approaches to writing—and language more generally—as well as with the dominant logic surrounding progression from school to university. They argue that the limited success of their enterprise came from working with, rather than challenging these understandings. A more genuinely transformative approach, they conclude, needs to involve work with teachers, exploring and developing their practices in order to understand and enhance the experiences of their students. Peake and Mitchell note the irony of reaching this conclusion, which—but for the persistence and power of dominant framings of literacy and deficit—they had known all along.

Transformation then is always an ongoing ideological tussle in which assumptions—one's own, one's students, one's collaborators, the institution's—need to be subject to scrutiny and discussion.

This section includes two *Reflections* pieces. The first is a conversation between Brian Street, Mary R. Lea and Theresa Lillis looking back at research which opened up the differing perspectives of students and of teaching staff in various disciplines, and considering the options it presented for taking a transformative stance towards what is possible in universities. Foregrounding the importance of ethnography as a way of making visible often taken-for-granted practices (see Sally Mitchell's comments on the importance of ethnography in the Introduction to the book; see also Reflections 2) they reflect that big institutional issues, such as access and success, are simply not fixed by deficit-driven skills-based approaches. They maintain that it is the impulse in Academic Literacies to question and contest that provides a basis for constructive ways forward in transforming institutions.

The book closes with Lucia Thesen who reminds us of how institutions are historically and geographically located and the consequences of such locations for the ways in which we seek to understand practice, pedagogy and theory. Thesen explores what a transformative agenda looks like from the perspective of the global south. Her Reflections touch on many of the themes raised in the book whilst engaging from the specific geohistorical location of South Africa. She foregrounds: the experiences and desires of students from communities historically excluded from higher education, the question of what it means to belong in academia, the potential threats to other senses of social belonging resulting from taking part in academia, the impact on meaning making of dominant academic literacy conventions and ideologies of knowledge. In a book where many of the contributions are from the global north, Thesen's Reflections remind us all of the need to engage in transnational conversations and, when doing so, to acknowledge the historical specificity of our speaking positions, seeking to develop shared understandings without masking difference.

CHAPTER 25

TRANSFORMING DIALOGIC SPACES IN AN "ELITE" INSTITUTION: ACADEMIC LITERACIES, THE TUTORIAL AND HIGH-ACHIEVING STUDENTS

Corinne Boz

Studies of transition to higher education highlight the fact that, in higher education contexts in the United Kingdom, undergraduate students receive limited one-to-one contact with academic staff. The lack of opportunity for regular, individualized contact with teaching staff can cause feelings of alienation and confusion about academic expectations (Anthony Cook & Janet Leckey, 1999) and can also be responsible for a lack of knowledge/understanding on behalf of the academic staff of students' personal/writing histories (see Ruth Whittaker, 2008). Ultimately, problematic student transitions may lead to issues with student retention (Mark Palmer et al., 2009). It has been argued that a more individualized educational experience would help to support students through those initial transition issues (Whittaker, 2008), although ever-expanding class sizes and increasing student-staff ratios arising from the massification of higher education would seem to make this an idealistic scenario.

The tutorial system at the Universities of Oxford and Cambridge (Oxbridge) affords the opportunity for close and sustained dialogue with tutors potentially providing ideal conditions for a supported and individualized transition from school to university. Given this potential, many people are surprised to find that a project supporting student transitions at the University of Cambridge exists at all. However, the following quotations from First Year undergraduates taken from our annual Undergraduate Learning Enhancement Survey illustrate that being prepared (Gillian Ballinger, 2003; Alan Booth, 2005; Maggie Leese, 2010), adapting to new expectations, particularly when they are often implicit (Theresa Lillis & Joan Turner, 2001), and understanding new discourses (David Bartholomae, 1986; Tamsin Haggis, 2006; Mary Lea & Brian Street, 1998) are significant challenges in our context also, reflecting experience across the UK higher education sector more widely:

> Although I think my essay writing skills were developed sufficiently in a certain way before I arrived, I have found that the difference in approach and style has been great and difficult to adapt to. (First year student)

> I often felt that my [tutor] was talking to me as if they were addressing a third year, not a first year fresh out of school who was confronting a subject for the first time in a completely alien manner, and in something close to a foreign language. Of course there is a jump between A-level and undergraduate study, but I often felt as though I was expected to have made that jump before I reached my first [tutorial]. (First year student)

> I felt very unprepared; the only advice given prior to university (and indeed throughout the year!) was that "people learn in different ways," without mentioning what these "ways" were. (First year student)

These comments are taken from students who have been very successful at A-level (or equivalent), they have met or exceeded academic expectations and have therefore been able to learn and, crucially, present knowledge in the ways that have been expected from them in their educational contexts to date. And yet, for some, our annual surveys reveal that the transition to university learning and writing is a greater challenge than expected.

In this chapter, I will discuss some of the issues surrounding transitions to academic writing at university for our high-achieving students and illustrate the ways in which we have incorporated the theoretical principles of an Academic Literacies approach into the design and delivery of our transitions project. In addition, I will demonstrate the ways in which the data, research and experience in our "elite" institutional context extends the boundaries of current Academic Literacies research to represent high-achieving students who have been underrepresented by the research to date (see Ursula Wingate & Christopher Tribble, 2012, for further discussion of Academic Literacies' focus on "non-traditional" students). For the purpose of this chapter, I am defining the university as "elite" in relation to its position in the world university rankings (see Times Higher Education, 2015). In defining our students as "high-achieving," I intend this to reflect their academic achievement at A-level. Of those students accepted for admission in 2014, 97.3% achieved the equivalent of A*AA or better counting only their best three A Levels (excluding General Studies and Critical Thinking) (University of Cambridge, 2015). In addition, I am consciously moving away from defining students with the dichotomous "traditional/non-traditional" label as it masks the diversity of the student population and has become increasingly meaningless (see Elaine Keane, 2011).

CONTEXT

The Oxbridge tutorial system is internationally renowned and commands "an almost mystic, cult status" according to David Palfreyman (2008). In Cambridge, the tutorial[1] constitutes the core of the educational provision provided by the 31 self-regulating colleges with curriculum, lectures, and practicals being provided by the central university via faculties and departments. Tutorials are described as follows:

> … a medium through which students learn to work autonomously, to learn with and from others, to argue and to present arguments, to handle problems, to question their own assumptions, and to meet deadlines. (University of Cambridge, 2009)

The tutorial is designed to allow tutors and students to discuss, explore and learn from each other (see Paul Ashwin, 2005, for a more detailed discussion of the Oxbridge tutorial and the qualitatively different ways in which it is perceived by undergraduates). The number of students within a tutorial most usually ranges from one to four or five depending on discipline and, in most cases, students will be required to produce a piece of work for each tutorial. It is significant to note that this tutorial work is formative and carries no summative assessment. Students are assessed by end-of-year examinations, in most cases.

Tutors are selected by the college and are responsible for the academic progress of their undergraduates. They may be eminent professors or first year PhD students and are selected for their disciplinary expertise. The system confers a large degree of freedom on tutors in terms of their approach to teaching, and this allows them to provide the conditions for an ideal dialogic learning situation where both tutor and student work towards creating new meanings and understandings through the process of critical discussion. The diversity of experience and pedagogical approach to teaching does, however, provide a challenge for the university in terms of accounting for quality of teaching and ensuring parity of experience for all its undergraduates.

Although it can be argued that the ideal Cambridge tutorial offers dialogic space for discussing/learning/creating subject content and knowledge, survey data from our context demonstrates that the same focus is not always given to dialogue around disciplinary writing practices and this can be problematic for students. Indeed, as David Russell et al. (2009) suggest, in their broader discussion of writing practices in HE, although the undergraduate courses of Oxford and Cambridge are "writing intensive" they are not necessarily "writing conscious" (p. 402). Students can find this lack of explicit writing focus challenging as they attempt to understand the requirements of genre and discipline, indicating that if this essential element is missing the dialogic situation is less than "ideal."

THE PROJECT

The Transkills Project was established in 2008, through the Teaching Quality Enhancement Fund (http://www.admin.cam.ac.uk/offices/education/lts/news/ltsn17.pdf). Occupying a collaborative space (resourced by the Education Section, Centre for Applied Research in Educational Technologies, and Personal and Professional Development) outside of faculty, departmental or collegiate structures, it emerged from institutional discourses centred upon student deficit and the recognition that the traditional academic socialization or apprenticeship model of writing support (see Lea & Street, 1998) might not address the needs of all students. Dominant perceptions were that first year students were no longer able to write on arrival at university, that this inability to write took time away from teaching disciplinary knowledge and tutors were becoming increasingly frustrated in dealing with issues that were perceived to be the responsibility of the school system. The initial aim of the project, then, was to investigate the experiences of first year students in their transition to undergraduate study at Cambridge and provide resources to support them, acknowledging that "transition support should not be extraneous to the mainstream activity of the institution, but integral to the learning experience" (Whittaker, 2008, p. 3). It was also our explicit aim for the project to support all incoming undergraduates and not just those considered to be "at risk" (see Wingate, 2012; see for discussion of 'risk', Thesen Reflections 6, this volume). In addition, we aimed to embed a scholarly model of support firmly based on our own institutional data and enhanced by current research into writing and transitions (see Anne Pitkethly & Michael Prosser, 2001).

In the Cambridge teaching system, texts are produced and discussed for and within the tutorial context and so enhancing student writing practices involved the tutorial, the tutor and the student. This engendered a move away from considering writing as a deficiency in the students' skill set towards an Academic Literacies perspective emphasising writing as a social practice in which meaning and text are constructed in dialogue and relations of power are implicated. In moving away from a traditional skills-deficit model of writing, our project became about, not only supporting students in learning to talk about and produce effective writing within their discipline at university, but also about developing tutors' understanding of student writing practices, of the ways in which the students' practices have been shaped by their previous A-level writing histories, and the tutor's own role in supporting student writers in transition. It provided an opportunity to support tutors in becoming more "writing-conscious" (Russell et al., 2009). This is where our project began to challenge the implicit institutional framing of academic writing. It is significant to note, however, that in attempting to address the challenge of supporting students in acquiring academic literacies, we were not attempting to spoon-feed for, as Ronald Barnett states, "A genuine Higher Education is unsettling; it is not meant to be a cosy experience. It is disturbing because ultimately, the student comes to see that things could always be other than they are" (Barnett, 1990, p. 155).

The design and delivery of our resources has been decided in collaboration with "experts" familiar with the requirements of each different context and as a result our provision has been varied in nature. However, we have found that the process represented in Figure 25.1 is most effective in bringing about changes in both perspective and experience and most closely reflects the principles of the Academic Literacies framework incorporated into our approach.

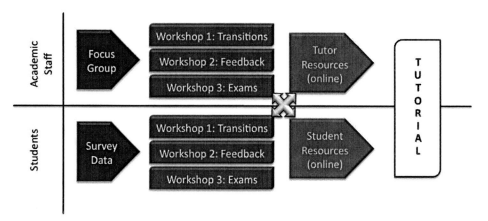

Figure 25.1: The Transkills Project—the process of creating dialogue around writing beyond the tutorial.

Figure 25.1 represents the process we have used to engage a range of faculties and departments, spanning Arts, Humanities, Social Sciences, and Biological Sciences, in enhancing writing support for first year students. Biological Sciences is used here as an illustrative example of a process used more broadly. In the first instance, we identified a group of Directors of Studies who were willing to act as a focus group. Issues raised at this initial discussion echoed the wider institutional discourse of student deficit with Directors of Studies highlighting the need for online writing support resources for students. Before developing these resources, however, the issues highlighted in the focus group discussions (see Figure 25.1) formed the basis of a series of workshops with tutors. These workshops were open to tutors of all levels of experience and not presented or perceived as initial "training" for new tutors but rather an opportunity for dialogue with peers around teaching practice.

To take into account the time pressures on academic staff, the workshops were delivered in a blended format with participants receiving an online pre-workshop resource in advance of a one-hour lunchtime session with a follow-up online resource delivered after the workshop. The pre-workshop resource was critical to the success of this process. Containing a short survey form, it asked participants to respond to questions pertinent to the upcoming workshop and relating to themes arising from the student survey data. Participant responses were then available to the workshop facilitators in advance of the session, allowing them to tailor the session to the specific group of people attending. This proved invaluable in ensuring that the sessions were perceived to be relevant to both individual and disciplinary context. The comments received via the pre-workshop package were collated and presented back to the workshop participants in the form of visual maps which provided an anonymized and less face-threatening way of beginning discussions around the workshop theme.

The outputs of the workshops, including student/tutor data, essay samples, and other documents used, were collated and sent out as a post-workshop resource. Significantly, however, the discussions and opinions captured at the tutor workshops were incorporated into designing the student workshops and online resources. As Figure 25.1 illustrates, as far as possible, the resources for staff and students were mirrored, both centring on the same themes drawn from tutor focus groups and student survey data (e.g., For tutors—Providing Effective Feedback /For students—Using Feedback Effectively). Some aspects of the content were also mirrored: the same authentic, first-year tutorial essays were included in both tutor and student sessions, for example. Quotations from tutors were also incorporated into the student resources and vice versa. This "mirroring" helped the project team to create an ongoing dialogue, a discussion around student writing outside of the tutorial context.

As the colleges of the university are responsible for teaching, the student workshops were delivered within the college rather than faculty/department. In the initial stages of the Transkills project, the project team delivered all workshops in collaboration with colleges. Later, the project team moved towards a model of facilitating workshops for college teaching staff who consequently delivered workshops to students within their own colleges. To date, 28 of the 31 colleges have been represented at these sessions.

DISCUSSION

In creating these new spaces for discussion of discipline-specific academic writing practices outside of the tutorial context, we provided an opportunity for tutors to consciously consider their students' writing histories (by highlighting A-level writing practices), to articulate their own framing of academic writing and have this debated by peers and to consider ways in which their own teaching practices could be adapted to support student writing in transition. Crucially, we also created space for explicit discussion of the dialogic nature of the tutorial and examined ways of best facilitating the types of learning situations "where pedagogic practices are oriented towards making visible/challenging/playing with official and unofficial discourse" (Lillis, 2003).

Feedback collected from tutors, both immediately following workshops and three to six months later, suggested that they had appreciated a focussed discussion on the recent changes to the A-level system and the implications this had for their teaching practice. Since attending the workshops many felt that they were better equipped to discuss writing in tutorials. In addition to these factors, however, one of the most common responses from the tutor feedback was that they valued the opportunity to talk with other tutors about their tutorial practices. The space these workshops provided has not traditionally existed within our institutional structures but was clearly valued by participants:

> Yes my [tutorial] practice has changed since attending the workshops. I have more confidence that the feedback I give students is constructive as I try to cover the various points covered in the feedback sheets supplied in the workshop i.e., structure, argument, content etc. I have also tried to use some of the techniques suggested by other [tutors] in the workshop. (College tutor)

> I have definitely adapted my tutorial practices since attending the workshops. I now give much more specific guidance to students about essay writing and in particular structuring their essays. (College tutor)

> I found the workshops very useful and they have had an impact on my [tutorial] practice, primarily in terms of the type of advice that I give regarding essay structure …. The workshops were also useful in confirming some of the things that I already do in [tutorials] … and this is useful because, to some extent, we tend to carry out [tutorials] in isolation as far as technique is concerned. (College tutor).

We also provided spaces for students to articulate their experience of the transition from A-level writing to disciplinary writing and provided opportunities beyond the tutorial where students could reflect, with peers, on the goals of their texts and their role as active participants in the feedback process.

CONCLUSION

In summary, an Academic Literacies framework has allowed us to begin to reframe discussion of academic writing practices within our institution. It has enabled us to move discussion away from shifting responsibility onto the students for arriving at University with a deficit skill set (the high-achieving profile of the students here makes this approach hard to justify, in any case). It has also helped to demonstrate that the traditional apprenticeship model of implicit induction, so often relied upon in the tutorial context, is not necessarily adequate even for high-achieving students. It has afforded us the opportunity to frame the discussion in terms of understanding both student and tutor practices, examining learner histories and the implications of A-level practices and the way these different factors interact. Discussions are not framed by deficiency in either students' or tutors' skills and therefore have not been initiated from a point of blame. This factor has been significant in fostering engagement across different contexts within the institution. The project has contributed towards changes in the nature of dialogue around writing and learning within our institution and, in doing so, has contributed towards changes in pedagogy at the level of the tutorial. Significantly, the work of the project has directly contributed towards the establishment of a new 'institutional space," the Teaching and Learning Joint Sub-committee of the General Board's Education Committee and Senior Tutors' Standing Committee on Education, a body with a specific remit to consider issues relating to the teaching and learning of undergraduates and act as an interface between the colleges and the university on study skills development, including support for transitions between school and university.

In addition to the ways in which an Academic Literacies framework has informed our institutional support of academic writing, I would argue that the pedagogical application of the approach in our context is significant in extending the practical and theoretical reach of the Academic Literacies perspective away from the focus of early Academic Literacies research (e.g., Lillis, 2001) on "non-traditional" students to illustrate its effectiveness in establishing transformational spaces in an "elite" context where all students are considered high-achieving.

NOTE

1. At the University of Cambridge, the one-to-one teaching for undergraduate students is called a "supervision." However, as in any other context this is called a tutorial, and, to ensure a clear distinction from graduate supervision, I will use "tutorial" and "tutor" to refer to the teaching session and the teacher.

REFERENCES

Ashwin, P. (2005). Variation in students' experiences of the Oxford tutorial. *Higher Education, 50,* 631-644.

Ballinger, G. J. (2003). Bridging the gap between A level and degree: Some observations on managing the transitional stage in the study of English Literature.

Arts and Humanities in Higher Education, 2(1), 99-109.

Barnett, R. (1990). *The idea of higher education.* Buckingham, UK: Open University Press.

Bartholomae, D. (1986). Inventing the university. *Journal of Basic Writing, 5,* 4-23.

Booth, A., (2005). Worlds in collision: University tutor and student perceptions of the transition to university history. *Teaching History, 121,* 14-19.

Cook, A., & Leckey, J. (1999). Do expectations meet reality? A survey of changes in first-year student opinion. *Journal of Further and Higher Education, 23*(2), 157-71.

Haggis, T. (2006). Pedagogies for diversity: Retaining critical challenge amidst fears of "dumbing down." *Studies in Higher Education, 31*(5), 521-535.

Keane, E. (2011). Dependence-deconstruction: Widening participation and traditional-entry students transitioning from school to higher education in Ireland. *Teaching in Higher Education, 16*(6), 707-718.

Leese, M. (2010). Bridging the gap: Supporting student transitions into higher education. *Journal of Further and Higher Education, 34(2),* 239-251.

Lea, M., & Street, B. (1998). Student writing in higher education: An academic literacies approach. *Studies in Higher Education, 11*(3), 182-199.

Lillis, T. (2003). Student writing as "academic literacies": Drawing on Bakhtin to move from critique to design. *Language and Education, 17*(3), 192-207.

Lillis, T. (2001). *Student writing: Access, regulation, desire.* London: Routledge.

Lillis, T., & Turner, J. (2001). Student writing in higher education: contemporary confusion, traditional concerns. *Teaching in Higher Education, 6*(1), 57-68.

Lowe, H., & Cook, A. (2003). Mind the gap: Are students prepared for higher education? *Journal of Further and Higher Education, 27*(1), 53-76.

Palfreyman, D. (2008). The Oxford tutorial: "Thanks, you taught me how to think." Oxford, UK: Oxford Centre for Higher Education Policy Studies.

Palmer, M., O'Kane, P., & Owens, M. (2009). Betwixt spaces: Student accounts of turning point experiences in the first-year transition. *Studies in Higher Education, 34*(1), 37-54.

Pitkethly, A., & Prosser, M. (2001). The first year experience project: A model for university-wide change. *Higher Education Research and Development, 2*(2), 185-198.

Russell, D. R., Lea, M., Parker, J., Street, B., & Donahue, T. (2009). Exploring notions of genre in "academic literacies" and "writing across the curriculum": Approaches across countries and contexts. In C. Bazerman, A. Bonini, & D. Figueiredo (Eds.), *Genre in a changing world. Perspectives on writing.* Fort Collins, CO: WAC Clearinghouse/Parlor Press.

Times Higher Education. (2015). World university rankings. Retrieved from https://www.timeshighereducation.co.uk/world-university-rankings/2015/world-ranking/#/

University of Cambridge. (2009). *The senior tutors' guidance to new tutors*. Retrieved from http://www.admin.cam.ac.uk/committee/seniortutors/guidance/

University of Cambridge. (2011). *Learning and teaching: Supervisions*. Retrieved from http://www.cam.ac.uk/univ/learning/univrole.html

University of Cambridge. (2012). *Undergraduate admission statistics: 2011 cycle*. Retrieved from www.study.cam.ac.uk/.../docs/admissionsstatistics2011.pdf

University of Cambridge. (2015). *Undergraduate admission statistics: 2014 cycle*. Retrieved from http://www.cam.ac.uk/news/2014-admissions-cycle-statistics-published

Whittaker, R. (2008). *Quality enhancement themes—The first year experience: Transition to and during the first year*. Glasgow, UK: Quality Assurance Agency for Higher Education (QAA). Retrieved from: http://www.enhancementthemes.ac.uk/docs/publications/transition-to-and-during-the-first-year.pdf

Wingate, U. (2012). Using academic literacies and genre-based models for academic writing instruction: A "literacy" journey. *Journal of English for Academic Purposes, 11*, 26-37.

Wingate, U., & Tribble, C. (2012). The best of both worlds? Towards an English for academic purposes/academic literacies writing pedagogy. *Studies in Higher Education, 37*(4), 481-495.

CHAPTER 26

THE POLITICAL ACT OF DEVELOPING PROVISION FOR WRITING IN THE IRISH HIGHER EDUCATION CONTEXT

Lawrence Cleary and Íde O'Sullivan

In 2007, when the authors of this chapter were being selected to get Ireland's first writing centre up and running, concerns about postgraduate writing for publication coincided with national and institutional drives to up-skill the population for participation in a knowledge economy. A feature of our context is that our institution began its life as a National Institute of Higher Education and maintains strong ties with local industry to this day. Student retention and transferable skills development were Higher Education Authority concerns that largely determined some goals for our target groups. Those groups included mature students, international students and students coming in through the Access programme as a consequence of low, or the absence of, Leaving Certification exam scores (http://www. examinations.ie/). The national discourse about writing at third level in Ireland up to that time was largely limited to talk about writing development for professional academic advancement.

Surveys conducted by Íde in 2005 and 2006 had given us some insight into teacher and student attitudes towards writing and the teaching and learning of writing, into the ad-hoc writing development initiatives that were already in play and into student and staff preferences for ways forward (see Lawrence Cleary et al., 2009). Both of the authors of this chapter come from backgrounds in applied linguistics with a focus on academic writing—Lawrence also having the additional, very positive experience of Janice Neuleib's undergraduate writing programme at Illinois State University. Given our backgrounds, we both had some idea of how to satisfy student and staff preferences, but as researchers charged with forming a systematic approach to writing development based on best practice for students and staff across four faculties, we had to do our homework.

Roz Ivanič and Mary Lea (2006) are keen to remind writing developers that choosing one pedagogical theory of writing over another "is always a political act"

(p. 14), even if it is rarely recognized as such. The reminder from Ivanič and Lea is reminiscent of an even earlier caution by James Berlin (1982, p. 765) that choosing one pedagogical theory of writing over another is more than just quibbling about which feature of the writing process to favour. "To teach writing," wrote Berlin (1982, p. 766), "is to argue for a version of reality, and the best way of knowing and communicating it." The writer-centred approach adopted by our writing centre is in many ways typical of writing centres in the United States. We do not intervene in students' papers, but into their processes (Stephen North, 1984), talking to them about strategies for reaching their writing goals. The *authority* over their paper is theirs. Our approach is largely eclectic, drawing on many traditions including ESP, EAP and corpus and systemic functional linguistics, each uniquely informing and thereby expanding our understanding of student writing and the writing of professionals in the disciplines. Crucial to our politics, however, we draw from the literature on Academic Literacies and one particular form of the US Rhetoric and Composition model, New Rhetoric.

This chapter explores the influence of Academic Literacies and New Rhetoric on the pedagogical approach to the development of writing in one higher education institution in Ireland, namely the University of Limerick. A single lesson in one writing Centre initiative will serve to illustrate how these two traditions can come together to foster the development of a writing tradition that provides writers with the tools and materials needed to evaluate any writing situation, to enter into the discourses relevant to that situation as critical agents in the creation of knowledge—rather than passive recipients of trickle-down ideological and epistemic values and to consider the implications of their lexical choices and structural strategies with respect to their credibility and the realities for which they advocate. Though focusing on a single tutorial, the demonstration reveals much about the politics of our eclectic approach.

POLITICS AND PEDAGOGICAL CHOICES

We suspect that most writing developers would struggle to relate Rhetoric and Composition studies with Academic Literacies studies, especially if their experience of Rhetoric and Composition is the ritualized curricula of the dominant Current-Traditional model that most people think of when they think of first-year composition. Sharon Crowley (1985) refers to such a model as the teaching of "a bizarre parody of serious discourse and the process by which it is produced" (p. 159). Correspondingly, John Heyda (2006) links the Current-Traditional model to earlier models of "vocationally-oriented instruction" that quickly proved capable of descending into "a writing-by-the-numbers charade" (p. 155). However, Rhetoric and Composition is not a theoretical monolith, but harbours many competing traditions. The value of integrating aspects of rhetorical theory, in particular the rhetoric advocated by Berlin (1982), Robert L. Scott (1967), Ann E. Berthoff (1978), Richard E. Young, Alton L. Becker and Kenneth L. Pike (1970) and Andrea Lunsford and Lisa Ede (1994), is not altogether inconsistent with the values honoured by Academic Literacies scholars and practitioners.

The earlier caution from Ivanič and Lea (2006, p. 14), about the politics embedded in writing pedagogy, results from their recognition that, to paraphrase Orwell's pigs: "All writing is equal, but some writing is more equal than other writing." Language is "the prime carrier of ideology" (Romy Clark a& Roz Ivanič, 1997, p. 29) and "[w]riting is of strategic importance to the outcome of those ideological struggles" (p. 21). There is resonance between Clark and Ivanič (1997), Brian Street (2003) and Paulo Freire (2000) with respect to their ideas about the socially situated nature of knowledge and the role of hegemonic forces in maintaining value for particular kinds of knowledge and ways of knowing, not least of which is the dominant educational practice which subordinates students (learners) to teachers (knowers). This recognition of the socially situated nature of language and struggles over how language and social practices mean in any given writing or teaching situation is reflected in the work of New Rhetoric scholars as well:

> Rhetorical theories differ from each other in the way writer, reality, audience, and language are conceived—both as separate units and in the way the units relate to each other. In the case of distinct pedagogical approaches, these four elements are likewise defined and related so as to describe a different composing process, which is to say a different world with different rules about what can be known, how it can be known, and how it can be communicated. (Berlin, 1982, pp. 765-766)

Berlin describes reality as one of the elements of the composing process, yet these components taken together "identify an epistemic field—the basic conditions that determine what knowledge will be knowable, and how the knowable will be communicated" (Berlin, 1982, p. 767). The reality we teach is determined by how we treat each component in the writing process. The New Rhetorician values a process of truth-making or meaning-making that makes room for each student's experience of reality and the perpetual transformation of those truths as a result of the dialectical interplay of writer, reality, audience and language. Truth in this view of the process is "always truth for someone standing in relation to others in a linguistically circumscribed situation" (Berlin, 1982, p. 744).

DO YOU WRITE LIKE AN ENGINEER?

Our demonstration of how the politics of the two traditions combine will be limited to a discussion of a single lesson in one particular provision, *ME4001*,

Introduction to Engineering, a compulsory module for first-year students in the *Engineering Choice* programme. The writing component of this module might best be described as a mini-module-within-a-module, comprised of four hours of lectures, entitled *Report-writing for Engineers*, and four *Do you write like an Engineer?* tutorial hours. The majority of students on this module are from traditional backgrounds, coming in directly from second-level education having scored well on Leaving Certification exams (see also Fischer Chapter 5, Paxton and Frith Chapter 11 this volume).

Students on this module write three papers for assessment that together constitute forty-five per cent of the student's total grade. The submissions are assessed by a postgraduate TA and, in the third paper, by two peers. Finally, for each submission, colour-coded feedback for self-assessment is provided by the writing tutor with the help of two postgraduate Engineering students.

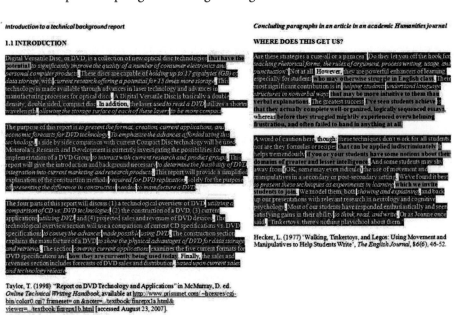

Figure 26.1: Comparison for clause-type preferences.

After asking "Why do reports from engineers and essays from students in the Humanities look different from one another?" in the first tutorial, the texts above are projected onto the screen at the front of the classroom. The tutor inquires into the differences in proportional representation of colour. Naturally, students point out the preference for red structures in the text to the left and for green structures in the text on the right. The text on the left is identified as being from an engineer's feasibility report, the one on the right as belonging to a teaching and learning specialist writing for an academic journal.

Groups of students are instructed to work together to determine the function of the red and the green with respect to whatever precedes or follows it, be it blue or green or another red strand. The tutor asks, "What is the passage in red or green doing?"

...they are powerful enhancers of learning, especially for students who may otherwise struggle in English class.

the laser used to read a DVD utilizes a shorter wavelength

Figure 26.2: Subordinate clauses versus non-finite verb clauses.

In the samples above, for instance, students are asked about the relationship between the green and the blue in the first sentence. Eventually, we work out that the green is defining *students*, answering the question: *Which students?* Interestingly, in the second sample sentence above, students work out that "used to read a DVD," in red, is doing the same thing, defining *the laser*. So the question becomes, if they do the same thing, why does this engineer choose red structures over green structures?

This is an opportunity for the writing tutor to model the kinds of inquiry with which good writers typically engage. Perhaps, if we could understand how the red and the green structures are different from one another, we could say why the engineer prefers the red structure. When asked about their thoughts on the differences between the two structures, students usually report that the red structure sounds more factual, more to the point. The tutor has learned that this understanding of the difference is intuited and has merit. He then shares two differences between the structures: firstly, that the green structure contains a conjunction, a word that expresses an explicit relationship—in the case above, a relative pronoun—and a verb marked for tense—time, person, number, and mood; in the second sample sentence, two non-finite verbs (a participle and an infinitive) are left to *imply* the relationship between the information in the red structure and that in the blue structure which precedes it.

If the green structure expresses the relationship more explicitly through the use of a conjunction, why does this engineer prefer the less explicit relationship expressed by the red structure, as in the second sample sentence, where the relationship needs to be inferred? After all, we usually think of engineers as embracing precision. Asking students to reformulate sentences, changing red structures into green structures and green structures into red structures, students come to see red structures require fewer words. Though less precise than green subordinate clauses, the red non-finite verb phrases and clauses allow for more information to be stacked up in a more concise way. Engineers, after all, love concision too. Students learn that there is a bit of a trade off when choosing this red structure: some precision in the expression of the relationship is sacrificed in the interest of concision. But why does the red structure sound *more factual* than the green structure?

At this point, students are informed that at the turn of the twentieth century, the writing of scientists and engineers looked more like the sample Humanities text (William Vande Kopple, 2003, pp. 370-371)—hardly any red structures, but lots of blue and green. What changed? Why the gradual increase in preference for red structures over green? Students may offer some theories, but it is not a question they are expected to be able to answer—the question is designed to intrigue them. Students are asked to speculate on the role of time, person, number, and mood absent from the structure currently preferred. Students often portray the red structures as communicating more factual information. An examination of the content, though, does not reveal more facts. However, that the structure *sounds* more factual, more *certain*, is clear. Despite not being marked for tense, the structure seems to imply modality or degrees of certainty.

If this structure is preferred by engineers, what allows today's engineers to express a greater degree of certainty than yesterday's engineers? In the tutorial, this question is usually followed by a long silence. Students must think about what has happened over the past one-hundred years. With time, someone volunteers an explanation. A typical response might be that today's engineers and scientists know more. "We know more facts" is how they often express it. Sooner or later, students volunteer that today's engineers have more knowledge to work with and that they have better, more precise tools. These conjectures agree with the conclusions in the literature: with more precise and reliable measurements, engineers today feel more confident about their results and more readily generalize their conclusions (Vande Kopple, 2003, p. 371). The tensed verb ties the empirical observation to a particular time, implying that the results cannot be generalized beyond its immediate context; a loss of tense has the rhetorical effect of communicating that the occurrence is typical.

These revelations about what the various clause structures communicate leads to a class discussion of cases where it might be inappropriate for an engineer to communicate such typification and of the effect that misrepresentations of degrees of certainty might have on the readers' sense of the writer's credibility. This is a rhetorical issue, but it is an issue that is basic to identity as well. If a writer wishes for a text to communicate something about herself, then the writer needs to consider not only how her language choices signify at the level of denotation, but what is implied and what acts are performed, if any, by those choices. The tutor argues that over- or understating the value of the findings in research undermines the reader's sense of the writer/researcher's credibility. Using a grammatical structure that incorrectly implies that a case is typical is to engage in faulty reasoning—not a method of justifying conclusions that we typically associate with scientists and engineers. If the degrees of certainty expressed are not reliable, it is only natural that readers would ask: What else is unreliable? What other evidence is not valid? Can I trust this writer? If I were to rely on this engineer's conclusions, how would I be viewed by the engineering community?

CONCLUSION

This mini-module on the writing for engineers does not challenge the episte-mology of science. Instead, we indirectly pose the question to students: Are pos-itivist values alone sufficient for dealing with each and every engineering writing situation? Is it enough to just be *factual*? Is that the only kind of knowledge that counts? We run across sentences like the following in the relevant literature:

> It would *appear* to be impossible to obtain J-c for tearing and cleavage for the same material—either it will fail by cleavage or tearing at $Q = 0$ giving either J-c or J-c; the other must be ob-tained from a theoretical model or by extrapolating experimental data. (O'Dowd, 1995, p. 463; *italics* ours)

And the great thing about having electronic texts projected onto a screen in class is that we can search for all sorts of examples of the language of uncertainty and condition, among other features. By asking students to write about issues rele-vant to professional development, looking at texts on engineering ethics, policy and education to see how engineers write about those kinds of issues, by delving deep into the implications of linguistic features common in engineering writing, we are asking students to reconsider the scope of what it means to be an engineer and to re-evaluate what counts as evidence in each rhetorical situation.

However, it is a little more difficult to engage young engineering students in discussions of how engineering practice is a social practice and about how they are positioned by the requirements of the module, the course, and the discipline/field, particularly with respect to how they are positioned by the process by which they satisfy (or fail to satisfy) those requirements. Though we do not explicitly inquire into how the values of science cohere with the cultural values students bring with them into this new third-level educational context, sometimes the inconsistencies come from the least expected places, and it is the job of the tutor to inquire into the social construction of the epistemological principles that constitute individual realities.

It is interesting that student responses to feedback on their writing—for exam-ple, requests for literary sources for particular claims or supporting information or objections to language that calls attention to the author's cognitive or affective processes or agency—are amongst the best opportunities for exposing some of the values that they do bring with them into university. Objections to citing and refer-encing requirements and to prohibitions against allusions to one's own agency are opportunities for a tutor to lead an examination of the confrontation between the language and methods whereby students expressed their authority and agency in the past and how it is expressed in the present writing context. Such objections are opportunities to examine the role of context in the way that knowledge is best positioned for rhetorical (argumentative) reasons and how audience and language function in this new context to affirm or negate the identity a student wishes to portray. Objectionable practices can become opportunities if viewed as rhetorical strategies for the creation of both knowledge and identity. A sanction invalidates; a strategy authorizes. Just as there is guilt by association, there is credibility by association. By avoiding language that suggests subjectivity, we conjure that sense of indifference that we commonly associate with the unbiased scientist, an identity to which the writer perhaps aspires. These are opportunities to examine the language writers use to establish identity, voice, tone, authority, etc. It is not the goal of our module on writing for engineers, however, to teach linguistic structures. The module, instead, demonstrates to students that they must assess how language is working in a given context in order to make the best determination of whether it is creating the reality for which they wish to advocate.

Just as the Academic Literacies approach has capacity also to value the roles played by the study skills and academic socialization models for writing development (Lea & Street, 1998), writing centres are "firmly grounded in an epistemological mix" (Eric Hobson, 2001, pp. 108-109). Both Academic Literacies and New Rhetoric approaches view each writing situation as a situated social practice "always embedded in socially constructed epistemological principles" (Street, 2003, p. 77) that determine "what can be known, how it can be known, and how it can be communicated" (Berlin, 1982, p. 766). Drawing on these insights, it is our writing centre's goal to teach a writing process that both foregrounds the writer's relationship with language, reality and audience in the meaning-making process and makes possible the conditions whereby she may consciously and critically transform the epistemic field into which she writes. The writer we hope is thus both informed and empowered.

REFERENCES

Berthoff, A. (1978). *Forming/thinking/writing: The composing imagination*. Rochelle Park, NJ: Hayden.

Berlin, J. A. (1982). Contemporary composition: The major pedagogical theories. *College English, 44*(8), 765-777.

Clarke, R., & Ivanič, R. (1997). *The politics of writing*. Abingdon, UK: Routledge.

Cleary, L., Graham, C., Jeanneau, C., & O'Sullivan, Í. (2009). Responding to the writing development needs of higher education students: A case study. *AISHE-J, 1*(1), 4.1-4.16. Retreived from http://ojs.aishe.org/index.php/aishe-j/article/view/4

Crowley, S. (1985). The evolution of invention in current-traditional rhetoric: 1850-1970. *Rhetoric Review, 3*(2), 146-62.

Freire, P. (2000). *Pedagogy of the oppressed*, (30th ed.) (Ramos, M. B., Trans.). London: Continuum International Publishing Group.

Heyda, J. (2006). Sentimental education: First-year writing as compulsory ritual in US colleges and universities. In Ganobcsik-Williams, L. (Ed.), *Teaching academic writing in UK higher education: Theories, practices and models* (pp. 154-166). Hampshire, UK: Palgrave Macmillan Publishing.

Hobson, E. H. (2001). Maintaining our balance: Walking the tightrope of competing epistemologies. In R. W. Barnett & J. S. Blumner (Eds.), *The Allyn and Bacon guide to writing center theory and practice* (pp. 100-109). Needham Heights, MA: Allyn and Bacon.

Ivanič, R., & Lea, M. R. (2006). New contexts, new challenges: the teaching of writing in UK higher education. In Ganobcsik-Williams, L. (Ed.), *Teaching academic writing in UK higher education: Theories, practices and models* (pp. 6-15). Hampshire, UK: Palgrave Macmillan Publishing.

Lea, M., & Street, B. (1998). Student writingin higher education: An academic literacies approach. *Studies in Higher Education, 23*(2), 157-172.

Lunsford, A., & Ede, L. (1994). On distinctions between classical and modern rhetoric. In T. Enos & S. Brown (Eds.), *Professing the new rhetoric* (pp. 397-411). Englewood Cliffs, NJ: Prentice Hall.

North, S. M. (1984). The idea of a writing centre. *College English, 46*(5), 433-46.

O'Dowd, N. (1995). Applications of two parameter approaches in elastic-plastic fracture mechanics. *Engineering Fracture Mechanics, 52*(3), 445-65.

Scott, R. L. (1967). On viewing rhetoric as epistemic. *Central States Speech Journal, 18*(1), 9-17.

Street, B. (2003). What's "new" in new literacy studies? Critical approaches to literacy in theory and practice. *Current Issues in Comparative Education, 5*(2), 77-91.

Vande Kopple, W. J. (2003). M. A. K. Halliday's continuum of prose styles and the stylistic analysis of scientific texts. *Style, 37*(4), 367-381.

Young, R., Becker L., & Pike, K. (1970). *Rhetoric: Discovery and change*. New York: Harcourt, Brace and Jovanovich.

CHAPTER 27

BUILDING RESEARCH CAPACITY THROUGH AN ACLITS-INSPIRED PEDAGOGICAL FRAMEWORK

Lia Blaj-Ward

In a 2007 article which they describe as part AcLits research overview, part position paper, Theresa Lillis and Mary Scott wrote:

> At this point, we consider that our aims should be to: … Sustain current support and critical discussion systems that exist for the development of researchers in academic literacies, acknowledging the marginal position of many in this field. (Lillis & Scott, 2007, p. 22)

This chapter addresses the aim identified by Lillis and Scott (2007) through exploring an initiative to support the development of research literacy among practitioners delivering English for Academic Purposes (EAP) provision for international students, in the UK higher education system and in other national higher education systems where non-native speakers of English participate in courses taught in this language. *Research literacy* refers to the ability to engage with existing research reports and to produce accounts of research that illuminate aspects of EAP practice in a rigorous, persuasive and engaging way.

The chapter opens with three scenarios of EAP practitioners preparing to undertake research; it describes the thinking behind a professional association's initiative to build an EAP researcher support network, partly in response to the three scenarios; it explores ways in which AcLits course design principles helped shape this initiative and suggests points for further consideration. The viewpoint reflected in the chapter is that of the coordinator of the events and follow-on resources which formed part of the researcher development initiative.

SCENARIOS

Alexandra works in a language centre in a UK university and teaches in-sessional EAP, i.e., non-assessed, non-credit-bearing language support for international students. She designs teaching materials which help international students develop their ability to write postgraduate dissertations. The students in one particular group she works with have different supervisors with different expectations about academic writing. Alexandra would like to interview the supervisors and report the findings in a more formal document, beyond integrating those findings into teaching materials. She is also considering starting a PhD to explore feedback strategies in more depth.

Brian is in charge of pre-sessional courses in a different university. Prior to starting their studies for an academic degree, a number of international students are required to take a pre-sessional EAP course and their acceptance onto the university degree course is dependent on successfully completing the pre-sessional. Brian would like to find out how his students subsequently perform on university courses, both in order to enhance the quality of the pre-sessional and to encourage subject lecturer input into the pre-sessional course content; he believes that subject-specific EAP provision is likely to increase students' academic performance at university.

Carina is the head of an EAP unit in a UK university. She needs to generate evidence to persuade senior management in her institution that an in-sessional course, delivered by the unit to support a particular Business programme, is fit for purpose and a justifiable expenditure. At the same time, she is reviewing staff development strategies within the unit she leads.

POINT FOR CONSIDERATION

Alexandra, Brian and Carina are qualified to master's level in their area, but not all have completed a research-based dissertation or have comparable experience of academic, practice- or policy-oriented research. Time for academic research and related publication activities is not formally built into their contracts and workloads. Their situations can, however, yield valuable insights not only for their immediate contexts but also for the wider professional community and to develop a theoretical knowledge base in EAP. *What support network can be made available to Alexandra, Brian and Carina to ensure that their questions are developed into projects with successful outcomes?*

INSTITUTIONAL SETTINGS FOR EAP RESEARCH

To place the above point for consideration into the institutional context in which Alexandra, Brian and Carina deliver EAP teaching, coordinate and/or are involved in strategic planning of EAP provision, the three scenarios outlined above are grounded in a UK higher education context, where links between academic research, on the one hand, and teaching and learning practice, on the other, are gradually becoming stronger, albeit not consistently so across academia. EAP provision is strongly embedded within institutional structures associated with teaching and learning; staff delivering EAP provision usually hold the status of teacher practitioners rather than discipline academics with research responsibilities. The nature of institutional mechanisms of reward for research (the UK Research Excellence Framework, www.ref.ac.uk) means that there may be limited institutional support for EAP practitioner research. The work of EAP practitioners is often invisible in high status research publications. Within their institutional context, EAP practitioners may have access to professional development related to the design and delivery of EAP provision, but it is less likely that they will be formally supported to plan and conduct research and they are not legitimate participants in the "research game" (Lisa Lucas, 2006) in academic life.

In the United Kingdom EAP-related research is conducted in Applied Linguistics departments, whereas research into the internationalization of higher education systems, which could potentially be informed by insights from EAP provision and in its turn have a bearing on international student support, is conducted in a range of other research-focused departments (e.g., Education, Sociology, Business). These areas have limited if any input from EAP practitioners like Alexandra, Brian, and Carina (a notable exception is a study by Diane Sloan and Elizabeth Porter, 2010).

RESTES: WITHIN/OUTSIDE INSTITUTIONAL FRAMEWORKS

BALEAP, *The global forum for EAP professionals* (www.baleap.org), has responded to the situations exemplified by the three scenarios by creating opportunities for the development of a support network, through setting up ResTES, a Research Training Event Series consisting of face-to-face one-day training events. Participants (presenters and audience members) have varying degrees of investment in research; they may be researching their own teaching practice, working towards a research degree, conducting institutional research for quality assurance purposes or interpreting research to construct policies. At the time of writing this chapter, five one-day face-to-face events have taken place. The events, hosted in 2011 and 2012 by universities in different locations in the United Kingdom, were open to an international audience of BALEAP members and non-members. The rationale behind the series is described as follows:

> The academic experience of international students in English-speaking countries has gained increased visibility as a result of new developments in government policy and legislation. Perhaps more so now than ever before, research into English for Academic Purposes (EAP) can and should inform decisions made not only in the context of individual academic practice but also at the level of institutional and governmental agendas on academic aspects of the

international student experience. (BALEAP, 2011, p. 207)

Each of the five events that constitute the research training initiative addressed a separate aspect of the research process: 1. Defining the research space: Literature reviews and research questions; 2. Methodologies for researching EAP contexts, practices and pedagogies; 3. Issues in EAP classroom research; 4. Qualitative data analysis in EAP research; 5. Quantitative data analysis in EAP research. The format for each of the first four events was half a day of input by an expert or experienced researcher in the field (a masterclass) followed by half a day of presentations of work in progress scheduled in a single strand. A call for presentations of work in progress was issued prior to each event. The fifth event was delivered as a one-day workshop on quantitative data analysis in an IT suite software.

In order to pre-empt projecting an image of the research process as a set of discrete stages through which researchers proceed linearly, resources from the series are available online (www.baleap.org). Event participants can thus revisit materials, and BALEAP members not taking part in face-to-face events can work through the material in an order and at a pace appropriate for their individual interests. The online resources bring events together as a coherent whole and showcase accounts of ongoing research.

The emphasis on presenting work in progress rather than finished accounts reflects the ResTES ethos of peer learning, i.e., "the sharing of knowledge, expertise, experience, highs and lows in practice and research, pedagogic principles and professional interests, curiosities and uncertainties" (BALEAP, 2011, p. 207). Participants at the events have varying degrees of experience of conducting research, which creates fruitful peer learning opportunities.

ACLITS: CHALLENGING INSTITUTIONAL FRAMEWORKS

A programme supporting the development of REF-type outputs such as academic journal articles (*Writing for Publication*), informed by AcLits and sponsored by an academic journal is discussed by Theresa Lillis, Anna Magyar and Anna Robinson-Pant (2010). The research outputs on which the ResTES work-in-progress presentations focus do not necessarily, however, fall within the Research Excellence Framework (REF) remit. Nonetheless, AcLits lends itself well as a basis for developing the ResTES, given that ResTES is intended as a catalyst for research and as a set of opportunities for practitioners to develop as researchers. This is due to AcLits' exploratory rather than prescriptive approach to literacy development and its emphasis on creating spaces in which institutional frameworks and expectations can be integrated and transformed.

One particular aspect of AcLits, namely the pedagogic principles for course design (Lea, 2004; Lea & Street, 2006), informed the development of ResTES. The origins of AcLits can be traced back to an endeavour to reframe student academic literacy not as a set of generic skills or as the object of straightforward enculturation into the practices of a specific academic discipline but as the site where individual identities, social practices and institutional frameworks interact and are reshaped in the process. AcLits has developed primarily in relation to assessed academic writing within university degree courses, where its perhaps most immediate relevance lies. The attention it pays to power, authority, institutional contexts, individual and social practices and identities, however, makes it a robust and flexible framework to explore ways of supporting EAP teacher practitioners to develop research literacy in relation to EAP.

In one of the key AcLits texts, Mary Lea (2004) discusses how she and her colleagues drew on the relationship between writing and learning identified through AcLits research to develop principles for course design, and illustrates these principles with the help of a case study of an online course delivered globally in English to a group of postgraduate students working in education-related roles. Four of the principles put forward by Lea (2004), in particular, resonated with the aims and the contextual specificity of ResTES. These four principles stipulate that the AcLits approach to course design

a. acknowledges that texts do more than represent knowledge,
b. involves thinking about all texts of the course—written and multimodal—and not just assessed texts,
c. attempts to create spaces for exploration of different meanings and understandings by all course participants,
d. sees the course as mediated by different participants. Allows spaces for this and embeds this in both the course content and the course design (Lea, 2004, p. 744).

The selection of four—rather than the wholesale adoption of all—principles listed in Lea (2004) is underpinned both by the ResTES designers' choice to explore the situatedness of AcLits and by AcLits' inherent flexibility as an enabling rather than prescriptive pedagogic framing. A later study by Mary Lea and Brian Street (2006) offers two examples of courses aimed at different audiences (a programme developing the academic literacy of pre-university students in the United Kingdom and a course aimed at supporting law academics to write introductory law course materials); in their 2006 study, Lea and Street further elaborate on the last principle selected for discussion in this paper (principle d, see above) by noting that the tutors and participants

> worked closely … to collaboratively investigate the range of
> genres, modes, shifts, transformations, representations, mean-
> ing-making processes, and identities involved in academic learn-

ing within and across academic contexts. These understandings,
when made explicit, provide greater opportunities for teaching
and learning, as well as for examining how such literacy practices
are related to epistemological issues. (Lea & Street, 2006, p. 376)

AcLits research and the AcLits design frame are closely interrelated, in that the former generates insights into literacy, teaching and learning which can inform further course development. The remainder of the chapter elaborates on the ways in which the four AcLits course design principles identified above are helping shape BALEAP's researcher development initiative; the "Points for further consideration" in the closing section of the chapter highlight aspects into which additional research is needed to take the ResTES forward and further refine its design.

ACLITS AND RESTES

While the overall framework of ResTES was inspired and informed by AcLits principles for course design, participants were not formally and explicitly introduced to these principles or to the research from which they were derived. AcLits underpinned the design of learning opportunities; it was not part of the content explored at ResTES events. Lea and Street (2006) also chose not to introduce the Law academics on the *Writing Level One Course Materials* workshops explicitly to the AcLits conceptual underpinning of these workshops, and instead enabled them to experience the AcLits approach through the activities designed. They found that this did not hinder fruitful discussion and academics' exploration of literacy as a situated social practice. In the case of ResTES, the implicit rather than explicit presence of AcLits within the series is partly explained by a desire to maximize the space for presenters and participants to negotiate their own understanding of what it means to develop as a researcher.

a. Texts do more than represent knowledge.

The research texts with which ResTES participants engage either as consumers (e.g., published research) or as producers (e.g., draft reports or writing produced for the award of a postgraduate degree) position participants as researchers in the field and the identity work involved in transitioning from practitioner to researcher is supported through opportunities to offer constructive critique of published work and feedback on work in progress. As well as prompting identity work, texts provide guidelines within which new knowledge can be created. In the inaugural ResTES masterclass, Ian Bruce, an established researcher in the EAP field (e.g., Bruce 2008, 2011) shared with the audience a literature review excerpt from one of his published texts and invited them to unpack the textual strategies he had used to position his work among existing research. In the second half of the event, as an audience member, he engaged with the "texts" which the presenters of work in progress contributed to the event (PowerPoint slides, oral commentary, handouts) and offered constructive feedback on how the projects could be shaped to reveal more fully the voice of the author, make claims of legitimate participation in the chosen research field and open avenues for further inquiry.

b. Think about all texts of the course—written and multimodal—and not just assessed texts.

While most of the EAP research shared at ResTES events may eventually be incorporated into written documents following institutionally-endorsed academic writing conventions, the aim of the series is to capture snapshots of various stages in the development of research projects, those stages which are frequently edited out of final published documents but which are central to developing research literacy. ResTES presenters may be working towards producing a piece of writing assessed as part of a postgraduate degree in a specific higher education institution, but within ResTES emphasis is placed on supporting the journey towards creating new knowledge. While masterclasses unpack published texts, work-in-progress presentations centre on draft texts which are transformed in the interaction between audience and presenters. To take just one example of how a multimodal text was used in the context of ResTES, one work-in-progress presenter at the third event (*Issues in EAP classroom research*) chose to communicate the milestones in his ongoing research journey through the medium of prezi (http://prezi.com/). When complete, his research will be reported in a master's dissertation. As a pedagogic tool to enable peer learning, the dynamic account of the research process captured the real research experience more effectively than a draft methodology section following accepted academic conventions.

c. Create spaces for exploration of different meanings and understandings by all course participants.

Unlike in the case described by Lea (2004), which involves a course delivered to a student cohort expected to engage in a pre-established number of teaching and learning activities for a delimited period of time, the coherence of the ResTES series comes not from the assessment element linked to the award of a degree but from participants' own choice about the level of investment they are prepared to make in this form of professional development. Event participants explore different meanings and understandings related to research methodology in the space of the face-to-face event; EAP professionals who access resources online can relate these to their own research experience or use them as a starting point for further involvement in/with research. For example, at the second ResTES event one of the presenters was an international student conducting doctoral research at a UK university on pre-sessional courses. The pre-sessional tutors and course directors in the audience were able to bring to the discussion a different set of understandings of the way in which access and researcher roles can be negotiated in such a situation. They were also able to take away a nuanced insight into how they could act as gatekeepers in their current roles or, had they been conducting similar research to that of the presenter, the implications of their own roles for gaining access to and reflecting on relationships in the data collection context.

d. The course is mediated by different participants. Allow spaces for this and embed this in both the course content and the course design.

As key stakeholders in the training event series, participants have a greater level of input into the content and focus of each event. Two levels of participation are associated with face-to-face ResTES events: presenting work in progress and participating as an audience member. Collaboration between tutors and students is taken one step further. While in the context of one particular higher education institution tutor and student roles are often hierarchical and formally assigned, in the learning and teaching space created by ResTES they become flexible and interchangeable; presenting participants become tutors, while at the same time receiving useful feedback from their audience. One ResTES participant at the fifth event (not a presenter) attended this event in order to consolidate his knowledge about quantitative research methodology and, for the benefit of others planning to engage in/with quantitative research, recommended a number of texts about quantitative methodology that he had found useful. While participant feedback from each event informed the design and delivery of subsequent ones, the evaluation sheet for the fifth event was redesigned in order to facilitate a greater level of participation in the series, beyond attending the face-to-face events. The redesigned evaluation sheet invited participants to annotate resources and share information about the likely extent of their involvement in research (and/or supervision of research projects) in the near future, as a basis for refocusing the ResTES in response to evolving researcher development needs.

REACHING OUT

Plans to evaluate the impact of the training series are in place, to learn how participants like Alexandra, Brian, and Carina in the chapter-opening scenarios benefitted from engaging in AcLits-informed development opportunities and to use the lessons learnt as a basis for taking the series forward. Meanwhile, an open access, online publication, *Snapshots of EAP Research Journeys* (Lia Blaj-Ward & Sarah Brewer, 2013), was chosen as a vehicle for disseminating, to a global audience, research experience narratives written by presenters and non-presenting participants at ResTES events. The choice was made in line with AcLits' emphasis on giving participants greater responsibility for mediating learning and teaching opportunities (in this case, by creating resources that can support the development of research literacy). It also reflected how

> the ResTES team (BALEAP's Research and Publications Sub-Committee) is looking forward to facilitating cross-border dialogue about supporting, generating, and using EAP research to enhance student experience in a global higher education community. (BALEAP Research and Publications Sub-Committee, personal communication, 16 September, 2011)

The current priority to facilitate cross-border dialogue means that in addition to being of value as a design frame, AcLits can offer a helpful tool for formulating questions in order to explore the politics of academic knowledge production (Lillis & Curry, 2010) in the global context and to collect scenarios of EAP practitioners based outside the United Kingdom which can inform the further development of ResTES. Some of these questions, based on discussions among ResTES designers and event participants, are phrased as points for further consideration below and will be addressed at forthcoming ResTES events and in related publications.

POINTS FOR FURTHER CONSIDERATION

- To what extent are conceptualizations of EAP shared in the global EAP professional context? What EAP aspects are EAP professionals researching?
- To what extent are EAP literacy, teaching and learning practices similar or different across the institutions in which EAP professionals work?
- What are the commonalities and differences in institutional support for EAP in the various institutional/national contexts in which EAP professionals work, both as regards teaching and as regards research?
- To what extent are EAP research methodologies transferable and translatable across institutional/national contexts?
- What languages and local academic conventions are privileged in the contexts in which EAP professionals disseminate their research findings?
- What kinds of research literacy do EAP professionals possess and what research literacy do they need to acquire, in order to make an impact in the contexts in which they work, as well as on a wider scale?

ACKNOWLEDGEMENTS

I am grateful to Sarah Brewer for her support in developing the ResTES, to members of the BALEAP Executive Committee, ResTES presenters and participants, and organizers in the host institutions for their contribution to the events.

REFERENCES

BALEAP (2011). Report on ResTES. *Journal of English for Academic Purposes*, *10*(3), 207.

Blaj-Ward, L., & Brewer, S. (2013). *Snapshots of EAP research journeys*. London: BALEAP. Retrieved from http://tinyurl.com/EAP-research-journeys

Bruce, I. (2011). *Theory and concepts of English for academic purposes*. Basingstoke, UK: Palgrave Macmillan Publishing.

Bruce, I. (2008). *Academic writing and genre*. London: Continuum International Publishing Group.

Lea, M. R. (2004). Academic literacies: A pedagogy for course design. *Studies in Higher Education, 29*(6), 739-756.

Lea, M. R., & Street, B. V. (2006). The "academic literacies" model: Theory and applications. *Theory into Practice, 45*(4), 368-377.

Lillis, T., & Curry, M. J. (2010). *Academic writing in a global context: the politics and practices of publishing in English*. Abingdon, UK: Routledge.

Lillis, T., Magyar, A., & Robinson-Pant, A. (2010). An international journal's attempts to address inequalities in academic publishing: Developing a writing for publication programme. *Compare: A Journal of Comparative & International Education, 40*(6), 781-800.

Lillis, T., & Scott, M. (2007). Defining academic literacies research: Issues of epistemology, ideology and strategy. *Journal of Applied Linguistics, 4*(1), 5-32.

Lucas, L. (2006). *The research game in academic life*. Maidenhead, UK: Open University Press.

Sloan, D., & Porter, E. (2010). Changing international student and business staff perceptions of in-sessional EAP: Using the CEM model. *Journal of English for Academic Purposes, 9*(3), 198-210.

CHAPTER 28

ACADEMIC LITERACIES AT THE INSTITUTIONAL INTERFACE: A PRICKLY CONVERSATION AROUND THORNY ISSUES

Joan Turner

SCENE ONE: AN EMAIL EXCHANGE

> Graduate School Representative (GSR): I wonder if we could meet to have a chat about the somewhat thorny issue of PhD students getting their theses proofread.

> Ac Lits Practitioner/Researcher (ALR): Yes, an extremely thorny issue. Main problem is usually what needs to happen isn't "proofreading" as in the sense of proofing an article before sending off to publication. Most changes involve clarification of meaning with the original writer, hence time (and money).

SCENE TWO

Some weeks later, a face-to-face conversation takes place. At the request of the academic literacies practitioner/researcher, this was recorded:

> ALR: Right, OK—so tell me from your perspective what the issues are.

> GSR: OK … This matter was raised as part of a supervisor workshop. One of the issues raised was about international students in particular having their theses proofread—um … not so much on the basis that their English language isn't up to scratch, but more to do with the fact that the student is perfectly capable of writing and articulating their research and their research outcomes in their own language, but no matter how good their English is, may not quite get it right in English …. I was hoping that a way

forward might be to have a small panel of proofreading organizations, that we can say to students "we don't recommend any one of these but pick from one of these, they understand what they can and can't do in terms of correcting your work and making suggestions," but then you start getting into where the boundaries are—and then I'm out of my comfort zone. So that's kind of where I'm at, really, but still having the same sort of queries from a lot of people, can I have my thesis proofread.

ALR: At what stage are they asking for that?

GSR: Quite late on.

ALR: The final stages … So, it's a big job then?

GSR: Yeh.

ALR: And of course it probably doesn't actually mean proofreading in the standard sense of proofreading—where you're submitting an article for publication and you're just making sure there isn't a typo or the paragraphs start in the right place or whatever.

GSR: (somewhat uncomfortable intake of breath) mmmhh, well you see, I don't know, you see, I would hope, perhaps naively, that it *would* be at that level, because if somebody's about to submit, then there should be a confidence that they're submitting something that's worth examining and that is going to pass …

ALR: Yeh, um, it is a terribly thorny issue. I mean I know because I've worked with a lot of PhD students across the college, and I found it was becoming such a … I mean I wasn't proofreading, I was trying to analyze their English and help them to formulate it so that they could actually say more clearly what it was they wanted to say—but that was with me reading the text, marking it up and then having one-to-ones with them …

GSR: So quite close reading then really.

ALR: Yeh, because you can read a text and you can change it and it can mean all sorts of different things. And also, you can change one word and it can change the emphasis.

SGR: Absolutely … and if you're one step beyond that, they've got to sit and defend that thesis in front of examiners who may or may not be friendly and supportive, and who may or may not pass them, or who may pass them with 18 months corrections or something.

ALR: So I think proofreading's the wrong term really. I suspect it's very seldom that proofreading's exactly what they require. They do require a lot more input …. It's a grey area. You have to say it's "all my own work"—well, is it all their own work? 'Cos the writing is quite an important part of the work.

SGR: It's tricky. I suppose … I can't see the wood for the trees at the moment …

I don't think there's going to be a straightforward answer, except to say that there is particular support for dyslexic students—and I wonder whether we can draw on that in some way …

ALR: (audible deep breath) but that's a different type of support really. I mean, we run in-sessional language support classes for PhD students, and my worry is that these students haven't really made use of those …

GSR: The more you think about it, the harder you try and deconstruct it—the harder it's got to put it together again—it almost feels like there's a PhD in there somewhere (joint laughter).

PROOFREADING: A THORN IN THE SIDE OF WRITING PEDAGOGY

While it was not explicitly stated in the above conversation, there seems to be an institutional expectation that the role of academic literacies practitioners is similar to that of proofreading, and that writing or language centres should either carry out or facilitate that role. This assumption is implied in Stephen North's 1984 proclamation, born of frustration, in a North American context, that: "[the writing centre] is a place for learning not a proofreading-shop-in-the-basement" (North, 1984). Similarly, Peter Spolc (1996), in an Australian context, discusses issues of responsibility when he finds that students expect writing specialists to offer proofreading services, a situation he describes wryly as "the skeleton in the academic skills closet." The continuing experience, internationally, of this assumption on the part of students has led to many writing and language centres explicitly making the negative statement on their websites or notice boards that they do not do proofreading. Discussions around what to do about the recurring institutional demand for proofreading also appear from time to time on mailbases such as BALEAP (the British Association of Lecturers in English for Academic Purposes) or EATAW (the European Association for the Teaching of Academic Writing). In these discussions, it is the principles of learning and pedagogical practice that are highlighted in contrast to proofreading, which entails neither (see also, Joan Turner, 2011). One participant in a focus group on the topic of proofreading, conducted by the author with writing practitioners, asserted vigorously:

> We should be working with students to highlight weak areas that need to be improved and giving them examples of how to improve it but we certainly shouldn't be going through crossing every "t" and dotting every "i," I absolutely don't think that is our job.

A HUMPTY DUMPTY EXPERIENCE

Given this rather fraught relationship between writing pedagogy, whatever the theoretical perspective, and proofreading, it may be seen as positive that the graduate school representative in the above conversation had prefaced her consultation on proofreading with the understanding that it was a "thorny" issue. This had not been her initial understanding, however. Rather she had come to see it as "thorny." In this respect, she has undergone a transformative learning experience, albeit one that leaves her somewhat "nettled." She has come to understand the difficulties of deciding "where the boundaries are" between proofreading and "making sugges-tions" for example. She gives the impression of having become increasingly exasper-ated by the fact that the simple solution, which "proofreading" appeared to present, has opened up more and more dilemmas. As she put it:

> the more you think about it, the harder you try and deconstruct it—the harder it's got to put it together again.

This expression evokes the "Humpty Dumpty" nursery rhyme, in which, after he falls off a wall and breaks apart, "all the King's horses and all the King's men couldn't put Humpty together again." The sentiment underlines the difficulty of posing proofreading as a solution to thesis completion and submission. It also jus-tifies the academic literacies critique of a "quick fix" approach to academic writing, discussed for example by Mary Lea & Brian Street (1998). The apparent "quick fix" has fragmented into a number of different "thorny" issues, which can no longer be re-integrated into a neat whole. Indeed, the "thorns" appear to accumulate rather than diminish. They include:

- establishing a boundary with the proof reader that includes spell checking and grammar checking but doesn't alter the content of the work;
- not removing or distorting the student's own voice;
- defending a thesis in a viva when the student hasn't had complete control over word choice;

- students must sign that a thesis is "all their own work," but does using a proofreader alter that?

These are all problem areas that an academic literacies practitioner would instinctively be aware of, hence the professional disassociation of their role with that of proofreader. These issues also place the practice of proofreading in relation to student academic writing within an ethical framework. Similar ethical concerns were voiced by proofreaders themselves in research undertaken by Nigel Harwood and others at the University of Essex in the United Kingdom (Harwood et al., 2009, 2010).

MEANING AND MASKING MEANING

In Lewis Carroll's (1871) *Through the Looking Glass*, Humpty Dumpty declares that words can mean anything he wants them to mean. In the above conversation, it is the academic literacies researcher who takes on the role of arbiter of the word "proofreading" and its meaning. She states:

Proofreading's the wrong term.

In fact, the ideological role of the use of the term "proofreading" in higher education needs to be unmasked. When it is used in the context of students needing to improve their writing, or bring a PhD up to submission standard, it indexes an insipid and diluted view of what's involved. It also risks denying those students who have put a great deal of effort into developing their writing and their English language proficiency, the educational importance of their achievement. At the same time, it masks deeper underlying issues of international higher education, and its multilingual student body, that institutions seem reluctant to address. For example, the institutional discourse around written English in higher education has not yet engaged with the wider debates circulating in relation to scholarly publication. These include the role of academic literacy brokers in the publication of L2 scholars (e.g., Christine Casanave 1998, John Flowerdew, 2000, Theresa Lillis & Mary Jane Curry, 2006, 2010); multilingualism in composition studies (e.g., Suresh Canagarajah, 2011; Christiane Donahue, 2009; Bruce Horner & John Trimbur, 2002) and the role of English as a Lingua Franca in English language teaching, where the acceptability of varying forms of English is promoted (e.g., Jennifer Jenkins, Alessia Cogo & Martin Dewey, 2011; Barbara Seidlhofer, 2005). It is incumbent upon an academic literacies perspective, which I have characterized as "an overarching framework, within which to embed a focus on the myriad processes and practices associated with reading and writing in contemporary higher education" (Turner, 2012, p. 2) to engage with these wider debates, and bring them into their practitioner, as well as institutional, discourse. The use of "proofreading" as a mechanistic solution to maintaining the status quo skates over all of these issues, and therefore needs to be resisted.

ENABLING THE TRANSFORMATIVE AT THE INSTITUTIONAL INTERFACE

One of the rationales for this edited collection is a focus on the relationship between academic literacies practices and their "transformative" potential. The notion of the "transformative" is a powerful one for higher education more widely, as can be seen for example in the following mission statement from my own university:

> We offer a transformative experience, generating knowledge and stimulating self-discovery through creative, radical and intellectually rigorous thinking and practice.

The above context of the transformative relates to student experience, and the proposed changes to their consciousness and thinking patterns as individuals. In their work from an academic literacies perspective, Ivanič (1998) and Lillis (2001) chart this kind of transformative development, as well as detail the struggles the students have with institutional expectations. A transformative trajectory need not only be one where students adapt to institutional expectations, or where students (and practitioners) reach a higher stage of learning, or renewed sense of identity, but can also be one where institutional assumptions and practices change. The exigencies of international higher education highlight the need for such institutional change. Echoing the "ideological stance" (Theresa Lillis & Mary Scott, 2007), which focuses on the transformative rather than the normative in academic literacies practice, the relevance of the above conversation may be seen in its attempt to encourage the transformation of mechanistic perceptions of the work of academic writing, which the use of the word proofreading suggests.

There is no claim here, however, that any institutional transformation was achieved in the above conversation. It is nonetheless important to have such difficult conversations, to resist solutions such as proofreading, which it seems writing practitioners are adjudged to be able to provide, and at the same time, to keep the conversation going. One outcome of the above conversation was the suggestion of further conversations, ideally with the graduate school board, and a presentation at a future meeting was proposed.

The institutional interface, then, is an important site for academic literacies work and its transformative agenda. However, the route to transformation is strewn with prickly thorns, and not one easily signposted to "mission accomplished."

REFERENCES

Canagarajah, S. (2011). Codemeshing in academic writing: Identifying teachable strategies of translanguaging. *The Modern Language Journal, 95,* 401-417.
Carroll, L. (1871). *Through the looking glass.* London: Macmillan and Co.

Casanave, C. P. (1998). Transitions: The balancing act of bilingual academics. *Journal of Second Language Writing, 12*(1), 175-203.

Donahue, C. (2009). "Internationalisation" and composition studies: Reorienting the discourse. *College Composition and Communication, 61*(2), 212-243.

Flowerdew, J. (2000). Discourse community, legitimate peripheral participation, and the nonnative-English-speaking scholar. *TESOL Quarterly, 34*(1), 127-150.

Harwood, N., Austin, L., & Macaulay, R. (2009). Proofreading in a UK university: Proofreaders' beliefs, practices, and experiences. *Journal of Second Language Writing, 18*, 66-190.

Harwood, N., Austin, L., & Macaulay, R. (2010). Ethics and integrity in proofreading: Findings from an interview-based study. *English for Specific Purposes, 29*, 54-67.

Horner, B., & Trimbur, J. (2002). English Only and US College Composition. *College Composition and Communication, 53*, 594-630.

Ivanič, R. (1998). *Writing and identity. The discoursal construction of identity in academic writing*. Amsterdam: John Benjamins Publishing Company.

Jenkins, J., Cogo, A., & Dewey, M. (2011). Review of developments in research into English as a lingua franca. *Language Teaching, 44*(3), 281-315.

Lea, M., & Street, B. (1998). Student writing and staff feedback in higher education: An academic literacies approach. *Studies in Higher Education, 23*(2), 157-172.

Lillis, T. (2001). *Student writing. Access, regulation, desire*. London/ New York: Routledge.

Lillis, T., & Curry, M. J. (2006). Professional academic writing by multilingual scholars. Interactions with literacy brokers in the production of English-medium texts. *Written Communication, 23*(1), 3-35.

Lillis, T., & Curry, M. J. (2010). *Academic writing in a global context: The politics and practices of publishing in English*. London: Routledge.

Lillis, T., & Scott, M. (2007). Defining academic literacies research: Issues of epistemology, ideology and strategy. *Journal of Applied Linguistics, 4*(1), 5-32.

North, S. (1984). The idea of a writing center. *College English, 46*(5), 433-446.

Seidlhofer, B. (2005). English as a lingua franca. *ELT Journal, 59*(4), 339-341.

Spolc, P. (1996). Proofreading: The skeleton in the academic skills closet? In K. Chanock, V. Burley, & S. Davies (Eds.).*What do we learn from teaching one-to-one that informs our work with larger numbers?* (pp. 153-168). Melbourne, AU: Language and Academic Skills Units, La Trobe University.

Turner, J. (2011). Re-writing writing in higher education: The contested spaces of proofreading. *Studies in Higher Education, 36*(4), 427-440.

Turner, J. (2012). Academic literacies: Providing a space for the socio-political dynamics of EAP [Special issue on English for academic purposes: Contributions from systemic functional linguistics and academic literacies]. *Journal of English for Academic Purposes 11*(1), 17-25.

REVISITING THE QUESTION OF TRANSFORMATION IN ACADEMIC LITERACIES: THE ETHNOGRAPHIC IMPERATIVE

Brian Street in conversation with Mary R. Lea and Theresa Lillis

Brian Street is Professor Emeritus of Language in Education at King's College London and visiting Professor of Education in the Graduate School of Education, University of Pennsylvania. His anthropological fieldwork on literacy in Iran during the 1970s and his theoretical work articulating an "ideological model" of literacy are foundational in literacy studies. Together with Mary R. Lea, he carried out ethnographic research on writing and reading practices in UK universities and their 1998 paper is highly cited and debated. In this extract from ongoing conversations, several of them recorded, Brian discusses with Mary and Theresa the impact of his disciplinary roots—anthropology—for studying literacy and his perspective on the transformational orientation of academic literacies research and practice.

Theresa: In reflecting on what academic literacies is, I think it's important to consider its strong ethnographic orientation. So I wonder if you can say something, Brian, about the importance of your own research and disciplinary background, in terms of anthropology and ethnography for developing this space—this particular approach to writing, reading and knowledge-making in the academy.

Brian: I think for me it emerged from having spent years working in New Literacy Studies which itself emerged from an anthropological perspective on language and literacy and in particular the idea of using ethnographic perspectives to try to understand what people are actually doing in reading and writing. In the dominant model—I work in development contexts, quite a lot, where the this model is very influential—the dominant view tends to be, "people are illiterate, what you need to do is pour literacy into them, and that once this is done other benefits will automatically happen—social, economic etc." The ethnographic approach says, "Hang on, look and listen to what literacy practices they're already engaged in." And very often, the response to that will be "they don't have any, they're illiterate, they're stupid." An ethnographic perspective forces you to suspend your own assumptions as to what counts as literacy and to listen to and observe what people are actually doing. So we've done a lot of that around the world in terms of the New Literacy Studies. It involves challenging what we refer to as the autonomous model of literacy, the assumption that literacy is just one uniform thing which happens everywhere, and instead adopting an ideological model, which states that the ways in which we understand reading and writing are always embedded in power relationships, ideologies, culture and meaning.

And that was the basis for looking inside our own systems, in universities and saying let's apply these ideas here. The dominant perspective here is not unlike the developing world which is, "Here are these students arriving. Students can't write". Lots of people say, "Nothing to do with me. I'm a tutor, I teach geography, economics. Send them off and fix them." Pour the literacy into them. And what we—Mary and I—began to develop—was an ethnographic perspective in the same way as we had done in international contexts. We said, "Let's see what the students are bringing with them." So one of the things that tells you is that firstly, students are coming with a variety of ways of addressing reading and writing. The second thing it tells you is that when they're in the universities in courses, the ways in which they're expected to read and write vary from one subject to another. The dominant model, the autonomous model says, literacy is literacy. When they arrive, if they can do it, fine, if not fix them. And the academic literacies' view I think says there are multiple versions of this thing "academic literacy"—most obviously that the writing and the reading requirements of the different disciplines vary. An example I remember from my own discipline, anthropology, was interviewing an anthropologist at a university who had marked a student essay and had written in red ink down the side at the bottom, "You cannot write. Get down to the study skills centre." And the student (we interviewed him as well) said, "I haven't a clue what they're talking about! My main major is history. I get good marks; my tutors think I can write. What's all this about?" And that's a classic example that what the disciplines expect is quite different. And it's at the level not just of skill but of epistemology. So in history when this student wrote an essay, the assumption was that you had a sequence and the sequence was of time across periods which you then connected in terms of causal events—what happened in nineteenth century England, the corn laws may affect them then parliamentary moves in the late nineteenth century. In anthropology, anthropologists are very wary of that sequential kind of evolutionary move because that's how very often people have seen *other* societies and anthropologists challenge this linear sequencing and say they don't want a sequence from, for example, so called primitive through to intermediate modern to postmodern. What we want instead are, if you like, structural, post-structural accounts of social institutions, meanings and people's *own models* of what goes on. And that's a big one, *people's own models.* So apply that to the different disciplines and the writing of the essay in anthropology, the epistemological, ideological, academic literacy perspective and assumptions are so different. And this student—and lots of students we encountered—have to learn to switch and very often their own tutors don't realize this because they're sitting in their own little edifice: the history guy sits here and anthropology there. And they say, "Nothing to do with me. I'm not a linguist I shouldn't have to teach academic literacy—they should know that already." What they don't necessarily recognize is that they are actually making epistemological, ideological literacy assumptions about what *they* think is a good essay—and the other tutor will have a different view. Students often recognize it slightly more— particularly if they're taking mixed degrees. You take business studies, you're doing economics one term, sociology another, business planning management another, and each of those will have their own conceptions as to what counts as thinking and what counts as writing. Now you know it sounds simple enough when I put it like that but actually, it does involve some kind of transformation of what counts as writing at university in the thinking and in the eyes of the tutors.

Theresa: So that kind of transformation is in terms of the tutors' own understandings of what's involved?

Brian: Yes and in fact that's one of the big issues. I taught a course at the University of Pennsylvania where we examined these issues with post graduate students and they began to unpick "hidden features" of academic writing (see Fischer this volume, chapter 5). They'd been told what the explicit features were you know, paragraphs, spelling, layout but there were also lots of hidden features—such as notions of tone, voice, and stance. Tutors implicitly used these hidden features to mark essays but they weren't made explicit. One point that this illustrates is that it's not just the students who need support—and if you like transformation—it's the tutors. And trying to take that idea into the universities and say, okay, you want to enhance the writing practices of students on degrees, so maybe it isn't enough just to address the students, maybe you also need to address the faculty and there you do come up against a block quite often (for further analysis and discussion, see also Tuck Chapter 14 and Roozen et al. Chapter 15 this volume).

Theresa: So, one goal of Academic Literacies drawing upon ethnography is to make visible the multiple literacies and the fact that in universities there are different practices, different rhetorical and epistemological practices associated with different disciplines. One pedagogical implication could be in terms of practice. That what tutors and students need to do is to make visible those conventions—as they currently exist—and to induct people into those practices. So to make visible, using whichever tools we have, and obviously there are strong traditions for doing this— like EAP, English for academic purposes and Contrastive Rhetoric—which have worked hard to identify, label, make visible and teach key textual and rhetorical features. So I'm just wondering, from your perspective, is there a difference in terms of what academic literacies seeks to identify, make visible or engage with?

Brian: Maybe there are two levels. The first is what we can think of as the access level so Academic Literacies isn't rejecting study skills, socialization—the other models—it is recognizing that those are necessary parts of the process, if you like, of academic socialization. But in order to accomplish them you also need transformation at two levels: one is transformation at the level where the tutors themselves recognize that they actually have a contribution to make to the teaching and learning of writing. That writing isn't something separate. This is something that for example Sally Mitchell and colleagues have worked very hard at and is obviously a key goal in WAC and WID (see Russell and Mitchell this volume, Reflections 2). But the other level—and the bigger one—which became very obvious when working with mature students (I think some of your work dealt with this, Theresa) where you get people in midlife coming back to university who've been writing in many ways—maybe they've worked as nurses and had to write reports—and maybe now they've hit university and the tutor says "you can't write". Gradually what comes out is the recognition that this is a different literacy practice and what you would hope is a kind of negotiation: the student saying "I'm not entirely convinced that the genre you're requiring for this discipline is actually the best way to go about it" and the tutor saying "I don't necessarily think that what you learnt in writing reports as a nurse is the same as what a degree requires which is reflexive critical, analytic writing." What I would say is, *Okay let's negotiate that difference.* That's a transformation. That's a totally different ideological relationship between tutor and student and between discipline and professional practice. From a literacies—and academic literacies view—we'd say let's look more closely at what the students are bringing and look more closely at what the tutors are expecting, then let's talk about how the two can mesh together.

Mary: I agree and this was my starting point in the early 90s (Lea, 1994). Now, I'm thinking about this question and notion of transformation—what it is and the extent to which it is a goal or value of Academic literacies research and pedagogy. Where do you see "transformation" in relation to our 1998 article?

Brian: I don't think that you and I were directly concerned with issues of transformation in the article but we were concerned with issues of power in and around student writing and in taking a specific institutional perspective. Our interest was in power as process rather than structure and our aim was to make this process evident. We were definitely articulating what we might call a "change agenda," which looking back on it now was quite strongly transformational—but maybe not quite in the Lillis and Scott (2007) sense.

There are probably always going to be tensions between the normative and transformative and how you actually instantiate what we called an academic literacies model in practice. In some ways, supporting people to access and engage in literacy practices that are valued, and ultimately powerful, may appear to be normative rather than transformative. So I think there are always going to be tensions between these perspectives. When we start looking at power it leads us to ask questions about who has control over resources, what counts as knowledge or how knowledge is articulated. I think both of us would say that it is issues of power that run through academic literacies' work in different contexts. That's where our key issues lay and this is what we were trying to tease out. Central to this, of course, was our institutional framing, which was not just about students and their writing. Maybe inevitably though—because the institutional lens is always on the student—it was that focus which got taken up and, of course, our three models were articulated around approaches to *student* writing.

Mary: Yes, I think our interest was as much with tutors and broader institutional practices as with students. One thing that happened was that in the interviews the tutors began to give us documents around writing as they talked about their practices. So we collected a vast range of unsolicited data, in terms of documentation, which foregrounded this institutional perspective. It was these documents, coupled with our observations within the different institutions, that made the institutional perspective so prominent.

Brian: Indeed. And our 1998 paper encompassed that institutional focus in the "academic literacies" approach, which we contrasted with "study skills" or "academic socialization." Our intention here was to foreground aspects of practice which had significant implications for teacher-student interactions around writing. In that respect we argued that practice around student writing is always located in relations of power and authority and never reducible to sets of skills and competences necessary for success in the academy. In fact, we recognized then, and it has been made apparent in subsequent work, that we should not simply separate the three "models" with water tight boundaries. They are not discrete, and indeed aspects of each may be evident in the others.

Mary: An important point. I think one way of understanding that relationship is to take a specific example, like "genre conventions." Traces of these are likely to be found in all three models in practice but what would be significant analytically is the way in which genre is being articulated, often implicitly, in different institutional contexts. "Study skills" can be identified through prescriptive attention to the formal linguistic features of genre conventions in generic models of academic writing, for example, "you shouldn't use the first person." "Academic socialization" could involve disciplinary specialists working with students to help them understand how to recognize specific disciplinary or subject based genres such as "writing about theory and practice in social work courses." Issues of genre can also be approached through an academic literacies lens. Rather than focusing on genre features or what they look like—teaching genres—an academic literacies perspective is concerned with revealing how genres create knowledge in particular ways. Or as Fiona English argues, (see Chapter 17) what genres actually do. From an academic literacies perspective, this involves working with both students and their teachers to make visible the different ways in which particular genres shape knowledge and, ultimately offer students more control over them and over meaning making processes. In each instance genre is made visible. The contrasting ways in which this is being done in relation to each of the three approaches, study skills, academic socialization, academic literacies, signals difference in the relationships of power and authority between the participants involved and their engagement and control over meaning making resources. None of this can be decoupled from institutional decision making about where and how to locate work around writing and the values and beliefs which underpin this. What we pointed to in the 1998 paper was that the analytical lens offered by academic literacies research makes the workings of such institutional practice visible. So this picks up on the question Theresa asks previously—"Is there a difference in terms of what academic literacies seeks to identify, make visible or engage with?"

Theresa: Yes indeed. Thinking again about the dominant model of literacy that you were problematizing in the 1998 paper—I'm wondering whether you see such a model adversely affecting students from all social groups. I'm thinking about literacy and language, and thinking both locally within the United Kingdom and then globally—if we think of the position of English in academia, both in publishing but also in its increasing use as a medium for higher education. If there's an ideological notion of a standard literacy/language doesn't this have particular negative repercussions for groups of people from particular social classes—working class— or backgrounds—users of English as a second language etc.

Brian: Maybe it worked under imperialism—the idea that, "we'll take this narrow standardized view of English and we'll make that the standard for people moving up the system." But this has never worked in actual communicative practice. For example, I was in Singapore at a project meeting where people were speaking versions of English and Hindi and Arabic; so what we actually ended up speaking around the table was a mix. At the same time, you can go into a UK classroom if the teacher is just trying to teach standard English; well these kids are coming from such mixed experience of everyday life that this standardized dominant model in southern England doesn't bear much relation to the world they are actually living in. So it becomes rather isolated. You can use it for a while to set supposed standards, tick for this kind of accent and this grammar but once they go out into jobs and start working, particularly international business it looks rather quaint and irrelevant and all the research shows that. I've more recently been working in Brazil where universities are expanding and you're seeing the usual statements and arguments, "Oh look, these nontraditional students, they can't write! Send them to the skills centre! What are we doing with them at university?"

An academic literacies view would say, hang on, slow down. Let's look more closely at what the students bring in. Then let's look at what the tutors are expecting. Then let's talk about how the two can mesh together. Let's negotiate this. And recognize that it will vary from one department to another, from one year to another, from one university to another. And that can create all kinds of resistance amongst those people who want to a have some kind of uniform standard. That is a big issue that needs addressing. You can have uniform standards that are, so to say, monolingual/monoliterate, or you can have uniform standards that involve multilingual variety and diversity. So there's a communicative point here, do we want people to communicate? Or do we want them to be able to tick boxes to say they've met some obscure but rather irrelevant standard?

Theresa: You've both been working this area—both in terms of new literacies and academic literacies—for some considerable time in a whole range of contexts. Are there particular challenges or priorities you see for people working in this area, both in terms of research and in terms of practice. Are there things you think we really need to pay significant attention to?

Mary: My concern is just how intransigent the deficit model is—even when people are using the term "academic literacies" to describe what they do, in practice there still seems to be slippage into "fixing" particular groups of student. More recently I've been working on literacies and digital landscapes and the use of the term "digital literacy/ies" is fraught with similar problems. I think that wherever "literacies" is taken up across post-compulsory education there is a real danger that it loses it critical edge and becomes decoupled from fundamental issues of power and authority. The challenge for me is how we can regain "literacies" and all that the plural use signals in terms of contested practice.

Brian: One metaphor I'd use comes from the person from Algeria who was appointed to follow Kofi Annan as the UN representative in Syria. He said, "All I can see in front of me is a wall but I know that walls have cracks in them and that's what I'm going to work on." So that's what we're doing. Universities look like walls but there are some cracks. The main cracks are the number of students who are seen as failing, who drop out. And the phrase that tutors in this country use as much as anywhere is that "students cannot write." So let's address that head on and say, what does that mean? And what we can do about it? And an academic literacies view I think can offer a much more constructive view than study skills, academic socialization, EAP—even some of the rhetoric in the United States which can get narrow—because academic literacies says "let's question our assumptions about what counts and how we've arrived at it." And it could be that by challenging our assumptions we can explain why large numbers of students who could otherwise do well are being thrown out of the system. So that's the little gap in the wall I think that we might make our way through.

REFERENCES

Lea, M. R., & Street, B. (1998). Student writing in higher education: An academic literacies approach. *Studies in Higher Education, 23*, 157-172.

Lillis, T., & Scott, M. (2007). Defining academic literacies research: Issues of epistemology, ideology and strategy. *Journal of Applied Linguistics, 4*(1), 5-32.

Lea, M. R. (1994). "I thought I could write until I came here": Student writing in higher education. In G. Gibbs (Ed.), *Improving student learning: Theory and practice*, 216-226. Oxford: Oxford Centre for Staff Development.

CHAPTER 29

RESISTING THE NORMATIVE? NEGOTIATING MULTILINGUAL IDENTITIES IN A COURSE FOR FIRST YEAR HUMANITIES STUDENTS IN CATALONIA, SPAIN

Angels Oliva-Girbau and Marta Milian Gubern

In 1999, 30 countries signed the Bologna declaration, which would set the grounds for the creation and development of the European Higher Education Area, aimed at making European universities more competitive by progressively eliminating the area's segmentation and by increasing student and teacher mobility (for details, see http://www.ehea.info). The subsequent process of adaptation caused a general upheaval in Catalan academia, as many students and teachers resisted what they perceived as a move towards the marketization of higher education. The Bologna process had a strong impact on the structure of new degrees and on the working patterns of university professors of all levels due to the introduction of seminar work at undergraduate level and more student-focused pedagogies. It also dramatically shifted the language balance towards English. As a result the already complicated balance between Catalan and Spanish in education and research is now being reconceptualized to make room for English and its prevalence as the academic language of prestige. These efforts towards internationalization have affected students' and faculty's relationship to their background languages and their self-image as members of academia.

This chapter looks at the effects on students' attitudes and beliefs, of learning to operate within academic genres in English. It focusses on a first year course in the Humanities designed to compensate for the lack of previous programmes in writing instruction and students' low English language proficiency whilst helping them develop an academic identity. Both ourselves and our students are members of a multilingual community in which a minority language (Catalan) coexists with Spanish and other foreign languages, a community that is being pressurised to adopt English as the key to internationalization. We argue that teaching methodologies based on an academic literacies approach can increase students' awareness of the elements that make up academic communication, help them analyze the inter-relationships between these elements, and challenge the status quo in which minority languages and their speakers are marginalized from the construction of knowledge. However, we acknowledge the difficulty of engaging students in contesting academic genres and roles at a stage when they are still struggling to become part of the academic community.

DEVELOPING ACADEMIC LITERACIES AT UNIVERSITAT POMPEU FABRA (UPF)

Within the Bologna process, the new Humanities degree at UPF (Barcelona, Spain) requires students to enroll in subjects taught in English to graduate. This degree starts with a two-year period of general courses, followed by a specialized second cycle. The general period includes two instrumental courses aimed at preparing students to deal with the genres of the different disciplines within the Humanities (Art, History, Literature, Philosophy, and such), one in Catalan/Spanish and one in English, both during students' first year. Both subjects need to overcome students' resistance to academic know-how courses.

In the new European context, academic literacy entails for our Humanities students the mastering of academic genres in students' two mother tongues (Catalan and Spanish), and in English, with German or French courses available as well. Academic genres, can be regarded as 1) the mediating instruments of academic interaction; 2) the prevailing form of assessment; 3) tools of learning and knowledge construction; and 4) marks of identity. Academic genres are students' key to their permanence at university and their long-term learning. Becoming participants in the academic community requires students to accept the entry rules of the community, have their participation sanctioned by the expert members of the communities, and actively participate in the exchanges of the community so as to be eligible for acceptance and show adherence to the community. Alongside and through academic genres, students are expected to acquire the community's collective goals and knowledge, and prove their value as valid members of this community.

> Academic writing, like all forms of communication, is an act
> of identity: it not only conveys disciplinary "content" but also
> carries a representation of the writer ... our discoursal choices
> align us with certain values and beliefs that support particular
> identities. (Ken Hyland, 2004, p. 1092)

However, the process of initiation can be problematic for students, as academic genres can sometimes contradict discourse practices that identify them as part of their home community, and therefore challenge their values and identity.

Because of the gradual process through which new members acquire the genres of a discipline, writing ends up seeming a transparent thing, the simple transcription of knowledge and research, what David Russell (1991) called the *myth of transparency*. As a result professors often misinterpret students' difficulties learning to read and use genres. The *myth of transience* (Mike Rose, 1985; Russell, 1991) helps the academics mask their lack of involvement in students' acquisition of academic genres behind the assumption that past students did not need any further instruction, and that it is a problem with the present students only. Such misconceptions about how students acquire discipline-specific ways of communicating can lead to a negative view of students' struggles to become part of the academic community, with language and literacy becoming visible only as a problem to be fixed through additional or remedial measures (Theresa Lillis & Mary Scott, 2007).

For non-native English speakers, academic literacy involves an extra challenge, as the practices of the different linguistic communities cannot be automatically transferred, even within the same discipline. Apart from the language-related issues they may find, students are hindered by their own rhetorical identities, which "may be shaped by very different traditions of literacy" (Hyland, 2004, p. 1091-1092), determined by often implicit cultural-specific issues that cause a "crisis of representation and associated instability of meaning" (Barry Smart, 1999, p. 38). Students' contribution to collective knowledge, and hence their value within the academic community, is thus undermined by their image as poor producers of academic discourse in the language of prestige (Aya Matsuda, 2003; Marko Modiano, 1999).

Based on her study of international students' writing in German, Stella Büker (2003) classified into four categories students' conflicts in writing academic papers in a foreign language: the content-specific level, the domain-specific procedural level, the level of cultural coinage, and the foreign language proficiency level. The first level covers subject knowledge, as first-year students feel extremely inexperienced regarding the knowledge of their discipline. Field-specific procedural knowledge refers to the generic conventions that characterize academic writing—students' need to employ the procedures typical of the field, even if they have not had any specific instruction in them. Regarding the problems derived from cultural coinage, the conventions of particular academic communities are strongly influenced by their different traditions, with, for example, the Anglo-American style being quite different from the Continental style of academic writing (see Lotte Rienecker & Peter Stray Jörgensen, 2003). Such cultural differences affect both the focus and the form of the academic genres members write in, and do not solely depend on the language they are written in. When writing essays, students need to cope with planning, revising, and putting down in words their ideas according to a topic and a set of formal rules they are new to. Simultaneously, they need to deal with their deficits in foreign language competence, even if they choose to do part of the task in their mother tongue to avoid this problem. However, the main issue regarding foreign language proficiency is that the students' language issues mask their difficulties at other levels, as we observed in a preliminary study (Angels Oliva-Girbau, 2011). Students writing in L2 tend to see their lack of competence in L2 as the only source of their problems in writing, disregarding the cultural, discipline-specific and procedural problems they may have.

ACTIVITIES TO DISPEL THE TRANSPARENCY OF WRITING

The materials for the first-year course on English for the Humanities are aimed at promoting students' explicit discussion and contestation of their own developing identities within the activity system of the Humanities as a way to scaffold their acquisition of the tools and goals of the academic community. It is our belief that such programmes should include not only textual and contextual work, but also opportunities to reflect on and negotiate identity issues, which can contribute to empowering students to see themselves as valid members of the academic community. During the first two years of the study, we interviewed volunteer students and distributed questionnaires in order to assess the materials and adapt them to the context of the new Humanities degree. However, the number of students who participated in the voluntary interviews was too low to be considered representative of the students' situation. Consequently, during the third iteration of the course, we decided to use students' writing on the course as data for our research as well, in order to provide us with an emic perspective of students' process of initiation. The reflective activities used in the course have two goals. First, to foster students' development of their academic persona through the study of academic genres in relation to the other components of the academic community. Second, to guide students towards awareness and reflective analysis of the ambivalence latent in their negotiation of difference between their previous identities and their academic ones, so that they may become capable of managing their construction of a new academic identity.

In order to reach these learning goals, the course instructors 1) teach students about the components of the academic community in which they intend to participate and offer them opportunities to reflect on them through the analysis of texts; 2) promote students' awareness of the cultural, ideological and linguistic aspects underlying the nature and mechanics of Anglo-American style genres in comparison to Continental genres and how these determine their relation to the other components of the academic community; and 3) provide room for discussing the conflicts students experience regarding the construction of their own identities in relation to their initiation into the academic community, contesting institutional views on literacy, knowledge, language choices and power relations.

Activities are intended to promote awareness, analysis and contestation. These responses do not exclude each other, but occur in a continuum, as awareness leads to analysis, and both are necessary to create opportunities for students to challenge their novice status, identity and possibilities within the system. Awareness activities refers to tasks aimed at raising students' awareness of the nature of the academic community and its components. Analysis refers to activities that guide students' analysis of the genres of the discipline and the underlying assumptions that determine their functions and features. The third category, contestation, covers activities that provide room for discussion and challenging of the academic community and its components, students' role, and their process of initiation. As an illustration, we present two activities that were carried out during the first weeks and the last weeks of the term respectively.

First, as follow-up to a whole-group discussion in seminar two, we designed a collaborative task in which students had to tell out of a list of descriptors which ones corresponded to canonical Anglo-American or Continental genres, regardless of the language in which they were written but on the basis of the contents, the writer's approach, structural features, and such. The list of descriptors was based on the work of Rienecker and Stray Jörgensen (2003), and adapted to students' language level. In an on-line forum, students presented one or two of the items they had chosen and justified their decision in a short paragraph. Firstly, we wanted students to become aware of the cultural differences across different discourse communities. Secondly, we wanted students to see the connection between the adoption of certain genres and the cognitive processes involved in the construction and communication of knowledge. And thirdly, we wanted them to develop their own approach to somewhere in the continuum between Anglo-American and Continental genres, and take control of their discoursal choices to construct their own identity as writers. When presenting the task in class, we used practical examples and students' own experiences to help them understand the descriptors. However, the exercise made students think that there is a prescriptive dividing line between genres in one tradition and another, and it made them link genres to the languages they are written in. Indeed, students viewed their own genres, cognitive processes and identities as defective and inadequate, in opposition to those of native English speakers. Writing in Catalan or Spanish became something wrong, something to be done as a last resort.

Towards the end of the course, our second activity was introduced. Based on Halliday's functional components of discourse, it aimed at raising students' awareness of the way genres do things with words, i.e., the functional components of genres and how they are realized by textual features. Additionally it aimed to expose the context beyond texts, and to look at the relationship genres establish between members of the community, between writers and their individual and collective goals, and between writers and their texts. The third goal was to help students reflect on the extent to which a writer's expert/novice status determines the choice of specific generic features, giving students the chance to challenge the transparency of writing by exposing the rules of the game. For every section of an essay (introduction, body and conclusion), students had to write a list of the functions that different sentences performed in it—such as attracting the readers' attention, illustrating one's arguments, acknowledging the limitations of one's research, and so on. These functions were then connected to a diagram showing academia as an activity system (Yrjö Engeström, 1995; Alexei Leontiev, 1978; David Russell & Arturo Yáñez, 2003) made up of subjects who share some common goals which they try to achieve using tools and patterns of interaction that are unique to that community. Students analyzed a sample paragraph from one of the three sections using the list of functions they had previously written, connecting linguistic resources to functions. At the end of the session, students were asked to guess the status of the writers, and their relationship to the other elements of the activity system, using quotes from the texts as evidence. For example, the use of hedging in the results section often signaled the writer's lack of commitment to the contents of the paragraph, and hence his/her novice status. The use of canonical ("expert") and non-canonical (written by previous students, for example) paragraphs provided students with a wide range of language resources to implement, and exposed the heterogeneity of academic genres regardless of their language and field of use. Though the activity also presented non-expert, non-native speakers as efficient communicators, we were interested to note that students' contributions systematically failed to acknowledge this, hence ignoring the gradual progress in their own and their peers' progress from novice to expert status.

GENRES, IDENTITY, AND THE BUILDING OF AN INCLUSIVE ACADEMIC COMMUNITY

The data we gathered through students' participation in these activities shows an increased awareness of other levels of difficulty besides their foreign language skills. Thus, their trouble understanding and producing such genres was no longer purely linguistic, but also determined by cultural differences, problems finding an audience, lack of content and procedural knowledge, status, and such:

> It's very difficult to change our way of thinking .... I start writing in English, but then I forget a lot of things that I wanted to write, therefore I first write in Spanish or Catalan and then I translate to English. Well, I know it's wrong but if I write directly in English I can't control my ideas.

When asked in different activities to reflect on their problems with academic genres in English, students realized that they lacked control over content, form, audience and reception. Even though this lack of control existed in their native language(s) too, it was exposed even more clearly by their deficiencies in writing in English, and because of the different planning and writing processes Anglo-American writing requires from them. As a consequence, their still insecure academic identity was undermined by their inability to communicate transparently using academic genres, certainly in their L1, but even more so in English where they struggled between their will to create and their will to communicate: "I can start writing only when my thoughts are totally structured and when I know how I am going to conclude. So I have the feeling of being paralyzed for a while before starting the writing"; "I often explain more things than are necessary and I often expand the topic and add some new ones, which is not correct in English texts."

Students' wish to contribute was still strongly individualistic, rather a personal challenge than a contribution to collective goals. They felt that they needed to assert the legitimacy of their belonging to the academic community, which depended solely on their ability to articulate their contributions in an academic manner and submit them to the approval of an audience superior in status to them. In this respect, academic socialization overlaps first-year students' entrance into maturity and their reach for new more powerful and independent roles. At this point, reasserting their academic identities was much more important as an individual goal than the collective goals and patterns of interaction established by the community; the social construction of knowledge is not feasible when one cannot see oneself as a legitimate member of the community. Students felt they were constantly in competition with one another: when asked about the functions of conclusions, their replies were "to undermine the opponent," "to defend your point of view," and "to completely convince your reader."

The data gathered during the final seminars of the course seems to indicate that students reached a later stage of their process of initiation. The students who were committed to the seminar work appeared to feel more confident regarding the legitimacy of their academic identity, and their capacity to participate meaningfully in the construction of the ideational contents of their area of interest. In the last questionnaire, one of the students stated that he/she felt:

> … prepared to write texts that have coherence, cohesion and a
> complete, clear sense. It is very important, because in this way
> we can express our opinion impersonally, and we will be listened
> to by the world.

Students' struggle with the acquisition of academic genres is tied up with the conflicts derived from their process of initiation into the academic community. Explicit discussion of this process helped deny the transparency of academic genres, and exposed students' difficulties, thus changing their focus from language to content, and from tools to goals, functions and relationships. By gaining a deeper understanding of how to use generic tools and how genres shape/are shaped by identity, students appeared to gain more control of the image they project and their relationship to the ideational contents of the Humanities and other members of the system. More control means that students may be able to make their own choices by connecting, through generic patterns, their construction of their academic identity and their representations of the elements that make up the community.

Language-wise, students started the term in denial of English and the genres they associated with this language. Then, as the term progressed, they reversed this attitude to place English as the only language of true academic communication, in opposition to the creative capabilities of their mother tongue and the genres associated with it, which students saw as relegated to private use. The contributions of students attending the seminars—and the silence of the absentees—evidence the fragility of students' academic identities. Students either discarded their previous identities (linked to their mother tongue) as inadequate, or refused to join the part of the academic community that regards English as its lingua franca. Throughout the course, we failed to engage students in the series of opportunities the materials offered for contestation: we found no evidence of a student daring to challenge the prevalence of English. On the contrary, students seemed to accept their subordinate position because of their inability to change their background, cognitive processes, and identities. Rather than challenging academic genres and the cognitive processes and values associated to them, the students who participated in the seminars embraced Anglo-American academic genres as the solution to their communication issues. Students linked their reading and writing problems to their identities as Catalan/Spanish writers. By rejecting genres in these languages, they distanced themselves from the apparently defective cognitive processes and status associated with users of less prominent genres and languages.

The increasing internationalization of academia and the widespread view of English as its lingua franca can create a barrier for students from other language backgrounds, preventing them from entering the new European university or leading them to view their own language and culture as inferior to it. However, students need not be acculturated into the system, as their other identities can contribute to enrich the academic community. In the new academic community, there should be room for different views, genres, languages and the different contributions all these can make. When designing materials for non-native speakers, it is important to emphasize the multiplicity of literacies in academia, and their corresponding cognitions, identities and goals. As discussed in this chapter, the course activities designed within a more genre-based pedagogy sometimes narrowed students' view of the components of academic communication, and mistakenly presented dominant academic genres as the only possible option. On the other hand, the materials designed according to the principles of academic literacies were successful in increasing students' awareness of and capacity to analyze the components of academic communication, and exposed to some extent the power relations that are established, negotiated and challenged using genres, between users, communities and languages.

Only within the context of plural literacies can minority languages retain their purpose and relevance. If we fail to enable students to challenge the status quo and lead them to accept English as the only language of academic communication, we are depriving their native tongue of prestige, and we are depriving them of the opportunity to create and contribute meaningfully to the social construction of knowledge. In fact, the notion of a unique academic literacy would create a linguistic elite and ignore valuable academic contributions just because they come from the fringes of the system.

REFERENCES

Büker, S. (2003). Teaching academic writing to international students: Individual tutoring as a supplement to workshops. In L. A. Björk, G. Braüer, L. Rienecker, & P. Stray Jörgensen (Eds.), *Teaching academic writing in European higher education* (pp. 41-58). Dordrecht, NL: Kluwer Academic Publishers.

Engeström, Y. (1995). Expansive learning at work: Toward an activity theoretical reconceptualization. *Journal of Education and Work, 14*(1), 133-156.

Hyland, K. (2004). *Genre and second language writers.* Ann Arbor, MI: University of Michigan Press.

Leontiev, A. N. (1978). *Activity, consciousness, and personality.* Englewood Cliffs, NJ: Prentice-Hall.

Lillis, T., & Scott, M. (2007). Defining academic literacies research: Issues of epistemology, ideology and strategy. *Journal of Applied Linguistics 4*(1), 5-32.

Matsuda, P. (2003). Proud to be a non-native English speaker. *TESOL Matters, 13*(4), p. 15.

Modiano, M. (1999). International English in the global village. *English Today, 15*(2), 22-8.

Oliva-Girbau, A. (2011). First-year students' conflicts during their construction of an academic identity in English as a foreign language: Implementing cultural-historical activity theory. *Bellaterra: Journal of Teaching and Learning Language and Literature, 4*(3), 38-52.

Rienecker, L., & Stray Jörgensen, P. (2003). The (im)possibilities in teaching university writing in the Anglo-American tradition when dealing with continental student writers. In L. A. Björk, G. Braüer, L. Rienecker, & P. Stray Jörgensen (Eds.), *Teaching academic writing in European higher education.* Dordrecht, NL: Kluwer Academic Publishers.

Rose, M. (Ed.). (1985). *When a writer can't write: Studies in writer's block and other composing-process problems.* New York: Guilford.

Russell, D. (1991). *Writing in the academic disciplines, 1870-1990: A curricular history.* Carbondale, IL: Southern Illinois University Press.

Russell, D., & Yáñez, A. (2003). Teoría de la actividad histórico-cultural Vygotski-ana y la teoría del sistema de géneros: Una síntesis sobre la escritura en la edu-cación formal y la escritura en otras pŕacticas sociales. *Entre Lenguas, 8*, 67-82.

Smart, B. (1999). *Facing modernity*. London: Sage Publications.

CHAPTER 30

ACADEMIC LITERACIES AND THE EMPLOYABILITY CURRICULUM: RESISTING NEOLIBERAL EDUCATION?

Catalina Neculai

Against an increasingly oppressive corporate-based globalism, educators and other cultural workers need to resurrect a language of resistance and possibility, a language that embraces a militant utopianism, while being constantly attentive to those forces which seek to turn such hope into a new slogan, or to punish and dismiss those who dare look beyond the horizon of the given.

– Henry A. Giroux, 2007

Academic literacies research (hereafter AcLits) has keenly scrutinized the rapport between the knowledge and pedagogies of academic writing in higher education institutions and the dominant "institutional order of discourse" (Theresa Lillis, 2001). This sustained scrutiny has produced an understanding of academic literacy that runs against and problematizes the dominant ideological basis of the academy. Moreover, AcLits has regarded the mainstream institutional outlook on academic literacy as a homogenizing force which appears to sand down the differentials in students' academic, social, and cultural writing practices and identities across the university. In response to this academic homogenization, AcLits has recognized the plurality and heterogeneity of academic literacy (see the AcLits special issue of *The Journal of Applied Linguistics* 4(1)) and offered solutions for active dialogic and transparent writing pedagogies (Lillis, 2001, 2005). Since the birth of AcLits in the 1990s, such theorizing has taken place against the backdrop of an increasingly neoliberal educational apparatus that has sought to link the formation and mutations of a particular subject—in university parlance, the formation of a particular graduate—with the economic system of business and enterprise. This neoliberal educational project has gained dominance by means of certain "techniques of the self" (Graham Burchell, 1996), amongst which the skills-driven curriculum of employability is the most evident.

While AcLits has not overtly engaged with the neoliberal essence of today's higher education institutional order of discourse (for a veiled attempt, see Paul Sutton, 2011), it may provide a solid research matrix for interrogating the neoliberal agenda, and particularly its underlying assumptions with regard to the teaching and learning of academic writing. AcLits may not offer an immediate solution or programmatic response to neoliberal institutional practices but it could help writing teachers and researchers in their various local contexts envisage possibilities for contestation, resistance or change (for "utopian pedagogies" of resistance against neoliberalism, see Mark Coté, Richard J. F. Day & Greig de Peuter, 2007). In this transformative spirit, two questions need to be asked: how can we make academic writing less instrumental in the reproduction of the neoliberal order? How can we shift our language and pedagogies in order to subvert rather than maintain this order?

In this chapter, I explore possible answers to these questions by focusing on a specific programme initiated at Coventry University, UK, which aims at increasing students' "employability" after graduation (for details, see http://www.coventry.ac.uk/study-at-coventry/student-support/enhance-your-employability/add-vantage/). This undergraduate scheme, referred to as Add+Vantage modules, includes modules on academic writing which are delivered by the Centre for Academic Writing (CAW) and in my discussion I focus in particular on a third year module, "Academic Writing: Your Dissertation or Final Year Project." In my analysis, I implicitly acknowledge the institutional, curricular, disciplinary, and social spaces of academic literacies afforded by the employability curriculum while trying to project a counterhegemonic stance in line with the AcLits position formulated at the start. My argument is that, in pertaining to the employability scheme, the teaching of academic writing suffers from an inescapable double bind of compliance and resistance with the neoliberal order. On the one hand, CAW's undergraduate writing provision mainly exists because of this neoliberal agenda whereby a new university like ours seeks to trace students' post-graduation career pathways. On the other hand, the very existence of this provision is vulnerable as it depends, in turn, on the existence of the employability scheme and on the ways in which the scheme chooses to define and make room for the teaching and learning of academic writing. This institutional vulnerability of our modules means that attempting to question or challenge the neoliberal status quo, its language and writing ideologies is fraught with difficulties.

At this point, a couple of caveats are worth noting. Firstly, I articulate the following viewpoints and interpretations in my capacity as convenor for the Dissertation module as well as a member of the team of lecturers at CAW who deliver the suite of academic writing courses (hence the use of the collective "we," representing our joint efforts to streamline the modules). Secondly, I avow an ideological bias against the dominant neoliberal values in higher education whereby the teaching and learning of academic writing are simply instrumental in the production of "commercially oriented professionals" (Kathleen Lynch, 2006, p. 2). Instead, I conceive of academic writing development as a process of consciousness-raising, a democratization of literacy practices, conducive to personal and collective intellectual, social and cultural development.

ACADEMIC WRITING IN THE NEOLIBERAL UNIVERSITY

The values, principles and relations in our society are dictated by the values, principles and relations in the marketplace. Succinctly put, this equation represents the nature of neoliberal ideology, which underlies the contemporary culture of commercial profit, entrepreneurship, commodification and flexible specialization (for a brief, yet compelling analysis of neoliberalism, see David Harvey, 2005). The implications for higher education in the trans-Atlantic space have been highly visible: the heavy privatization of its resources (Lynch, 2006), the unabashed promotion of a market-driven and market-targeted educational system, the loss of critical literacy (Henry A. Giroux, 2011), "the cult of expertise" (Giroux, 2008, p. 1), increasingly blunted capacities for democratization, civic engagement, and academic freedom from the constraints of the market (Giroux, 2008). Academic "performativity" (Stephen J. Ball, 2012), audit and measurements of impact, satisfaction, and performance have become unquestioned systemic currencies in the neoliberal academy.

One of the local consequences of the neoliberal order has been an institutional concern with employability as a set of formally acquired skills, knowledge and competences. According to this agenda, reaching "the positive destination" at the end of the university degree is more than an accidental or implicit bonus of learning and participating in the university cultures, of studying a discipline or a number of interrelated disciplines. Employment is regarded as the net result of strategic teaching and learning of work-related skills, supplemented by privileged access to the world of employers and employment throughout the duration of the degree. In the United Kingdom, new universities which, historically, have a vocational orientation, have been even more attuned to the employability programme. Coventry University, in particular, has introduced the Add+Vantage scheme in line with its corporate mission: "employability, enterprise and entrepreneurship" (Coventry University, 2012b). While the university prides itself on its entrepreneurial achievements, it also measures its success by the support offered to its students and by aiming to create cohesive communities and viable local and trans-local partnerships. This apparent antinomy between a calculative, market-driven institutional spirit and a humanistic inclination is also built into the university's undergraduate employability curriculum.

The Add+Vantage scheme is intended to add employability value in two ways. Firstly, it seeks to cultivate in students a set of personal competences required in the labour market, such as flexibility, decisiveness, self-confidence, or reflectiveness, alongside a set of pragmatic abilities such as problem solving or written/oral communication skills. Secondly, it attempts to produce a number of pre-defined selves: the "global," the "creative," the "entrepreneurial," the "influential," the "community-focused," or the "e-graduate" (Coventry University, 2012a).

The range of themes under which the various modules are offered include: work experience and skills, global languages and perspectives, enterprise and entrepreneurship, professional accreditation and development, and research skills. While the scheme is administratively coordinated by the Careers Office, its component modules are designed and delivered by academic staff in faculties and departments. Departmental boards of study assure the quality of the module design, delivery and assessment while student surveys measure satisfaction rates. Add+Vantage serves all three years of study and although peripheral to the degree curriculum, it is both a credited and mandatory programme for all undergraduate students; in other words, it is a prerequisite for graduation. Students enroll on the programme at the start of every academic year and can choose a different module each year. Students' registration takes place on a first-come, first-served basis, which means that they may not always be able to attend the module of their choice. Class numbers are limited to 24 students, with a module spanning ten weeks, in two-hour weekly iterations.

In the Add+Vantage programme, the modules offered by CAW sit under the rubric of research skills. By taking part in the scheme alongside the other faculties, the Centre for Academic Writing has gained a foothold in one strand of the university curriculum which has opened up possibilities for participation in a faculty board and in departmental affairs, for the creation of a new platform publicizing and promoting the other kinds of writing facilitation at CAW as well as mediated access to departmental resources and inside writing practices. Active cross-fertilisations happen between the teaching of writing through the scheme, the academic writing tutors' one-to-one work with students and the lecturers' consultations with academic staff on their teaching of writing in the disciplines. Thus opportunities for a systemic, more complex approach to writing instruction within the university become available to CAW (for a full profile of CAW, see Mary Deane & Lisa Ganobcsik-Williams, 2012).

CHALLENGING DESIGN: WHICH LITERACY? WHOSE LITERACY?

In a neoliberal understanding, academic and workplace literacy are regarded as co-extensive and become reified into something that is always already there in the form of standards, norms, rules or correctness, said to be defined and dictated a priori by employers (Romy Clark & Roz Ivanič, 1997, pp. 214-215; Fiona Doloughan, 2001, pp. 17, 24). Thus, literacy has become a catalyst in "the production of particular kinds of knowledge and *sanctioned knowers*" (Cindi Katz, 2005, p. 231—emphasis mine), which places universities unapologetically, "at the heart of the knowledge economy" (David Blunkett, as cited in Jonathan Rutherford, 2001; Katharyne Mitchell, 2003, p. 397). It is in this sense that the pedagogization of employability cannot be severed from "the pedagogization of literacy" (Brian Street,

1995, p. 113) whereby instilling knowledge of writing legitimates and scaffolds graduates' future writing-intensive roles in the service economy. The production of writing in the knowledge economy, characterized by a global reach and trans-national networked practices, is often seen, by employers and academic institutions alike, to rest on a generic, stable literacy infrastructure which could be transferred successfully from locale to locale due to the erosion of national economic and industrial boundaries. Employers' demands for demonstrable writing abilities are thus oblivious to the contexts of various communicational acts (Doloughan, 2001, p. 24) and writing practices. Such disregard for writing in context may in fact preclude transferability and render the undifferentiated instruction of academic and workplace literacies an unaccomplished project from the start.

The writing ideology of transferability and objectification transpires in the ways CAW is called upon to build and teach its three-year set of Add+Vantage modules, which, upon first reading, represent everything that the AcLits paradigm has sought to debunk in the writing-*qua*-skills model. Firstly, the recruitment process seldom permits students' enrolment on the CAW writing modules for three consecutive years, which thwarts possibilities for creating a developmental framework akin to an undergraduate writing curriculum. Secondly, randomized enrolment results in amalgamated cohorts of students with different disciplinary affiliations that are difficult to manage pedagogically. Yet, these two insufficiencies of design have not remained unchallenged. Historically, we have made efforts to channel the enrolment process and cluster students in keeping with *meaningful* differences and disciplinary affiliations. As a result, the former first year module "Introduction to Writing at University," a generic, rite of passage-type of module, was divided into three distinct paths: "Academic Writing for (Applied) Sciences," "Academic Writing for Social Sciences," "Academic Writing for Arts and Humanities." While we acknowledge the internal variations of these makeshift disciplinary formations (Mike Baynham, 2000), controlled heterogeneity has secured a commonality of students' academic affiliations, an academic lowest common denominator, which has helped forge a more cohesive writing community with each Add+Vantage module and class. Furthermore, in order to articulate the cultural and critical underpinnings of literacy practices, another first year module has been developed: "English Academic Writing in a Global Context." However, unlike year one provision, in the second and third years, "Developing Academic Writing Skill" and "Academic Writing: Your Dissertation or Final Year Project" do not, as yet, follow a disciplinary logic.

There are also other, more subcutaneous ways in which we have questioned the neoliberal underpinnings of the employability programme. Each module descriptor (see Table 30.1) addresses the employability agenda in an oblique way by highlighting the contribution of academic writing to students' developments in their own fields of study while the lexicon of neoliberalism is almost absent in these descriptors, thus creating a type of resistance through indifference. By engendering an elsewhere and a pretext for student writing that intersects with the curricular space of subject degrees, the CAW writing modules also draw upon, help build or even challenge disciplinary writing spaces. Moreover, through a series of "codes," such as *genre*, *criticality*, the concept of *writing as a process* and as *discourse*, the module descriptors also create a space for academic writing as a field of knowledge and practice in its own right. This epistemological space is further expanded and explored through the writing-infused lexicon of the syllabi and assignment briefs, and through the relational, writing-aware nature of seminar activities and assignment production. Fully articulating and accounting for the disciplinary hybridity of students as well as for the inherent variations in their individual writing expertise and practice still remains a utopian project. However, the changes in design and practice show that the CAW modules are not stagnant curricular and pedagogical constructions.

THE DISSERTATION: ADVANCING INTELLECTUAL LITERACIES

One example of non-compliance is the third year module, "Academic Writing: Your Dissertation or Final Year Project." This is a peculiar case in point not only because of its great success amongst students (six different iterations are currently being taught, with only three two years ago) but also due to its temporal proximity to graduation and therefore to the much invoked "positive destination" (see for example of this employability discourse http://www.pkc.gov.uk/CHttpHandler.ashx?id=13188&p=0). Designed as a companion to students' processes and practices of dissertation writing in their own subjects, the title unsettles the stability of the dissertation genre by allowing for alternative final year research projects beside the conventional dissertation. In some disciplines, such as engineering or performance studies, the alternatives to dissertations are the report on design or the so-called long essay. During the module, covert tensions exist, at times, between entrenched, legitimized dissertation writing conventions, such as the classical IMRaD macro-structure (Introduction, Methods, Results, Discussion), and their disciplinary or individual project variations, or between IMRaD structures in the social sciences and thematic mappings in arts and humanities projects. Inevitably, departmental academic writing cultures and departmental guidelines (where these exist) also come into play, making the Add+Vantage module a site of debate over more stable, consistent meanings of dissertation writing as product, process and practice. In a sense, the module's success also stems from students' desire for coherent and consolidated textual and research practices. That is why, turning atomized literacy practices into synergetic ones, without homogenizing writing teaching and learning, is a primary pedagogic challenge.

Table 30.1: Academic writing vs. neoliberal focus in selected module descriptors

Module Titles	Overt Academic Writing Lexicon	Covert Neoliberal Lexicon
Year 1 Academic Writing for: • Sciences • Health and Social Studies • Arts and Humanities	• learning about academic genres and cultures associated with degree subjects • researching, planning, revising and editing texts • interrogating genre conventions of argument-based essay writing, report writing, reflective writing and case studies	developing students' employability in subject-related careers by enhancing their written communication in relevant genres
Year 2 Academic Writing: • Developing Skill in Academic Writing	• reviewing the concept of writing as a process • introducing strategies for structuring and developing academic papers • analyzing written texts • assessing a range of sources when researching • constructing an academic argument • learning appropriate reflection and referencing skills using *The Coventry University Harvard Reference Style* • writing as a primary medium through which students' knowledge is developed and assessed	contributing to Personal Development Planning (PDP)
Year 3 Academic Writing: • Your Dissertation or Final Year Project	• conceptualizing, planning, drafting, revising and editing final-year projects and dissertations • focusing on "evaluate," "synthesize," "argue" and "reflect"—articulating the place of these types of discourse and practices in academic communication	acquiring and developing competences that contribute to academic development and, implicitly, to future workplace roles that are increasingly writing intensive.

In order to respond to this challenge, the main thrust of the module, which guides my work as a pedagogue, is the advancement of *intellectual literacies* as a complex set of literacy practices that are not simply entrenched in and determined by academic, institutional imperatives. The logic is that by enhancing the intellectuality of my teaching of writing, I implicitly minimize or disregard the mercantile attributes of the neoliberal order. This task is even harder and very sensitive to openly acknowledge in formal institutional settings, such as boards of study, since the neoliberal educational status quo is generally maintained covertly through the marketing of academic writing as a set of transferable, trans-local and trans-disciplinary competences. In its attempts to probe the depths of final year academic writing for research, the module draws attention to the linkages that exist between modes of active reading, active thinking, and active writing inside and outside of academia. The dissertation becomes then a pretext for such probing. I do not wish, however, to invalidate the importance of students' preparation for their graduate careers, but simply to plead for a holistic, non-segregationist approach to student career development that could also feature in the teaching and learning of academic writing *through* the disciplines. This possibility is, in fact, granted by the relational nature of academic literacies: the relations between texts and students, between students' identities and the conventions of their research writing, between students' thinking, reading, and writing practices.

During the ten weeks of the module, students bring to the table the diversity of their individual research projects, the heterogeneity of their writing knowledge and experience, the fluidity of their disciplinary affiliations. Their intellectual labour is only pre-coded in the themes of the syllabus (see the second column in Table 30.2) which include: macro and micro-level modes of textual construction; register, writerly identity, and voice; problem identification, definition, and exploration; critiquing; methodological frameworks; peer reviewing, addressing feedback through revising and editing. This generic "technological" design becomes a unifying principle in class, thus creating a commonality of literacy practices and a matrix of shared goals. The workshop activities, on the other hand, (the third column) are centred on the students and propose a relational, constructivist mode of engagement with writing.

Furthermore, three features of the "Dissertation" module make of it a more complex matrix of teaching and learning than the neoliberal skills-driven model might indicate. First, class activities frame individual writing practices and processes dialogically: discussing in pairs or collectively emotional and cognitive aspects of academic writing in general, and of dissertation writing in particular, exploring individual knowledge of writing, expectations, frustrations, and challenges through dialogue and keeping dissertation writing diaries. These are complemented by a session dedicated to the double peer-reviewing of the coursework draft assigned for summative assessment. In conjunction with this, formative written feedback to writing is complemented by "talkback" (Lillis, 2005) in class and during office hours, thus generating opportunities for one to one tutorials to accompany class

Table 30.2: Sample syllabus—"Your Dissertation or Final Year Project"

Module Outline (N.B. Seminar themes and workshop activities may be subject to change, depending on your writing requirements, class interactions and discussions.)		
Week:	Seminar themes	Workshop activities
1.	The module: workshops, assignment, deadlines; dissertation writing vs. other writing.	Warm-up discussions and reflections.
2.	The process, practice and genre of dissertation writing: from proposal to project.	Discuss the role the following factors may play in your dissertation writing: your dissertation proposal, your own writing practices and knowledge of academic writing, your colleagues and your supervisor, your interest in your subject, your vocational aspirations.
3.	Style and language use: words, sentences and paragraphs.	Use and analyze formal features of academic writing in contrast with other writing.
4.	Working with the dissertation structure: why introductions come first and conclusions last.	Analyze samples of dissertation structures; write an outline of your own dissertation structure, detailing the role of each section.
5.	Reading for the dissertation (1): summaries, arguments and critiques.	Write a summary and critique of an article which you will use for your dissertation, and will have read in advance of the seminar.
6.	Reading for the dissertation (2): the literature review as intellectual dialogue.	• Write a mock literature review based on two articles that you will use in your dissertation and will have read in advance of the seminar. • Analyze literature review samples.
7.	Your dissertation: So what? Questions, niches, problems and claims; analyzing introductions.	Identify topics, questions and problems in sample dissertation introductions; identify your own dissertation topic, main questions and potential problem to solve.
8.	Working with evidence: research methods, data analysis, the ethics of research.	• Identify and write the rationale for choosing your research methods and type of data analysis; reflect on the ethical dimensions of your research. • Planning your assignment with a view to producing a draft by next week.
9.	Peer reviewing week	Bring a draft of your assignment to class for peer reviewing
10.	Abstract writing and executive summaries/Assignment editing and revising.	• Analyze abstracts and executive summaries. • Revise and edit your assignment draft.

interactions. Second, differences in disciplinary discourses are actively brought to bear upon discussions by: teasing out variations in formal conventions (structuring and style in particular); highlighting the tight connection between producing and interrogating knowledge in students' particular subjects and dissertation projects; constructing problems and critiquing academic literature from within disciplinary frameworks, whereby students are asked to explore and share articles relevant to their work. Last, the module construes academic writing as a subject of knowledge, reflection and evaluation. Students are thus inducted into a new discipline, a functional field with its own meta-codes, discourses and community of practice. This transformation of academic writing from an infrastructure of support into a discipline is achieved in at least two ways: through an assessment design that is analytical and reflective in nature, either focusing on comparing and analyzing student and published writing, reflecting on the complex dimensions of one's own dissertation writing or comparing previous coursework writing with dissertation writing; by means of a reading list that telescopes the field's recent incursions into academic writing as product, process and practice. These two approaches come together in the requirement that students substantiate their analyses and reflections on writing through recourse to academic writing literature.

CONCLUSIONS

The neoliberal order of discourse and its educational corollaries have already started to produce a body of research into writing for employability or writing for the knowledge economy, in its milder, non-politicized variety (Deborah Brandt, 2005; University of Bath, 2011-2012; Juliet Thondhlana & Julio Gimenez, 2011) or research into the collusive relations between literacy and neoliberalism, in its more radical and ideologically resistant form (David Block et al., 2012; Christian Chun, 2008). This paper aligns itself with the latter strand of research with the hope of recapturing the role of academic literacies in "creatively transforming human culture" (The Miami Plan as cited in Jill Swiencicki, 1998, p. 27) with its diverse voices and identities as those found in the academic writing class. Through some of AcLits' valuable formulations, I have sought to indicate how the academic writing employability modules delivered by the Centre for Academic Writing at Coventry University minimize and disrupt the workings of the neoliberal Add+Vantage teaching scheme, thus making academic writing less instrumental in the reproduction of the neoliberal order of discourse. In my analysis, I have adopted the combined position of a "long-marcher," who voices an ideological Marxist critique, and of a "whistle-blower," who interrogates the incorporation of academic writing from within a corporatized framework of teaching writing (Dyer-Witheford, 2007, p. 49). Ethical dilemmas abound, but so does the hope that academic writing will eventually build its own spaces of knowledge-making and practice-honing, free of neoliberal dictates.

REFERENCES

Ball, S. (2012). Performativity, commodification and commitment: An i-spy guide to the neoliberal university. *British Journal of Educational Studies, 60* (1), 17-28.

Baynham, M. (2000). Academic writing in new and emergent discipline areas. In M. Lea & B. Stierer (Eds.), *Student writing in higher education* (pp. 17-31). Buckingham, UK: The Society for Research into Higher Education/Open University Press.

Block, D., Gray, J. & Holborow, M. (2012). *Neoliberalism and applied linguistics.* London: Routledge.

Brandt, D. (2005). Writing for a living: Literacy and the knowledge economy. *Written Communication, 22* (2), 166-197.

Burchell, G. (1996). Liberal government and techniques of the self. In A. Barry, T. Osborne, & N. Rose (Eds.), *Foucault and political reason* (pp. 19-36). Chicago: University of Chicago Press.

Chun, C. (2008). Contesting neoliberal discourses in EAP: Critical praxis in an IEP classroom. *Journal of English for academic purposes, 8,* 111-120.

Clark, R., & Ivanič, R. (1997). *The politics of writing.* London: Routledge.

Coté, M., Richard, J. F., & de Peuter, G. (Eds.). (2007). *Utopian pedagogy: Radical experiments against neoliberal globalization.* Toronto: University of Toronto Press.

Coventry University (2012a). *Add+Vantage scheme.* Retrieved from http://www.coventry.ac.uk/study-at-coventry/student-support/enhance-your-employability/add-

Coventry University (2012b). *The university.* Retrieved from http://www.coventry.ac.uk/culc/study/why-choose-culc/

Deane, M., & Ganobcsik-Williams, L. (2012). Providing a hub for writing development: A profile of the centre for academic writing (CAW), Coventry University, England. In C. Thaiss, G. Bräuer, P. Carlino, & L. Ganobcsik-Williams. *Writing programs worldwide: Profiles of academic writing in many places* (pp. 189-201). Fort Collins, CO: WAC Clearinghouse/ Parlor Press.

Doloughan, F. (2001). *Communication skills and the knowledge economy: Language, literacy and the production of meaning.* London: Institute of Education.

Dyer-Witheford, N. (2007). Teaching and tear gas: The university in the era of general intellect. In M. Coté, J. F. Richard, & G. de Peuter, G. (Eds.), *Utopian pedagogy: Radical experiments against neoliberal globalization.* (pp. 43-63). Toronto: University of Toronto Press.

Giroux, H. A. (2011). Beyond the limits of neoliberal education: Global youth resistance and the American/British divide. *Campaign for the public university.* Retrieved from http://publicuniversity.org.uk/2011/11/07/beyond-the-limits-of-neoliberal-higher-education-global-youth-resistance-and-the-american-british-divide/

Giroux, H. A. (2008). Academic unfreedom in America: Rethinking the university as a democratic public sphere. *Works and Days, 51/52* (26), 5-27.

Giroux, H. A. (2007). Utopian thinking in dangerous times: Critical pedagogy and the project of educated hope. In M. Coté, J. F. Richard, & G. de Peuter, G. (Eds.), *Utopian pedagogy: Radical experiments against neoliberal globalization* (pp. 25-42). Toronto: University of Toronto Press.

Harvey, D. (2005). *A brief history of neoliberalism.* Oxford, UK: Oxford University Press.

Katz, C. (2005). Partners in crime: Neoliberalism and the production of new political subjectivities. In N. Laurie & L. Bondi (Eds.), *Working the spaces of neoliberalism: Activism, professionalisation and incorporation.* Special Issue of *Antipode* (pp. 227-235). Oxford, UK: Blackwell.

Lillis. T. M. (2001). *Student writing: Access, regulation, desire.* London: Routledge.

Lillis, T. M. (2005). Moving towards an "academic literacies" pedagogy: Dialogues of participation. In L. Ganobcsik-Williams (Ed.), *Teaching academic writing in UK higher education: Theories, practices and models* (pp. 30-45). Basingstoke, UK: Palgrave Macmillan Publishing.

Lillis, T., & Scott, M. (2007). Defining academic literacies research: Issues of epistemology, ideology and strategy. *Journal of Applied Linguistics, 4*(1), 5-32.

Lynch, K. (2006). Neo-liberalism and marketisation: The implications for higher education. *European Educational Research Journal, 5*(1), 1-17.

Mitchell, K. (2003). Educating the national citizen in neoliberal times: From the multicultural self to the strategic cosmopolitan. *Transactions of the Institute of British Geographers, 28*(4), 387-403.

Rutherford, J. (2001). The knowledge economy vs. the learning society. *Signs of the Times, May.* Retrieved from http://www.signsofthetimes.org.uk/knowledge.html

Street, B. (1995). *Social literacies: Critical approaches to literacy in development, ethnography and education.* London: Longman.

Sutton, P. (2011). Re-crafting an academic literacies approach to pedagogic communication in higher education. *Teaching and Learning, 4*(2), 45-61.

Swiencicki, J. (Ed.). (1998). *College composition at Miami 1997-98* (Vol. 50). Oxford, OH: Miami University.

Thondhlana, J., & Gimenez, J. (2011). Academic literacies and graduate employability: In search of a link. In G. Baker (Ed.), *Teaching for integrative learning: Innovations in university practice* (pp. 136-142). Nottingham, UK: Centre for Integrative Learning.

University of Bath (2011-2012) *Developing writing in STEM disciplines.* Retrieved from http://hestem-sw.org.uk/project?id=5

CHAPTER 31

A CAUTIONARY TALE ABOUT A WRITING COURSE FOR SCHOOLS

Kelly Peake and Sally Mitchell

… in which two optimistic writing developers seek to work with students to develop their writing, and find themselves thwarted by myriad conundrums, unknowns and disappointments, until finally they abandon their efforts and rethink their position …

On and off over the last four years, we[1] have been working on various writing development projects with sixth form[2] students from local schools as part of our university's outreach and access programme which aims to encourage and enable students across its neighbouring communities to go on to higher education. Our remit within this programme was to focus on students' problems with academic writing. The core of our work with schools began as a "writing course." Since its first iteration we have changed the course significantly, relocating it from inviting students from multiple schools to our university campus to going to teach students from a single school in their own setting, and also refocusing it in terms of content. Our initial approach sought to draw students' attention to the features of writing that are often valued at university level, experimenting with types of texts, then linking these to writing students brought with them from school. Then as we became familiar with the students' writing, we began to hone our approach to draw on Language Awareness (Rod Bolitho et al., 2003; Leo van Lier, 1995) and to focus largely on the linguistic expression of, and linking between, ideas in written texts. We felt that it was here that the students often had fewest resources, and that without these resources they were unable to participate fully in the "types of text" activities we had first offered them.

Although the funding context which initiated our work has changed, the university where we work remains committed to widening participation. The course too, in its various forms, remains part of what the university is happy to offer; it is, moreover, "an offer" that schools are happy to take up. At face value, therefore, we have been successful in our attempt to work with writing in schools; schools are keen to invite us in and we have had positive feedback on the materials we have developed. Nonetheless what we are doing with this course continues, despite the changes we have made, to strike us as a flawed approach to writing development in schools (and, indeed, more widely). In this paper—which we think of as a cautionary tale—we explore our thinking around these flaws. To ground our discussion we first ask you to consider the course as enacted in two short vignettes drawn from our experiences this year.

LOCATION 1

A new sixth form in an urban school. We meet the Head of Sixth, tell her what we've done previously, show her our materials, get a sense of how they might fit in to what the students are doing; she is generally enthusiastic, assures us it will be relevant and useful. We agree to offer a five week course adapting our materials to take into account the students' needs, and helping them work on the writing they are doing in their classes. We plan for a meeting with a wider spread of teachers prior to starting, but it is postponed and not re-scheduled. As a result we start the course without much sense of what the students may be doing and what teachers are hoping for from us.

We arrive and sign in. Students start to appear but are shepherded by the Head of Sixth, who sets to work directing them to the various tables. We have no register, and miss an opportunity to establish contact with the students ourselves. We get on with the lesson but students are tired, distracted, chatty among themselves. We are struck by how at home they are with one another and as a result, how little attention we are getting. They grumble that the exercise is similar to one they've done in English lessons, and when asked to write are fidgety and reluctant: "Can't you just give me a sentence to start, Miss?"

The following week very few students appear. Some are evident outside the window on the street; there is waving. Questioned why there are so few, a boy explains "They're not here because they got out before they were caught." So, the end of the school day is a race to escape. "It's like a prison here," he says. We find out that the workshop was compulsory, when we'd thought of it more loosely as "recommended" perhaps.

The next two weeks are better, more focused, although the students are still reluctant to work on their own writing. The final week numbers are right down again; we'd planned to start with them looking at their own writing, but the four students who've turned up haven't brought any: unbeknownst to us they had an essay deadline the previous week, and now they are not doing writing; they'd rather start preparing a presentation. Our course now feels like a homework club.

LOCATION 2

A large sixth form college that feels like a campus. We are asked to work with their honours programme students, a group of academically high achieving students who have been identified as likely to go to university; this is a different approach for us, we feel positive. It's challenging though, as it means delivery to the whole group—120 students—but we work with this, agree to have tables set up in the hall, that teachers and college tutors will participate, that we will pass on our materials for them to use in their teaching. We redesign the course for the larger numbers and different environment. We meet with a couple of teachers and some tutors a couple of weeks before we start—they are very positive about our focus and approach.

We arrive to find the hall unprepared. When the session is due to start one (lone) student has arrived, former students employed as "college mentors" are milling about; they suspect students have gone off to get lunch. We wait, a handful of students drift in, mentors go off to telephone the rest. After half an hour we decide to start—we have 28 students, a nice class size. It emerges that no students can stay for the planned hour and a half so we cut back our plan. Students have brought a range of writing—personal statements, scholarship applications, a science report, English essays. It's a good session with focus that leaves us generally feeling energised. No teachers attend.

No teachers next week either. We find ourselves in an out of the way classroom, again starting late—and working now with only seven students out of our possible 120. Lots—we find out circuitously from one of the college tutors—may have gone off to visit various universities, our own included. Everything about this planned course seems to have crumbled, except for the fact that we turn up, but the fact of our turning up has no impact on anything much—the action is all elsewhere. As this course was promised to be literally much more centre stage, what, we ask, has shifted between the enthusiastic planning and take-up and the reality?

The third and final week. We arrive, expecting little, having decided to run a much shorter class in case no one turns up. Six of last week's students have returned and two from the first week; they have all brought work, all listen and participate in the discussion around the activity which gets them looking at tone and formality. There is concentration, quiet discussion, reviewing and rewriting sections of their texts. Two girls in particular make significant changes, really finding focus in the claims they are starting to make. We are all surprised by the end of the hour. It feels like, for these few students, it is finally coming together, just as we are about to leave.

THE COURSE AS "AUTONOMOUS" AND THEREFORE PERIPHERAL

To unpack a little of what is going on in these vignettes and why our experiences felt so unsatisfactory, we've found it helpful to engage with Street's distinction between autonomous and ideological models of literacy (Brian Street, 1984; see

Chrissie Boughey, 2008). We see that problems with the course in both instances stem from its separation from the locations' practices, purposes and players. By creating a course on writing that stands outside of mainstream activities, subjects and the timetabled hours of the school, we inadvertently reinforce a notion of writing as an autonomous entity that is separable from the actual context in which writing takes place and has meaning (as, for example, "assignment" or "homework" or "exam"). In designing materials for such a course, we are in a sense forced to see them this way too, as autonomous, detached from the teaching and learning happening in school. It follows that, of necessity, we treat the writing that students bring to work on in the course largely autonomously; we can be no real judge of its quality, if quality is in reality determined by assessment frameworks which we do not employ. As such our teaching and materials, when they work, are, we could argue, only accidentally successful; their effectiveness intrinsically and inevitably limited by the conditions of their use. It is the autonomous nature of the course, we conclude, that makes it peripheral and largely inappropriate or irrelevant as a vehicle to achieve transformation.

WRITING IN SCHOOLS IS A SOCIAL PRACTICE AND WE NEED TO RECOGNIZE THIS

Against this, the experience we capture in the vignettes prompts us to recognize that writing is already a part of "social practice," or what James Gee calls "Discourse"—"not language, and surely not grammar [which he differentiates as discourse], but *saying(writing)-doing-being-valuing-believing combinations*" (1990, 1994, p. 142)—and therefore ideological. Discourse or social practice here is not a cool, theoretical concept, but something highly complex, instantiated, and dependent on the messy and changeable relationships of participants to each other, to themselves, to their space, to their texts. It creates insight around the moment, for instance, when one of "our" students resisted rewriting a short text by a fellow student because that student was known in the year group as "a really good writer." "Writing" here clearly emerged as part of social practice, of "having one's being" at this particular school, in this particular peer group. If we were to have any purchase in that classroom, we needed to recognize this.

A SOCIAL PRACTICE LENS ALERTS US TO LIKELY DISJUNCTIONS IN OUR UNDERSTANDINGS

Outside of a social practice perspective, our course might be expected to have run relatively smoothly: it was something that was perceived by teaching staff and by ourselves—both parties experienced in education—as meeting the identified needs of the students. The teachers and advisors we spoke to in setting up and developing our approach gave us lists of concerns (structure, formality, argument) that were familiar to us; they also sometimes seized upon our materials as addressing precisely the problems they encounter in reading their students' scripts. We know little, however, about whether and how these materials might translate into their regular subject teaching. A social practice lens suggests that the apparent unity in our goals may well gloss disjunctions in our experiences and understandings that would show themselves only in local contexts of use. For example, we would not expect materials used in a classroom that sits outside the social practices of a school and by teachers—ourselves—who are also outsiders, to carry the same meanings if employed by subject teachers in subject classes for subject-based assessment ends.

ACTIVITIES AND OUTCOMES ARE LINKED BUT THIS ISN'T ALWAYS RECOGNIZED

Such intimate linking of goals and activities is not, though, convenient for educational planning, particularly where an apparently clear "issue" such as "student writing" has been identified. Nicholas Burboles in his paper "Ways of thinking about educational quality" (2004) observes that models of education that emphasize outcomes (which most models do, even if only weakly), often omit to recognize that outcomes are related to practices; they assume, that is, that one can substitute any kind of practice without affecting the achievement of the outcome. In fact, as we've noted, neither goals nor practices are autonomous: "Activities do not simply aim at goals, they partly constitute and reconstitute them" (John Dewey 1899/1980, glossed by Burboles, 2004). There can be different players in these processes of constitution and reconstitution too; the agency is not solely that of those invested with authority. So for example the students in our first location who came to the final week of the course, successfully resisted our plans for a writing exercise, and used the time instead to get ahead with their homework, something they'd earlier complained the course was preventing them from doing. Their expressed aim was always in any case different than ours—not an abstract "write better," but a clear "write better in exams."

WRITING IN TRANSITION IS A QUESTIONABLE NOTION

When we began our work with schools we framed it as being about "writing in transition"—an invitation to students to come, after school, into our university context, largely to think about writing in the ways we think about it. However the very notion of transition, resting on moving uni-directionally from one known to another known, came to seem problematic: we didn't really know much about the writing done in schools; at the same time, we were aware that any generalized notion of "writing in universities" was flawed. In addition, we noted with some unease a tendency in discussions of "transitions work" (e.g., Ursula Wingate, 2007) to characterize what goes on in universities in terms of highly valorized activities (criticality, argument, research)—and by implication to suggest that none of these qualities are present or developed in pre-university education. We saw such characterisations as potentially contributing to a strongly teleological model of education in which long-term extrinsic goals (graduate employability for example) come to dominate the here-and-now experiences of students and their teachers, creating an instrumentality for writing we would not want to promote (see Mitchell, 2010). We picked up that others were voicing related concerns: Carol Atherton (2003), for example, pointed out that A-level English is not just a preparation for university English: many students don't go on to university or if they do, study different subjects. And Michael Marland (2003) was asserting that A-level experiences needed to be recognized as intrinsically valuable, and that the needs of higher education should not be allowed to obscure them. This thinking sensitized us to the limitations—and potential harm—of framing our work in schools as "transitions work."

CONCLUSION: WE NEED TO MOVE TOWARDS "TALKBACK"

Even practices that apparently achieve their intended goals, Burboles (2004) cautions, may have other unintended or unarticulated consequences. The more we have thought about our writing course whether offered at the university or—in an attempt to get closer to "where students were at"—in schools, the more we are persuaded that we need to attend to a more complex notion of both practice and consequence. We conclude that we cannot separate writing from its social practice; we must work within the contexts in which writing is produced and becomes meaningful, acknowledging "the values and attitudes towards print, and the socially embedded understanding of the purposes of a text these values and attitudes give rise to" (Boughey, p. 194). In practical terms this more ideological stance means working with teachers to understand and enhance *their* practices, rather than with handfuls of individual students. Our aim, we feel, should be a recasting of Lillis' "talkback" dialogue (2003, 2006) where we move away from interaction whereby we, the "HE experts," dispense the advice which will help "solve" students' easily defined writing "problems" to one in which the purposes of the school are primary, the responsibility is the teachers' and our role is to facilitate processes by which they can select, adapt and incorporate ideas and materials around writing into their everyday teaching and curriculum. This positions the students' and teachers' A-level experiences as being intrinsically valuable, and does not allow the needs or expertise of higher education to obscure them (following Marland, 2003). We feel we should—and do—resist offering even a set of recommendations on how to accomplish this type of dialogic relationship, as to do this would yet again detach writing from its social practice.

WHY OUR CONCLUSION IS NOT MORE OBVIOUS

Ironically, what we describe here as an aspiration for our work with schools is the position we have always taken in our work in writing and curriculum development at our university (see e.g., Teresa McConlogue, Sally Mitchell, & Kelly Peake, 2012; Sally Mitchell & Alan Evison, 2006). We are intrigued to recognize that in our work with schools we adopted a model (the stand-alone course) that in other contexts we would have argued vociferously against. But the situation is instructive; it points, we think, to the persistence of a skills-based, decontextualized conception of writing and "problems with writing," and the instrumental value of this conception—even to us—as a way to make writing visible. Creating a course enabled us to begin to participate in the institutional framing and funding of widening participation work which is measured by the participation of individual students. It enabled us to respond to the attractiveness both to the university and to schools of an identifiable product that could be offered and taken up. In contrast to this "something for nothing" deal, the challenge of getting involved in complex school contexts and finding time and space to work with staff who are already working at full capacity, would probably have been beyond us. (This remains a significant challenge, after all, for many writing developers within their own institutional contexts.) Four years on, however, we are in a stronger position; in dialogue with teachers and university colleagues about our cautionary insights, equipped with a flexible/challengeable body of ideas around writing at A-level, and clearer and more adamant that the way forward for working on writing in schools is through embedded partnership *within their* myriad social practice contexts.

NOTES

1. Based at a large UK HE institution in the East End of London, we are part of Thinking Writing, a small team of educational developers who work primarily with academic staff around the roles that writing can play in learning in the disciplines.

2. The term "sixth form" refers to a non-compulsory two year course that students can choose to take at the end of secondary education in England and Wales; it often offers a route into further or higher education. The most common qualification that students work towards in that time is the "A-level."

REFERENCES

Bolitho, R., Carter, R., Hughes, R., Ivanič, R., Masuhara, H., & Tomlinson, B. (2003). Ten questions about language awareness. *ELT Journal*, *57*(3), 251-259.

Boughey C. (2008). Texts, practices and student learning: A view from the South. *International Journal of Educational Research*, *47*, 192-199.

Burboles, N. (2004). Ways of thinking about educational quality. *Educational Researcher*, *33*(4), 4-10.

Dewey, J. (1899/1980). *School and society*. Carbondale, IL: Southern Illinois University Press.

Gee, J. (1990/ 1994). *Social linguistics and literacies: Ideology in discourses*. Basingstoke, UK: Falmer Press.

Lillis, T. (2003). Student writing as "academic literacies": Drawing on Bakhtin to move from critique to design. *Language and Education*, *17*(3) 192-207.

Lillis, T. (2006). Moving towards an "academic literacies" pedagogy: Dialogues of participation. In Ganobcsik-Williams, L. (Ed.), *Teaching academic writing in UK higher education: Theories, practice and models* (pp. 30-45). London: Palgrave MacMillan Publishing.

Marland, M. (2003). The transition from school to university: Who prepares whom, when and how? *Arts and Humanities in Higher Education*, *5*, 201-211.

McConlogue, T., Mitchell, S., & Peake, K. (2012). Thinking Writing at Queen Mary, University of London. In C. Thaiss, G. Bräuer, P. Carlino, & L. Ganobcsik-Williams, L. (Eds.), *Writing programs worldwide: Profiles of academic writing in many places* (pp. 203-211). Fort Collins, CO: WAC Clearinghouse/Parlor Press.

Mitchell, S. (2010). Now you don't see it; now you do: Writing made visible in the university. *Arts and Humanities in Higher Education*, *9*(2), 133-148.

Mitchell, S., & Evison, A. (2006). Exploiting the potential of writing for educational change at Queen Mary, University of London. In L. Ganobcsik-Williams (Ed.), *Teaching academic writing in UK higher education: Theories, practice and models* (pp. 68-84). London: Palgrave Macmillan Publishing.

Street, B. V. (1984). *Literacy in theory and practice*. Cambridge, UK: Cambridge University Press.

Van Lier, L. (1995). *Introducing language awareness*. London: Penguin.

Wingate, U. (2007). A framework for transition: Supporting "learning to learn" in higher education. *Higher Education Quarterly*, *61*(3) 391-405.

REFLECTIONS 6

"WITH WRITING, YOU ARE NOT EXPECTED TO COME FROM YOUR HOME": DILEMMAS OF BELONGING

Lucia Thesen

Lucia Thesen has been working in academic writing development at the University of Cape Town since the mid 1980s. In that time the institution has changed profoundly in some ways, providing access to historically excluded students, but not in others. The complexities of the shift from apartheid to a democractic South Africa underpin Lucia's practical and theoretical work and are reflected here in her exploration of the meanings of transformation.

TRANSFORMATION FROM A SOUTHERN PERSPECTIVE

What does the transformative agenda in Academic Literacies look like from a cluster of neo-classical buildings that cling to a mountain, facing north, from the southern-most university on the African continent? My starting point is the quote in the title: "With writing you are not expected to come from your home." These are the words of Sipho, a student (quoted in Gideon Nomdo, 2006) who is reflecting on his university experience.[1] As a first generation working class black student in a historically English speaking, white, elite university,[2] a profound political transformation has created policy space for him that was not possible under apartheid. But for students granted entry through new policy spaces, formal access does not easily translate into what Wally Morrow calls epistemological access (2007). After a false start as a student of economics, he leaves the university, returning later to major in drama where he finds a disciplinary shelter, if not a home, from which he goes on to become an accomplished actor and director.

His words have stayed with me since I first read them in Nomdo's piece. The modality is strong, conveyed in the present tense as a statement of fact and generalized to "you." Is this true for the universal "you," or is it more of an expression of a particular moment, for a particular person? What about the expectations of writing that he refers to? How negotiable are they? Is there something necessarily estranging about the semiotic act of writing? Or is it only academic writing that he is speaking about—what Kate Cadman (2003) calls "divine discourse"—a project of the Enlightenment that claims the capacity to be neutral, to be able to generalize and speak across contexts? Is it possible/necessary that in the act of academic writing we feel that we belong? What would we belong to, which places, histories, conversations? Does belonging matter for the academic literacies stance and does a better understanding of how we (both students and academics) might see ourselves as belonging contribute to its transformative agenda?

Academic literacies continues to offer an important academic shelter in my life as a teacher-researcher as it values situated practice. In the introduction to our book, *Academic Literacy and the Languages of Change* (Lucia Thesen & Ermien van Pletzen, 2006) we reflect on how our work at a South African university has been caught up in wider circles of context, foregrounding the political transformation from apartheid to the democratic era. The word transformation is widely used in all areas of public life in this country and it is always sharply loaded and contested. It is strongly associated with the historical break with apartheid, following the "elite pacting" (Linda Chisholm, 2004) of the early 1990s. There is no doubt that we have undergone a profound political transition from a pariah state to a nervous but so far resilient democracy where intense processes of negotiation between competing values and practices are the norm. It is hard to describe just how significant this shift has been at the symbolic level; at the same time, it is important to acknowledge how incomplete, uneven and problematic aspects of this transition remain, many of which are still the subject of on-going contestation. The gap between symbolically impressive policy and practice on the ground is particularly important. There are no easy answers about the role of education in these processes: all decisions seem to require a deep engagement with a series of dilemmas where superficial answers will surely let us down.

ACADEMIC LITERACIES: LAYERS OF MEANING

I think of academic literacies as theoretically informed activism to change practice. My understanding has been honed through years of convening a master's level semester-long course that focuses on academic literacies. Students who register for this course are typically academics from a range of disciplines, school teachers (the term academic literacy has recently made its way into schooling) or adult educators with an interest in language in the educational process. I tell students my value system regarding student text: I am not interested in hearing whether this piece of writing is wrong or right: I want to hear you say, "That's *interesting*. Why does it look like that? Has it always been like this? What is the writing/drawing/text doing? Is it fair? How might it be different? What would we need to know and do for it to be different?"

Through working with students I have identified three different intersecting, sometimes competing, angles on academic literacies. First is academic literacies as a *shorthand for academic literacy practices*: this is a descriptive term for the vast and changing history of how the academy comes to value some forms of communication above others in different disciplines. These practices were there long before us, and they will remain long after we have gone, in forms that may be hard to imagine now. For now, writing is most strongly caught up in assessment and how the university communicates research. It hasn't always been like this. At times the oral has held sway over the written (William Clark, 2006). The written form is paramount, but digital literacies are escalating changes in both written and oral forms, shrinking the academic world in some ways but widening rifts in others. There is a geographical as well as historical dimension to these changes, as the anthropological tradition in Literacy Studies has shown so clearly. From a southern African perspective, time and space meet in colonialism and the end of apartheid, and the processes of postcolonial emergence are what shape us most strongly, as I shall expand on later. This foregrounds the dilemmas that come with writing and is what makes the student's comment about writing and home so resonant.

The second meaning of academic literacies refers to a *form of pedagogical work* that has a direction towards some ideal notion of the conventions of "good writing" in English. While we know from Meaning 1 that there is no settled unitary version of good writing that can be taught once and for all, there are many aspects of convention that can and must be taught if we are to embrace the access challenges of massification. We can't open the doors of learning and then let new students fail. Academic literacy/ies as work responds to the institutional refrain that "students can't read and write." This is the meaning that defines a crisis, that creates a problem to be solved, that raises state funding and pays my salary to do the kind of work that we do. In South Africa, this work has been tied to a political project of the transformation of higher education since the mid-1980s, to admit historically excluded working class black students to the university, and to make sure that although the playing field is not level on entry, we do enough to make sure that they graduate strongly enough to make meaningful choices at the end of the degree, some joining the university as the next generation of academics. This meaning is sustained by the myth that writing problems can be fixed (Brian Street's 1984 autonomous model). A distinguishing feature of academic literacy/ies locally is that it also involves systemic policy work. Our group helps shape policy, create flexible routes through the degree process, and in a recent language and academic literacy implementation plan, commits to working in partnership with academics in the disciplines. Academic literacy/ies is everyone's responsibility.

The overarching meaning of Academic Literacies (with capital letters) as *epistemology and a methodology* (Theresa Lillis & Mary Scott, 2007) is a cluster of tools and methods (and people), an emerging sub-discipline that takes a critical stand on communicative practices (particularly writing) in the changing university. It does not look only at induction to high status academic literacy practices of the day, but looks at practice and how notions of reading and writing are expressed in particular time/place arrangements. Crucially, it is also interested in alternative, more socially just, innovative practices where new forms of hybrid writing can take hold. This meaning is most effective as a research-in-practice lens that ideally brings the first and second meanings of the term academic literacies into a productive relationship with one another.

And here I want to reflect on the student Sipho's words through the Academic Literacies lens to argue that a key part of transformative practice is a *process of engagement* that asks questions about belonging. This belonging refers to both global and local elements. It doesn't aim to settle these questions of belonging. If we are to take transformation further, we have to understand how students (and academics) engaged in knowledge-making weigh up their commitments to what they bring along, and where they hope to go, and what they want to be. Transformative practice calls for deep conversations about hopes and fears and attachments. This conversation needs openness to risk and risk-taking (Lucia Thesen and Linda Cooper, 2013). I begin by situating the quote from Homi Bhabha below in analysis of writing practices in the post-colonial university. This foregrounds the dilemma that underlies the comment about writing and belonging. You have to engage with academic writing, but if you succeed, you may have sold out or lost out on something valuable and defining that will also have implications for what counts as knowledge.

"ANGLICISED BUT EMPHATICALLY NOT ENGLISH" (HOMI BHABHA, 2004, P. 125)

Homi Bhabha explains the concept of the mimic man, how colonialism makes subjects who are almost the same, but just different enough for the difference to matter, to need "civilizing." The phrase "Anglicised but not English" signals the importance of postcolonial studies in trying to understand what transformative writing practices could look like. While speech is a universal human capacity, writing is not. Its materiality as inscription played a key part in colonialism. As Adrien Delmas writes, "Writing was the medium by which Europe discovered the world" and in the process it took on a range of "top down" technical, administrative, religious, scientific, and educational functions (2011, p. xxviii). The state of being ambivalent, torn between discourses, is what the postcolonial subject has to come to terms with. This ambivalence has arguably been relevant for a long time, and is certainly relevant since the inclusion of working class and women students in the academy. If the postcolonial situation is the condition of the majority of students now participating in higher education globally, it may be a perspective that has far more global relevance than either the Academic Literacies or composition studies traditions have thus far acknowledged.

The idea that writing pedagogy takes place in multilingual, diverse, contested, and congested "contact zones" (Mary Louise Pratt, 1999) is beginning to take hold in many settings. The contact zone is increasingly the norm as universities become more diverse with massification. Examples are Theresa Lillis and Mary Jane Curry (2010) in academic publishing and Xiaoye You's (2010) history of English composition in China, which argues that writing in what is locally called the devil's tongue (English) is actually writing in *our* tongue, as nobody "owns" a global language like English. You's history of composition is one way of making academic literacy work more "ethically global."

Bhabha argues that if we want to understand the global, we need to start with the local. The term "local" resonates in Academic Literacies, with its connections to the New Literacy Studies. The "second wave" of research (Mike Baynham & Mastin Prinsloo, 2009) in the literacy studies tradition with which the Academic Literacies position is associated pushed for studies of local literacy practices. As a South African writer, I have always struggled with this: on the one hand everything we do is so strongly situated in the local context. If one backgrounds context, reviewers and readers often ask for more local setting. But the more context is given, the more likely one's research is to be read as exotic, tragic, or lacking. We want to "come from home" but also to be read as contributing to global conversations. Achille Mbembe helps to explain this ambivalence in his thought-provoking piece on African "self-writing": discourses on African identity force people into "contradictory positions that are however concurrently held" (2002, p. 253). The shadow side of the Enlightenment has ascribed to Africa a meaning that is inferior—"something unique, and even indelible … and has nothing to contribute to the work of the universal" (p. 246). This inferiority bleeds into territory. African identity is translated in local, territorial, terms, but always in a racist discourse that creates the dilemma for writers: I am in/from/of Africa but I am also part of the world.

So "to come from your home" is not a straightforward matter of belonging. It points to territory, an earthing that gives one some recognition, but at the same time it racializes identity. So belonging is for many writers in the postcolonial university a space full of contradictions and dilemmas. Using Bhabha's concepts of "unhomed" and "hybridity," Bongi Bangeni and Rochelle Kapp (2005) have explored the experience of black students in a historically white institution looking at their state of being in-between, and how it changes over time, as they make their way through the undergraduate degree in the social sciences. The data for their paper is drawn from the richness of conversations generated by the question "What was it like to be at home during the vacation?" While the interviews they report on in this paper do not focus specifically on writing (they focus more on students' non-academic lives), there are moments where one of the students, Andrew, talks about how writing reflective pieces in various courses helped to achieve some kind of integration and sense of a coherent self. Similarly, Sipho in Nomdo's article also finds a form of writing that he feels more comfortable with. This form is achieved through a combination of his writing and performance in Drama:

> I try to create a new form, even to recreate my own self because I feel I've been clouded by other things. There's a lot of things I need to unlearn. Writing actually gives me that opportunity. The pen, I don't use it that much, I use it in point form, this is the situation Drama gives me the physical ability to recreate myself, for example, playing somebody else that I'm not everyday but that I might be inside. (Nomdo, 2006, p. 200)

This is a different view of writing not as alienating, but as a tool for the project of the self, an exploratory, reflective and reflexive form of writing that is low stakes, and may or may not be part of assessment practices. It is also interestingly secondary to the primary means of communication, which in the discipline of Drama, is the body. Most importantly, it is feeling towards new forms, experimenting, imagining. Insights such as this remind us of the importance of hearing what projects of the self students are busy with, and how they bring their histories to the academy. The concept of "risk" and "risk taking" can help open up this kind of discussion and insight (Thesen and Cooper 2013).

A final reflection on my own theoretical belonging: the three angles I identify that make up Academic Literacies—changing practices, pedagogy, and emerging discipline—sometimes work together, and sometimes don't, and I'm comfortable with the tensions between them. I find them risky, but productive. I suggest that by belonging to the community of teacher-researchers in the Academic Literacies field, I am also able to belong to other theoretical conversations, in particular in this piece, to conversations about postcolonial ambivalence. Given that practices are so strongly rooted in historical and geographical (including translocal) contexts, it is important to keep the academic literacies approach alert and responsive, through deep conversations with others who are interested in the possibilities of the transformative "acts" in practice.

NOTES

1. The dilemmas experienced by the student Sipho (a pseudonym) are described in Nomdo (2006) who uses Bourdieu to show how issues of class, race and language work for different students participating in a US-funded scholarship programme for black senior undergraduates..

2. The terms of racial classification, central to apartheid's project, are still relevant in public life, 20 years after democracy.

REFERENCES

Bangeni, B., & Kapp, R. (2005). Identities in transition: Shifting conceptions of home among "black" South African university students. *African Studies Review, 48*(3), 1-19.

Baynham, M., & Prinsloo, M. (2009). *The future of literacy studies*. Basingstoke, UK: Palgrave Macmillan Publishing.

Bhabha, H. (2004). *The location of culture*. Abingdon, UK: Routledge.

Cadman, K. (2003, November). *Divine discourse: Plagiarism, hybridity and epistemological racism*. Paper presented at LED 2003: 1ˢᵗ International conference on language, education and diversity, University of Waikato, Hamilton, NZ. Retrieved from http://hdl.handle.net/2440/39833

Chisholm, L. (Ed.). (2004). *Changing class: Education and social change in post-apartheid South Africa*. Cape Town/London: HSRC Press/Zed Books.

Clark, W. (2006). *Academic charisma and the origins of the research university*. Chicago: University of Chicago Press.

Delmas, A. (2011). Introduction: The written word and the world. In A. Delmas & N. Penn (Eds.), *Written culture in a colonial context: Africa and the Americas 1500-1900* (pp. xvi-xxix). Cape Town: UCT Press.

Lillis, T., & Curry, M. J. (2010). *Academic writing in a global context: The politics and practices of publishing in English*. Abingdon, UK: Routledge.

Lillis, T., & Scott, M. (2007). Defining academic literacies research: Issues of epistemology, ideology and strategy. *Journal of Applied Linguistics, 4*(1):5-32.

Mbembe, A. (2002). African modes of self-writing. *Public Culture, 14*(1), 239-273.

Morrow, W. (2007). *Learning to teach in South Africa*. Cape Town: Human Sciences Research Council Press.

Nomdo, G. (2006). Identity, power and discourse: The socio-political self-representations of successful "black" students. In L. Thesen & E. van Pletzen, (Eds.), *Academic literacy and the languages of change* (pp. 180-206). London: Continuum International Publishing Group.

Pratt, M. L. (1999). Arts of the contact zone. In D. Bartholomae & A. Petrosky (Eds.), *Ways of reading: An anthology for writers* (5th ed.). New York: Bedford/St Martins.

Street, B. V. (1984). *Literacy in theory and practice*. Cambridge, UK: Cambridge University Press.

Thesen, L., & Cooper, L. (2013). *Risk in academic writing: Postgraduate students, their teachers and the making of knowledge*. Bristol, UK: Multilingual Matters.

Thesen, L., & van Pletzen, E. (Eds.). (2006). *Academic literacies and the languages of change*. London: Continuum International Publishing Group.

You, X. (2010). *Writing in the devil's tongue: A history of English composition in China*. Carbondale, IL: Southern Illinois University Press.

AC LITS SAY ...

Imperatives that have shaped my academic life (with apologies to Paul Morley and Katherine Hamnett). These T-shirts were designed by Peter Thomas and presented in a symposium at EATAW 2015: 8th Biennial Conference of the European Association for the Teaching of Academic Writing, held at Tallinn University of Technology, Tallinn, Estonia, in June 2015. Image provided by Peter Thomas, Middlesex University, UK (p.thomas@mdx.ac.uk).

LIST OF CONTRIBUTORS

Joelle Adams, Santa Monica College, United States

Cecile Badenhorst, Memorial University of Newfoundland, Canada

Beverley Barnaby, Middlesex University, United Kingdom

Lia Blaj-Ward, Nottingham Trent University, United Kingdom

Helen Bowstead, Plymouth University, United Kingdom

Corinne Boz, Anglia Ruskin University, United Kingdom

Kate Chanock, La Trobe University, Australia

Lawrence Cleary, University of Limerick, Ireland

Lisa Clughen, Nottingham Trent University, United Kingdom

Lynn Coleman, Cape Peninsular University of Technology, South Africa

Matt Connell, Nottingham Trent University, United Kingdom

Jane Creaton, University of Portsmouth, United Kingdom

Isabelle Delcambre, Université de Lille, France

Christiane Donahue, Dartmouth College, United States

Jennifer Dyer, Memorial University of Newfoundland, Canada

Fiona English, UCL, Institute of Education, United Kingdom

Adriana Fischer, Universidade Regional de Blumeneau, Brazil

Vera Frith, University of Cape Town, South Africa

Julio Gimenez, University of Westminster, United Kingdom

Jennifer Good, University of the Arts, London, United Kingdom

Marta Milian Gubern, Universitat Autónoma de Barcelona, Catalonia, Spain

Kathy Harrington, London Metropolitan University, United Kingdom

Bruce Horner, University of Louisville, United States

Julian Ingle, Queen Mary University of London, United Kingdom

Cecilia Jacobs, Stellenbosch University, South Africa

Kathrin Kaufhold, Stockholm University, Sweden

Sonia Kline, University of Illinois at Urbana-Champaign, United States

Gillian Lazar, Middlesex University, United Kingdom

Mary R. Lea, The Open University, United Kingdom

Maria Leedham, The Open University, United Kingdom

Theresa Lillis, The Open University, United Kingdom
Cathy Malone, Sheffield Hallam University, United Kingdom
Laura Mc Cambridge, University of Jyväskylä, Finland
Colleen McKenna, Higher Education Consultant, United Kingdom
Andrew Middleton, Sheffield Hallam University, United Kingdom
Sally Mitchell, Queen Mary University of London, United Kingdom
Cecilia Moloney, Memorial University of Newfoundland, Canada
Morgan Murray, Memorial University of Newfoundland, Canada
Catalina Neculai, Coventry University, United Kingdom
Makiko Nishitani, La Trobe University, Melbourne, Australia
Angels Oliva-Girbau, Universitat Pompeu Fabra, Catalonia, Spain
Íde O'Sullivan, University of Limerick, Ireland
Moragh Paxton, University of Cape Town, South Africa
Kelly Peake, Queen Mary University of London, United Kingdom
Claire Penketh, Liverpool Hope University, United Kingdom
Paul Prior, University of Illinois, United States
Kevin Roozen, University of Central Florida, United States
Janna Rosales, Memorial University of Newfoundland, Canada
Diane Rushton, Sheffield Hallam University, United Kingdom
David Russell, Iowa State University, United States
Mary Scott, UCL, Institute of Education, United Kingdom
Tasleem Shakur, Edge Hill University, United Kingdom
Fay Stevens, University College London, United Kingdom
Brian Street, King's College London, United Kingdom
Lucia Thesen, University of Cape Town, South Africa
Peter Thomas, Middlesex University, United Kingdom
Jackie Tuck, The Open University, United Kingdom
Joan Turner, Goldsmiths, University of London, United Kingdom
Sylvia Whitmore, La Trobe University, Melbourne, Australia
Rebecca Woodard, University of Illinois at Chicago, United States
Nadya Yakovchuk, University of Surrey, United Kingdom

Lightning Source UK Ltd.
Milton Keynes UK
UKOW04f1454131115

262600UK00002B/83/P